MILLENNIUM PARK

MILLENNIUM PARK

Creating a Chicago Landmark

Timothy J. Gilfoyle
in association with THE CHICAGO HISTORY MUSEUM

The
University of
Chicago Press
Chicago and
London

TIMOTHY J. GILFOYLE
is professor of history at
Loyola University in Chicago
and the author of *City of Eros:
New York City, Prostitution, and the
Commercialization of Sex, 1790–
1920* and *A Pickpocket's Tale:
The Underworld of Nineteenth-
Century New York.*

The University of Chicago Press, Chicago 60637
The University of Chicago Press, Ltd., London
© 2006 by The University of Chicago
All rights reserved. Published 2006
Printed in the United States of America
15 14 13 12 11 10 09 08 07 06   1 2 3 4 5
ISBN: 0-226-29349-1 (cloth)

MANUFACTURED BY R. R. DONNELLEY

Library of Congress Cataloging-in-Publication Data

Gilfoyle, Timothy J.
    Millennium Park : creating a Chicago landmark / Timothy J. Gilfoyle ;
    in association with The Chicago History Museum.
        p. cm.
    Includes bibliographical references and index.
    ISBN 0-226-29349-1 (cloth : alk. paper)
    1. Millennium Park (Chicago, Ill.)—History. 2. Millennium Park Project.
    3. Chicago (Ill.)—History I. Chicago Historical Society. II. Title.
    F548.65.M55G55   2006
    977.3'11—dc22   2005034630

♾ The paper used in this publication meets the minimum
requirements of the American National Standard for Information
Sciences—Permanence of Paper for Printed Library Materials,
ANSI Z39.48-1992.

TO NEWT AND JO, *who made this book possible*

CONTENTS

FOREWORD

Millennium Park is the future. Its design, funding, and construction signal a sharp departure from our beloved nineteenth-century city parks exemplified by Chicago's many magnificent urban landscapes—Grant, Edison, Lincoln, Wicker, Douglas, Horner, Garfield, Washington, and Humboldt parks, to name only a few. Critically acclaimed as a unique fusion of art, architecture, and landscaping; embraced by diverse Chicagoans as a park for all people; and promoted to tourists as the crowning glory of a beautiful world-class city, Millennium Park has, in many ways, won Chicago the honor as the city of the century.

But every place has a past. And no piece of land in Chicago has a history quite as complex and as intriguing as Millennium Park. Newton and Josephine Minow knew this better than anyone else. When the Minows approached the Chicago Historical Society (CHS) in fall 2000 to publish a history of the site that was to become Millennium Park, it was a troubled project. The transformation of the 24.5-acre property on the north end of Grant Park into the urban park and garden design that mayor Richard M. Daley unveiled in 1998 had already missed its original 2000 completion date, and nobody would venture a guess when it would finally be finished. But the Minows believed in the park from its beginning, and their enthusiasm did not flag. As devoted Chicagoans they had placed bets before on the future of the city, and as lifelong champions of history they understood the value that the lens of the past brings to the present and to the future. As Jo Minow expressed it, "We love Chicago, where our great-grandparents settled when they and the city were very young."

The Chicago Historical Society eagerly embraced this book project as a unique opportunity to fulfill its mission to remain a major research center and to make current scholarship more broadly accessible to the public. Equally important, CHS has for decades been committed to documenting and collecting drawings and papers of architects, real estate firms, and contractors to create an archive of Chicago's evolving built environment. Material relating to the history of this important lakefront site and to the history of Millennium Park promised to add significantly to that collection. We were especially eager to excavate the rich layers of history lying beneath the park to describe not only how this land was used over time, but also why it assumed its successive urban forms.

The Minows recommended professor Timothy J. Gilfoyle of Loyola University Chicago to write the book. In choosing an urban historian rather than an architectural historian, they revealed a clear grasp of the challenge the book presented: this site has historically been a hotly contested place embroiled in legal disputes and political debate; telling this complex history would require a historian skilled in political, economic, social, and cultural history. Urban historians are especially adept at synthesizing these multiple perspectives into a cogent and candid story, and the choice of Professor Gilfoyle was ideal. We were delighted to build on our strong relationship with Professor Gilfoyle, who has written histories of CHS's Making History awardees for *Chicago History* magazine for more than a decade. His skillful interviews of those Chicagoans prepared him well for the rigors of researching the many stories behind Millennium Park.

Complementing Professor Gilfoyle's work are the stunning images by Hedrich Blessing, the nation's most prestigious architectural photography firm. As another long-term partner of CHS—Hedrich Blessing has donated to CHS some 500,000 images that span the firm's work from 1928 to 1979—we were thrilled to include their newly commissioned images along with historic maps and photographs drawn from CHS's extensive collection in the book.

If Millennium Park is the future, the past often intrudes: the Peristyle from the Millennium Monument, the Lurie Garden, the Jay Pritzker Pavilion, the *Crown Fountain*, and *Cloud Gate* reflect the intersection of the past and the future. The earliest park designs were inspired by Daniel Burnham's vision of Chicago and A. Montgomery Ward's imperative to keep the lakefront "forever, open, clear, and free"; for these architects, and for many who followed, the future meant completing plans from the past. The triumph of Millennium Park, however, is in its straddling the past and the future. We are grateful to the Minow Family Foundation for generously supporting this book; without the Minows' foresight and ongoing enthusiasm, it would not have come to fruition. *Millennium Park: Creating a Chicago Landmark* is an evocative account of how this part of Chicago evolved into a new kind of park for the twenty-first century, and the Chicago Historical Society is proud to be copublisher.

GARY T. JOHNSON, *President*
RUSSELL LEWIS, *Executive Vice President and Chief Historian*
Chicago Historical Society (now Chicago History Museum)

PREFACE

Upon opening on July 16, 2004, Chicago's Millennium Park was hailed as one of the most important millennium projects in the world. For some, the new park embodied the intersecting relationship between municipal politics and urban culture. Perhaps no one believed this more than the project's instigator, Chicago mayor Richard M. Daley. The city's chief executive insisted that culture—visual art, literature, music, architecture—was a primary agent of personal expression and social cohesion. Artists, he believed, were more responsible than any other group in building bridges among the disparate and diverse social groups that comprised the American metropolis at the millennium. "Politicians come and go; business leaders come and go," he proclaimed, "but artists really define a city."[1] Millennium Park, in Daley's mind, embodied Chicago at the turn of the twenty-first century.

Millennium Park was born out of civic idealism, raised in political controversy, and matured into a new symbol of Chicago. The combined park, outdoor art museum, and cultural center included an unprecedented combination of distinctive architecture, monumental sculpture, and innovative landscaping. An exceptional collection of world-renowned artists and designers, including Frank Gehry, Anish Kapoor, Jaume Plensa, Thomas Beeby, and Kathryn Gustafson, transformed a largely unused railroad yard. The new park was built and financed by an alliance of municipal government, global corporations, private foundations, and wealthy civic leaders. For some, Millennium Park epitomized not only the benefits of public and private cooperation in a civic project, but a new kind of cultural philanthropy.[2]

Millennium Park's space, bounded by Columbus Drive, Monroe Street, Michigan Avenue, and Randolph Drive, illuminates not only the political and artistic cultures of Chicago at the millennium, but the larger physical history of the city. Before 1850, the waters of Lake Michigan covered these acres of land. Then for over a century, the Illinois Central Railroad Company literally created the land and determined its use, at just the moment the railroad transformed Chicago. The gradual creation of Grant Park after 1900 and the growing prominence of the automobile reshaped both design and traffic at the site over the course of the twentieth century. Finally, as the industrial city gave way to the service-oriented, high-tech metropolis, the aging, rust-belt landscape was reconstructed into a cultural center. The site of Millennium Park embodies this economic and spatial restructuring of Chicago, a local history lesson writ small.

The forces that generated Millennium Park are a reflection of nearly two centuries of Chicago history, politics, and culture. Before the creation of the park, Lake Michigan, the Illinois Central Railroad Company, the automobile, and city officials determined the evolution of the site. As Grant Park developed during the twentieth century, civic leaders envisioned the park as a cultural center. The desire for a state-of-the-art music pavilion shaped this debate. Following the construction of the Grant Park bandshell in 1931, more than fifteen designs for such a venue were proposed, including designs by Richard Bennett, Bruce Graham, C. F. Murphy, and Gene Summers. One such proposal—Lakefront Gardens in 1977—came close to realization. The failure of public and civic leaders to build a permanent music pavilion along Chicago's lakefront set the stage for Millennium Park.

The sale of the site by the Illinois Central Railroad after 150 years of control inspired Richard M. Daley to complete the final corner of Grant Park, Chicago's "front yard." He quickly recruited architect Adrian Smith of Skidmore, Owings & Merrill, who developed the initial comprehensive plan. But the project was transformed when Daley invited Sara Lee CEO John Bryan to lead a private campaign to raise $30 million to landscape a park above the new parking garage. Bryan quickly invoked Daniel Burnham: "Make no small plans." The chief executive not only raised over $235 million from the private sector, but along with other Millennium Park officials successfully recruited some of the world's leading artists and architects to design the major "enhancements" in the park. To support the construction of these grand amenities, Bryan exploited the corporate, cultural, and philanthropic networks he had developed during his quarter-century residence in Chicago.[3]

The addition of new, larger, and more expensive enhancements in the park, however, dramatically increased expenses. Millennium Park was soon embroiled in controversy. Negative media coverage transformed the public debate over the park during the final three years of construction and after. For better or worse, Millennium Park came to symbolize the inspirational vision and "I Will" forbearance of Richard M. Daley, and the dark underside of his legacy.

Millennium Park chronicles the creation of this major urban public space. For more than a century, most of the twenty-four acres of the park were part of a rail yard that separated the city from the lakefront. From 1998 to 2004, Chicago recaptured that private space and transformed it into a cultural and civic center. But Millennium Park is more than just a new park. It represents the globalization of art, the historical legacy of Richard M. Daley, the influence of corporate philanthropy, the use of culture as an engine of economic expansion, and the nature of political power in Chicago. Millennium Park embodies the transformed relationship of public art, private philanthropy, and urban cultural development at the onset of the twenty-first century. What follows is that story.

PART ONE HISTORY

Chapter 1

BEFORE GRANT PARK

By the end of the twentieth century, Grant Park was Chicago's "front yard." More than any other piece of Chicago real estate, the park's 319 acres along Lake Michigan immediately east of the city's Loop embodied the city's civic heart. Here Chicagoans came to witness the public appearances of famous people, celebrate special events, attend major festivals, and patronize leading museums. Traditional neighborhood and recreational activities—softball, ice skating, tennis, even promenading—were daily and seasonal events throughout the park.[1] The completion of Grant Park's final twenty-four acres—Millennium Park—in 2004 reinforced the centrality of the site in the cultural life of the metropolis.

Unlike the canonical events of Chicago history—the Great Fire of 1871, the World's Columbian Exposition of 1893, Daniel Burnham and Edward Bennett's 1909 *Plan of Chicago*, the race riot of 1919, the Century of Progress International Exposition of 1933–34—Grant Park evolved over the course of an entire century.[2] The park never had one comprehensive plan, nor was it the brainchild of a single architect. Rather, Grant Park developed in a gradual, piecemeal fashion, the combined product of various and sometimes unrelated architects, landscape designers, planners, artists, and business leaders.[3] The creation of Millennium Park was shaped by this 170-year tradition.

The overlapping histories of Grant and Millennium parks constitute more than the simple introduction of "nature" into the urban fabric. While both landscapes reflect the influence of the pastoral ideal and the parks' movement over time, they also embody the transportation innovations that defined the nineteenth- and twentieth-century city—canals, railroads, and automobiles.[4] Equally important, both park spaces exemplify places of civic, public, and artistic activity, and thereby represent changing ideas of culture in Chicago.

Before 1850, most of the future site of Grant Park was water—Lake Michigan. A portion of what became Millennium Park was a sand bar extending from the current entrance of the Chicago River as far south as the future location of Washington Street.[5] In 1836, the Board of Canal Commissioners responsible for raising money to construct a canal between the Mississippi River basin and the Great Lakes organized a public auc-

[Grant Park's] nearest counterpart is the Tuileries, the front yard of Paris, in which the Seine is the lake and the Rue de Rivoli, Michigan Boulevard. Grant Park is the nexus of the region, the "fabulous front yard."

HARRY WEESE, 1968

tion to sell Chicago's first city lots. Prominent citizens, fearful of commercial lakefront development, lobbied the commissioners to set aside open space along the lakefront. In response, the commissioners left the land from Randolph Street south to Park Row (11th Street) and east of Michigan Avenue undivided with the notation on the map designated "Public Ground—A Common to Remain Forever Open, Clear and Free of Any Buildings, or Other Obstruction, whatever."[6] No other document proved as influential in shaping the future development of Grant and Millennium parks.

Over the next decade, the lakefront land remained relatively untouched. In 1844, the canal commissioners transferred control of the open, undeveloped space to the City of Chicago; three years later, the narrow strip of land east of Michigan Avenue was designated "Lake Park" (although over the next half century, Chicagoans used both "Lake Park" and "Lake Front Park" to describe the area).[7] The small park proved to be among the most popular public places in the city, "the only breathing-space in the city," wrote one resident. Others compared Lake Park to New York's Battery, Boston's Tremont Street Mall, Philadelphia's Fairmount Park, and Charleston's Battery. Promenading, traditionally an elite custom limited to the upper classes of Chicago, became commonplace, bringing together Chicago's emerging middle classes. Boosters and promoters of Chicago even identified Michigan Avenue and the lakefront as "the Battery of Chicago."[8]

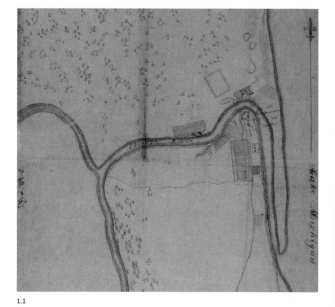

1.1

1.2

1.3

1.4

1.1. Hand-drawn U.S. government map of Chicago (1818). One of the earliest maps to include the future site of Millennium Park, this federal document illustrates various structures associated with one of the United States' first settlements—Fort Dearborn.

1.2. Detail from Joshua Hathaway, Jr., "Chicago with the School Section, Wabansia and Kinzie's Addition" (1834). Pine Street (later Michigan Ave.), labeled on the north, was later extended through the Fort Dearborn site. The sandbar that extended south and protected the entrance of the Chicago River bisected the future location of Millennium Park.

1.3. Detail of the Illinois and Michigan Canal Commissioners map, "Chicago with the Several Additions" (1836). This map, perhaps the most influential document affecting the development of Chicago's lakefront, set aside a portion of the lakefront south of the Chicago River as "Public Ground—A Common to Remain Forever Open, Clear and Free of any Buildings, or Other Obstruction, whatever." This area became Grant Park in the twentieth century.

1.4. The city of Chicago in 1855.

1.5. Chicago in 1872. Although the Michigan Avenue waterfront was associated with "Lake Park," some mid-nineteenth-century maps did not even identify Lake Park. Other renderings labeled the lakefront from Randolph Street to Harmon Place simply as "public ground." Figs. 1.4 and 1.5 both show that the area immediately south of Randolph Street remained water up to 1872. The 1872 map depicts only the area from Park Place (11th Street) to Peck Court (roughly Polk Street) as "Lake Park."

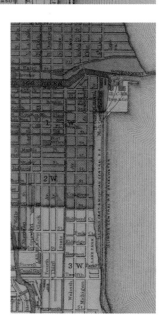

1.5

Lake Park and Michigan Avenue, however, were frequently threatened by the fierce winter storms off Lake Michigan. To prevent the park and the upscale street from washing into the lake, the city cut a deal. In 1852, the Illinois Central Railroad agreed to construct a protective breakwater in the lake north of Twelfth Street, thereby protecting Chicago's most expensive residential real estate along Michigan Avenue. In return, the city council granted a right-of-way to the railroad to enter the city along the breakwater. Over the next four years, the Illinois Central, Michigan Central, and Chicago, Burlington

1.6.
Stereographic view of Michigan Avenue and Lake Front Park looking north, 1868–1869.

1.7.
Michigan Avenue from Park Row in 1866.

1.8.
Michigan Terrace on Michigan Avenue (between Van Buren and Congress streets) in 1863. One of the city's elite residential blocks, Michigan Terrace (or Terrace Row) was designed by William W. Boyington.

1.9.
Lake Park with Great Central Depot in background (undated). Lithographic views of Lake Park depicted the site as a place for promenading. In contrast with Michigan Terrace, this undated photograph reveals an ill-kept and rutted landscape along Lake Michigan.

1.10

1.11 | 1.12

1.10. Charles Shober's "View of Illinois and Michigan Central Depot" (1860) from corner of Madison Street and Michigan Avenue.

1.11. Stereoscopic view of the Great Central Railway Station from the south rail yard (1860s).

1.12. The Great Central Railway Station from the south shortly after opening (1856).

1.13. These images depict the Illinois Central Railroad's Great Central Depot designed by architect Otto Matz. Considered one of the largest man-made structures in Chicago by the era of the Civil War, the terminus was 504 feet long and 166 feet wide. The truss arches protected eight lines of track and were considered the longest span constructed up to that time, illustrating Chicago's importance as the nation's rail center. Located on South Water Street, the headhouse served as both passenger depot and railroad company headquarters.

& Quincy railroads erected the barrier, creating an attractive and peaceful lagoon along Michigan Avenue. The protected and accessible basin of water was soon transformed into a center for recreational and casual boating.[9] The cooperative agreement between the city's public and private sectors was a portent for the future Millennium Park site.

Construction of the breakwater, however, proved to be a Faustian bargain. By 1857, the area north of Randolph Street stretching to the Chicago River was filled with railroad terminals, passenger facilities, warehouses, and other industrial structures. The most impressive of these structures was the Great Central Depot, a four-story, five hundred-foot-long terminus designed by Otto Matz that opened in 1856. Journalists immediately hailed the depot as one of "the finest passenger structures in the United States," and "the finest of the kind in the West." During the 1860s, the future site of Millennium Park filled with railroad tracks. Fearing that Michigan Avenue was becoming a "railroad avenue," well-to-do residents soon moved away from the lakefront. "Wealth and fashion," wrote James Sheahan in 1866, "have gone elsewhere."[10]

For the remainder of the nineteenth century, the Illinois Central Railroad was the key variable in the evolution of Lake Park. During the 1860s, with the expansion of terminal and freight facilities around the Great Central Depot, a switchyard fanned out to the east between Randolph and Adams Streets. In time, the right-of-way grew from two hundred feet at Adams to thirteen hundred feet at Randolph. Needless to say, the grade-level location of the tracks greatly impaired views of Lake Michigan. Only in 1919, when the tracks were finally lowered below street level, did the vista from the Michigan Avenue

1.14

1.15

promenade improve. Eventually four vehicular bridges and four pedestrian bridges were constructed above the tracks.[11]

Equally important were efforts by the Illinois Central to control development along the lakefront. In 1869, the Illinois legislature passed the Lake Front Act over the veto of governor John M. Palmer. The law granted the City of Chicago the full title to land earlier dedicated to the Illinois and Michigan Canal commissioners and confirmed to the Illinois Central the right to use certain submerged lands east of the lakeshore. Critics dubbed the legislation "the lakefront steal" because the Illinois Central, Michigan Central, and Burlington railroads gained the right to erect new stations east of Michigan Avenue between Randolph and Monroe Streets, then referred to as "the three blocks" and today the site of Millennium Park. Only strenuous public opposition discouraged the railroads from developing the land, and in 1873, the state legislature repealed the statute.[12]

These setbacks, however, never dampened the Illinois Central's enthusiasm for acquiring more lakefront real estate. In 1881, the railroad proposed extending the rail lines another one hundred feet into Lake Michigan, creating a three-hundred-foot rail bed parallel to and immediately east of Lake Park. With 170 trains "passing both ways over these tracks daily," argued Benjamin F. Ayer of the Illinois Central, commercial development was a necessity. Opponents like G. J. Lydecker of the Army Corps of Engineers concluded that such proposals would simply turn the lakefront and Lake Park into "a vast railroad yard."[13]

1.14. Alexander Hesler photograph of Lake Front Park and Great Central Depot (1858).

1.15. Michigan Avenue (1866) from the Lake and Great Central Depot. Figures 1.14 and 1.15 illustrate the close physical relationship of Lake Park and the railroad throughout the nineteenth century. Note the elegant homes along Michigan Avenue during the 1850s and 1860s. By 1873, the erection of the Inter-State Industrial Exposition and various railroad structures dramatically changed the vista. The rail lines in front of the station occupy the site of Millennium Park.

1.16. "Bird's Eye View of Chicago, 1857." This view captures the industrial nature of the Millennium Park site in 1857. The wall protecting the rail lines from Lake Michigan was the inspiration for the "seam" in Millennium Park's Lurie Garden.

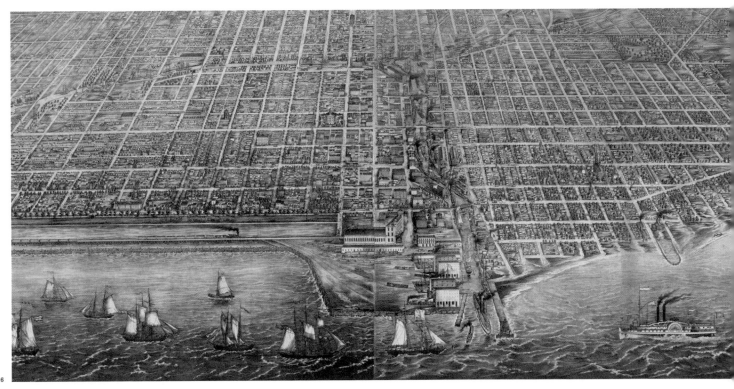

1.16

Equally important was the impact of the Great Fire of 1871. In addition to the destruction of Grand Central Depot north of Randolph Street, the area between Michigan Avenue and the railroad breakwater became a landfill site for charred rubble. Over the next twenty years, the lagoon was filled in and, for the first time, land east of the railroad trestle was created. Much to the chagrin of many citizens, however, the site was used primarily for dumping garbage, transforming the lakefront into an unsightly open space.[14]

More significant, in the haste to rebuild Chicago in the aftermath of the fire, a number of structures appeared in Lake Park, directly violating the "open, clear and free" provision. In 1873, the 165-feet-high Inter-State Industrial Exposition Building (1873–91), designed by W. W. Boyington just south of Monroe Street (at the future location of the Art Institute), inaugurated Chicago's first exposition and proclaimed the city's recovery from the fire.[15] At approximately the same time, the Illinois Central built an additional freight depot adjacent to the exposition building. Based on legislation passed in 1869, the railroad was granted "in fee" the land between Randolph and Monroe Streets and Michigan Avenue and the railroad tracks. From 1874 to 1891, the Illinois Central leased the property to the Baltimore and Ohio Railroad.[16] Finally, in 1881, municipal authorities granted the federal government the right to construct two armories in the park.[17]

In addition to providing space for business and industrial purposes, Lake Front Park also hosted professional sports. In 1871, the city leased the northern part of the park to Albert G. Spaulding, owner of the Chicago White Stockings of the National League (forerunners of the Chicago Cubs, not the White Sox). Spaulding promptly built the Union baseball grounds. Situated in the relatively narrow space between Michigan Avenue and the Illinois Central tracks north of Madison Street, the grounds seated seven

1.17. The Great Central Depot of the Illinois Central Railroad lay in ruins after the Great Fire of 1871.

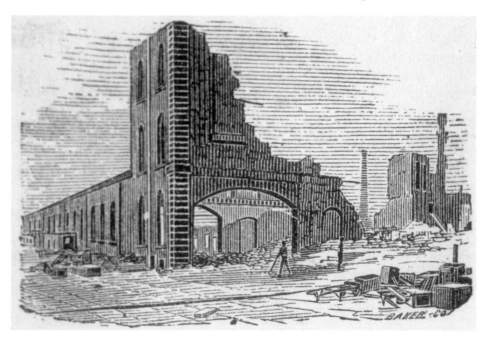

1.18. Inter-State Industrial Exposition Building (1873).

1.19. Map showing the B&O Depot (1886).

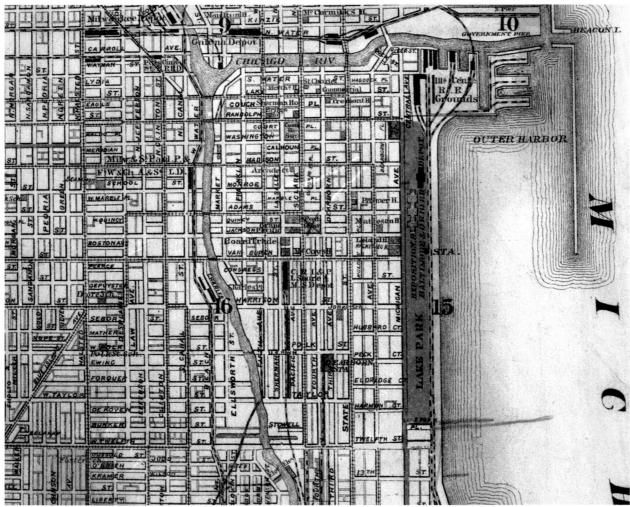

1.20. Pauline Dohn Rudolph, "Inter-State Industrial Exposition" (1873). In the aftermath of the fire, a number of structures were built in Lake Park, in apparent violation of the earlier restrictions. The most prominent was the Inter-State Industrial Exposition Building in 1873, designed by William Boyington and occupying the site of the future Art Institute. From 1883 to 1891, the Baltimore and Ohio Railroad Depot leased a "first-class" brick freight warehouse (fig. 1.19). Millennium Park's *Crown Fountain*, Chase Promenade, and Lurie Garden now occupy this space.

thousand spectators with the main grandstand behind home plate located along Randolph Street. A few months after the field opened, the entire structure was incinerated by the Great Fire.[18]

Baseball did not rebound as quickly as the rest of Chicago. A professional team did not reappear until 1874, and Spaulding did not rebuild the grounds until 1878. This time, he reconfigured the field, locating home plate near the corner of Madison and Michigan Avenue. The playing area was, by later standards, cramped; the foul lines measured only 180 feet in left field, 196 in right field, shorter than some Little League fields today. Outfield fences were so short that balls hit over them were deemed ground-rule doubles, not home runs, prior to 1884. When such out-of-the-park hits were defined as home runs, Chicago slugger Ned Williamson established the single-season home-run record of twenty-seven. That remained the standard until 1919 when Babe Ruth hit twenty-nine.[19]

The baseball grounds were considerably improved in 1883, doubling the seating capacity to eight thousand. The *Chicago Tribune* and *Harper's Weekly* each proclaimed the "palatial" structure to be the best in the country, if not the world. The field's proximity to the retail district of State Street and the team's success (winning three consecutive National League championships from 1880 to 1882) made the site a popular entertainment venue. In 1882, the team averaged three thousand spectators per game, reportedly

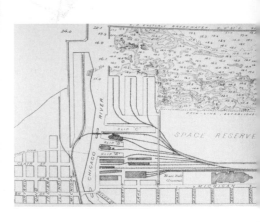

1.21. Interior view of baseball grounds, looking south. Lake Park hosted professional baseball from 1874 to 1883. After 1878, the grandstand was located on the south end of the field.

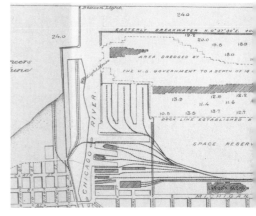

1.23
—
1.24

1.22. Detail from Theodore R. Davis, "Bird's-Eye View of Chicago" (1871). This view shows the Central Elevator on the Chicago River, Great Central Depot north of Randolph Street, and the "White Stocking Base-ball Ground."

1.23, 1.24. Lake Front Park and Chicago Harbor, 1883 and 1884. The 1883 map, published by the U.S. Army Corps of Engineers, shows the baseball grounds. By 1884, the grounds were removed from Lake Front Park.

1.25. Currier & Ives, "The City of Chicago" (1892). Despite the dismantling of the baseball grounds in 1884, Currier & Ives lithographs such as this one published nearly a decade later in 1892 included the grounds. From 1878 to 1883, the grandstand was located on the south end of the field, not the north end as depicted here. Note the unidentified structure between the baseball grounds and Exposition Building, most likely the B&O depot.

"made up in good part of the better classes of the community." Reporters believed that attendance at the lakefront field surpassed that of any other city in the United States. Such success, however, proved short-lived. At the end of the 1884 season, Spaulding's squad was forced out. Since the land was given to the city by the federal government with the stipulation that no commercial venture could use it, the team was compelled to move to a new facility on the South Side.[20]

Debates over lakefront development rights entered a new phase after 1890. In 1892, the United States Supreme Court finally ruled that the state of Illinois did not have the authority to grant lakefront water rights or control to the Illinois Central. In fact, such power belonged to the city "in trust for public use." Under this public trust doctrine, as it became known, the municipality owned all the filled land east of Michigan Avenue between Park Row (previously Eleventh Street) and Randolph Street, including the land on which the railroad had its right-of-way.[21] That same year, the Illinois Central Railroad Company demolished the passenger station north of Randolph Street in anticipation of the opening of the new terminal south of Lake Park at Twelfth Street. A smaller facility for suburban trains replaced the old depot, which some described as a "ruin" and "an eyesore." The remainder of the site was thereafter devoted primarily to freight service.[22]

In anticipation of the World's Columbian Exposition in 1893, the World's Congresses Building was erected in the park along Michigan Avenue, just south of Monroe Street. Designed by Shepley, Rutan and Coolidge (the successor firm to Henry Hobson Richardson), the building was the one fair structure located in the park after planners rejected Lake Park as the site for the exposition. The edifice, which replaced the Inter-State Industrial Exposition Building, housed a variety of exhibits on religion, folklore, and music. More significant, the Congresses Building was the first structure to obtain unanimous approval from property owners along Lake Park, a precedent that proved critical in the creation of Millennium Park a century later. The park's newest building became the permanent home of the Art Institute of Chicago at the conclusion of the fair.[23]

Among the property owners who approved the plan to construct the Art Institute was Aaron Montgomery Ward. More than any other lakefront landlord, Ward disapproved of the park's unsightliness. In 1890, he initiated the first of a series of lawsuits to keep the park free of new buildings, specifically the wooden shanties, garbage, and other refuse that littered the site. Ward argued that Michigan Avenue property owners held an easement on this property and that the city was responsible for preventing encroachments. A decade later, the Illinois Supreme Court expanded Ward's claim in concluding that all landfill east of Michigan Avenue was subject to the same dedications and easements. In 1909, the Illinois Supreme Court further reinforced Ward's opposition to development in the park when he sought to prevent the erection of the Field Museum of Natural History in the center of the park.[24]

Ward's litigation attracted increasing attention and gained importance after the World's Columbian Exposition. By 1896, when state and city legislation placed Lake Front Park under the control of the South Park Commissioners, the municipality was

1.26. New Illinois Central station at Michigan Avenue and Park Row (1892).

1.27. Randolph Street Passenger Station (1895). In 1893, the Illinois Central Railroad opened a new terminal at the south end of Lake Park (fig. 1.26). The erection of this new modern passenger facility on Park Row necessitated the destruction of the old station at the northern end of the park, which was replaced with a more modest facility (1.27).

1.28. View of Lake Park with train (1891). The railroad remained an ongoing industrial presence in Lake Park throughout the nineteenth century.

1.29. "Map of the Lake-Front from the Chicago River to 16th Street Showing the Original Shore-lines and lands reclaimed by the Illinois Central Rail Road" (ca. 1894). This map depicts various landfill and structural additions from 1836 to 1894 on the future site of Millennium Park.

1.26

1.27

1.28

1.29

1.30. "Railroad Ownership" (1913). Few maps better illustrate the role of the railroad in the physical and economic development of Chicago. By 1890, railroad corporations not only controlled the most valuable property along the lakefront and the future site of Millennium Park; they were also the dominant real estate interests in land surrounding the Loop.

1.31. Aaron Montgomery Ward. "Here is park frontage on the lake, comparing favorably with the Bay of Naples, which city officials would crowd with buildings, transforming the breathing spot for the poor into a showground of the educated rich. I do not think it is right." Mail-order king Ward thus defended his then-unpopular lawsuit to prevent the erection of the Field Museum in the center of Grant Park.

1.32. The Art Institute of Chicago shortly after construction in 1892.

1.33. Aerial view of north end of Grant Park (1919).

1.34. Aerial view of north end of Grant Park, looking northeast (1929). These aerial views of the future site of Millennium Park show the original peristyle along Michigan Avenue and the massive lakefront rail yard to both the north and south of Randolph Street. The beginnings of the Monroe Street parking lot and the landfill for Grant Park are evident. Note that the original Randolph Street viaduct (in the center of 1929 photograph) was only one level. Millennium Park sits on the area to the right (south) of the viaduct.

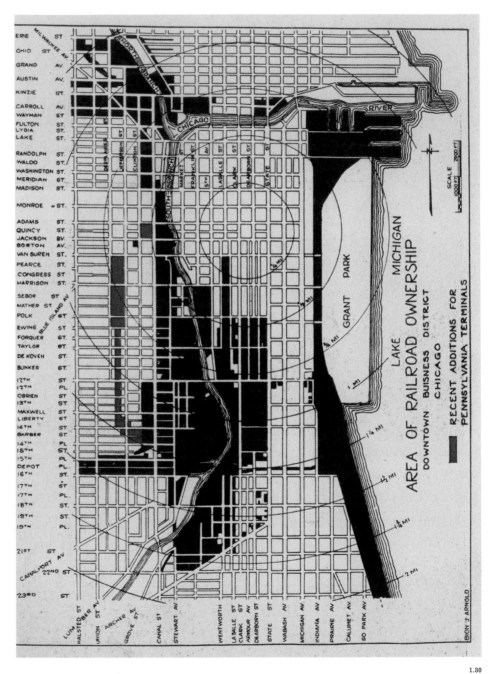

1.30

creating parkland east of the Illinois Central tracks. Although the process was slow—6 acres by 1898, 26 acres by 1901, 49 acres by 1903—by 1910, the park comprised 205 acres. The additions included a beachhead east of Michigan Avenue and Washington Street which later became the Richard J. Daley Bicentennial Plaza and Millennium Park. [25]

1.34

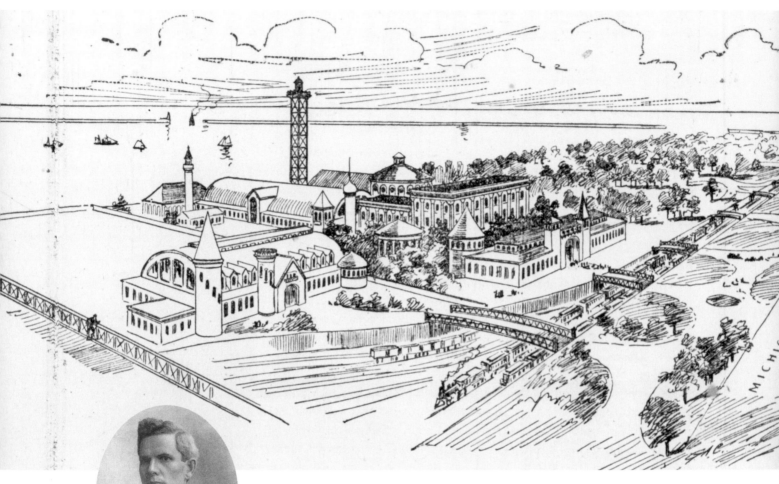

2.1. Martin Madden's plan for a
new lakefront park (1894). The
alderman's scheme proposed lower-
ing the Illinois Central tracks, filling
in Lake Michigan 750 feet east of the
tracks and from Randolph Street to
Park Row. The new park would include a parade ground, armory, and
permanent exposition buildings.

2.2. Alderman Martin B. Madden
was among the earliest to plan the
development of Lake Front Park into
a grand civic center.

Chapter 2

CREATING GRANT PARK

The closing of the World's Columbian Exposition of 1893 stimulated a movement devoted to lakefront improvement. Why not, asked some civic leaders, create a monumental Court of Honor like the one that graced the fair adjacent to the business district along the magnificent Lake Michigan shoreline? In December 1894, alderman Martin B. Madden proposed such a design. Predicting that the site "would be the greatest park in America," Madden proposed filling in Lake Michigan east of the Illinois Central Railroad tracks and creating a new, two-hundred-acre landscape that would feature an armory, a parade ground, and permanent exposition buildings. The alderman's proposal was the first of many over the ensuing century to envision Chicago's lakefront as a civic center.[1]

Madden's plan quickly generated a public debate. On August 9, 1895, Peter B. Wight, working on behalf of the Municipal Improvement League and the Illinois chapter of the American Institute of Architects, presented a competing plan. Wight envisioned a 140-acre park with an open center and monumental architecture located around the edges of a central formal lagoon. Structures included a ten-thousand-seat amphitheater rimmed with a peristyle and topped with a triumphal arch, an exposition building, an armory, a police and fire building, a city hall, the Crerar Library and the Field Columbian Museum. Rendered in a classical style, the plan expressly reflected the influence of the World's Columbian Exposition.[2]

We believe that an opportunity here exists to produce a park and a water front that will have no equal in the world.

FERDINAND W. PECK (1895)

2.3. Peter Wight's "Proposed Plan for Lake Front Park, Chicago" (1895).

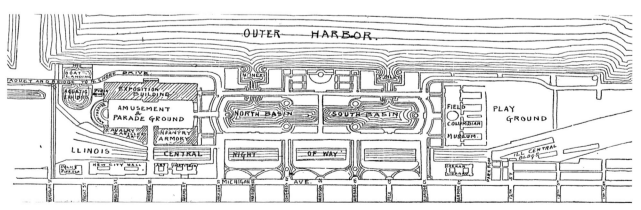

Like Madden, Wight suggested depressing the Illinois Central's railroad tracks, elevating the park grade, and crossing the tracks with bridges at all streets. Wight also recommended a "lake drive" connecting the North and South sides of the city. "This grand drive will be like the famous Rotten Row of London," Wight predicted, eventually becoming "the most fashionable drive of the city."[3]

Both Wight's and Madden's visions challenged prevailing views that parks should provide pastoral respites from the grime and contagion of the city. The park's location along the lakefront, insisted Wight, demanded a different strategy. He argued that any new lakefront park would depart in both character and form from other city parks. Chicago did not need another Lincoln or Jackson Park in the heart of the city. "It is not simply that the city needs another park," insisted Wight; "it needs another sort of park." Because of the park's waterfront location, the opportunity to create a civic and cultural center—"a greater court of honor," in Wight's words—should not be squandered. "Here art should predominate over nature, and symmetry take precedence over picturesqueness."[4]

Although largely forgotten today, the Wight or Municipal Improvement League plan proved to be far more prophetic of Chicago's lakefront development than the much ballyhooed *Plan of Chicago* (1909) by Daniel Burnham and Edward Bennett. Wight envisioned numerous features later implemented in Grant Park and along the lakefront. First, the construction of *Buckingham Fountain* reflected the adoption of a formal, classical design with an open center. Second, the creation of a lakeshore drive connecting Chicago's north and south park systems and the sinking of the Illinois Central Railroad tracks below grade addressed traffic concerns. Third, the Field Museum and various playing fields were located on the southern end of park. Fourth, a "Government Pier" was placed where Municipal (Navy) Pier was later situated. Finally, a large outdoor bandshell was placed at the north end of park, an unwitting precursor to Frank Gehry's Pritzker Pavilion a century later.

In 1895, Daniel Burnham and Charles Atwood authored a competing design that echoed the Municipal Improvement League plan. All these designs retained the classical architectural schemes and envisioned a lakefront park as Chicago's civic center. In addition, each reflected Dwight Heald Perkins's claim a decade later that "Chicago cannot move the Illinois Central road, but it can move the shore line eastward." The Burnham-Atwood plan, however, featured a significant difference: it placed the large,

2.4. Burnham and Atwood lakefront plan (1895). By 1895, Chicago civic leaders were debating how to improve the lakefront. Daniel Burnham proclaimed: "The front of our city should be very beautiful, and it can be made so. From a disgusting ash-heap, fringed with rotten piers and unsightly fishermen's derricks, should spring within the next few years, lagoons and wooded terraces unsurpassed in loveliness."

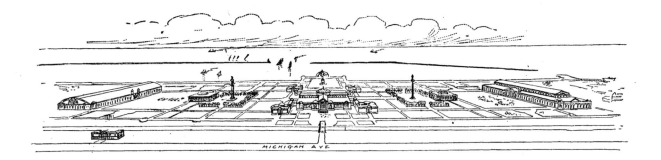

MICHIGAN AVE

neoclassical Field Museum in the center of the park, flanked by formal plazas and long, rectangular buildings at the extreme ends. Addressing the South Park Commission in 1897, Burnham proposed a grand scheme that would "make Chicago so beautiful that it will out-rival Paris."[5]

In 1903, the city commissioned Olmsted Brothers to develop a series of plans for the park, renamed Grant Park in 1901 in honor of Ulysses S. Grant. By this time, Burnham had been chosen as the architect for the Field Museum. The state legislature's Museum Act of 1903 allowed for tax revenues to build and maintain both the Field Museum and the Crerar Library in Grant Park, with the former occupying a central position within the park. Wight immediately criticized the Field Museum's proposed central location, and this issue ultimately generated the precedent-setting lawsuit by Montgomery Ward. Furthermore, the plans and models Olmsted Brothers developed recalled both Versailles near Paris and the McMillan Plan of Washington, D.C. (1901) with their formal layouts, classical-style buildings, symmetrically laid-out gardens, and rejection of commercial structures.[6]

Within this classical framework, however, Olmsted Brothers suggested different alternatives for the north and south ends of Grant Park. One plan adopted a naturalistic form, landscaping both ends of the park as pastoral settings. Whereas the four entrances to the Field Museum looked out on statuary, the northern and southern thirds of the park would be "meadows" with irregular plantings of trees and bordered by two columns of trees on their perimeters.[7]

This vision of the park as a place of contemplative reflection (as embodied in the meadows), however, was later replaced with a second Olmsted Brothers plan that envisioned a more associational and less bucolic park. Large playfields, surrounded by a border of trees, replaced the meadows. In the area immediately east of the Art Institute (Butler Field today), Olmsted Brothers envisioned a "Concert Grove" that included a round, raised bandstand surrounded by four encircling rows of trees. While the land-

2.5. Chicago Architectural Club Plan (1896). This unattributed design was the product of a music pavilion competition sponsored by the Chicago Architectural Club and the Illinois Chapter of the American Institute of Architects. The pavilion was to be a semi-circular, roofed theater with a seating capacity of 3,000 and a stage capable of holding 75 musicians.

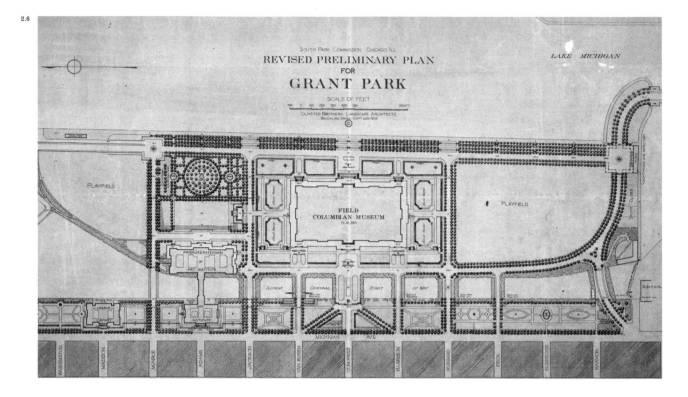

2.6

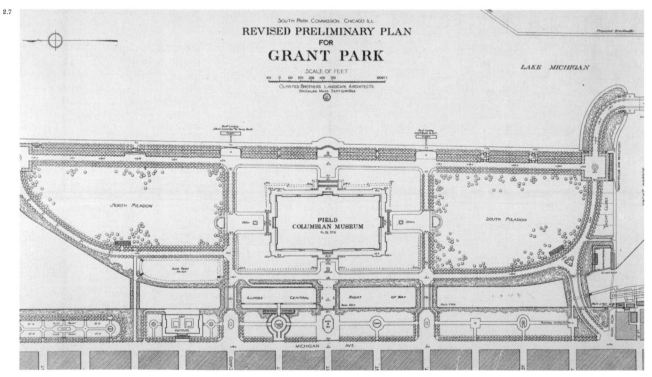

2.7

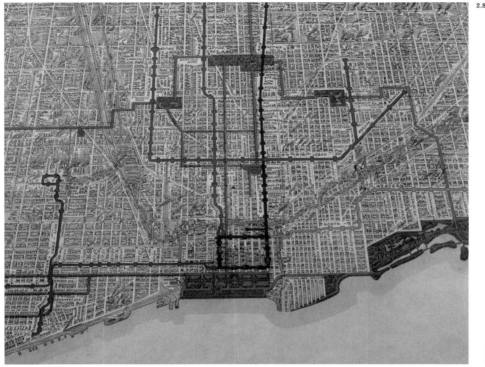

scaping was formal, the absence of any permanent seating indicated that the Olmsteds anticipated an informal setting for concerts and other musical events.[8]

These designs and the later *Plan of Chicago* (1909) envisioned a new, inner-city core organized around a grand boulevard, and classical and monumental cultural institutions. This vision relegated the commercial district to a decidedly secondary position. Burnham, in particular, expressly sought to create a civic center. The institutions of government, literature, art, and culture would serve as the common ground for harmonizing individual and class interests. In reaction to two decades of violent labor struggles, Chicago's civic elite embraced the City Beautiful movement because of its visible emphasis upon order and control. The City Beautiful designs featured statues and monuments, both heroic and allegorical, reinforcing the social ideals of the movement: classical designs, civic unity, and American nationalism.[9]

Burnham's vision, however, proved secondary to Aaron Montgomery Ward's. The mail-order entrepreneur sued to prevent the erection of the Field Museum or any similar structure in the park. In 1911, the Illinois Supreme Court ruled in Ward's favor. But all was not lost. New landfill at the southern end of the park from 1911 to 1915 allowed for the construction of the Field Museum (1915–1919), and eventually the John G. Shedd Aquarium (1929) and the Adler Planetarium (1930).[10]

The resolution of the Ward litigation and the publication of Burnham and Bennett's *Plan of Chicago* allowed city officials to begin the major construction of Grant Park. In

2.6. Olmsted Brothers, "Revised Preliminary Plan for Grant Park" (Sept. 22, 1903), no. 20.

2.7. Olmsted Brothers, "Revised Preliminary Plan for Grant Park" (Sept. 22, 1903), no. 31. Olmsted Brothers completed a series of plans for the lakefront. One plan featured a playfield and concert grove, while another included a simple meadow and a more pastoral setting.

2.8. J. B. McComber, "Birds-Eye View of the Elevated Railroads, Parks and Boulevards of Chicago," 1910 (detail). The earliest maps of Grant Park sometimes depicted a nonexistent landscape. This view, for example, includes the Field Museum in the center of the park. Furthermore, Grant Park extends from 11th Street immediately north of the Illinois Central Station to Lake Street on the north end. This rendering not only replaced the existing Illinois Central rail yards between Randolph and Lake streets with a landscaped park, but also completely covered over or eliminated the exposed tracks of the railroad extending through the park.

1913, mayor Fred A. Busse created the Chicago Plan Commission, a 328-member organization responsible for implementing the *Plan of Chicago*. Bennett served as consulting architect for the commission from 1913 to 1930 and the South Park Commissioners relied on him for design ideas after 1915. Over the next decade, Bennett completed a number of plans for various features in the north end of Grant Park. Development, however, was repeatedly postponed until after World War I because of resistance by property owners and legal difficulties.[11]

Between 1917 and 1929, Bennett and his new partners, William E. Parsons, Cyrus Thomas (both trained, like Bennett, at the Ecole des Beaux-Arts in Paris), and Harry T. Frost, developed a variety of plans, sketches, and drawings. These designs reflected the influence of earlier classical plans by Wight, Burnham, and others, while adding French garden and French Renaissance features. Bennett's first Grant Park project was the north section between Randolph and Jackson Streets along Michigan Avenue between 1915 and 1917. The beaux arts classical balustrades along the Michigan Avenue promenade were later replicated over the Congress Drive, Balbo Drive, Jackson Drive, Van Buren Street, and Harrison Street bridges. In 1927, the completion of *Buckingham Fountain* gave the park a magnificent centerpiece.[12]

The French Renaissance elements in Grant Park emphasized symmetrical spaces, axial views through the landscape, formal rows of trees and hedges, terraces, recessed lawn panels, fountains, classical architectural details, and sculpture. Spaces within the park became "rooms" with clear shapes and configurations (usually squares or rectangles), much like the *salles* of French formal gardens. Ornamental trees, paths, and hedges further subdivided these rooms. The principle element used to articulate the formal design of Grant Park was (and remains) the tree, specifically the American Elm, which created an imaginary envelope of approximately fifty feet above grade throughout Grant Park.[13]

Because of its piecemeal development, however, Grant Park never achieved the symmetry that was originally envisioned. Butler Field on the north end of the park, for example, was originally designed to mirror Hutchinson Field to the south by being three blocks in length, but that plan was abandoned when the city extended Monroe Drive from Michigan Avenue to Lake Shore Drive. The area north of Monroe and east of Columbus remained an unsightly, open parking lot from 1921 to 1976, when Richard J. Daley Bicentennial Plaza and a two-level, underground garage opened.[14]

Grant Park's architectural style also changed over time. During the 1930s, art deco designs supplemented the earlier classicism. Bennett's initial plan for the Outer Drive Bridge, for example, followed a classical form, but was abandoned for an art deco style with heavy square pylons, smoother surfaces, and streamlined incised details. Similarly, the Christopher Columbus sculpture at the south end of Grant Park was placed on an art deco pedestal, and the new bandshell (1933–1978) in Arvey/Hutchinson Field was modeled after the Hollywood Bowl. Finally, the Monroe Drive Bridge (1939) assumed an art deco style, replacing an earlier classical bridge.[15]

In a comparison that would have pleased both Daniel Burnham and Edward Bennett, Chicago Park District officials still liken Grant Park to Versailles. The park represents the city to the world, just as Versailles does France. Both were reclaimed land, built with landfill on a flat terrain. They provide settings for spectacles, a logical system of outdoor spaces in various sizes, and different levels of formality to accommodate public events, and they extend the formal order of the city into the garden. In the words of park district officials, the park serves as "the interface between Culture, the city and Nature," the French countryside in the case of Versailles, Lake Michigan for Chicago.[16]

As Bennett and his colleagues designed the park, a new invention was transforming not only Grant Park but the American city—the automobile. In 1908, park superintendent J. F. Foster attended the first International Road Congress in Paris to learn the latest developments in road making in order to adapt Chicago parks for increasing automobile use. As early as 1910, the city installed "automobile-proof pavement"—concrete two inches thick—in Grant Park. Although the automobile was still in its infancy when Burnham and Bennett authored the *Plan of Chicago*, they nevertheless envisioned Grant

2.9. This 1929 aerial view depicts the uncompleted Grant Park at the onset of the Great Depression. The recently constructed *Buckingham Fountain* (1927) stands out amidst a treeless, barren plaza. To the right is the future site of Lake Shore Drive. Northeast of the fountain sits Augustus Saint-Gaudens's sculpture of *(Seated) Abraham Lincoln* (cast 1908, erected 1926) facing the future site of the Court of Presidents. Columbus Drive bisects this portion of the park. At the north end of the park is the Art Institute and its expanded facility over the Illinois Central tracks, the Illinois Central yards, and the Monroe Street Parking Station.

Park as part of a metropolitan park system linking the North and South sides of Chicago along the lakefront and then to the suburbs via parkways and highways.[17]

In 1923, architect Eliel Saarinen proposed a vast underground parking structure in Grant Park that included a bus and auto terminal beneath the landscape. While it was never built, Saarinen proved to be an astute soothsayer, recognizing the automobile's future as the dominating influence on Grant Park's twentieth-century development. "The shape my plan has taken is in large measure influenced by traffic problems," wrote Saarinen, "more especially the solution of the automobile traffic problem." Concerned with the flow of traffic through Grant Park and along Michigan Avenue, Saarinen envisioned a twelve-lane, 120-foot-wide sunken highway located roughly where Columbus Drive sits today. More ambitiously, he included a three-story, underground, 47,000-car "parking terminal" under Grant Park to accommodate automobiles from outlying suburbs. Saarinen wanted to eliminate car traffic in the park, except along the shore close to the lake. All of this was feasible by extending Grant Park with landfill generated by the parking terminal's construction. The income from parking fees would support the plan financially. "The park should be reserved as a recreation and promenade ground for citizens," insisted Saarinen.[18]

2.10

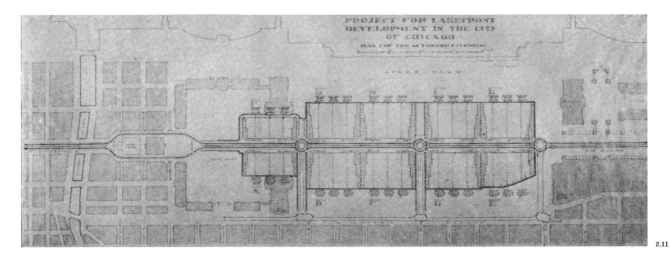

2.11

2.12

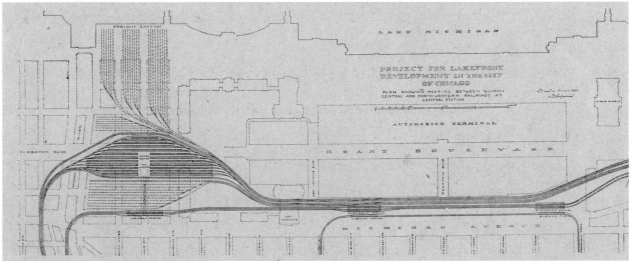

2.13

2.14. Aerial view of the Illinois Central terminal site between the Chicago River and Monroe Street. Saarinen's was not the only plan that transformed the industrial and warehouse facilities south of the Chicago River. This 1929 proposal shows a completed Lake Shore Drive, an extended Wacker Drive, a series of high-rise structures reminiscent of those depicted in Burnham and Bennett's *Plan of Chicago* (1909), a completed Grant Park east of the peristyle, and a new outdoor concert venue between Monroe and Washington Streets.

2.15. Monroe Street Garage in Grant Park, 1928. By the late 1920s, cars were starting to fill the northern end of Grant Park. Note the peristyle in the left background.

2.16. Aerial view of construction of Lake Shore Drive and bridge, 1937. The construction of Lake Shore Drive during the 1930s increased both the flow of traffic through Grant Park and the usage of the Monroe Street Parking Station. Note the construction of the Randolph Street viaduct, the beginnings of the S-curve of Lake Shore Drive (which was reconfigured in 1986), the erection of the bridge over the Chicago River, and the presence of the peristyle.

2.17. Projected aerial photograph of Randolph Street Railroad Terminal (1933).

2.18. Architectural drawings of facade of proposed Randolph Street Terminal.

Like many of his generation, Saarinen was entranced by the skyscraper. He framed the north and south ends of Grant Park with two high-rises, the Grant Hotel at Randolph and Grant Boulevard (Columbus today) and Chicago Tower to the south, correctly foreseeing that the Illinois Central's property would become too expensive for manufacturing. Culture tied all of this together. The lakefront was to be a monumental space dedicated to art and cultural expression. Grant Park would, in Saarinen's words, "become to Chicago and America what the Louvre with Place de la Concorde and Champs Elysees is to Paris and Europe."[19]

Saarinen was undoubtedly responding to the dramatic changes taking place within the Loop and the Grant Park area. Parking and traffic control were major public concerns after 1920. In 1921, the first parking lot was added to Grant Park—the Monroe Street Garage (later called the Monroe Street Parking Station). In 1925, traffic control signals were installed in the Loop. A year later, the city banned all commercial vehicles from the Loop unless they were making deliveries or pickups, while angular parking anywhere in the city was prohibited. In 1928, parking was prohibited in the Loop during the working day. And between 1926 and 1939, Chicago constructed one of the nation's first roads designed primarily for automobile traffic—Outer Lake Shore Drive, extending from Jackson Park to Foster Avenue.[20]

In 1933, the Railway Terminal Committee of the Chicago City Council offered a plan to consolidate all of the city's passenger terminals at the existing Illinois Central freight station north of Randolph Street. Authored by Edward Noonan, a consulting engineer, the plan proposed eliminating the three major passenger terminals then in existence south of the Loop, which critics claimed physically blocked commercial development in that area. According to Noonan, the Randolph Street site offered numerous advantages: accessibility to vehicular traffic along Lake Shore Drive and to mass transit in the Loop; little construction interference with existing railroad operations and vehicular traffic; and the segregation of freight traffic and related freight warehouses. Most significantly, the report was one of the earliest to acknowledge that the Illinois Central no longer used much of the land north of Randolph Street, since the construction of Wacker Drive in the 1920s had forced the relocation of the large produce–freight business.[21]

While the railway terminal proposal was never executed, the Illinois Central opened

2.16

2.17

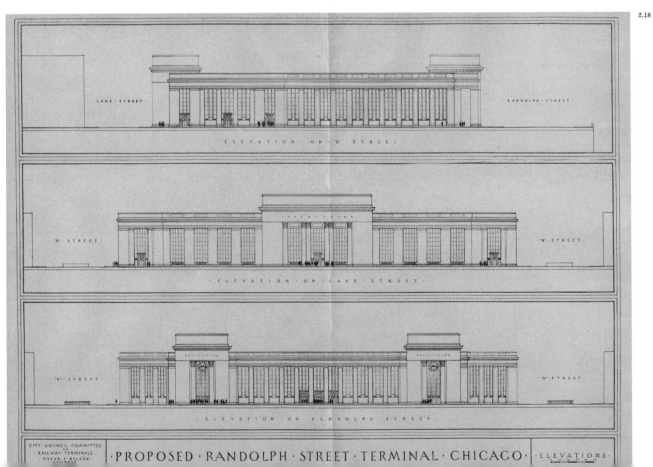

2.18

ELEVATION ON 'B' STREET

LAKE STREET

RANDOLPH STREET

ELEVATION ON LAKE STREET

'D' STREET

'B' STREET

ELEVATION ON RANDOLPH STREET

'B' STREET

'D' STREET

CITY·COUNCIL·COMMITTEE
ON
RAILWAY·TERMINALS
OSCAR·F·NELSON
CHAIRMAN

PROPOSED·RANDOLPH·STREET·TERMINAL·CHICAGO

ELEVATIONS

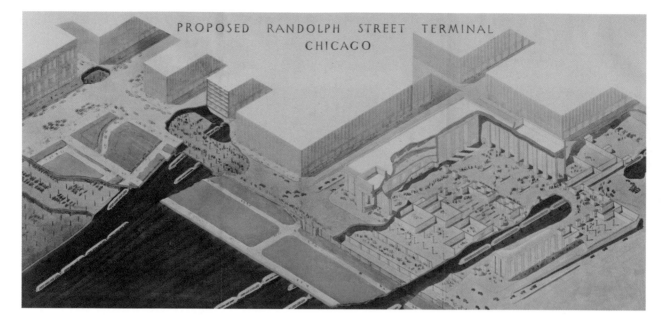

PROPOSED RANDOLPH STREET TERMINAL
CHICAGO

2.19. The influence of both Daniel Burnham and Eliel Saarinen appear in the 1933 plan of the Railway Terminal Committee of the Chicago City Council authored by Edward Noonan. Noonan envisioned a new central station for all passenger service at Randolph Street and recognized the changing land use in the vicinity. The prospective renderings in figs. 2.17, 2.18, and 2.19 show the terminal located at just east of the future site of Prudential Plaza and the Aon Building with a proposed park and plaza over the future site of Millennium Park.

a new, reconstructed suburban passenger terminal at Randolph Street in 1931. The project also resulted in reconstructing the Randolph Street viaduct into a three-deck, 128-foot-wide roadway. The viaduct, in fact, formed the structural framing and part of the roof of the station building. By this time, the Illinois Central carried nearly forty million suburban passengers annually, most of whom passed through the Randolph Street terminal.[22]

After World War II, the impact of the automobile at the northern end of Grant Park grew more visible. By 1946, the Chicago Park District operated three parking lots in Grant Park, effectively renting public property for automobile space: the Monroe Street Parking Station (1921), the Goodman Theatre lot (1937), and the Soldier Field lot (1946). The parking station, completed in 1938, was particularly noteworthy. The twenty-four-hour, 85,000-square-yard facility with a capacity of 3,500 cars remained the largest single-fee parking facility in the United States into the 1950s. More significantly, annual usage doubled from 1936 to 1946, rising from less than 500,000 cars to over 1.1 million a decade later. By the 1970s, the annual number of automobiles parking in Grant Park topped 2.5 million; by the 1980s, 3 million (see appendix 2). [23]

The growing reliance upon the automobile forced city officials to find more parking spaces in Grant Park. In 1952, the city issued $8.3 million in revenue bonds for the construction of a 2,359-vehicle underground garage in the park. Designed by Ralph Burke, the former chief engineer of the Chicago Park District, the facility (later designated the Grant Park North Garage) opened on September 1, 1954. By 1957 and after, the garage accommodated more than 1.6 million cars annually and averaged about 4,400 daily. In a development that significantly influenced Millennium Park a half century later, the construction of the garage resulted in the elimination of the Edward Bennett–designed peristyle.[24]

2.22

2.20, 2.21, 2.22. The Illinois Central yard between Monroe and Randolph Streets, 1951. These views show the future site of Millennium Park. The Monroe Street Parking Station is visible in 2.21, separated from the Illinois Central yards by the former seawall that is now represented by the "seam" in Millennium Park's Lurie Garden. The Randolph Street viaduct appears in the rear, as well as the Furniture Mart (now 680 N. Lake Shore Drive). The Tribune Tower stands behind the Pabst sign in 2.20. Figure 2.22 shows the yards looking south from the Randolph Street with the Art Institute in the background. Note the numerous trailers in the yard, signaling the declining importance of the railroad and the rise of automotive trucking.

The Grant Park underground garage reflected a larger, national trend of how municipalities accommodated the automobile. The first underground, underpark garage appeared beneath San Francisco's Union Park in 1940 with spaces for 1,700 cars. After World War II, Los Angeles's Pershing Square (1951) and Pittsburgh's Mellon Square (1953) opened similar facilities with capacities for 2,150 and 896 cars, respectively. By 1992, nearly a dozen such inner-city structures were found throughout the United States (see appendix 3).[25]

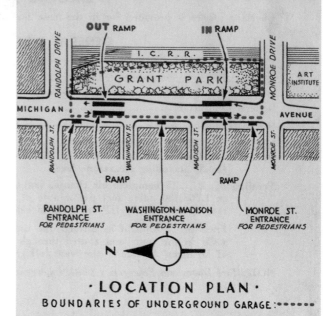

2.23

2.24

2.25

2.23. Design drawing of Grant Park Underground Garage.

2.24, 2.25. The construction of the Grant Park North Underground Garage began in 1952. The garage was reconstructed in 2000–2001 as part of the Millennium Park project.

2.26, 2.27. Grant Park with the peristyle (1952) and without (1953). The 1952 photograph includes the future site of the Prudential Building, the Randolph Street viaduct extending over the Illinois Central railroad lines, and the peristyle in Grant Park. A year later, construction of the Prudential Building and the construction of the Grant Park North Garage had commenced, resulting in the destruction of the peristyle. The construction of the garage (1952–1954) and the Prudential Building (1952–1955) marked the onset of a half-century-long transformation of the area from a railroad and warehouse district to a skyscraper and recreational center, culminating in the construction of Millennium Park.

2.26

2.27

2.28

2.28, 2.29, 2.30.
With the completion of the Grant
Park North Garage in 1954, trees were
planted in the reconstructed portion
of Grant Park. Note the absence of the
peristyle at the northern end of the
park, the Prudential Building under
construction, and the Randolph Street
viaduct extending over the Illinois
Central rail yards. The foreground is
now occupied by the *Crown Fountain*.

2.29

2.30

By 1960, some complained that Grant Park was a park in service to the automobile. "You seldom see people in the beauty spots of Grant Park," wrote Harold Moore, chairman of the Central Area Committee, adding that only fifty thousand people used the lakeside area of Grant Park annually. The combination of railroad tracks and increasing motor traffic discouraged pedestrian movement from Michigan Avenue to the lakeside, complained Douglas Schroeder of the Chicago Heritage Committee. An estimated 34 percent of Grant Park was now devoted to traffic and parking. Grant Park, concluded reporter Ruth Moore in 1961, "largely belongs to the automobile."[26]

Such criticism, however, did little to deter this pattern of park use. In 1965, the Grant Park South Underground Garage opened, providing space for still another 1,241 vehicles. In less than a decade, the park district paid off the existing debt on both Grant Park underground garages, eleven years early because of the large profits the facilities generated. Not surprisingly, such economic success stimulated similar growth. In 1977, the Monroe Street Underground Garage beneath the new Daley Bicentennial Plaza opened and replaced the old Monroe Street Parking Station. With a capacity of 3,700 vehicles, the new facility more than doubled the total automobile capacity of Grant Park to more than 7,000. By 1981, the three Grant Park garages provided 20 percent of all parking spaces in the Loop.[27]

The growing presence of the automobile in downtown Chicago and Grant Park generated proposals to reconfigure traffic patterns. One solution was to move Lake Shore Drive. In 1958, the Department of City Planning, and in 1960, the Central Area Committee proposed relocating Lake Shore Drive in Grant Park, eliminating the S curve just south of the Outer Drive Bridge and constructing a curving, high-speed thoroughfare over the existing Illinois Central terminals. These plans envisioned the drive passing Randolph Street, skirting the edge of the triangular patch of the Illinois Central, and becoming a depressed highway parallel to the east side of the Illinois Central tracks and continuing south past the Field Museum. Planners believed that the addition of new pedestrian overpasses in Grant Park would not only remove the drive as a barrier between the lakefront and recreational areas of Grant Park, but also provide better vehicular access to the Loop. The lakeside, without the drive, could be transformed into a promenade featuring plazas, gardens, restaurants, and new pedestrian spaces. At the north end of Grant Park, the Illinois Central tracks would be decked over with a new parking lot, while the roof of the Monroe Street Garage would become a sunken tennis stadium and a wintertime ice skating rink. At the south end, the new traffic pattern would reduce noise and allow for construction of a new music bowl at the current site.[28]

Ultimately, private real estate generated physical change in the northern end of Grant Park. The construction of the Prudential Building (1952–1955) marked the beginning of the transformation of the Randolph Street viaduct area from industrial to service-oriented uses. Between 1852 and 1900, the Illinois Central had purchased most of the real estate extending from Randolph Street to the Chicago River, from east of Michigan Avenue to Lake Michigan. For more than a century, the Illinois Central's rail yard and freight

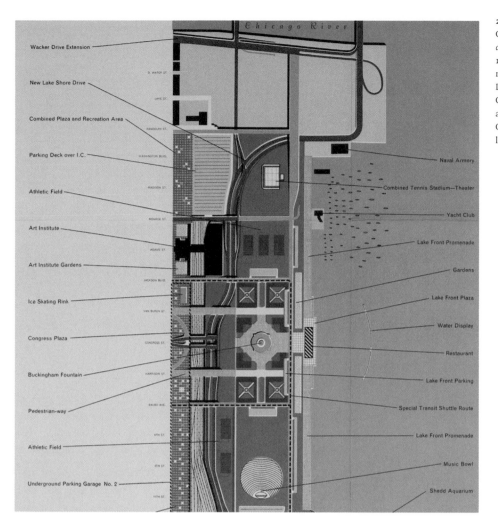

Wacker Drive Extension

New Lake Shore Drive

Combined Plaza and Recreation Area

Parking Deck over I.C.

Athletic Field

Art Institute

Art Institute Gardens

Ice Skating Rink

Congress Plaza

Buckingham Fountain

Pedestrian-way

Athletic Field

Underground Parking Garage No. 2

Naval Armory

Combined Tennis Stadium—Theater

Yacht Club

Lake Front Promenade

Gardens

Lake Front Plaza

Water Display

Restaurant

Lake Front Parking

Special Transit Shuttle Route

Lake Front Promenade

Music Bowl

Shedd Aquarium

2.31. Detail from map in Chicago Central Area Committee, *Grant Park and Burnham Park Study* (April, 1960). During the 1950s, city planners envisioned moving Lake Shore Drive to the site of present-day Columbus Drive and building a parking deck over the Illinois Central Railroad tracks, now the location of Millennium Park.

terminal occupied the large, eighty-three-acre site. Although observers predicted that high-rise structures would be built over the Randolph Street terminal and the Illinois Central site as early as 1931, only in 1951 did the company sell the air rights at Michigan Avenue and Randolph to the Prudential Insurance Company.[29]

When the Prudential Building was completed in 1955, the forty-one-story, 601-foot structure was the tallest in Chicago and included one of the city's largest built-in garages for a single office building, with 350 vehicle spaces. Although development of the area proceeded slowly because of the high costs of both obtaining and building over air rights, by 1959 Illinois Central officials acknowledged that the air rights of the railroad were worth more than the entire railroad system.[30]

The construction of the Prudential Building stimulated the construction of offices, stores, hotels, and residences on the site of the former Illinois Central rail yards and warehouses. Over the next three decades, the Illinois Central sold not only air rights

2.32, 2.33, 2.34.
The Prudential Building and the Illinois Central Railroad yards. The construction of the Prudential Building embodied the decline of the railroad along Chicago's lakefront, a necessary prelude for the creation of Millennium Park. Fig. 2.33 is from the top of the Prudential Building and depicts the future site of Millennium Park with Montgomery Ward Gardens on the right, and Monroe Street and the Art Institute at the top.

north of Randolph Street, but the ground as well.[31] In 1963, construction began on the Outer Drive East Apartments, just east of Lake Shore Drive on Randolph Street. Upon completion a year later, the $27-million, 940-unit structure was the world's largest residential structure. In 1970, One Illinois Center, designed by Mies van der Rohe, opened along East Wacker Drive. By 1972, city officials and developers Lawrence Lawless of the Illinois Center Corporation and Bernard Weissbourd of Metropolitan Structures proposed adding 140 acres of park land, including twenty additional acres in Grant Park, by covering the Monroe Street parking lot. Mayor Richard J. Daley termed the development, valued at more than $1 billion, "the greatest real estate deal in history."[32]

Daley may have been guilty of hyperbole, but only a little. This pattern of enormous, densely packed development continued for the remainder of the century. A series of additional high-rises went up north of Randolph Street, including hotels such as the Hyatt Regency (1974), the Fairmont (1987), and Swissotel Chicago (1989). The most prominent structures, however, were Edward Durell Stone's Standard Oil Building (1974)—later renamed the Amoco Building and then the Aon Building, which in 2005 remained the second-tallest Chicago skyscraper—and Loebl, Schlossman & Hackl's Two Prudential Plaza (1990). South of Randolph Street, the city opened the Richard J. Daley Bicentennial Plaza above the new underground parking facility in 1977.[33]

2.35, 2.36. Construction of the Randolph Street viaduct, 1962 and 1963.

2.37. Illinois Central rail lines and Monroe Street Parking Station with Prudential Building and Outer Drive East Apartments in 1964. A decade after the construction of the Prudential Building, the first major apartment building on the site of the old Illinois Central rail yards was completed. The Outer Drive East Apartments were located east of Lake Shore Drive, which was later reconfigured to the east of the apartment complex. The new structures stimulated office, hotel, and residential construction in the area. The three levels of roadway in the Randolph Street viaduct later proved critical in Millennium Park's intermodal transit system.

2.37

Almost simultaneously with the opening of Daley Bicentennial Plaza, a group of civic activists advocated completing the remainder of Grant Park wit h a spectacular garden and music venue over the Illinois Central rail yards and tracks. The proposed Lakefront Gardens was advertised as the completion of Daniel Burnham's vision for Grant Park. The project would help transform the Illinois Central rail yard into the new skyscraper

2.38. Construction of Richard J. Daley Bicentennial Plaza in 1976.

development of Illinois Center while providing a permanent home for the Grant Park Orchestra and other small performing groups in an attractive, state-of-the art urban garden setting. Proponents argued that plans for a year-round theater and restaurant and the location of nearby cultural activities in the Loop would stimulate even more economic and cultural development. Planners optimistically predicted that site acquisition, fundraising, and designs would be completed by June 1978, construction by June 1980.[34] When mayor Michael Bilandic endorsed the project, Lakefront Gardens supporters were ecstatic. "It is a clear win," wrote architect and civic activist Harry Weese.[35]

Weese was quickly proven wrong.

Chapter 3

THE GRANT PARK PROBLEM

From inception, Grant Park was more than a park. Nineteenth- and early twentieth-century landscape architects like Frederick Law Olmsted, Calvert Vaux, and Jens Jensen promoted naturalistic and pastoral designs. By contrast, Chicago planners envisioned Grant Park as an educational and cultural center. Influenced as much by City Beautiful ideas as the park movement, the first plans that emerged from the ateliers of Daniel Burnham, Charles Atwood, Normand Patton, Peter Wight, and others included magnificent sculptures, monumental plazas, and edifices for libraries, museums, armories, and municipal services. Such structures, argued the *Chicago Tribune*, would "indicate a superior civilization."[1]

Controversies initially centered on the inclusion of monumental structures in this lakefront civic center. For more than a decade, Aaron Montgomery Ward's battle over the placement of the Field Museum dominated the development of Grant Park, specifically preventing the erection of any building blocking the vista of Lake Michigan from Michigan Avenue. Historical discussions of the Field Museum debate, however, ignore a longer and equally divisive conflict regarding the purpose and role of Grant Park in Chicago's civic life. More than any other type of structure located within the park, concert venues generated the most acrimonious and ongoing controversy. City planners such as Daniel Burnham envisioned a lakefront civic center as a physical common ground to harmonize both individual and class interests.[2] But for more than a century, proposals to erect a significant music pavilion in Grant Park generated more contention than harmony.

The earliest plans for a significant lakefront park that appeared after the World's Columbian Exposition of 1893 included music halls, amphitheaters, and other concert-related facilities. The Municipal Improvement League's 1895 plan included two potential music venues. On the north end of the park, a peristyle and arch faced an open-air amphitheater designed to seat ten thousand spectators. The enormous enclosed space measuring 400 by 1,125 feet in size was also envisioned as a parade ground for the adjacent armory. In the center, just east of a large lagoon, was an open-air bandstand or music pavilion. Here another peristyle, 350 feet long, served as the backdrop, while the

3.1. Detail from Peter Wight's "Proposed Plan for Lake Front Park, Chicago" (1895).

3.2. Detail from Chicago Architectural Club Plan (1896). The earliest plans for a civic center and park on the lakefront included a concert venue. Wight's design on behalf of the Municipal Improvement League and later the Chicago Architectural Club plan both included an amphitheater on the north side of the park with seating for ten thousand attached to an amusement and parade ground. A music pavilion or "band stand" facing the "Grand Plaza" and "Grand Drive" anticipated holding up to a thousand performers and three hundred musicians.

3.3. Detail from Burnham and Atwood lakefront plan (1895). Burnham and Atwood also placed a music hall at the north end of the park. Compared to the schemes of the Municipal Improvement League and the Chicago Architectural Club, this plan was more modest in scale.

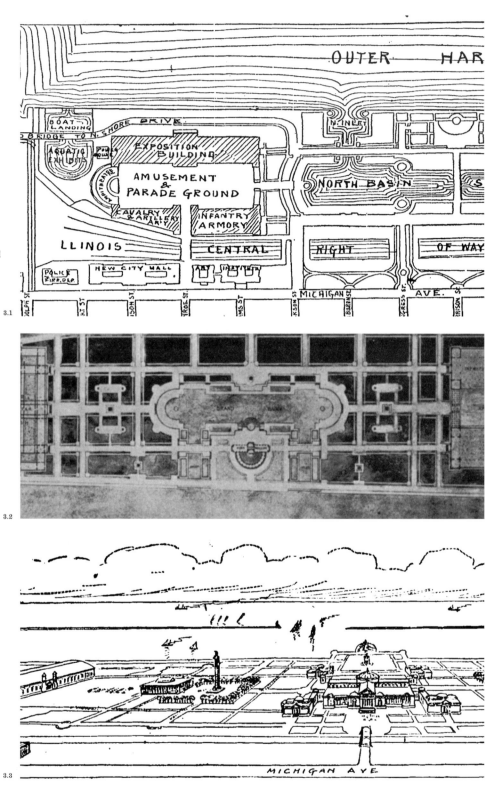

3.1

3.2

3.3

80-foot stage anticipated accommodating a thousand singers and three hundred instrumental performers. The pavilion looked onto a grand plaza, 400 by 250 feet in dimension. A design released in 1896 by the Chicago Architectural Club incorporated similar features.[3] By comparison, Burnham and Atwood's enclosed music hall at the north end of the park was considerably more modest. Burnham nevertheless bragged that Chicago's status as home to the greatest orchestra in the United States necessitated the inclusion of a magnificent concert structure.[4]

A decade later, many of the numerous plans developed by Olmsted Brothers included no concert venue of any sort. One, however, located an outdoor concert area on the north side of the park. The scale of the Olmsted Brothers plan was comparatively inconspicuous, with a small music stand situated in a grove of circular rows of trees. The considerable foliage would have hindered sight lines and acoustics, perhaps because the Olmsteds imagined the grove as a site of tranquil serenity, not large concerts.

Significantly, the famed *Plan of Chicago* (1909) authored by Daniel Burnham and Edward Bennett included no music pavilion in its vision for Grant Park. Instead, Burnham and Bennett proposed a lakefront civic center composed of the Field Museum in the center, flanked by equally monumental structures to the north and south, one of which was to be the Crerar Library. For Burnham and Bennett, the lakefront was a single composition devoted to the arts, letters, and natural sciences. The three classically styled groups were combined with broad terraces, walks, driveways, and trees. But nowhere was there a space for music.[5]

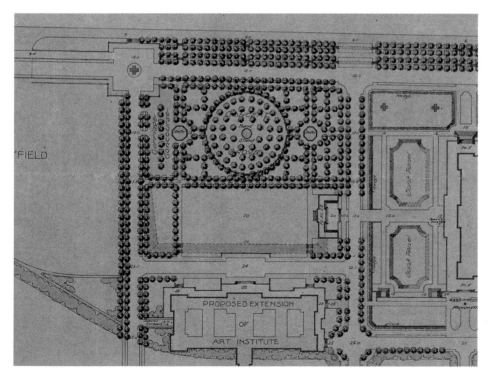

3.4. This detail from one of Olmsted Brothers numerous plans for developing Grant Park (1903) included a design for an outdoor concert area in the park. Situated on the future site of Butler Field, the grove included a small music stand (possibly a gazebo) in the center, surrounded by four circular rows of trees. Two other potential stands were located at the ends of the larger square. The large number of trees indicates that the Olmsteds envisioned the site as a place of quiet, contemplative repose, not one for the large concerts envisioned by Wight, Burnham, Atwood, and others.

3.7

3.8

3.9

3.5. Aerial map of proposed Grant Park in *Plan of Chicago*.

3.6. North end detail of proposed Grant Park in *Plan of Chicago*. The most influential document in the history of urban planning in Chicago, Daniel Burnham and Edward Bennett's *Plan of Chicago* (1909) included no design for a music pavilion or concert area. Instead, they envisioned a Grant Park dominated by three classical, beaux arts structures devoted to "Letters" on the south, "Arts" on the north, and the Field Museum of "Natural Sciences" in the center. Figures 3.5–3.6 provide different vantages of a monumental lakefront park and civic center.

3.7, 3.8. The Grant Park Bandshell under construction, 1931.

3.9. Hollywood Bowl (undated). The first concert venue in Grant Park, inspired by the Hollywood Bowl in Los Angeles, was erected in 1931 in anticipation of the upcoming Century of Progress Exposition in 1933–1934.

The incremental, piecemeal construction of Grant Park and perhaps the ongoing influence of Burnham and Bennett's *Plan* prevented the erection of any concert venue, large or small, until 1931. In anticipation of the Century of Progress International Exposition in 1933–1934, the city erected a temporary, forty-three-foot-high bandshell on the south end of the park. Chicago mayor Anton Cermak envisioned the bandshell, modeled after the Hollywood Bowl in Los Angeles, as a venue for free band concerts, reportedly "to lift the spirits of Depression-ridden Chicagoans." On July 4, 1935, the first Grant Park concert took place.[6]

From 1935 to 1970, the Grant Park summer concerts ranked among Chicago's most popular cultural events. The eight-week season usually included between thirty and forty concerts featuring classical music and popular selections from contemporary composers. Between 1935 and 1941, the free concerts attracted between 2.1 million and 3.5 million people annually, more than double the annual number of visitors to the Art Institute

3.10. Grant Park concerts in the 1950s.

3.11. For over four decades, concerts in Grant Park were among the most popular cultural events in Chicago.

3.12. The Grant Park bandshell looking north (1955).

3.12

or spectators attending Soldier Field events (see table 1). In 1940 alone, the park sponsored 101 concerts. Their popularity ultimately led to the establishment of the Grant Park Symphony Orchestra in 1944 with featured soloists and famous guest conductors.[7]

TABLE 1. GRANT PARK ATTENDANCE STATISTICS, 1900-2000

Year	Adler Planetarium	Art Institute[a]	Concerts	Soldier Field	Field Museum	Shedd Aquarium
1900	-------	577,421			275,653*	-------
1910	-------	668,555			218,047	-------
1920	-------	1,136,174			3,745[b]	-------
1930	570,871	916,816			1,332,799	2,323,133
1935	217,728	919,620	2,100,000	417,000	1,182,349	593,016
1940	74,156[c]	1,041,763	3,500,000	937,000	1,450,685	955,309
1945	194,463	1,085,000	782,800	639,000	1,070,678	606,126
1950	242,522	NA	460,000	1,014,894	1,173,661	708,250
1955	301,610	994,495	396,700	2,686,918	1,072,676	666,507
1960	413,893	700,000	269,000	415,900	1,244,374	912,856
1966	552,655	2,506,000	388,300	409,327	1,787,174	1,027,588
1970	617,761	1,760,332	300,000	223,201	1,645,198	966,006
1975	586,989	NA	460,000		1,116,207	974,417
1980	787,779	1,339,000	600,000		1,339,702	1,091,127
1985	728,688	1,334,000	NA		1,089,127	899,968
1990	654,466	1,410,951			1,465,938	1,288,965
2000	465,299	1,240,431			2,363,752	1,720,174

SOURCES: Art Institute of Chicago, *Annual Reports* (Chicago, 1934–2002) Vera Lechner Zolberg, "The Art Institute of Chicago: The Sociology of a Cultural Organization" (Ph.D. thesis, University of Chicago, 1974), 151 (for selected years from 1930–1971); Chicago Park District, *Annual Reports* (Chicago, 1936–1988); Field Columbian Museum, *Annual Report of the Director* (Chicago, 1895–1960); Field Museum Yearly Attendance, 1960–1995 (provided by Christine Giannoni); Chicago Office of Tourism (1998, 2003); Adler Planetarium statistics (provided by Bill Wilhelm); Shedd Aquarium statistics (provided by Joan Tomlin); *Crain's Chicago Business*, 3 May 2004, 21 Feb. 2005; *Chicago Tribune*, 7 Feb. 2005.

NOTE: For the purpose of brevity, I included only five-year intervals of data. Since no data on concerts was available for 1965, I included 1966. No precise concert data was available after 1988.

*Approximation.

[a]Before 1915, Art Institute statistics covered from June to June, so 1895 is really 1894–95.

[b]The 1920 annual report included attendance from only January to February, after which time the facility closed and the collections were moved to the new building which opened in 1921.

[c]Closed for repairs 29 April to 20 Oct. 1940.

The large number of spectators at the Grant Park concerts generated interest among park district officials in building a permanent lakefront music pavilion. One proposal, Sid Minchin's Open Air Music Garden and Amphi-Theatre (1936), was located immediately east of the Art Institute on what became Butler Field. The structure included 37,298 permanent seats along with another 8,120 movable ones, for a staggering capacity of 45,418—slightly more than Wrigley Field or Comiskey Park. The stage, backing up to Columbus Drive and facing west, accommodated 1,000 musicians or 1,500 vocalists. The sunken amphitheater occupied nearly the entire block, allowing only the music shell and the entrances to rise above the sidewalk elevation. Gated and surrounded by a wall of

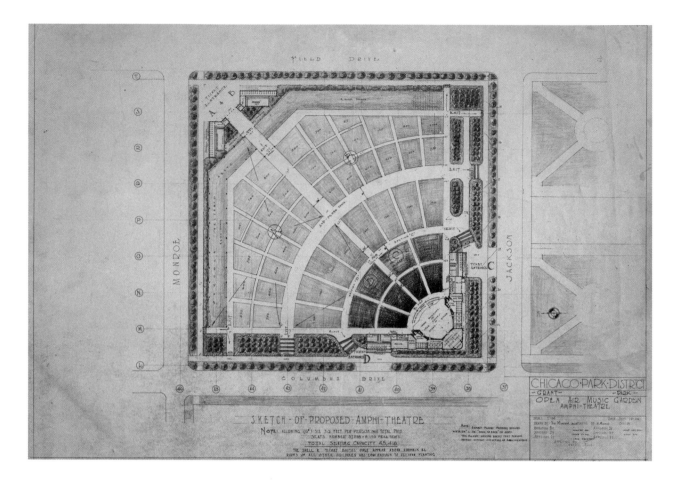

3.13. Sketch of Proposed Open Air Music Garden and Amphi-Theatre, 14 Sept. 1936.

trees, the planned amphitheater included ticket booths, indicating its potential use for commercial purposes.[8]

Another park district scheme in 1936 envisioned a sunken, outdoor amphitheater at the southern end of the park, now Hutchinson Field. Designed to conform with the beaux arts style adopted by Edward Bennett in the early development of Grant Park, the proposal included an enormous 162-foot-wide stage in front of a classically styled structure. A short, rising lawn and then several rows of trees surrounded the oval-shaped amphitheater. A baseball field sat immediately north of the proposed amphitheater.[9]

Between 1934 and 1941, Ralph Burke, the chief engineer of the park district, submitted a series of plans for a musical arts center in Grant Park. Much less ambitious in scope, these proposals provided for approximately five thousand permanent seats and capacity for another ten thousand behind them. The bandshell, shaped like a parabolic arch, rose over a stage with an eight-foot elevation. The amphitheater sloped outward from a five-foot elevation in front of the stage to a forty- to fifty-two-foot elevation in the rear.[10] Like earlier proposals, these plans generated neither political support or funding.

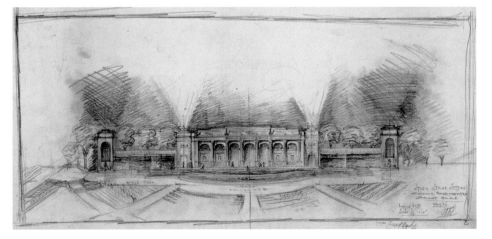

3.14. Model of Outdoor Amphitheater in Grant Park, Chicago, undated [1936?].

3.15. Study of Outdoor Amphitheater, Grant Park, 24 Feb. 1936.

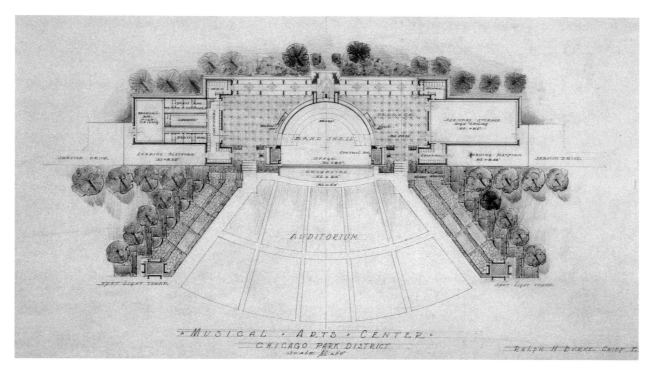

3.16. Ralph Burke's Proposed Musical Arts Center, undated.

3.17. Ralph Burke's bandshell drawing, undated.

The end of World War II renewed interest in building a permanent music structure in Grant Park. In 1945, park district architects proposed a music court and amphitheater directly east of the Art Institute. This pavilion included a 100-foot-wide, 50-foot-deep stage facing west. A sunken amphitheater with a capacity of approximately twenty thousand occupied a space measuring 820 by 785 feet. A grove of trees situated on a raised berm then separated the amphitheater from Columbus Drive to the west. The most in-

3.18, 3.19. Models of Proposed Music Court and Amphitheater, Grant Park, 1945, with its canopy closed (3.18) and open (3.19).

novative element of the proposal included a movable canopy that covered the stage and ten thousand permanent seats during inclement weather.[11]

In 1961, the park district and the A. Montgomery Ward Foundation proposed a solution to Grant Park's thirty-year bandshell dilemma. Each offered $1.5 million to construct a $3 million memorial bandshell dedicated to Aaron Montgomery Ward on Butler Field, between the Art Institute and Lake Shore Drive. The park district, collaborating with architect Richard Bennett of Loebl, Schlossman & Bennett, made several proposals which addressed concerns of various Michigan Avenue property owners, musicians, and conductors. The park district instructed Bennett to design a new music center that would not be a "structure," in accordance with the Montgomery Ward restrictions.[12]

In October 1962, the park district released a design. Bennett proposed a twenty-thousand-seat amphitheater adaptable for ballet, orchestral concerts, musical comedies, and opera. Surrounded by formal gardens, two circular reflecting pools, trees, and winding paths, the amphitheater stage faced west, enabling the audience to look out onto Lake Michigan during performances. Most important, the amphitheater design addressed the height concerns of Michigan Avenue property owners. Wide, sloping, and fan-shaped, the facility dropped twenty-nine feet in order to remain below the forty-foot tree level of the park.[13]

At first, the proposal was warmly received by the media and drama critics. Indeed, some viewed the bandshell issue as a wake-up call to Chicago. New York's Lincoln Center for the Performing Arts, costing nearly $150 million and considered by some to be

3.20. Preliminary Bird's-Eye View of Proposed Chicago Park District Amphitheater, 22 Dec. 1961.

3.21. Proposed Chicago Park District Amphitheater, 19 March 1962. These collaborative proposals by E. V. Buchsbaum and Richard Bennett considered a music amphitheater resting on Butler Field. Like the 1936 Park District proposal, the amphitheater extended west from Lake Shore Drive and rose to a 45-foot berm along Columbus Drive. In this proposal a canopy was suspended from a series of cables which extended to the outer edge of the seating structure. The stage platform was designed to raise, lower, and rotate, allowing for flexible and multiple uses.

3.22. Proposed Music Amphitheater, Grant Park, 1961, E. V. Buchsbaum, architect. Buchsbaum and Bennett revised their design during 1961 and 1962. The seating rose to an elevation of 67 feet, which (because of the depressed center) remained below the 40-foot tree line of Grant Park. A series of pools was placed outside the pavilion structure. Another proposal included a canopy over a traditional stage facing west. At the western edge of Butler Field, a series of berms was added to muffle sound coming from Columbus Drive.

3.23, 3.24. Conjectural photograph of A. Montgomery Ward Memorial Amphitheater, October 1962. In the final plan for the Ward Amphitheater, the stage was set below street level, insuring that the roof was no higher than 56 feet above Chicago city datum. Proponents argued this meant the facility was 11 feet lower than the current bandshell and 42 feet below the highest level of the Art Institute.

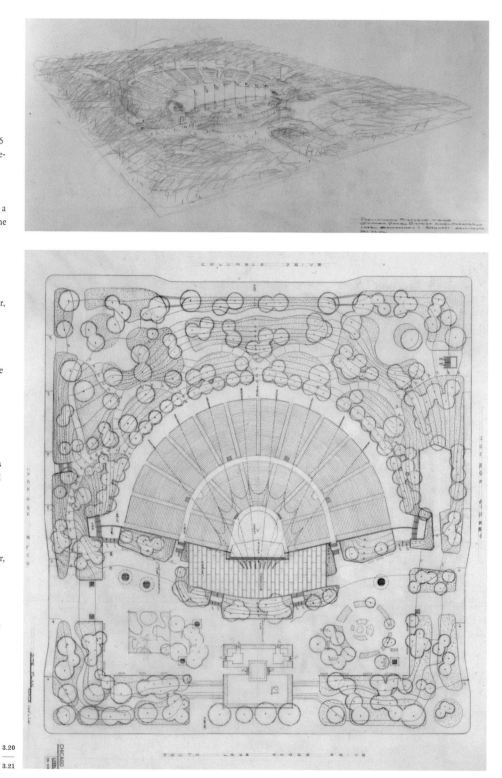

3.20
—
3.21

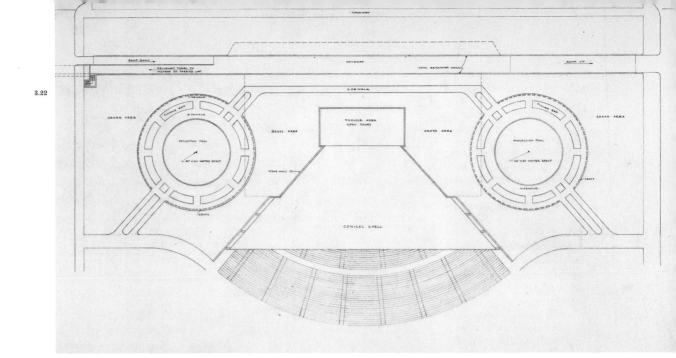

3.22

3.23 | 3.24

the world's first modern performing arts facility, was about to open in 1962. Other cities, notably Los Angeles and Washington, D.C., were well advanced in building similar new cultural centers. "The facts are impossible to dismiss," declared one critic. "Chicago has no resident ballet, no repertory drama, no secondary opera company, and no theaters to befriend them if they did exist." Chicago, feared some, was on the verge of becoming a cultural wasteland. A new Grant Park bandshell would address this problem; it was potentially a "new jewel for the lakefront," proclaimed the *Chicago Daily News*.[14]

Such concerns, however, paled before the growing number of bandshell critics. A coalition of ten civic groups led by the Metropolitan Housing and Planning Council and the City Club charged that the park district plan violated the Ward court rulings. Several Michigan Avenue property owners joined in opposition. Criticisms focused on numerous issues: the replacement of 20 percent of the green space in Grant Park with concrete, poor acoustics, and the short season in which the venue would be available.[15] The City Club proposed that the Monroe Street parking lot be replaced with a two-story underground garage, topped with a recessed music shell. But Chicago Park District Commission president James H. Gately remained steadfast, defending the Butler Field location with the impolitic proclamation that "you can have too much green grass." Even after capacity was reduced to 10,700 seats, failure to win unanimous approval of all property owners ensured the proposal's defeat.[16]

Opposition to this and later park district designs stemmed not just from a stubborn refusal to allow any new structure in Grant Park. Indeed, most critics supported construction of a new bandshell. Rather, after 1960, many planners, architects, and civic groups increasingly attacked the incremental development of the lakefront in general and Grant Park specifically. Robert McRae of the Chicago Community Trust, one of the bandshell opponents, described the proposal as "spot planning" for failing to consider other facilities in the area. Others argued that skyscraper development east of outer Lake Shore Drive—notably Lake Point Tower in 1965—raised "special problems" and threatened public access to the lakefront. "Grant Park," argued architect Stanley Tigerman, "is an essential core of downtown Chicago and it must be treated with reverence and understanding."[17]

A variety of proposals sought to address Grant Park planning in a comprehensive manner. One, authored by architect Harry Weese and landscape designer Dan Kiley on behalf of the Michigan Boulevard Association, presented a design for a music bowl on the Monroe Street Garage site. Like other municipal plans, traffic control was a key element in the Weese-Kiley proposal. Weese argued that a "final solution" to Grant Park traffic was a necessity, fearing that Lake Shore Drive would become a high-speed highway traversing the front yard of Chicago. By accommodating vehicular traffic, not eliminating it, Weese believed Grant Park would be saved. Rejection of the automobile was foolhardy. "Parks without cars," Weese argued, "are Forest Preserves."[18]

The most influential plan, however, emerged from the offices of Skidmore, Owings & Merrill (SOM) and Charles Murphy Associates. In 1963, the two firms joined forces under the leadership of SOM's Bruce Graham (later the designer of the Sears Tower and the John Hancock Center) as the primary architects of the Illinois Center development north of Randolph Street. On behalf of the three primary developers of the Illinois Center site, Graham proposed a direct answer to New York's Lincoln Center—an elaborate multipurpose cultural center just north of Randolph Street between the Prudential Building and Lake Shore Drive. Consolidating the street rights-of-way into a public plaza , the proposal included a new Orchestra Hall, a university music school, a high school for the

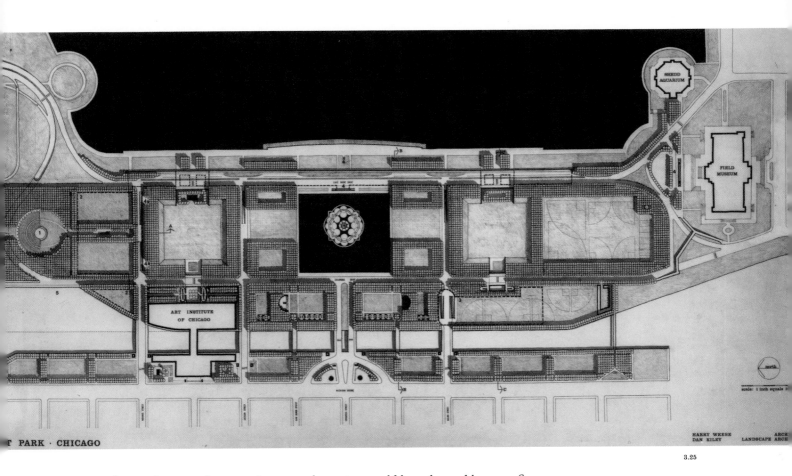

HARRY WEESE   ARCH
DAN KILEY   LANDSCAPE ARCH

3.25

arts, and an underground garage. Access to the center would be enhanced by reconfiguring Lake Shore Drive, splitting the thoroughfare into two one-way streets, one going south on Columbus Drive and the other going north on the current Drive. On the other side of Randolph, forty-seven feet high at this point, a cascade of steps would lead down to park terraces and lawns, with a music bowl located on Butler Field or fitted into the area then occupied by the Monroe Street Garage.[19]

By 1966, the Central Area Committee and Chicago Community Trust endorsed a revised version of the SOM/Murphy plan that included a small music bowl recessed in the slope of Randolph Street. With a ten-thousand-seat capacity, this amphitheater was surrounded by terraces for informal seating, cascading staircases, and planted terraces. The new music venue was situated over a parking garage large enough to accommodate eight thousand automobiles. Furthermore, a variety of groups, including the Metropolitan Housing and Planning Council, the Welfare Council's Openlands Project, the Chicago Central Area Committee, and the Chicago Community Trust, called for decking over the Monroe Street Parking Station. While some labeled the comprehensive report "the new Burnham plan," the Chicago Park District ignored the proposals.[20]

The city's failure to adopt any plan for a new outdoor facility only generated more

3.26. Map of proposed cultural center north of Randolph, terrace over Monroe Street Garage, music bowl on Butler Field, and a reconfigured Lake Shore Drive (1963). Park District planners considered building a terraced deck and gardens over the Monroe Street Parking Station, and thereby linking the proposed Ward Amphitheater to a new proposed cultural center on Randolph Street.

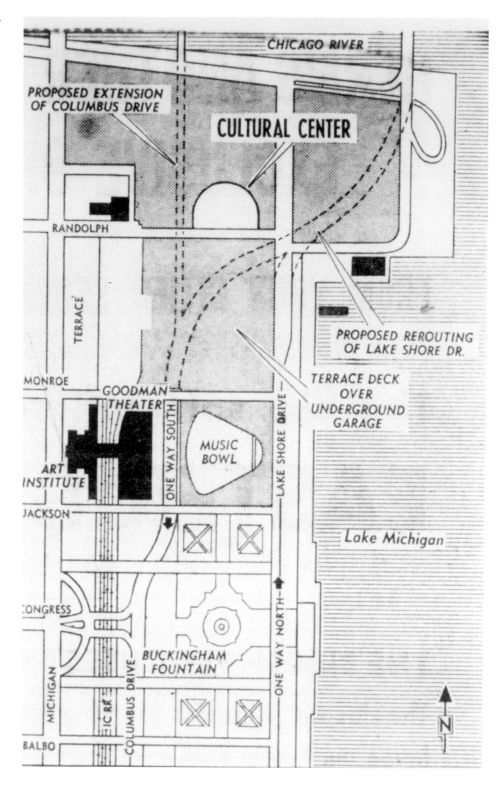

complaints about the existing bandshell. The sound was so poor, wrote one sardonic spectator, that listeners believed "that the inventor of outdoor concerts must have hated music." Musicians complained about noise from nearby Lake Shore Drive, Columbus Drive, and Soldier Field, as well as the blinding sun during rehearsals. Even worse, the bandshell was physically deteriorating. Splinters and plaster fell on peoples' heads during performances. By the 1970s, an assortment of stagehands, performers, and even grand pianos had fallen through the stage floor. David Zinman, principle conductor of the Grant Park Orchestra, likened the structure to the "57th Street men's toilet in New York City."[21]

In June 1972, the park district finally responded. Gene Summers of C. F. Murphy Associates proposed an eighty-five-foot, translucent, half-coned bandshell over a new 3,700-car underground garage on the existing twenty-two-acre site of the Monroe Street parking lot (which then held 2,700 cars). The bandshell was composed of fiberglass and acrylic plastic infill panels supported by black steel beams anchored to six-foot-high, reinforced concrete abutment walls. The facility included 3,000 permanent seats and room for another 9,000 on a sloping lawn. The projected $31 million cost would be paid for by park district bonds and $1.5 million in private grants and bequests.[22]

3.27. Model of north end of Grant Park with proposed outdoor concert venue (1966). Reflecting the influence of the Burnham Plan, the Illinois Central Air Rights Project envisioned completing the north end of Grant Park as part of the transformation of the area north of Randolph Street from a railroad, freight, and warehouse facility to a mixed-use skyscraper neighborhood filled with office towers, apartment buildings, and hotels.

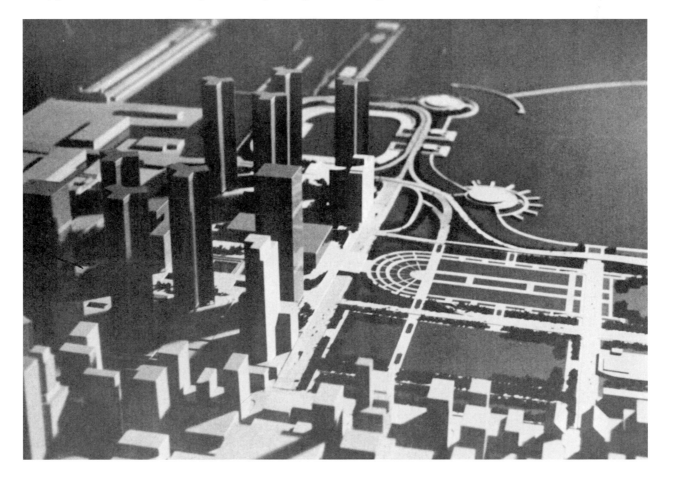

3.28 | 3.29

3.28. This 1972 prospective view of a bandshell designed by Gene Summers of C. F. Murphy Associates included the Standard Oil of Indiana (now Aon) Building under construction.

3.29, 3.30. Various prospective views of the luminescent bandshell proposed by architect Gene Summers in 1972 on the twenty-two-acre site of the Monroe Street Parking Station. Summers was best known as the architect of McCormick Center south of Grant Park.

3.30

The Metropolitan Housing and Planning Council (MHPC) and other critics immediately mobilized various constituencies in opposition to the Summers proposal. While acknowledging that a music pavilion was desirable, opponents complained that the eighty-five-foot-high design violated the Montgomery Ward court orders and blocked sight lines within the park. Furthermore, the 250-foot-long and twenty-seven-foot-high retaining walls hindered pedestrian movement within the park. The bandshell would be underused, open only during the summer months, and with a capacity of only 10,000, it was too small.[23]

Defenders of the park district proposal, including the *Sun-Times, Tribune, Daily News,* and the Michigan Boulevard Association, challenged such criticism. First, a revised proposal cut the bandshell size by twenty-six feet, making the new structure only fourteen feet higher than the existing one and twenty-three feet shorter than the Art Institute (which was eighty-two feet high). When average elevation was taken into account, the bandshell remained below tree level. The proposed bandshell occupied less than 4 percent of the twenty-acre site, less space than the water area of *Buckingham Fountain.*[24]

The MHPC remained steadfastly opposed, and issued a counterproposal to resolve what it identified as "the Grant Park problem." The civic group advocated decking over the entire site between Lake Shore Drive and Michigan Avenue, covering both the Monroe Street parking lot and the Illinois Central tracks with a forty-acre addition to Grant Park. On top of this, the MHPC proposed installing a demountable tent and portable

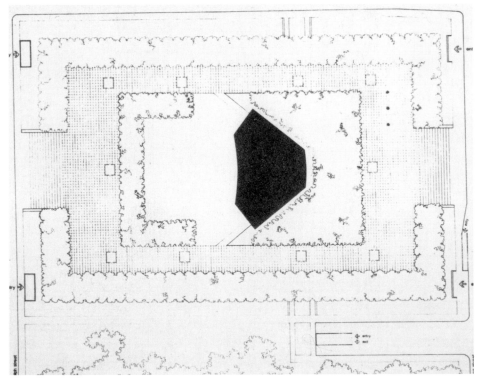

3.31. Gene Summers's "Site Plan."

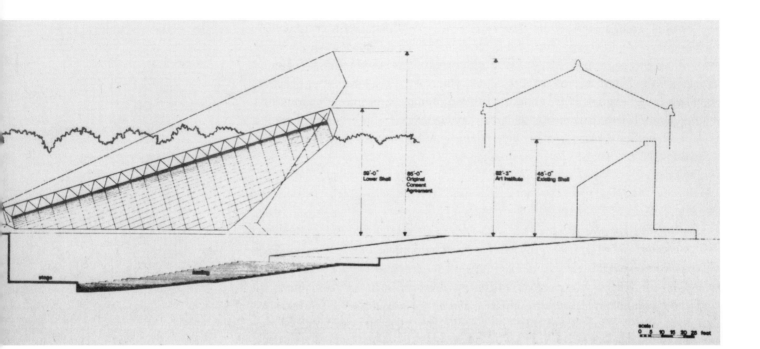

3.32. "Comparative Heights" shows Summers's initial eight-five-foot-high proposal and then the fifty-nine-foot alternative. The site plan in fig. 3.31 displays the bandshell in black and surrounded by a border canopy of trees. The comparative drawings reveal the initial eight-five-foot-high proposal and the revised fifty-nine-foot plan in relation to the eight-two-foot height of the nearby Art Institute and the forty-five-foot-tall existing bandshell.

3.33. Summers's design for a new music pavilion on the site of the Monroe Street Parking Station included an underground garage which increased parking capacity at the site from 2,700 to 3,700. Although the pavilion was never built, the garage plan was later constructed beneath the Richard J. Daley Bicentennial Plaza.

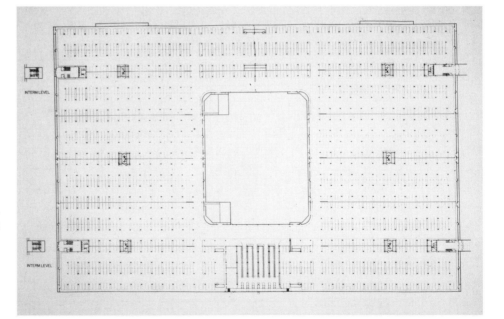

stage for the summer months, transforming the site into a "downtown Ravinia Park" with 60,000 to 75,000 seats on the grass. Grant Park would become "a 365 day-a-year living park" or "a park for all seasons."[25]

Park district officials, however, displayed little sympathy or interest in "outside" proposals. By the 1970s, a variety of civic and political reform groups complained that the Chicago Park District was administered more like a political patronage army than as a public service. Civic activists like Lois Weisberg and Cindy Mitchell (who together founded Friends of the Parks in 1975) charged that park district officials were simply unresponsive to a wide array of public needs and complaints. A new bandshell proposal was just another example of the park district's lack of interest in citizen input. In November 1972, when the park district leadership concluded that the necessary unanimous approval from the Michigan Avenue property owners was an impossibility, plans for the Summers-designed bandshell were abandoned.[26]

Lakefront Gardens

Five years later, the tension between civic groups like the MHPC and the Chicago Park District briefly lifted. On February 10, 1977, the park district acceded to MHPC demands, presenting a scheme for a "demountable" and portable bandshell. More important, the park district announced that informal discussions with the Michigan Boulevard Association, representing property owners who had previously vetoed proposals, indicated that Michigan Avenue landlords were willing to endorse the new bandshell to be located in Butler Field.[27]

Bandshell proponents emphasized the need to accommodate the Grant Park Orchestra, primarily for two reasons. First, for over four decades the orchestra had stood as "a symbol of artistic democracy," providing free concerts to anyone wishing to hear symphonic music. Second, Chicago and New York were the only cities in the country with two orchestras. Without the new structure, some feared, the Grant Park Orchestra would go out of business. Indeed, attendance to the Grant Park concerts was in a free fall. Before 1960, single concerts sometimes attracted fifty thousand people. In 1972, however, the best-attended concerts drew only twenty-five thousand spectators. On average, fewer than ninety-five hundred showed up to concerts at the bandshell.[28]

Park district officials felt pressure to overcome the growing perception that Grant Park was a disorderly, if not an outright dangerous, place. The nationally televised violence associated with antiwar demonstrations during the Democratic Party Convention in 1968 occurred in front of the Hilton Hotel along the edge of the park. Two years later, after the rock group Sly and the Family Stone failed to appear for a Grant Park concert, frustrated spectators rioted; over 100 were injured and another 150 arrested. Governor Richard Ogilvie later complained that "every dropout, kickout and throwout in the city of Chicago was there." In 1973, two women were murdered in the park.[29]

George Ranney, Jr., president of the Metropolitan Housing and Planning Council and an Inland Steel Corporation executive, began mobilizing civic groups two days before the park district released the plan. He immediately called Julian Levi, chair of the Chicago Plan Commission and one of his former teachers at the University of Chicago Law School, complaining that the park district was bypassing the proper review. Levi

3.34. George Ranney, Jr.

reassured Ranney and concurred with many of his objections. Shortly thereafter, a coalition of private citizen groups and civic organizations—Friends of the Parks (whose president was Victoria Ranney, George Ranney's wife), the Openlands Project, and the Chicago chapter of the American Institute of Architects—joined forces with the MHPC. Sometimes referred to as the "civics," the coalition began working on a counterproposal, spurred in part by a request from the Chicago Plan Commission.[30]

Ranney came from a family prominent in Chicago civic affairs. His grandfather, Edward Ryerson, also an Inland Steel executive, was instrumental in creating the Metropolitan Planning Council in 1934 and Chicago's public television station WTTW. Ranney's mother, Nancy Ryerson Ranney, was also active in Chicago philanthropy. Ranney, Jr., had graduated from Harvard College and the University of Chicago Law School, where he was editor-in-chief of the *Law Review*. After clerking with the U.S. Court of Appeals in Washington, he returned to Illinois as the deputy director of the state's Bureau of the Budget. From 1973 to 1986, he served as a counsel and vice president at Inland Steel.[31]

Ranney, the MHPC, and other Chicago Park District critics did not object to relocating or rebuilding the bandshell. Any new bandshell, Ranney insisted, should generate more cultural activity such as music, dance, and theater, making Grant Park a summertime focal point. Ranney admitted, "We wanted a change in the tone and character of downtown Chicago with a heavy tilt toward culture and civilized conduct."[32]

Ranney also realized that the civic groups needed to offer a viable alternative to the park district proposal. Ranney approached Robert A. Hutchins, one of his college classmates at Harvard and then a thirty-seven-year-old architect working at Skidmore, Owings & Merrill. On October 6, 1977, bandshell opponents led by the MHPC publicly offered Hutchins's counterproposal: a $10 million, twenty-acre landscaped park decked over the Illinois Central Railroad tracks, as well as over the then-planned Columbus Drive on the east side of the park. For the first time, the MHPC endorsed not only a new bandshell, but other "permanent structures" in the park. The music facility contained ten thousand fixed seats and an adjoining garden capable of holding another twenty thousand. The southern part of the park plan included a small outdoor theater, a courtyard restaurant, and skating rink. The plan was dubbed "Lakefront Gardens for the Performing Arts."[33]

The Lakefront Gardens proposal represented the culmination of nearly two decades of plans to dramatically transform the northern end of Grant Park. Proponents described the scheme as "an enviable example of urban cultural development." Going beyond just physical development, defenders of Lakefront Gardens emphasized the importance of the Grant Park Orchestra, the need for daytime and widely varied programming, and the desirability of an administrative, not-for-profit organization to oversee the operation. Like Frank Lloyd Wright's Midway Gardens (1913–1929) on the South Side, Lakefront Gardens combined a music pavilion, eating facilities, and multiseason use. Not only would the blight of parked automobiles, freight trains, and warehouse terminals be removed from sight, but Lakefront Gardens would transform the park into a year-round performing arts, recreation, and entertainment facility.[34]

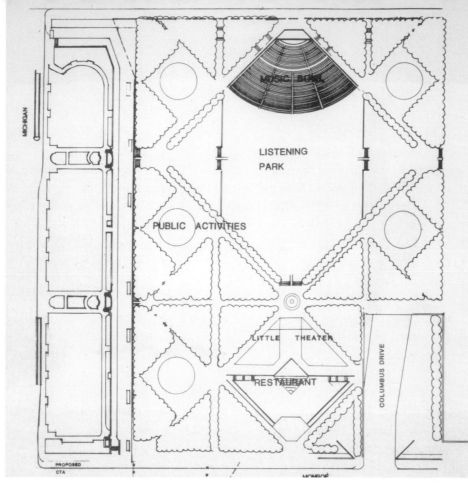

3.35. Robert A. Hutchins.

3.36. Illustrative Plan of Lakefront
Gardens, 6 Oct. 1977.

3.36

The Illinois Central Railroad played a critical role in generating support for Lakefront Gardens. Since 1852, the Illinois Central's "perpetual operating easement" was tantamount to ownership. By the 1970s, however, the railroad's maintenance operations had shifted to the south of Grant Park, eliminating the need to bring freight into the north end of the park. The Illinois Central maintained one spur, running an occasional train along it so that undeveloped portions of the property north of Randolph Street were still classified as rail yards for tax purposes. But a recent Supreme Court decision made railroad land no longer tax exempt. When Ranney and Hutchins met with Illinois Central president Bill Johnson, the executive reportedly promised to help raise $2 million to purchase the railway right-of-way.[35]

When Hutchins and Ranney released the details of Lakefront Gardens to the public in October 1977, support for the proposal was immediate. The Friends of the Parks, the Openlands Project, and the Chicago chapter of the American Institute of Architects offered their endorsements, as did Chicago's three daily newspapers. Stanley Freehling, past president of Ravinia and a trustee at the Art Institute and the Chicago Symphony Orchestra, described Lakefront Gardens as "the finest, most sophisticated outdoor urban facilities for music of any city in the nation."[36]

Chicago Park District officials, however, remained obstinate. For several months prior to the Lakefront Gardens announcement, park district and MHPC officials battled

3.37. Photograph of the prospective site of Lakefront Gardens.

3.38. Photograph with prospective color rendering of Lakefront Gardens. The earliest plans for Lakefront Gardens included decking over the entire area, including the Illinois Central railroad tracks and much of Columbus Drive.

FESTIVAL
PERFORMANCE
CENTER

LAKEFRONT
GARDENS

each other. MHPC officials complained that Chicago Park District superintendent Edmund Kelly and his protégés ignored public input. Kelly simply "didn't like the civics," admitted John McDonough, a Sidley & Austin attorney and MHPC official. Frequently mentioned as a possible mayoral candidate, Kelly ran the public agency like a personal patronage machine. Harry Weese described the park district as "an incompetent dictatorship" and a "fiefdom operating outside the political process."[37]

The conflict between the park district and the citizens' groups had reached an impasse when, on October 18, 1977, mayor Michael Bilandic intervened. Partly moved by Levi's suggestion that Lakefront Gardens could be "the ornament of his administration," Bilandic ordered the Chicago Plan Commission to stay its ruling in favor of the Butler Field bandshell in order to give the Lakefront Gardens proposal an adequate hearing, and he ordered the commission to form two committees to address the various issues of conflict.[38]

Events moved quickly. On November 7, one committee endorsed Lakefront Gardens, arguing that the plan represented the completion of Burnham's vision for Grant Park and would transform the Illinois Central rail yard into the new skyscraper development of Illinois Center, "a vital and impressive urban cityscape." Three days later, the Plan Commission approved a four-year, temporary plan that included a demountable bandshell with large, cement, underground facilities for storage, restrooms, and lockers. In the summer, the facility would be used for the orchestra, in the winter as a warming house for ice skaters. The total price tag was initially estimated to be between $1.4 million and $1.6 million (although by February 1978, the cost had escalated to $2.6 million).[39]

Proponents of Lakefront Gardens, however, soon realized that the Chicago Park District had gained what it wanted: a demountable bandshell and a permanent building in

3.39. Frank Lloyd Wright's Midway Gardens (1913–1929) served as an inspiration for the multipurpose goals of Lakefront Gardens.

3.40. Lakefront Gardens Plan, 7 Nov. 1977. This revised plan eliminated the complete decking over Columbus Drive (which saved $3.7 million) and substituted a bridge at the Madison Street axis connecting the Gardens to the new garage and park east of Columbus Drive. The plan also eliminated the complete decking over the Illinois Central tracks (which saved $8.6 million), thus shrinking the size of the three plazas on the west side and leaving a 65-foot-wide opening exposing the IC tracks below. On both sides of the Gardens acoustic control berms cut noise levels on the east and west sides of the Gardens.

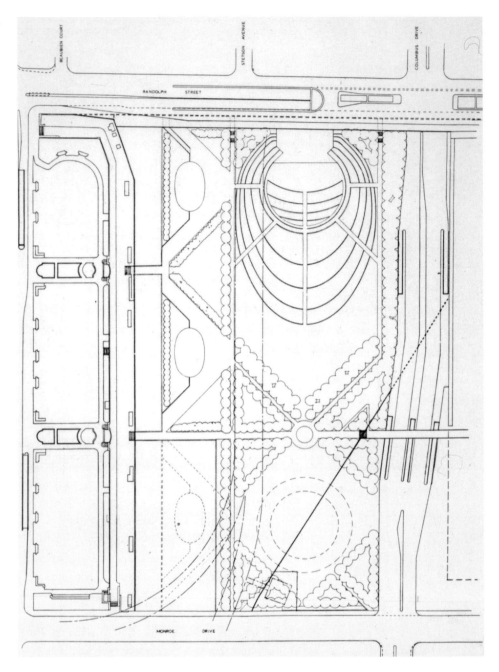

the park. When the new bandshell was constructed, the *Tribune* predicted "that the 'temporary' bandshell will become a permanent part of the Chicago scene." They were right. Even before the shell went up, park district president Patrick O'Malley refused to spend park district funds to dismantle the structure. "The MHPC will have to go down there and do it themselves," he insisted. Sure enough, park district superintendent Edmund

3.41. The "temporary" pavilion became the Petrillo Music Shell in 1976. It was still standing after the completion of Millennium Park in 2005.

Kelly refused to allocate the $389,000 for demounting the shell in the fall of 1978, a task he described as "putting money in the sewer."[40]

Park district recalcitrance aside, the not-for-profit organization Lakefront Gardens, Inc., was established to raise money and obtain federal funding. Officials were optimistic. Early proponents identified a variety of federal park, conservation, and highway programs as potential funding sources. Julian Levi took charge of private fundraising. As director of the Southeast Chicago Commission (the planning agency established by the University of Chicago in 1952 to act on behalf of its real estate interests), Levi had engineered what was then the largest gift ever for the University of Chicago—$12 million from the Pritzker family in 1969. His strategy for Lakefront Gardens was to locate one large gift to stimulate similar contributions from other private sources, including corporations. These gifts, in turn, would allow for larger matching funds from the federal government.[41]

Within months, Lakefront Gardens supporters presented the plan to the Commercial Club of Chicago, while professional fundraiser James Feldstein met with U.S. secretary of commerce Philip A. Klutznick of Chicago, in hopes of garnering support. Initial study grants came from the Chicago Community Trust (for $50,000) in 1978 and then from the John D. and Catherine T. MacArthur Foundation in 1981. In return for a major gift, Lakefront Gardens officials even offered to name the new park "MacArthur Gardens." By then, Lakefront Gardens, Inc., had developed a scenario where the organization would purchase the railroad easement from the Illinois Central Railroad for $1.25 million on

3.42. The Lakefront Gardens site looking north above the Art Institute.

3.43. Lakefront Gardens rendering by Slutsky, January 1981. Lakefront Gardens promised to dramatically transform the site of the Illinois Central rail yard.

3.44, 3.45. Lakefront Gardens plan, 4 November 1980. These plans eliminated the three garden plazas on the western edge, leaving a wider cut for the exposed IC tracks and a smaller Lakefront Gardens.

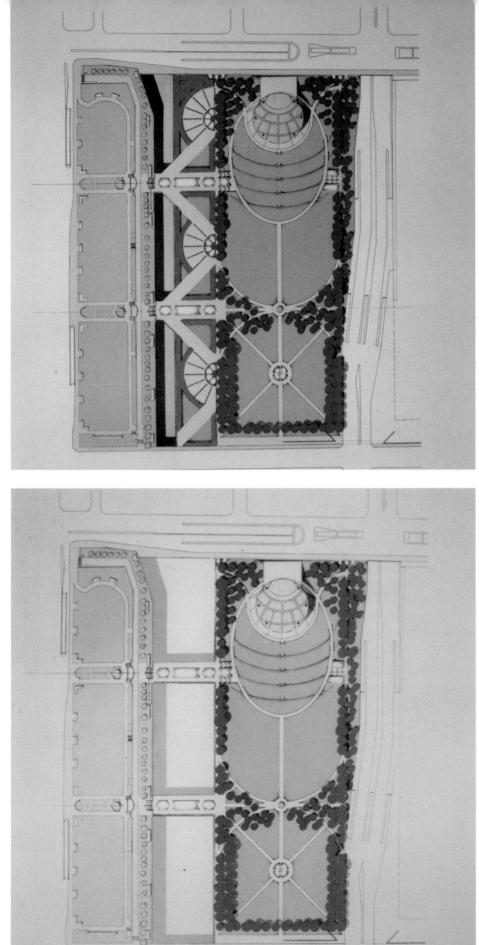

3.46. Lakefront Gardens: Functional and Construction Elements, SOM, 30 April 1983. Although the design plans for Lakefront Gardens went through a variety of changes from the initial proposal in 1977 to 1982, each proposal included the following design features: (1) a pavilion with 2,500 covered seats, (2) a stepped, grass terrace around the pavilion for seating an additional 8,500 people, (3) listening gardens beyond the terrace for an additional 30,000, (4) a formal or sculptural garden in the southern third of the park, (5) three garden plazas on the western edge of park divided by bridges at Madison and Washington streets connecting the park to the already existing portion of Grant Park.

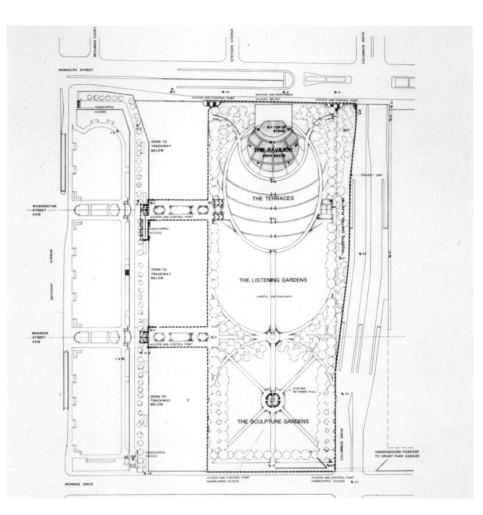

behalf of the city of Chicago, which in turn would lease the site to the park district for one dollar per year. The park district and Lakefront Gardens would then jointly design and construct a performance facility and gardens for an estimated $25 million.[42]

Then the problems began. Shortly after he endorsed the project in 1977, mayor Michael Bilandic admitted that the cost of Lakefront Gardens could reach $30 million. After Jane Byrne defeated Bilandic in his reelection bid in 1979, Robert Drevs, president of Lakefront Gardens, met with the newly elected mayor, who voiced her support for the plan. Later communications between Byrne and Lakefront Gardens officials, however, generated little progress. Worse yet, the budget cutbacks of Ronald Reagan's administration curtailed potential federal funding sources. These combined developments upset efforts by Levi, Feldstein, and others to raise money. Lakefront Gardens never mounted a formal campaign to finance the project.[43]

Consequently, a revised proposal in 1983 called for cutting the size of the park by diminishing the acreage to 10.25 acres. The new plan sandwiched Lakefront Gardens

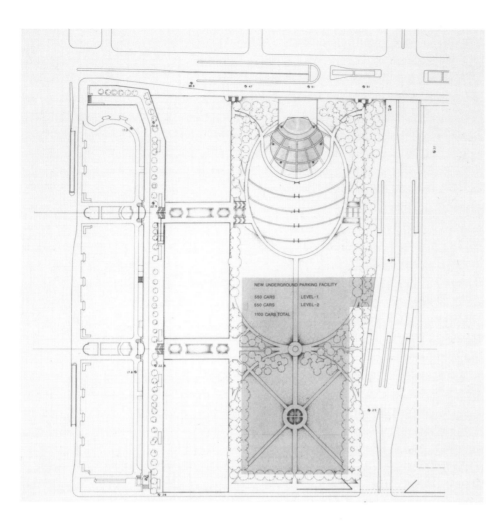

3.47. Lakefront Gardens: Revised Scheme Showing Parking Garage Alternative, May 1988. The Lakefront Gardens plan remained unaltered until 1988, when SOM added a new underground parking facility beneath the southern half of Lakefront Gardens. The two levels of parking would hold 1,100 vehicles.

between the Illinois Central tracks on the west and the new Columbus Drive on the east. The railroad tracks remained exposed but for two walkways that extended from Washington and Madison streets. Furthermore, the restaurant and ice skating rink at the southern end of the park were now replaced with a sculpture garden. The anticipated cost was $15 million.[44]

The revised proposal fared little better. Hutchins continued to lobby on its behalf, and in 1992 offered still another revision. In "Grant Park: A Vision for the NorthWest Corner," he suggested creating a Michigan Boulevard Promenade in the existing section of Grant Park along Michigan Avenue between Randolph and Monroe Streets. This would serve as a "cultural corridor" for booksellers, musicians, artists, and street performers, while simultaneously serving as an entrance to Lakefront Gardens. The memo also called for rebuilding the Grant Park North underground parking garage, leasing the new facility to a private operation and thereby generating revenue for Lakefront Gardens. This was among the earliest proposals to suggest funding the garage and Lakefront Gardens with capital bonds. In 1992, largely through Hutchins's efforts, Lakefront Gardens was incorporated into the city's master plan for the northwest quadrant of Grant Park.[45]

These changes, however, masked the lack of progress on Lakefront Gardens. A 1985 transportation study commissioned by the Central Area Committee did not even discuss, much less propose, any structure on the proposed site of Lakefront Gardens. After 1985, the Lakefront Gardens board no longer met. Only the activism of individual proponents, notably Robert A. Hutchins, generated the impression that Lakefront Gardens, Inc., was more active than it really was. By 1992, Hutchins was discouraged, conceding that if meaningful public and private support was absent, the corporation should, in his words, "fold tent."[46]

FOR MORE THAN A CENTURY, proposals to create a world-class cultural and musical center in Grant Park attracted the interest of Chicago's leading architects. Beginning with Daniel Burnham and Olmsted Brothers during the 1890s and extending to Richard Bennett, Bruce Graham, Harry Weese, and Gene Summers in the second half the twentieth century, multiple proposals suggested ways to transform Grant Park into a musical venue (see table 2). The most ambitious plan, Lakefront Gardens, generated support from the city's leading civic groups: the Metropolitan Housing and Planning Council, the City Club, Friends of the Parks, the Chicago chapter of the American Institute of Architects, and the Openlands Project. By the 1980s, the Lakefront Gardens board of trustees included executives from leading Chicago corporations—Continental Bank, Peoples Gas, Marshall Field's, First National Bank of Chicago, Commonwealth Edison, Johnson Publishing, Inland Steel, Quaker Oats, and Sears, Roebuck. Elite families long associated with Chicago industry and philanthropy were represented by the McCormicks and Ryersons. Prominent public officials voiced their support, including mayor Jane Byrne, Illinois governor Richard B. Ogilvie (1969–1973), and Chicago's cultural affairs director Joan Harris. None of these plans, however, were ever realized.[47]

Why was Lakefront Gardens never built? In retrospect, the timing for such a civic cultural center was never worse. From the 1960s to the mid-1980s, the Chicago Park District resisted external input and citizen participation. Political turmoil in Chicago made Edmund Kelly as politically powerful as mayor Michael Bilandic, "as we learned to our regret," George Ranney later admitted.[48]

Equally important was the political poker game public and private officials played with each other over Lakefront Gardens. As early as 1978, city architect Jerome R. Butler warned that "the City won't act until the private sector takes the initiative." Other city planning officials concurred. Yet potential private benefactors were reluctant to give their support without prior government approval. When the park district underwent political reform after 1980, specifically under the leadership of Raymond F. Simon, Walter Netsch, and others, the resulting political turmoil made political consensus virtually impossible. Between 1976 and 1983, Chicago elected four different mayors, a sharp departure from the two decades of political continuity under Richard J. Daley from 1955

TABLE 2. MAJOR GRANT PARK BANDSHELL PROPOSALS, 1930-2004

SOURCE / YEAR	LOCATION	ARCHITECT	HEIGHT	SEATS	LAWN CAPACITY	TOTAL CAPACITY	GARAGE CAPACITY	COST	FEATURES
CPD 1933–1977	Hutchinson Field	E. Buchsbaum	43	12,000					Hollywood Bowl model
CPD 1936	Butler Field	Sid Minchin		37,298	8,120	45,418			
CPD 1935–40?	Hutchinson Field								
CPD 1935–40?	Butler Field	Ralph Burke		5,000	10,000	15,000			
CPD 1945	Butler Field			10,000	10,000	20,000			
CPD 1953			42						
City Planning Dept. 1958	Hutchinson Field		40–50 ?						
CPD/Ward Foundation 1961–62	Butler Field	Richard Bennett	Sunken bowl rising 25	20,000; 10,700				$3 million	
City Club 1962–63	Monroe St. Garage		Sunken bowl				3,000 on 2 levels		
City Planning Dept. 1963	Monroe St. Garage/ IC tracks		Sunken bowl						Based on 1958 plan
SOM/ C. F. Murphy 1963	Monroe St. Garage/ IC tracks		Sunken bowl						Based on Burnham Plan
Harry Weese 1963–68	Monroe St. Garage	Harry Weese & Dan Kiley	Sunken bowl	12,000	12,000	24,000			Greek amphitheater
CCAC/CCT SOM/Murphy 1966	Monroe St. Garage	C. F. Murphy/ Bruce Graham							
CPD 1972	Monroe St. Garage	Gene Summers	85 (orig.), 59 (revised)	3,000	6,000–9,000	9,000–12,000	3,700	$31 million	Translucent shell
MHPC 1972	Butler Field & IC tracks		Demountable shell		60,000–75,000	60,000–75,000	3,000–4,000		
CPD 1977	Butler Field	Maurice Thominet						$1.5 million	
MHPC 1978	IC tracks	Robert Hutchins	Sunken bowl	2,000	8,500 & 30,000	40,500	None	$10–21 million	Lakefront Gardens
MHPC 1983	IC tracks	Robert Hutchins	Sunken bowl	2,800	7,200 & 30,000	40,000	None	$15 million (private)	Lakefront Garden revise
CPD 1978–2002	Butler Field		Demountable shell	4,000	6–7,000	10–11,000	2,400		J. Petrillo bandshell
Millennium Park 2004	IC tracks	Frank O. Gehry	over 100	4,000	7,000	11,000	4,160 (2,260)	$63 million	

to 1976. Furthermore, the election of Harold Washington in 1983 ushered in a period of intense conflict between the mayor and the city council. In 1986, these so-called "council wars" spread to the park district when the Washington-appointed park district board stripped Kelly of his powers. These events limited the ability of Lakefront Gardens proponents to achieve meaningful support from key parts of the city's political establishment.[49]

Appeals to private donors illustrated this predicament. In 1983, a group of Lakefront Gardens supporters spearheaded by Nancy Ryerson Ranney, the mother of George Ranney, Jr., met with Joseph Regenstein seeking a major gift. Nancy Ranney promised Regenstein that if he donated between $5 million and $10 million, part of the park would be named after his family and matching funds would then be raised. George Ranney, who was present at the meeting, remembered Regenstein saying, "This sounds just wonderful. We'd love to be involved, but what can you tell us about the city's and the park district's support?" The Ranneys admitted such support was tentative. Potential donors like the Regensteins simply refused to support any proposal that was unproven and politically controversial.[50]

Fundraiser James Feldstein later concluded that in any public/private partnership, officials need to get beyond the chicken-and-egg scenario to determine who goes first. Lakefront Gardens never enjoyed a base of public support, much less the projected garage revenues, that Millennium Park did. If it had, believed Feldstein, "it would have been a very different situation."[51]

In 1977, at the height of enthusiasm for the project, George Ranney proclaimed that Lakefront Gardens would give Chicago "an outdoor music facility that will excite the admiration of major cities throughout the world." In 1994, however, proponents conceded that the project was doomed, and the board elected to dissolve the not-for-profit corporation. "Lakefront Gardens was a wonderful idea, with many prominent endorsements," wrote John McDonough, "but it never got off the ground." McDonough wrote a check to the Metropolitan Planning Council for $4,368.54, the last remaining assets of the corporation. Lakefront Gardens was history.[52]

PART TWO POLITICS

Chapter 4

SKIDMORE, OWINGS & MERRILL'S MASTER PLAN

By 1997, most Chicagoans had forgotten Lakefront Gardens. It might have stayed that way but for the mayor's teeth. Every six months, mayor Richard M. Daley visited his dentist, whose office overlooked Grant Park. From there, Chicago's most important elected official regularly peered down upon the unsightly railroad cut between Michigan Avenue and Grant Park, a visual pox on what Daley called "the people's country club"—Chicago's lakefront. Then one day, Daley summoned Edward Bedore, mayoral advisor and the city's former chief financial officer, to his office. "Ed," he said, "this is something I've been wanting to do for a long time. See what can be done." Thus was born Millennium Park.[1]

The story of the mayor's dental visits, however, oversimplifies the origins of the project. Daley was moved to act because a historic but little-known event was transpiring at the Illinois Central rail yard. For several months, Chicago Park District general counsel and lakefront director Randy Mehrberg had been secretly engaged in an investigation. Like Daley, Mehrberg was disturbed by the unattractive rail yard in Chicago's major park; it was, in his words, a "very unhappy use of the land." As a railroad law attorney at Jenner & Block, Mehrberg observed employees of an Illinois Central Railroad subsidiary parking their cars free of charge at the site. "I always wondered how they got free parking," he later remarked.[2]

Mehrberg's curiosity was piqued. He soon learned what many considered common knowledge: the railroads had filled in the lakefront in the mid-nineteenth century, laid track, and built the railroad. In return, they received title to the land. Consequently, the Illinois Central had controlled the land for almost 150 years. But Mehrberg also realized that important elements of this story were little more than "folk law." His investigation found a more complicated reality.

Mehrberg discovered that the city had not relinquished complete ownership of the lakefront property to the Illinois Central Railroad in 1848. Rather, the railroad company was awarded an easement for the land south of Randolph all the way to 11th Street specifically for railroad purposes. The city still retained title to the land, despite the long-held misperception that the railroad owned it. More important, Mehrberg realized that most of the property was now an unpaved, unstriped parking facility, not a railroad yard.

Conditions in Chicago are such as to repel outsiders and drive away those who are free to go. The cream of our own earnings should be spent here, while the city should become a magnet, drawing to us those who wish to enjoy life. DANIEL BURNHAM AND EDWARD BENNETT (1909)

4.1. Randall Mehrberg.

"They left in one track on the eastern border of the property to maintain the pretense that it was for rail operations and they parked one or two old box cars, and just left them there," explained Mehrberg. "That was their way of saying it was being used for rail purposes."[3] In reality, concluded Mehrberg, the Illinois Central was technically violating the law.

The railroad, however, was not about to relinquish prize real estate without a fight. By the 1990s, automobile parking was the most lucrative use of the property. But Mehrberg recognized that the railroad was powerless to build anything on the site because they did not own the air rights above the property. When negotiations broke down, the park district filed a lawsuit against the Illinois Central, declaring that the easement was terminated because the company had abandoned rail operations.[4]

Fortune shone on Chicago. Shortly after the city and the Illinois Central began negotiations, the Canadian National Railway (CNR) began exploring the possibility of purchasing the Illinois Central. Upon learning of CNR's interest, park district officials approached their counterparts at the Illinois Central, suggesting that they donate their limited property rights to the city. Such an action would result in a tax deduction, boost their earnings, and increase their sale price. The railroad executives quickly recognized the benefit of making the transaction "as expensive as possible and to give as much away as possible." In retrospect, Mehrberg believed the pending offer from the CNR transformed negotiations between the city and the Illinois Central.[5]

But Chicago wanted more than just the property between Monroe and Randolph Streets. The city was formulating plans for an intermodal transit link—a series of multiple transportation systems integrated into one location—connecting McCormick Place with the parking facilities at the north end of Grant Park, the Metra terminus at Randolph Street, and nearby hotels. "This was a two-pronged approach," recounted Mehrberg. "We asked them to give us all of their interests, not only with regard to what is now going to be Millennium Park but also all the way down to McCormick Place." In December 1997, the railroad donated its rights, title, and interest in the property extending from McCormick Place to Randolph Street.[6]

In a matter of months, Randy Mehrberg had accomplished a feat that had stymied generations of city officials for more than a century: he enabled the city to regain control of the prime downtown, lakefront land that was ostensibly owned by the Illinois Central Railroad. This single, little-known event thrust into motion the forces leading to the creation of Millennium Park.

Daley administration officials immediately recognized a unique opportunity. For years, city authorities and private-sector planners had envisioned the area south of Randolph Street as part of an intermodal transit site.[7] Some, like mayoral advisor Edward Bedore, had worked on various schemes to enhance and improve Soldier Field since 1990, including more off-site parking. The city's repossession of the Illinois Central yards offered a new potential parking opportunity. But the Randolph Street viaduct between Michigan Avenue and Columbus rose to nearly fifty feet—the equivalent of a four-to-five-story building.

Bedore's solution was an underground parking garage topped by a park. Bedore approached several parking companies to determine potential usage and revenue streams. He learned that the city could construct a garage for approximately $150–200 million.[8] Bedore called a meeting with city and park district officials. While going over the spreadsheets, the park district's director of research and planning, Ed Uhlir, scribbled some calculations of his own on the back of an envelope. "We could probably build the parking structure and maybe put grass on top and fund it through the garage revenue," he concluded.[9]

Uhlir's nonchalance masked the significance of the suggestion. George Ranney, Jr., a leading proponent of Lakefront Gardens twenty years earlier, remembered that when the garage under Daley Bicentennial Plaza opened in 1977, the demand for parking was so low that the new garage had "a tough time filling up," a fact that later contributed to the lack of support for Lakefront Gardens. Funding the construction of the garage with parking fees, Ranney believed in retrospect, was "the conceptual breakthrough" that allowed for the creation of Millennium Park.[10]

4.2. Richard M. Daley.

Daley agreed. For the mayor, completing the final element of Grant Park represented the ideal millennium project. During his decade-long mayoralty, Daley had consistently espoused environmentally sensitive programs. To his supporters, he was "the green mayor." Throughout the 1990s, the park district planted an estimated 7,000 trees annually in city parks, totaling approximately 300,000 between 1989 and 2002. Denuded streets such as Ashland, Western, and Irving Park were transformed into attractive boulevards with trees, shrubs, and flowers in median planters and along the sidewalks. By 2003, sixty-three miles of Chicago streets included new median plantings. From 1997 to 1999, under the Campus Parks Program, Chicago built or restored fifty-five school parks. Daley also installed a roof garden on top of City Hall as part of an innovative energy-saving project, and helped establish the Chicago Center for Green Technology, a former brownfield site that was transformed into a model for sustainable environmental design. His boldest example—and perhaps most controversial—of executive environmentalism came under cover of darkness on March 30, 2003, when city contractors tore up the Meigs Field airplane runway, the first step in converting Northerly Island into a ninety-one-acre nature park.[11]

Daley also believed that a millennium gift had to be located downtown. "It's not a millennium gift to the people if it's in one section of the city," Daley insisted. "Downtown comprises everyone so it was perfect." Daley's ebullience for the idea was described by one corporate official involved in discussions with the mayor as an "almost boyish" enthusiasm.[12]

A park also made economic sense. For more than a decade, park advocates argued that parks and open space not only benefited the urban environment, but also promoted community investment, contributed to a city's unique character, and linked surrounding buildings to create a sense of place. History offers many lessons, claimed planner Alexander Garvin. New York's Central Park, for example, stimulated a ninefold increase

4.3. Adrian D. Smith.

in property values in the three wards surrounding Central Park in the fifteen years after park development began. Entrepreneurial planners such as Garvin believed that well-planned parks generated long-term private investment, encouraged residential use, cultivated social interaction, and transformed the character of everyday life.[13]

Finally, constructing a park on top of a garage converged with Daley's larger development goals of encouraging more residential, commercial, and even cultural activity in downtown Chicago. Projects such as the reconfiguration of Lake Shore Drive at the southern end of Grant Park and the creation of the Museum Campus (comprising the Field Museum, Shedd Aquarium, and Adler Planetarium), the renovation of Soldier Field and Navy Pier, the rebuilding of the Roosevelt Road bridge and corridor between Halsted Street and Michigan Avenue, the renovations of the Harris and Selwyn theaters (as the new Goodman Theatre in 2000), the Ford Oriental Theater (1998), and the Cadillac Palace (1999), and the openings of the Shakespeare Theater (1999) at Navy Pier and the Lookingglass Theatre (2003) at the Water Tower Pumping Station encouraged both tourists and area residents to visit center-city Chicago. The construction of new residential units and renovation of older buildings (more than five thousand units in 1997 and 1998 in the vicinity of the Loop) attracted commercial enterprises such as supermarkets, pharmacies, convenience stores, and restaurants. A new park would further contribute to what some described as "the cosmopolitanization of central Chicago."[14]

After Daley assigned the task of building a park and garage on the site of the Illinois Central tracks to Ed Bedore, he approached architect Adrian Smith of Skidmore, Owings & Merrill (SOM) to develop some preliminary plans. Smith was an obvious person to assign to the task. He not only knew Bedore well, but SOM was the best-known architectural firm in the city, if not the world. Founded in 1936, SOM architects had undertaken more than ten thousand architecture, engineering, interior design, and urban planning projects in more than fifty countries.[15] Smith was personally responsible for designing skyscrapers ranging from Chicago's NBC Tower (1989) and the AT&T Corporate Center/USG Building (1989) to the United Gulf Building (1987) in Bahrain and Shanghai's Jin Mao Tower (1999). Smith was active in Chicago planning, collaborating on the Chicago Central Area Plan in 1987, the proposed Chicago World's Fair for 1992, and the Lakeshore East Master Plan (2001). He was the design partner for the State Street renovation, only two blocks west of the Millennium Park, from 1995 to 1996. From 1997 to 1998, he chaired the Chicago Central Area Committee.[16] Smith even worked with Sara Lee CEO John Bryan and Chicago Symphony Orchestra officials in the renovation of Symphony Hall during the 1990s.[17]

Smith was also active in developing alternative parking plans for Soldier Field. By some accounts, SOM was awarded the early commission as a reward for the unused 1996 designs for Soldier Field.[18] "One study led to a conceptual view of a larger area than Soldier Field, which then led us into looking at Grant Park for more parking," Smith remembers. According to Bedore, Smith used the underpark garage at Post Office Square in Boston as a possible model.[19] Smith and Bedore also explored linking Grant Park

4.4. Boston's Post Office Square served as a model for park district and city officials in developing plans for an underpark garage at the site of Illinois Central rail yard.

parking to Soldier Field by an express bus on the existing railroad track right-of-way. Only after these issues were discussed, Smith claims, did "the energies start shifting towards a band shell in this northern area of Grant Park."[20]

Smith had his own ideas about a millennium project for Chicago. He toyed with constructing the breakwater Burnham and Bennett envisioned in their *Plan of Chicago*, while including a massive arch extending from Navy Pier on the north to Adler Planetarium on the south. He also proposed enlarging Chicago's harbor basin, ideal for the city's growing boating and waterfront activity, which could finance the cost of the project. Smith even joined some park district officials and contractors to price the project. But with an estimated $93 million price tag, such an idea was too expensive.[21]

When Daley approved construction of a park, Smith began working on a master plan. He was joined by fellow SOM architects Robert Wesley and Leigh Stanton Breslau, the latter a senior designer in the expansion and renovation of Chicago's Symphony Center who was familiar with musical venues at Ravinia in Highland Park, Elmhurst College, San Jose Symphony Hall, and Jazz at Lincoln Center and Avery Fisher Hall. Their initial schemes included a new bandshell, a seating area, a garden, an ice skating rink, and a promenade area.[22]

SOM's master plan reflected two important influences. First, Smith and his team adhered to the classical beaux arts elements of Burnham and Bennett's *Plan of Chicago*

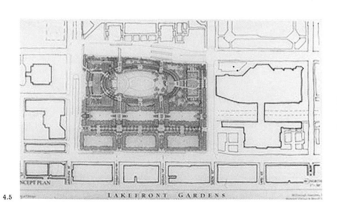

4.5   LAKEFRONT GARDENS   4.6

4.5. This design for Lakefront Gardens in SOM's archives served as a guide in early proposals for Millennium Park.

4.6. Aerial view of SOM's model looking from the north. The initial models for Lakefront Millennium Park (as the project was called) followed much the same schematic format and landscape program as the Lakefront Gardens proposals in the 1970s and 1980s.

(1909), emphasizing symmetry and formality, and conforming to the grid by visually extending the streets (Washington and Madison) as promenades. At the suggestion of developer Al Friedman, Millennium Park planners reintroduced Edward Bennett's peristyle, which had sat in the northwest corner of the park from 1917 until 1953 when it was removed for the construction of the Grant Park North garage. "I viewed it [the plan] as the completion of Grant Park," Smith later acknowledged.[23]

The second influence was Robert Hutchins's designs for Lakefront Gardens. Although few Chicagoans remembered the Hutchins plans, SOM incorporated elements from a 1988 revision with a two-tiered garage capable of holding 1,100 vehicles. The 16.5-acre plan included a performance bandshell to accommodate ten thousand spectators at the north end of the park; immediately south was a listening park for larger audiences. Access to the bandshell for equipment and performers came from the lower levels of Randolph Street. Sitting on a higher grade than the bandshell and south of Randolph Street was a reflecting pool that doubled as a skating rink in winter. SOM also included a three-hundred-seat theater for small or midsize musical and theatrical companies, and a small outdoor amphitheater for informal performances. Like the promoters of Lakefront Gardens twenty years earlier, SOM envisioned the park as a year-round facility.[24]

Most significantly, SOM's scheme addressed the earlier concerns regarding the height of any music pavilion. The shell was designed as a grotto buried in the cavity created by the Randolph Street viaduct. The result was a three-story stage below the level of Randolph Street and a flat landscape on top with few protruding structures. SOM envisioned a modest, understated music pavilion landscaped in stone and surrounded by a series of sculptures or a sculpture garden. The construction of the bowl at a lower elevation and over the railroad tracks insured that the park would remain "open, free, and clear," preserving lake views from Michigan Avenue and the Loop.[25]

Although specific elements in the SOM master plan were later altered or discarded, the fundamental scheme remained intact. The entrances and exits, the promenade, the

skating rink, the location of the fountains, the peristyle, the great lawn, the garden, and the music shell were conceived as a unit by SOM. The final overall layout of Millennium Park retained most of the features of the original SOM design. Architect Michael Patrick Sullivan, later one of the designers of the new peristyle, noted that SOM's plan created zones that allowed for potentially conflicting elements (such as the classical peristyle and a Frank Gehry-designed music pavilion) to exist in proximity to each other.[26]

SOM also considered placing the bandshell along Monroe Street at the south end of the park, facing north, a dramatic departure from Robert Hutchins's Lakefront Gardens concept twenty years earlier. "I don't know why they wanted to change that initial concept but they insisted on putting it down the south end," remembered Millennium Park project manager Ed Uhlir. Fearing reverberations off the Prudential Building, Aon Center, and other skyscrapers, Uhlir rejected the proposal unless approved by an acoustician. "I thought this was a totally stupid idea," he later declared.[27]

The key component in this early SOM plan was the garage. Planners were less concerned with the park and various cultural amenities and more attuned to issues revolving around physical planning and infrastructure. Not only did the project's $120 million cost make the garage the most expensive public investment, but the projected 2,500 parking spaces located underneath Millennium Park were both its financial and structural support. These concerns were more pronounced with the inclusion of an intermodal

4.7. Model of SOM's proposed music pavilion.

4.8. SOM envisioned a modest music pavilion in the early renderings for Millennium Park. The design sought to alleviate any objections to blocking vistas of Lake Michigan from Randolph Street or Michigan Avenue.

4.9. SOM's model of the garden, lawn, and music pavilion from south.

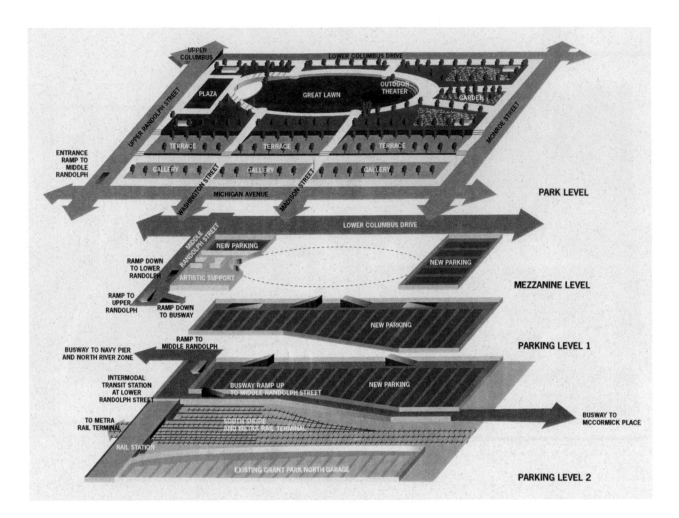

Labels within the figure:

UPPER COLUMBUS

LOWER COLUMBUS DRIVE

PLAZA

GREAT LAWN

OUTDOOR THEATER

GARDEN

UPPER RANDOLPH STREET

MONROE STREET

ENTRANCE RAMP TO MIDDLE RANDOLPH

TERRACE

TERRACE

TERRACE

GALLERY

GALLERY

GALLERY

WASHINGTON STREET

MADISON STREET

MICHIGAN AVENUE

PARK LEVEL

LOWER COLUMBUS DRIVE

MIDDLE RANDOLPH STREET

NEW PARKING

RAMP DOWN TO LOWER RANDOLPH

NEW PARKING

ARTISTIC SUPPORT

MEZZANINE LEVEL

RAMP TO UPPER RANDOLPH

RAMP DOWN TO BUSWAY

NEW PARKING

RAMP TO MIDDLE RANDOLPH

BUSWAY TO NAVY PIER AND NORTH RIVER ZONE

PARKING LEVEL 1

INTERMODAL TRANSIT STATION AT LOWER RANDOLPH STREET

BUSWAY RAMP UP TO MIDDLE RANDOLPH STREET

NEW PARKING

TO METRA RAIL TERMINAL

SOUTH SHORE AND METRA RAIL TERMINAL

BUSWAY TO McCORMICK PLACE

RAIL STATION

EXISTING GRANT PARK NORTH GARAGE

PARKING LEVEL 2

4.10. A schematic drawing of the Intermodal Transportation Center.

transportation center below the park. The center linked automobile, bus, and rail traffic, while the underground pedways connected the Metra station, Butler Field, Daley Bicentennial Plaza, the Art Institute, the Cultural Center, and the Monroe Street Garage. City and planning officials recognized that the garage's revenue potential was enhanced if it served as a remote parking facility for Navy Pier, the Museum Campus, Soldier Field, and McCormick Place, all of which were to be linked together with a "lakefront busway." At conception, the Lakefront Millennium Project was as much a transportation project as it was a new park space.[28]

By the 1990s, various planning institutions complained that the central lakefront area, despite remaining an open, public place surrounded by world-class cultural institutions, suffered from poor transit services. The lakefront busway was the solution. More significantly, the busway reflected an emphasis on physical planning, vehicle movement, and congestion control in the earliest plans for Millennium Park. This was hardly surprising given the debates in the half century after World War II over developing

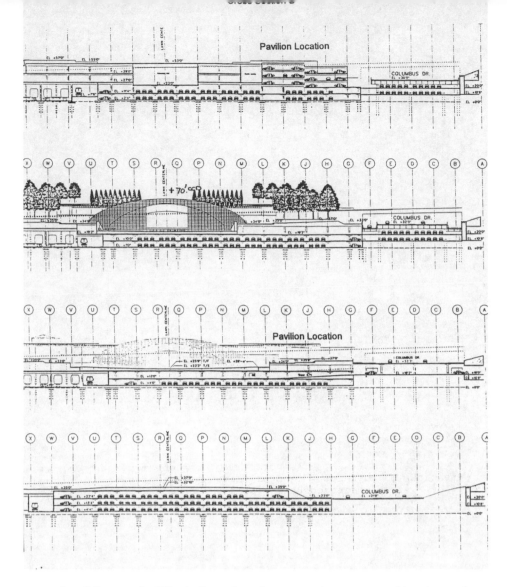

a transit rail line on the Illinois Central tracks, or creating segregated bus lanes along Columbus Drive. Proposals linking the Randolph Street area to McCormick Place were hardly new. In 1962, for example, Minnesota developer Dennis Scanlan proposed constructing a monorail connecting McCormick Place to Lake Shore Drive just south of the Chicago River. Scanlan's transit link would have extended through Burnham Harbor, across the Adler Planetarium peninsula, and through the harbor adjacent to Meigs Field before reaching the east side of McCormick Place.[29]

By the end of 1997, various city and lakefront institutions were actively planning for a new segregated, two-lane, subsurface, limited-access road running on an old Illinois Central Railroad right-of-way. The proposal had several advantages: grade separation with no traffic crossing, convenient access to McCormick Place, a connection to Randolph Street at the north terminus, and potential stops at the Museum Campus, Soldier Field, and Navy Pier. Chicago Transit Authority and charter buses would travel from Randolph Street, continue south in a trench between Columbus Drive and Michigan

4.11. Cross sections of Intermodal Transportation Center looking north, from the Chicago Plan Commission. Millennium Park planners hoped the inclusion of an intermodal transit station would generate more pedestrian traffic and usage of the park all year round.

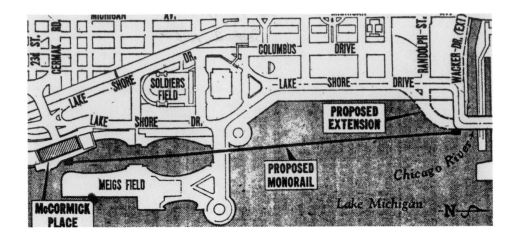

4.12. Dennis Scanlan's monorail proposal.

Avenue, pass underneath the Art Institute, and terminate at McCormick Place. City officials believed that linking Millennium Park with McCormick Place would eliminate considerable traffic congestion, thereby making McCormick Place competitive with other midsize convention centers nationwide. When the Metropolitan Pier and Exposition Authority (MPEA) expressed a willingness to sell the construction bonds in early 1998, the project gained further momentum. "Our single largest problem is during any of the major festivals," complained Jack Johnson, director of governmental and community affairs for the MPEA. "Streets are closed and buses are forced into traffic jams." The busway was funded with $100 million in revenue bonds issued by the MPEA.[30]

ON MARCH 30, 1998, mayor Richard M. Daley announced the Lakefront Millennium Project, with John Bryan to serve as the chief fundraiser for the donors group. "Every year, millions of people come to Grant Park to our festivals, gardens, and lakefront," proclaimed Daley. "Now they'll have another reason to come. The Lakefront Millennium Project will be free—a place for families and another destination for visitors which will generate convention and tourism jobs for people who live in Chicago's neighborhoods—all at no cost to taxpayers."[31]

Daley's remarks embodied the vast cultural terrain city officials crossed in the final quarter of the twentieth century. In 1973, the Metropolitan Planning and Housing Council complained that "the cultural institutions [of Grant Park] are not talking to each other." From traffic solutions to attracting more patrons, the city and its leading cultural institutions did little to promote themselves or Chicago to the outside world.[32]

Prior to 1990, Chicago tourism was the stepchild of the convention and trade show business. While the city was the premier convention center in the United States, and for a time boasted the only convention center with more than one million square feet of space, Chicago and Illinois did little to promote theater, historic preservation, or cultural tourism. In 1987, the Regional Agenda Project reported that while Chicago possessed some of the world's most important cultural resources, the city ineffectively promoted the region, and its resources were not recognized as major contributors to the city's quality of life. "Public and private agencies promoting tourism, business and economic development," the report argued, "do not exploit the potential of our cultural wealth."[33]

On the lakefront, the Grant Park Cultural and Educational Community, a not-for-profit umbrella organization for cultural and educational institutions in the Grant Park vicinity, was established in the 1980s to develop public awareness of Grant Park, specifically the ongoing and special events offered by member organizations. Certain events—the Taste of Chicago, Jazz Fest, Fourth of July fireworks—attracted large crowds, but the public remained largely ignorant of the many daily events sponsored by Grant Park institutions. Because the various institutions had limited advertising funds, they were compelled to focus on events that attracted the largest crowds. In 1986, the organization developed a marketing plan to promote the area, while working to improve relations and communications with the Chicago Transit Authority, METRA Commuter Rail Service, and various radio stations. Their stated goal was to promote tourism, culture, and leisure activities in the Grant Park area.[34]

Nothing better illustrated the impact of tourism—indeed the changing nature of Chicago's economy—than Navy Pier.

During the 1970s, with the completion of McCormick Place, the decline in Great Lakes shipping, and the relocation of the University of Illinois at Chicago (1966), Navy Pier became dormant. Although the tall ships docked there in 1976 during the national bicentennial celebration and various festivals continued on the pier (Lakefront Festival in 1976, Chicagofest from 1978 to 1982), the pier was an underused facility.

Some planners recognized Navy Pier's potential, especially when linked with Grant Park. Architect Harry Weese, for example, advocated turning the Loop "into a happy place, its throngs lured downtown by free transit to the region's largest shopping center, with Grant Park a frontispiece and gateway and Navy Pier a veritable Tivoli." Weese noted that the leading metropolises of Europe followed such development schemes. Navy Pier, in Weese's vision, should become an urban pleasure garden, an inner-city theme park.[35]

In 1980, the city signed a five-year contract with the Rouse Corporation to redesign the pier for a mixed-use commercial development. Rouse had attracted international attention by transforming Boston's Faneuil Hall/Quincy Market (1976), Baltimore's HarborPlace (1980), and New York's South Street Seaport (1983) into major tourist destinations. Six years after opening, HarborPlace had tripled the number of tourists in the Inner Harbor area of Baltimore. Boston's Faneuil Hall attracted 12 million tourists in 1995.[36] Chicago officials hoped Rouse could work the same magic on Navy Pier.

But in 1984, those plans fell apart and the city closed Navy Pier.[37] A year later, a mayoral task force identified the pier as "one of Chicago's greatest treasures," but the facility remained "undiscovered for much of the public." As one of the most visible elements of Burnham and Bennett's 1909 *Plan of Chicago*, the pier had the potential to showcase Chicago in a way no other public space could match.[38] The task force recommended redeveloping the pier as a multiuse public facility for expositions, the performing arts, museums, theaters, parks, sports, marinas, restaurants, and small retail establishments. In effect, the pier was to serve "as a stage for a multitude of compatible activities that would create an exciting place for people to visit, explore and use."[39]

In 1989, the city of Chicago and the state of Illinois created the Metropolitan Pier and Exposition Authority and committed $150 million for the reconstruction of Navy Pier. From 1992 to 1995, Benjamin Thompson & Associates embarked on a $196 million facelift. Almost overnight after opening in 1995, Navy Pier became Chicago's new "fun zone." In July 1997, Navy Pier's Children's Museum, Ferris wheel, IMAX Theater, outdoor Skylight Stage, numerous restaurants, cruise ships, and many shops attracted 1.2 million visitors, an average of 80,000 on Saturdays, and 30,000 on weekdays. Officials estimated that 40 percent were from outside the Chicago area, 30 percent from the city, 26 percent from suburbs, and 4 percent from foreign countries.[40] By the end of 1997, an estimated 7 million had visited Navy Pier, more than double Chicago's second-leading attraction—the Lincoln Park Zoo, with 3 million annual visitors.[41] With a new garage in 1998 increasing parking to 1,740,[42] and the opening of the Shakespeare Theater in 1999, the numbers only rose: in 2001, Navy Pier attracted 9 million visitors.[43]

Chicago's central lakefront institutions benefited from this resurgence. By 1995, the area running from the Museum Campus to Navy Pier attracted more than 10 million annual visitors, greater than the Grand Canyon and Yosemite National Park combined.[44] These new or newly discovered recreation and cultural facilities reportedly enticed more people to live in downtown Chicago. In 1980, only 6,400 resided in the area bounded by Lake Michigan, the Chicago River on the north and west, and Congress Parkway on the south. By 2000, the number reached 16,000, with projections doubling that figure by 2020.[45] Outside of Manhattan, "Chicago is where we are seeing the largest growth in population within the vicinity of downtown," claimed Michael Beyard of the Urban Land Institute in 2003. "It seems that good public planning and a good real estate market and changing demographics are all driving people into the city."[46]

The growing emphasis on tourism by municipal and planning officials coincided with a dramatic change in the city's political landscape. Since 1980, with the election of president Ronald Reagan and the ensuing cutbacks in federal government programs, municipalities had discovered that little, if any, money was available for public housing, urban renewal, slum clearance, or other types of physical civic improvement. According to one analysis, the federal government cut financial aid to cities by 46 percent between 1980 and 1990.[47]

Declining federal support was magnified by the growing resistance of taxpayers to supporting many of the programs associated with Lyndon Johnson's Great Society. Beginning with California's Proposition 13 in 1978, "taxpayer revolt" was a frequently repeated mantra describing citizen resistance to municipal and other government expenditures. And for good reason: by one estimate, taxes declined nationwide by about 25 percent from 1970 to 1990. In American cities, property taxes dropped from 48 to 31 percent of municipal revenues.[48]

American city officials such as Richard M. Daley were compelled to find new revenue sources and develop creative development strategies. "The urban landscape is changing," Daley told the Civic Federation in 1991. "American cities face greater problems— crumbling infrastructures, soaring crime rates, and troubled schools." These were, in Daley's mind, "the indisputable facts of life in Chicago." Daley insisted he had to challenge the status quo: "The truth is, we have no choice."[49]

During the 1990s, Daley and other big-city mayors like Rudolph Giuliani of New York, Richard Riordan of Los Angeles, Edward Rendell of Philadelphia, and Stephen Goldsmith of Indianapolis adopted programs of fiscal frugality, crime reduction, encouragement of corporate and transnational investment in center cities, and collaborative public-private partnerships. Hotel and commercial developments in downtown areas, upscale residential construction in former industrial neighborhoods, mixed-use sporting and high-tech entertainment venues, and the privatization of city services were typical results of these strategies. Such policies intended to prevent middle-class migration to the suburbs, encourage private capital investment, and cut back municipal supervision. "Our goal is to bring down the walls of regulation on businesses," Daley proclaimed.[50]

By 1994, Daley had privatized more than forty city services, reportedly saving the city $20 million.[51] Private contractors were hired to trim trees, remove tree stumps, fix traffic lights, clean sewers, and polish the floors of City Hall. Within the next decade, the city's data processing operations, the public school system's capital improvement program, abandoned-automobile towing, janitorial services, parking fine collection, and the daily operations of Midway Airport and the International Terminal at O'Hare Airport were ceded to private companies. At the Chicago Park District, from 1993 to 1998, Daley's former chief of staff turned superintendent Forrest Claypool hired private companies to operate the parking garages at Soldier Field and other district-owned lots, as well as marinas and golf courses. In 2004, on the eve of the opening of Millennium Park, Daley announced plans to privatize certain parts of the city's public school system.[52]

Privatization marked a dramatic transformation in the structure of political power in Chicago. The twin foundations of Richard J. Daley's power—municipal patronage and labor union support—were no longer necessary ingredients for political success. Indeed, privatization was designed to eliminate labor costs and jobs, the essence of both patronage and organized labor. At times, Richard M. Daley even blamed budget-balancing municipal layoffs on unions and their work rules, even threatening to privatize union-protected services and jobs. "He thinks more like a businessman than a politician," reported Marshall Holleb, an attorney active in city development issues. "His dad ran the city on patronage; he's running it like a business."[53]

This new approach to municipal governance in the final decade of the twentieth century induced Chicago and other U.S. cities to campaign aggressively for the tourist dollar, a competition that some likened to nineteenth-century cities competing for railroad lines. Municipal planners increasingly followed "niche strategies"—incremental development organized around cooperation between public and private participants. Many projects were designed to encourage tourism, leisure activity, and recreation: building or expanding convention centers, constructing stadiums and arenas for sporting and other entertainment events, and identifying certain neighborhoods as historic districts.[54]

Promoting cultural institutions was one conspicuous example of this strategy. From 1996 to 2001, mayor Edward Rendell and developer Willard G. Rouse III combined public and private forces to build the Kimmel Center for the Performing Arts, which opened in Philadelphia (2001). In Los Angeles, mayor Richard Riordan enlisted the help of Eli Broad to raise the necessary private funds to complete the Walt Disney Concert Hall (2003) when that project nearly fell apart in 1994. The Seattle Symphony's Benaroya Hall (1998) was built with $99 million in private funding, $19 million in public funds. And in an effort to revitalize downtown Newark, the New Jersey Performing Arts Center raised $187 million in public and private funds prior to opening in 1997.[55]

Exploiting cultural institutions to enhance a city's visibility and global identity was hardly unique to American cities. Glasgow advertised itself as the "City of Culture," especially with the opening of the Royal Concert Hall (1990), the Gallery of Modern Art (1996), and the Glasgow Auditorium (1997).[56] Shanghai's renovated Concert Hall and Dramatic Arts Center and new Grand Theater were constructed with significant state subsidies to attract foreign visitors.[57] And the opening of the Frank Gehry–designed Guggenheim Museum in Bilbao, Spain (1997), transformed that little-known city into a major tourist destination.

Some early observers described Millennium Park as a project in search of a "Bilbao effect," creating an architectural trophy that would transform an abandoned industrial site into a tourist destination. Daley emphatically denied this. Gehry's Guggenheim Museum undoubtedly had a great impact on the economically depressed waterfront area of Bilbao. But Chicago was different. "We didn't need that," insists Daley. "Bilbao needed that. There is no other identity to it."[58]

Daley was right. The "Bilbao effect" involved more than simply generating more tourism. With the Guggenheim Museum in Bilbao, Gehry created not simply a place, as he did with his Loyola Law School campus design in the 1970s—transforming the entire character of a one-block site in a gritty Los Angeles neighborhood—but a destination for tourists from around the world. In Daley's view, Chicago already was a tourist destination, and a city with a complex and global identity.[59]

Cultural tourism, the privatization of municipal services, and the changing economy of postindustrial Chicago thus gave rise to the Lakefront Millennium Project. The success of Navy Pier and the Museum Campus convinced public and corporate officials that commercialized culture and recreation were necessary elements of lakefront economic life. The Lakefront Millennium Project, city officials envisioned, could be a new tourist engine. An Arthur Andersen study predicted that such a park would generate between two and three million additional tourists annually. Even with a modest $50 expenditure per visit, that meant $100–150 million in new tourist revenue. Alderman Burton Natarus bluntly proclaimed that Millennium Park not only would create "a Mecca for culture," but would be a leading tourist destination.[60]

But such a development strategy required a major political reorientation for mayors like Richard Daley. American taxpayers historically displayed little toleration for using municipal funds for new cultural projects. While some limited subsidies or tax incentives were acceptable, the bulk of support had to originate from the private sector. Daley, for example, feared taxpayer wrath were he to spend $30 million on a simple park above the Millennium Park garage. Consequently, forging alliances with downtown corporate communities was a necessity. Indeed, Daley had little choice if he wanted Chicago to attract financial capital, economic investment, and visiting tourists. The mayor's desire to avoid conflict and encourage cooperation with the corporate sector led one writer to dub the era the age of "Pax Daleyorum."[61]

Few questioned this development strategy, evidenced by the numerous civic groups which quickly endorsed the Lakefront Millennium Project. The Chicago Central Area Committee (CCAC) noted their long-time support for such a proposal.[62] Benjamin E. Alba of the Grant Park Advisory Council described the proposal as "the most sweeping addition to Grant Park in the last century." Friends of the Parks endorsed the plan as "a remarkable affirmation of the efforts initiated by the Friends of the Parks and the Metropolitan Planning Council in 1976 to create a performing arts center and new parkland above the Illinois Central and METRA railyards." Jonathan Beck, coordinator of the Openlands Project, concluded that the project "will make the city more desirable and a better place to live." The Sun-Times editorialized, "What's not to like?"[63]

Even criticism of the park plan was muted. The Tribune argued that the overall design failed "to meet the practical needs of the city." With only 3,800 seats, the overwhelming majority of patrons would have to sit on the grass. Echoing past complaints, the Tribune believed Grant Park needed a single, all-encompassing venue as a home for both the Grant Park Symphony and the highly popular summer festivals. "The operative model should be the Hollywood Bowl, not the gardens of Versailles," argued the editorial board, and recommended increasing seating capacity to 20,000 with room for another 20,000 on the grass. Reservations aside, the Tribune described the initial design as "a visual knockout" and "a dramatic opportunity."[64]

Few observers paid any attention to the cost or funding mechanism at the time. Garage revenues would ultimately pay for the bonds floated by the city to construct the garage. But what about the park? Daley's answer was the private sector, specifically asking John Bryan of the Sara Lee Corporation to lead a campaign to raise $30 million to construct a park on top of the garage. Daley emphasized that "the city's historic commitment to investing in neighborhoods will not be diminished by the project." The garage and park, Daley reminded Chicagoans, would not require regular taxpayer funds, adding that from 1989 to 2000, his administration would spend almost $4.5 billion in neighborhood schools, libraries, streets, parks and other community projects.[65]

City officials went to work immediately. The Chicago Department of Transportation was named to oversee the project. A $6 million contract—some labeled it the largest "no bid contract" in city history—was awarded to McDonough and Associates, who immediately named SOM as a design subconsultant. On May 14, 1998, six weeks after Daley had publicly announced the project, the Chicago Plan Commission approved the Lakefront Millennium Project. "This is a long-awaited project," summarized transportation commissioner Tom Walker. "Daniel Burnham had a vision for the entire lakefront and this has been a longstanding gap in the completion of that vision."[66]

Walker, Daley, and other city officials, however, were unaware that John Bryan had dramatically different Burnhamesque ambitions for Millennium Park.

Chapter 5

SHOOTING FOR THE MOON

Nobody had bigger plans for Millennium Park than John Bryan. The Sara Lee CEO was attending a breakfast reception for the mayor of Mexico City at the Mid-America Club in the Amoco (now Aon) Building on September 4, 1997, when mayor Richard M. Daley pulled Bryan over to the window. To their left, Lake Michigan shimmered in the morning sunrise. Michigan Avenue's magnificent skyscraper streetwall, often compared with the great urban streetscapes of Venice, Shanghai, and Edinburgh, stood to their right. Inevitably their eyes wandered to the ground below. To their left and across the street was Bicentennial Plaza, named after the mayor's father, Richard J. Daley.

But none of this interested Daley. He directed Bryan's attention to what lay immediately in front of the Amoco Building: the largely empty former yard of the Illinois Central Railroad. "We should build a park there," Daley dreamed. Bryan nodded in agreement.[1]

Bryan gave little thought to the mayor's wish. But six months later, Daley summoned Bryan to City Hall. "He wanted to undertake this project to build this garage and a park," remembered Bryan. "He wanted me to be in charge of the enhancements on top of the garage." Daley was confident that all that was needed was $30 million from the private sector. Could Bryan raise that sum of money on his own, Daley inquired? Bryan said yes.[2]

But on the way back to his office, Bryan upped the ante. He envisioned both a larger project, with private-sector donors playing a more significant role. Traveling with Judith Paulus, another Sara Lee officer, Bryan proclaimed, "If the Mayor wants thirty [million], we're going to have to raise sixty [million]." Bryan was, in the words of Marshall Field V, going "to shoot for the moon."[3]

Bryan was a logical choice for such an assignment. During the 1990s, he had been an instrumental force in raising money to renovate Chicago's Lyric Opera House and Orchestra Hall. That capital campaign floundered in the beginning, notably when Bryan failed to secure a large grant from the MacArthur Foundation. Unflustered, Bryan turned his sights to Chicago's corporate elite. One day, he paid separate visits to three of Chicago's leading chief executives: Laurance Fuller of Amoco, Richard Thomas of the First National Bank of Chicago, and Patrick Ryan of the Aon Corporation. Bryan made a personal appeal to each one, persuading all three to provide major financial contributions.

> The donors "didn't want to put an ordinary park on that piece of land. They said, "gee, if we're going to do this, then we've got to shoot for the moon."
>
> MARSHALL FIELD V

5.1. John Bryan.

"So in one day, I had $30 million to start," Bryan gushed, and the campaign was on.[4]

By 1993, Bryan and his colleagues had raised $100 million on behalf of the Lyric Opera and Chicago Symphony. With major contributions from thirty-three corporations and foundations, the sum was believed to be the largest amount of money ever given by a business community in support of a local cultural project.[5] The campaign proved to be a dress rehearsal for Bryan's fundraising strategy in Millennium Park.

Yet John Bryan's pedigree made him an unusual choice to lead a campaign on behalf of the city of Chicago. A fifth-generation southerner whose ancestors fought in the Civil War siege at Vicksburg, Bryan grew up in a small Mississippi town dominated by his family's business. Bryan Brothers Packing Company was one of the largest combined livestock and meatpacking concerns in the South. Upon graduation from Southwestern (later Rhodes) College in Memphis, Tennessee, in 1958, Bryan returned home, and shortly after was named the company's new chief executive. He was only twenty-three. In 1968, Bryan negotiated the merger and sale of Bryan Foods with the Consolidated Food Corporation of Chicago run by Nathan Cummings.[6]

But it was not only Bryan's business acumen that attracted attention. Rather, Bryan's support of Martin Luther King, Jr., and the civil rights movement made him a target of scorn by many of his white, southern neighbors. During his tenure at Bryan Brothers, the young Bryan desegregated water fountains, restrooms, cafeterias, and white-collar positions. Then he joined the black community and sued the local school board for closing the public schools rather than submit to integration. When town officials closed the community swimming pool to prevent African Americans from using the facility, Bryan personally built a new one. When the previously all-black elementary schools finally reopened, Bryan's children were among the students.[7]

In 1974, Bryan was named president of Consolidated Foods and moved his family to Chicago; a year later, he was promoted to chief executive officer. Over the ensuing two decades, Bryan transformed the company. In 1985, Bryan persuaded shareholders to change Consolidated's name to the Sara Lee Corporation. More important, Bryan recognized the limits for future expansion in the food industry due to the slow growth of the American population. Bryan initiated a series of daring moves to diversify the enterprise. From 1990 to 1995, Sara Lee acquired more than $4 billion in European assets. Furthermore, Bryan moved the corporation into new markets. By 1994, for example, Sara Lee was the largest apparel company in the United States. When Bryan retired in 2001, Sara Lee was a diversified, global consumer packaged goods company with over $20 billion in annual revenues. The firm employed 139,000 workers, maintained operations in over 40 countries, and marketed products in over 140 nations.[8]

Bryan's success generated invitations to serve on the boards of directors of Goldman Sachs, Bank One, General Motors, and BP. More significantly, Bryan's "reinvention" of Sara Lee was emblematic of a transformation in the global economy: a new generation of companies was organized around a structure of low assets. Corporations like Sara Lee, Dell, Disney, and Merrill Lynch were increasingly, in Bryan's words, "assetless companies"—outsourcing virtually all production, concentrating on managing brands, helping customers decide what they need, and tailoring products and services to satisfy them. For Bryan, the vertically integrated corporation was a relic.[9]

But Bryan was about more than making mammon. As he had done in his native Mississippi, Bryan transformed Sara Lee into a corporate model for breaking down gender and racial barriers. He instituted a diversity program ensuring the representation of women and minorities at all levels of the company. From 1991 to 1996, he chaired Catalyst, a nonprofit research organization for women. Bryan impressed former Atlanta mayor and U.S. ambassador to the United Nations Andrew Young. "Bryan should not only be judged by the financial bottom line," declared Young, "but also by the moral bottom line because he makes fairness to minorities and women the major part of the business of his corporation."[10]

Bryan also possessed a keen passion for the arts. Some described the Sara Lee official as possessing an artist's sensibility, exemplified by his expertise in European decorative art and textiles, and as a collector of Gustav Stickley–designed furniture. Bryan eventually combined his cultural pursuits and administrative acumen by serving on the board of trustees of the Chicago Symphony, the University of Chicago, and the Art Institute of Chicago, including the chairmanship of the latter. Bryan's cultural interests were an ideal fit at Sara Lee. Since the days of Nathan Cummings, the company had possessed one of the largest art collections of any U.S. corporation, and was a leading contributor to cultural institutions. During Bryan's tenure, the corporation donated substantial portions of its collection to art museums. In 1998, Sara Lee was awarded the National Medal of Arts for its altruistic corporate policies.[11]

Bryan, like Adrian Smith and Richard M. Daley, also advocated commemorating the millennium in a concrete way. On November 18, 1997, in his acceptance speech for the Daniel H. Burnham Award from the Chicagoland Chamber of Commerce, he proposed building a monument to the millennium. He had already informally discussed ideas regarding Chicago's need for a signature structure. Bryan even suggested constructing a massive breakwater off Grant Park in Lake Michigan to complete Daniel Burnham and Edward Bennett's vision, as captured in their *Plan of Chicago* in 1909.[12]

Furthermore, Bryan adopted Burnham and Bennett's view of the city as a work of art, viewing the lakefront as an artistic composition as envisioned in *Plan of Chicago*. He called upon Chicago residents and public officials to build "a structure which would become *the* defining symbol of Chicago to all the world—a symbol designed with the very real expectation that it would become Chicago's signature." As examples, Bryan cited the Eiffel Tower, the Leaning Tower of Pisa, the Washington Monument, the Statue of Liberty, the Gateway Arch, and the Sydney Opera House, all of which are "*great physical structures . . . able to capture the imagination of people, and in one breath, tell all about a place and give a city great distinction.*"[13]

Bryan was hardly the first to publicly advocate a millennium project for Chicago. In 1996, John McCarter, president and CEO of the Field Museum, began organizing "The

5.2

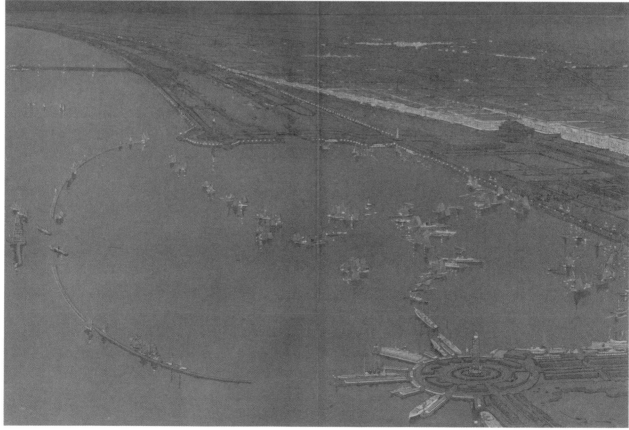

5.3

5.4

Millennium Project," a metropolitan program for 130 to 140 cultural and educational institutions. McCarter targeted 1999 instead of 2000 because he feared the public was "supersaturated" with the media hype surrounding the new century. During 1999, the project sponsored a series of educational and entertainment programs under the theme of the millennium, linking the programming of the various institutions, building databases, sharing information, and stimulating attendance at the smaller institutions. "The effort was perhaps irrelevant to some of the larger institutions," noted McCarter, "but the smaller institutions thought it was an important thing."[14]

McCarter also suggested a physical design to memorialize the millennium, specifically that the city implement Burnham and Bennett's plan for a southern lakefront park similar to Lincoln Park on the North Side. When that proposal attracted little attention, McCarter considered art gallery director and collector Richard Gray's idea that Chicago needed a distinct icon. In 1997, Claes Oldenburg, at the request of Gray and the Chicago Humanities Festival, proposed a basketball and hoop sculpture located off the coast of Chicago in Lake Michigan; the design later became the poster image for the festival's theme of "Work and Play." Oldenburg, a former Chicago resident given to fantastic and controversial sculptures, is best known in Chicago for his sculpture *Bat Column* (1976). Gray suggested taking Oldenburg's drawing and building upon the recent success of the city's professional basketball team led by Michael Jordan. "Chicago—the Basketball Capital of the World—this will be the millennium icon," Gray proclaimed.[15] In the end, however, these proposals attracted little support.

When Daley appealed to Bryan to lead the fundraising effort for Millennium Park, the Sara Lee executive was unfamiliar with the project. Bryan knew nothing about the

5.2–5.4. Aerial views of the proposed breakwater east of Grant Park in *Plan of Chicago*.

5.5. Claes Oldenburg,
Bat Column (1976).

early efforts by planners to provide more parking for Soldier Field. He knew little about the preliminary plans of the Daley administration. Only on March 18, 1998, less than two weeks before Daley made the first public announcement on constructing Millennium Park, did Bryan see the master plan devised by SOM.[16] But selecting John Bryan to lead the private sector's fundraising campaign changed everything.

Daley and Bryan believed privatization was a means to cut municipal expenditures in constructing the park. Daley associates remember that the mayor was adamant about avoiding tax revenues to build Millennium Park. "The mayor was determined to privatize it and make it run in the most efficient and revenue-generating way possible," remembered the city's former budget director Ed Bedore. Relying upon anticipated user fees from a three-story underground garage, Bedore and others convinced Daley that no tax dollars would be needed.[17]

Chicago was hardly unique in turning to the private sector to build a park. Since 1981, federal government support for local parks and open space (through the Land and Water Conservation Fund state grant program) had been slashed. A National Recreation and Park Association study in 1994 estimated that $30.7 billion of state and local recreational investment was needed between 1995 and 1999 just to meet the public demand.[18]

For these reasons, stakeholder-driven, public-private partnerships became increasingly common in urban park creation and renovation. Freeway Park in Seattle (1976), Hawthorne Park (1996) and Turtle Park (1997) in Kansas City, Missouri, and Mill Race Park in Columbus, Indiana (1992) were built with private subsidies accounting for 50 percent or more of the cost. The most notable example, however was Boston's Post Office Square (1992), a $75 million, 1.7-acre project that proved to be not only the city's deepest excavation, biggest garage, and most expensive park, but also one of the first park projects in U.S. to sell stock and offer investors interest. Friends of Post Office Square (1983) initially consisted of CEOs of neighboring corporations. The unique financing allowed the city of Boston to earn $1 million for ownership interest in the site, as well as annual property taxes of $1 million. The city also avoided operational expenses for the garage, and made sure that excess revenues were directed to maintaining neighborhood parks. When all the debt and equity was repaid in the future, ownership of the park and garage would return to the city.[19]

Neither Daley nor Bryan envisioned Millennium Park as a profit-making venture, but construction of the park demanded minimal public expense. Consequently, Adrian Smith's design envisioned a simple park costing $23 million with a $7 million endowment for future maintenance.[20]

Bryan believed that goal was too modest. His experience in raising $100 million for the Chicago Symphony and the Lyric Opera convinced him that he could raise a much larger sum than $30 million. Bryan quickly hired James Feldstein as a fundraising consultant and began exploiting the network of contributors he had fostered in that earlier campaign. Bryan formed a private "Blue Ribbon Committee" of corporate officials with extensive experience in civic and cultural affairs: Marshall Field V, Edgar Jannotta of William Blair & Company, James O'Connor of Commonwealth Edison, Richard Thomas of the First National Bank of Chicago, and Deborah DeHaas of Arthur Andersen. Donna LaPietra of Kurtis Productions joined Bryan as cochair of the committee. In time, the committee evolved into the Millennium Park Board of Directors.[21]

The Lakefront Millennium Project, however, confronted a different set of fundraising hurdles. Support for the Lyric/Symphony campaign originated from corporations, many of which enjoyed long-time and historic relationships with both institutions through various executive officers who served on their boards. By contrast, Millennium Park was a new entity with no history. Richard Thomas openly worried that Millennium Park faced additional obstacles, including the loss through mergers and acquisitions of several firms that had contributed generously to the Lyric and the Symphony. The challenge, conceded James Feldstein, was "to create an instant constituency."[22]

This was no small task. Even the name of the park was undecided. Bryan remembered that in the beginning, "the biggest concern we had, strangely enough, was that Millennium Park was a park within a park and we had been told that we couldn't use the name 'park.'" Some feared that having a small park in the larger Grant Park was both contradictory and confusing. Others worried that associating the park with the millennium would hinder fundraising. Market research found that the public was tired of

5.6. James Feldstein and John Bryan.

the ever-increasing attention on the millennium, and that the idea might be perceived as "tacky." Consequently, some of the earliest plans identified the park as "Lakefront Millennium Gardens," "Lakefront Gardens" and "Lakeside Gardens." Leo Burnett's research team even recommended naming the park the "Garden of the Arts." But Bryan astutely concluded that such a name sounded elitist, and would weaken support. In the end, proponents concluded that "it's not just a garden." Bryan rejected the studies and persuaded his associates to stick with Millennium Park.[23]

None of this discouraged Bryan. "In fundraising," he argued, "everything is about strategy." The key for Bryan was determining how to make Millennium Park highly appealing to potential donors. At first, Bryan and Feldstein entertained a broad-based campaign with large and small donations. "We would sell bricks," remembered Bryan, "like they did with Ellis Island." But as the campaign planning evolved, Bryan, Feldstein, and several others met with Daley, who vetoed such a plan. The mayor feared that such a campaign was unwieldy, and that smaller gifts ought to go to people giving to their own communities.[24]

Bryan then devised a two-pronged strategy. First, he would identify individuals, families, and corporations with historic attachments to Chicago and ask them to contribute a gift valued in excess of $5 million to develop a space in the park. In return, they would enjoy a "naming opportunity" and participation in the development of that space. Second, Bryan asked Marshall Field V to lead a fundraising drive for "smaller" $1 million gifts. These donations would be inscribed in stone on the peristyle in the northwest corner of the park, a roll call of Chicago's "modern day Medicis," according to Donna LaPietra.[25]

The most daring element in this strategy was that Bryan believed he could double the goal established by Daley, promising to raise $60 million in private-sector gifts. With more financial resources, Millennium Park would be able to attract higher quality and internationally acclaimed artists, designers, and planners. "We wanted to make it at the highest level," insisted Bryan. "We wanted everything to be using the best that we have today."[26]

Based on history, specifically Chicago's failure to create a suitable musical venue in Grant Park, Bryan's goal seemed like hubris. Why would any individual or institution agree to part with $1 million, much less $5 million or $10 million? Bryan offered a ready and repeated answer: "You are going to be responsible for creating the most beautiful space, ornament or building that is going to define Chicago for the next century. It will have your name on it, and it will be a gift to the people of Chicago from those people who were successful and prominent at the time of the millennium."[27]

"The pitch," as this philanthropic boosterism became known among Bryan admirers, worked. Bryan's southern charm, aesthetic erudition, and modest eloquence combined with his familiarity with Chicago's intersecting corporate, political, and cultural subcultures. The art gallery director Richard Gray described Bryan as extremely engaging, persuasive, and civic-minded. "People just flock to him," stated Gray. Daley believed that Bryan was so respected internationally and in Chicago that "we needed something like this that would really help the city." Commonwealth Edison's James O'Connor in-

sisted that Millennium Park was never "an ego thing" for Bryan. "I don't know anyone else in our community who could have done what he did."[28]

Millennium Park's location also played a key role. Marshall Field V remembered committee members recognizing that the site was the "finest piece" of undeveloped real estate left in Chicago. "They didn't want to put an ordinary park on that piece of land." For Bryan, Field, and other committee members, the goal was to attract the best and

5.7. An early aerial map with a projected view of Millennium Park.

most creative artists in the world at the time of the millennium, and invite them to design different elements of the park.

ON JUNE 16, 1998, Bryan convened a citizens' committee of civic and business leaders. Meeting over breakfast in the Chicago Cultural Center, they overlooked the physically repulsive rail yard that Bryan and Daley were determined to transform. In the distance sat the Petrillo bandshell; already a large crowd had gathered to celebrate the Chicago Bulls and their sixth National Basketball Association championship.[29] Bulls fans suspected that this might be the last hurrah, the grand finale, for the legendary teams of the 1990s led by Michael Jordan. It was. No one realized, however, the same was true for the Petrillo bandshell.

Chapter 6

ART IN THE PARK

John Bryan recognized he had to make Millennium Park original and unique to attract potential donors. That meant art. Bryan's emphasis on public art reflected how certain forms of culture had become an increasingly important element in urban planning.[1] It was not always like that.

When Pablo Picasso's untitled sculpture was unveiled in Chicago on August 15, 1967, public reaction was mixed. Art experts believed the sculpture looked like an abstract version of a woman's face, perhaps Picasso's mistress Jaclyn. Others described it as a baboon with wings or an Afghan hound. A *Tribune* editorial mocked it as a "predatory grasshopper." Art critics described the sculpture as "grotesque" and "obscene." Others speculated that the five-story, 162-ton object was a hoax—since Picasso had declined a commission and offered it as a gift, the artist must be playing a joke on the city. Alderman John J. Hoellen introduced a resolution to have it removed.[2]

But not only did the Picasso sculpture become a symbol of Chicago, as mayor Richard J. Daley predicted, it stimulated greater demand and appreciation for public art. In the final decades of the twentieth century, Chicago boosters invoked examples of public art to promote and even identify Chicago: Alexander Calder's *Flamingo* (1974) in Federal Plaza, Marc Chagall's *Four Seasons* (1974) at Chase Tower, Joan Miró's *Chicago* (1981) across from the Daley Center, Ellsworth Kelly's *Curve XXII* or *I Will* (1981) in Lincoln Park, Jean Dubuffet's *Monument with Standing Beast* (1984) in the Thompson State of Illinois Center, and Richard Hunt's *Freeform* (1993) on the restored State of Illinois Building.

This renaissance of public art was stimulated, in part, by municipal activism. In 1978, Chicago's "Percent for Art" Ordinance stipulated that a percentage of the cost of construction and renovation of municipal buildings include the acquisition of artworks for those structures. The legislation made Chicago one of the first cities and the nation's largest to incorporate public art into a municipal building program. By the 1990s, with over a hundred works of public art adorning downtown streets and plazas, the Loop was sometimes described as an outdoor sculpture gallery. The ordinance not only generated more commissions, but proved to be a model for similar statutes nationwide—over two hundred cities had similar programs by 2004.[3]

It is not simply that the city needs another park; it needs another sort of park. . . . Here art should predominate over nature.

PETER WIGHT (1895)

6.3

6.4

Bryan's goal was to find an artist (or several artists) so significant and a sculpture so distinctive that Millennium Park would become a destination for both residents and visitors to Chicago. In Bryan's plan, the interests of art, philanthropy, and planning all coalesced. Good art, he believed, "does something to the spirit of the city that almost is impossible to define."[4]

Bryan organized two committees: one for art and one for the garden. According to Judith Paulus, Bryan believed that the role of the private sector was to provide direction regarding the art and architecture in the park, both "to give it some expertise that wouldn't necessarily reside within the city, and to also raise the dollars that would be needed to make sure this would be an urban space without equal."[5]

Bryan's strategy built on the earliest historic designs for Grant Park, which included sculpture and statuary. Burnham and Atwood's 1895 plan, for example, wanted to reconstruct Frederick MacMonnies's *Columbian Fountain*, while including monuments dedicated to Columbus, Lincoln, and Grant. While Burnham and Atwood's vision was never realized, the impetus to include impressive and monumental statuary remained a staple of Chicago park planning, much of it privately funded. Eli Bates provided the gift that led to Augustus Saint-Gaudens's *Standing Lincoln* (1887) and Frederick MacMonnies's *Storks at Play* (1887), both in Lincoln Park. In 1905, lumber merchant Benjamin F. Ferguson bequeathed $1 million for the construction of monuments and statues in Chicago parks. Beginning with Lorado Taft's *Fountain of the Great Lakes* (1913), the Ferguson Fund sponsored seventeen projects from 1913 to 1980, which today represent some of the most prominent examples of public art in Chicago. And in the early twentieth century, Katherine Buckingham's gift in memory of her brother led to the construction of *Clarence Buckingham Fountain*.[6]

6.1. Pablo Picasso's *Untitled* (1967) in Daley Center Plaza.

6.2. Marc Chagall's *Four Seasons* (1974) at Chase Tower.

6.3. Joan Miró's *Chicago* (1981) across from the Daley Center Plaza.

6.4. Ellsworth Kelly's *Curve XXII or I Will* (1981) in Lincoln Park.

6.5. Jean Dubuffet's *Monument with Standing Beast* (1984) in the Thompson State of Illinois Center.

6.6. Richard Hunt's *Freeform* (1993) on the restored State of Illinois Building.

6.7, 6.8. Early maps of the proposed Lakefront Millennium Park. The first was unlabeled and used in fundraising literature for Millennium Park, Inc. The second map identified specific enhancements within the proposed park.

Relying upon SOM's master plan and Edward Bennett's Grant Park design, Millennium Park officials divided the park into sections. The initial scheme included a three-section terrace over the railroad tracks that repeated the "salons" or "rooms" in Montgomery Ward Gardens along Michigan Avenue, a reflecting pool and skating rink, a music pavilion, a "great lawn," a small outdoor amphitheater, and a garden. When the reconstruction of the Grant Park North Garage was absorbed into the Millennium Park construction, the three salons in Ward Gardens were incorporated into the park plan with a courtyard, skating rink, and water fountain. The now-elevated terrace immediately east and above the railroad tracks would serve as the center of a large, park-long promenade. The eastern half of the park would be divided into a music pavilion and a garden, separated by a great lawn. These sections were referred to as "enhancements."[7]

Chicago's director for public art and Millennium Park art committee member Michael Lash pointed out that from conception, the park was envisioned to have art in it. The Montgomery Ward Gardens along Michigan Avenue extending from Randolph to Monroe Street were increasingly used as an exhibition space after 1990: Keith Harring's

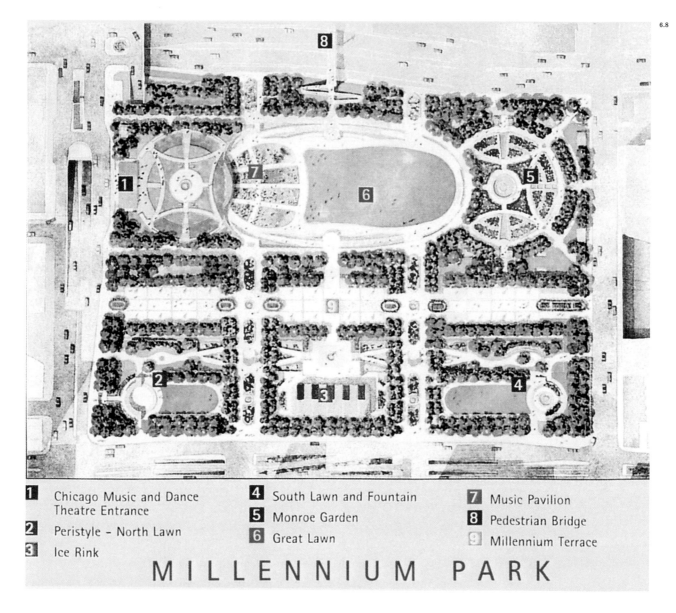

1 Chicago Music and Dance Theatre Entrance
2 Peristyle – North Lawn
3 Ice Rink
4 South Lawn and Fountain
5 Monroe Garden
6 Great Lawn
7 Music Pavilion
8 Pedestrian Bridge
9 Millennium Terrace

MILLENNIUM PARK

mural, Fernando Botero's "Botero in the Park," exhibits from Gallery 37, Summer Dance with Dan Peterman, and exhibitions by Barry Flanagan, Deborah Butterfield, and others. "People loved coming out there having lunch, having an arts experience," believed Lash. This part of Grant Park in the 1990s effectively replicated the nineteenth-century practice of promenading and lounging in the park surrounded by art. Planners wanted the same to continue in Millennium Park.[8]

On July 10, 1998, the Millennium Park Art Committee convened for the first time. At first, Bryan described the committee as "a bunch of people getting together to talk about contemporary artists and make lists." Committee member and art dealer Richard Gray remembered that much of the discussion revolved around whether the selected artists should have significant international reputations, or more local and regional identifications. Eventually, the committee agreed that some form of worldwide distinction was a requirement.[9]

Considerable debate centered upon the selection process. At one point, the committee considered including as many as six different pieces in the park. In Gray's opinion, the selection process came to a standstill because committee members had different and sometimes conflicting aesthetic interests. Finally, Gray offered a solution: empower officials from the Art Institute to make a series of recommendations to the committee. "Nobody could say no to that," remembers Gray. "That was like talking about God and country."[10]

Shortly thereafter, Art Institute curator Jeremy Strick assembled a list of world-renowned artists and photographs of their monumental outdoor art. Committee members became particularly enthusiastic about the artist Jeff Koons. "I'd been to Bilbao and I had seen the Jeff Koons puppy," remembered Bryan. "Lew Manilow had sent me a postcard telling me that the puppy was available and Lew was a good friend of Jeff Koons." Bryan later admitted he was initially "excited about the puppy." But he and other committee members soon realized that they should not mimic Bilbao. Instead, they needed to find a proposal unique to Chicago.[11]

Eventually, the ideas of a competition and multiple pieces of art were abandoned. Instead, the committee elected to commission two sculptures: one in the garden just across from the Art Institute and another in the middle of the park near the skating rink. For the two spaces, they invited proposals from two artists: Koons and the Indian-born British sculptor Anish Kapoor.[12]

By this time, Bryan had successfully attracted the first major gift for Millennium Park: Patrick Ryan, the founder, president, and chief executive officer of Aon, and his wife Shirley. Both enthusiastically agreed in 1998 to sponsor the garden, shortly after Bryan began his fundraising campaign. The Ryans had met as undergraduates at Northwestern during the 1950s. Shortly thereafter, Patrick founded a two-man company specializing in selling life insurance products to automobile dealers. By 1998, through mergers and acquisitions, Ryan had become a twentieth-century Horatio Alger. His companies included Aon Risk Services, the fastest growing global broker; Aon Re Worldwide, the world's largest reinsurance intermediary; Aon Services Group, the largest U.S. wholesale insurance brokerage operation; and Combined Insurance, the largest issuer of individual accident policies in the United States, Canada, Australia, and Ireland. With 40,000 employees and four hundred offices in eighty countries, Aon was one of Chicago's major global financiers.[13]

Bryan and the garden committee gave the Ryans authority to choose a landscape architect in return for financially supporting the garden. The Ryans quickly commissioned a design by Deborah Nevins. Described as "the sage of luxury landscapes" by the *New York Times*, Nevins was renowned for creating extraordinary landscapes in the most ex-

6.9. Patrick and Shirley Ryan.

tensive baronial estates around the world—from a farm in Dutchess County, New York, to entertainment mogul David Geffen's ten acre mansion in Beverly Hills. Her clients included Rupert Murdoch, Paul Walter, Henry Kravis, and others who allegedly swore her to secrecy. Trained in art and architecture at Columbia University, Nevins possessed a broad understanding of gardens and a distinctive historical perspective that made her one of the most sought-after landscape designers among the rich and famous.[14]

6.10. An early rendering of the Millennium Park Garden.

6.11. SOM's proposed pavilion.

The Ryans liked Nevins because of a personal experience. In 1979, the Ryans' new-born and youngest son was diagnosed with cerebral palsy. Their parenting experiences over the next several years motivated Shirley Ryan to establish the Pathways Center for Children (1985) to provide therapy for children with birth-related neurological, sensory-motor, learning, or communications disorders. When the Ryans began renovating and landscaping their three-acre North Shore home to accommodate their child, they were introduced to Nevins. They were impressed with her garden plan, which not only meshed with the French manor house designed by architect Thomas Beeby, but included wide paths to accommodate wheelchairs and featured wheelchair-accessible vistas from every window.[15]

Deborah Nevins proposed several plans for Millennium Park. The most popular one among garden committee members, remembered John Bryan, included "a symmetrical dropping of trees," which conformed with SOM's original design.[16]

While the art committee debated what public art was appropriate, another Millennium Park group focused on the music pavilion. SOM's initial design included a modest musical space—"a plain grotto in the ground," according to John Bryan. Adrian Smith suggested embellishing the pavilion with decorative sculptures on different parts of the structure; he even contacted the well-known Chicago sculptor Richard Hunt to determine his availability. These discussions convinced Bryan that the pavilion design was becoming more complicated, so he formed an architecture committee specifically to determine the design and purpose of the pavilion. Committee members, however, continued debating Smith's suggestion of adding a sculpture. Then Adrian Smith suggested Frank Gehry.[17]

Bryan recalls that he "lit up" at the idea of using Gehry, "because Frank was rather sculptural. . . . Maybe he'd design one of his patented fish to put on the sides." Smith and Gehry had recently collaborated in the design of the Guggenheim Museum in Bilbao, Spain, with SOM serving as the structural engineer. Recruiting Gehry to the project did not seem to be a far-fetched dream.[18]

More important, Bryan believed attracting Gehry would transform the park into an iconic symbol of Chicago at the turn of the millennium. Bryan, like many others, considered Gehry the most important, if not the greatest, architect of the time. Largely ignored during the 1950s and 1960s, Gehry began attracting attention in the 1970s with his unorthodox and eccentric renovation of his house in Santa Monica. The design reflected Gehry's interest in moving beyond the accepted aesthetic and technical constraints of twentieth-century architecture. Then in 1997, with the opening of the Guggenheim Museum in Bilbao, Spain, Gehry became a household name and an international celebrity. The Guggenheim in Bilbao was described as "a miracle," "a life-transforming experience," and "the greatest building of our time." The museum even transformed the city into a tourist destination, spawning the concept of "the Bilbao effect" among city planners and business leaders. Advertisements for Apple computers soon plastered Gehry's photograph with the caption "Think Different," similar to earlier ads with Albert Einstein and John Lennon.[19]

But one committee member was particularly disturbed by the music pavilion debate. "I disliked everything about it," remembers Cindy Pritzker in reference to SOM's bandshell design. "It was completely traditional." Pritzker objected to the linear emphasis in the design, as well as the sound system that she considered little more than a series of poles sitting on the lawn. "It was just awful."[20]

Pritzker also believed that efforts to recruit an artist to simply decorate the pavilion were misguided. "We would put a piece of sculpture on this side and we'd put a piece of sculpture on that side of the band shell so that we could be artsy," complained Pritzker. "I immediately thought that was really a dumb idea."[21]

Pritzker had her own brainstorm. If Millennium Park planners really wanted an artistic statement for a bandshell, why not ask Gehry himself to design it? More important, Pritzker and her family had been close personal friends of the architect, ever since he had received the Pritzker Prize in 1989, considered by many to be the "Nobel Prize of architecture." Although the Pritzker family had no influence in awarding the prize, they had taken an immediate liking to Gehry. Pritzker jokingly refers to herself as Gehry's "wife No. 2." She believed that Gehry was just the ingredient to transform the park into something unique, so she approached another member of the art committee, her friend and John Bryan's chief fundraiser, James Feldstein. "If they get somebody like Frank Gehry," Pritzker insisted, "the band shell would be the art and you don't need all of this stuff."[22]

6.12

6.13

6.14

Pritzker's opinion carried influence in Chicago. After growing up in Chicago's Kenwood and Hyde Park neighborhoods in the 1920s and 1930s, she married Jay Pritzker in 1947 and moved to the North Shore to raise her five children. In the meantime, her husband's Hyatt Hotel chain and Marmon Group became one of the most successful family empires in the United States.[23]

In 1979, the family moved back to Chicago, and Pritzker became involved in a wide range of activities: the board of directors and chair of the President's Council at the Museum of Science and Industry, the Women's Board of the Lyric Opera, and the establishment of the Pritzker Prize in Architecture. Pritzker's most noteworthy activity, however, came when mayor Harold Washington appointed her to the Chicago Public Library Board. At that time, the library was in poor shape and little regarded among Chicago civic institutions, "virtually a homeless waif," according to one newspaper.[24]

Cindy Pritzker changed that. She cofounded and served as president of the Chicago Public Library Foundation, which continues to raise private funds for library services and programs. By 1991, Pritzker had helped raise $8 million for books, while organizing an endowed fund with Citicorp Savings of Illinois to annually purchase 4,000 to 4,500 new children's books for the central library.[25]

Most notably, Pritzker was instrumental in building a new central library. She not only helped raise private money, but persuaded her family to donate $1 million to assist in the library's construction. She worked extensively with the Chicago architect Thomas Beeby, who was chosen after a highly publicized international competition. In 1991, the Harold Washington Library Center opened with 756,640 square feet over ten floors and seating for 2,337 readers—the world's largest municipal library building. Cindy Pritzker, the *Sun-Times* editorialized in 1998, was "responsible for turning what was once a neglected, even pathetic, civic institution into a nationally acclaimed asset." The building carried the name of Harold Washington, opined the *Sun-Times*, "but within this magnificent structure beats the heart of Cindy Pritzker."[26]

6.12. Frank Gehry's fish lamp (1983–1986).

6.13. Guggenheim Museum, Bilbao, Spain.

6.14. Cindy Pritzker.

During the summer of 1998, Feldstein organized a meeting with Pritzker and Bryan. At first, Bryan thought Pritzker wanted to invite Gehry to design a decoration for the proscenium over the music pavilion. But Pritzker quickly disabused Bryan of that idea. "If you guys are serious about getting Frank Gehry involved, let's not get him to decorate the proscenium," she insisted. "Let's get him to really do something here, and if you're serious about that we'll pay for it."[27]

By this time, Pritzker had had persuaded her family to support such a plan. Her husband Jay had recently suffered a stroke, but was included in the deliberations, as was her eldest son Tom, who had assumed much of the management of his father's business concerns. Pritzker believed the family would be encouraged—if not expected—to make a major contribution to the park. "We're going to have to give something anyway," Pritzker told her family, "and it seems to me that if we could get Frank in here, it could really be very exciting." They agreed.[28]

But Pritzker recognized she could not personally extend the invitation, or even attempt to recruit Gehry. That was the responsibility of Millennium Park officials. Since SOM was the architect of record, Adrian Smith first approached Gehry to design a fish sculpture on the front of the bandshell stage. "I said I really didn't want to do that," remembers Gehry. "That's not what I do." Smith added that there could be more to it, and that he would call Gehry about it. "Then he never called me," claims Gehry. "The months passed, and I just forgot about it." He proceeded to accept a number of other commissions.[29]

Back in Chicago, Millennium Park officials grew concerned. SOM was responsible for contacting and recruiting Gehry, remembers Feldstein, "but nothing had happened." He was also convinced that the scope and nature of the Millennium Park project hinged on attracting Gehry. "I'm not a person who begs for things very often but I really was at the point where I was convinced that it wasn't going to happen," remembers Feldstein. He further believed that in fairness to the Pritzkers, Millennium Park and city officials had to make a sincere effort to interest Gehry.[30]

Feldstein did not want to involve the Pritzker family directly, so he contacted Ed Uhlir, the Millennium Park project manager and Daley's representative. On December 11, 1998, Uhlir and Feldstein embarked on a day-long "secret mission" to Santa Monica to persuade Frank Gehry to design the music pavilion in Millennium Park. Feldstein believed Millennium Park fundraising was at a critical point, and securing Gehry's participation was necessary to stimulate donations.[31]

If anyone had asked Ed Uhlir during the Christmas season of 1997 where he would be in one year, the list of possibilities would have never included Frank Gehry's office. Uhlir was a life-long Chicagoan, the son of a Chicago cop and the grandchild of Bohemian and Lithuanian immigrants. After growing up in several Northwest Side neighborhoods, Uhlir graduated from Lane Tech High School in 1962. He went on to major in architecture at the University of Illinois at Chicago and work for the famed Chicago architectural firm of Graham, Anderson, Probst & White. In 1973, Uhlir joined the Chicago Park District as a senior architectural designer. Over the next twenty-five years, he advanced up the park district hierarchy to chief architect, director of engineering, and finally director of research and planning.

Uhlir's quarter century with the Chicago Park District provided abundant experience in construction. At various times, he oversaw the agency's annual $30 million construction program. From 1993 to 1995, he implemented a special $40 million capital program, a task which included supervising a staff of forty architects, engineers, surveyors, and planners. In 1990, his office was recognized by the National Trust for Historic Preservation for the restoration of Café Brauer in Lincoln Park. Uhlir's career path gave him unique expertise: a detailed knowledge of the history and management plans for Chicago's many parks, including protecting many landmark properties; acting as a liaison between community groups and government agencies; and acquiring, disposing, and maintaining everything from real estate to public art. In his final decade at the park district, Uhlir was the chief negotiator for the agency's acquisition of more than 250 acres.[32]

6.15. Edward Uhlir.

More critical at this moment, as he sat in the office of the world's most celebrated architect, was Uhlir's ability to negotiate among the specialized fields of architecture, planning, and art. At different times, he had served as chairman of the Joint Review Board for Tax Increment Financing, vice president of the Landmarks Preservation Council of Illinois, a member of the Mayor's Public Art Committee, and a member of the technical advisory committee of the Northern Illinois Planning Commission. But Uhlir's best-known work was in directing and authoring several award-winning municipal park plans: the "Grant Park Design Guidelines" (1992), "Lincoln Park Framework Plan" (1993), the "Shoreline Reconstruction Plans for Chicago" (1993), and "City Spaces—Turning Abandoned Land into Green Assets" (1998).[33]

Uhlir now called upon these experiences to answer perhaps the most important question of his career: why should Frank Gehry bother to design a music pavilion in Chicago? Gehry and his team of architects were extremely busy at that moment, attracting commissions from around the world. In the back of their minds, Uhlir and Feldstein recognized that the $15 million gift from the Pritzker family was dependent on persuading the architect to accept a Millennium Park commission. "She didn't necessarily tie her $15 million gift to actually hiring Frank Gehry," admitted Uhlir, "but it was implied." They had to convince Gehry that Millennium Park represented a unique opportunity. But, admitted Feldstein, "we had to describe the site and I couldn't have done that."[34] That task fell to Uhlir.

Gehry knew little about the project.[35] Uhlir proceeded to explain the unique qualities of the site: the historical importance and symbolism of the rail yard, the proximity to the Michigan Avenue streetwall, the role of Grant Park as "Chicago's front yard," and the impact of Lake Michigan in shaping that part of the city. Gehry listened patiently, while examining the site plans and maps laid out on the table before him. The architect began asking a few questions. Uhlir quickly noticed Gehry's interest in the projected bridge connecting Millennium Park to Daley Bicentennial Plaza over Columbus Boulevard. Uhlir asked the architect if he wanted to design the bridge.

"I've never done a pedestrian bridge," Gehry replied.

"Well, you've got it," was Uhlir's immediate response.

Feldstein then jumped in and explained the Pritzker offer, "that we were there with their blessing." It "made a huge impact on him," remembers Feldstein.[36] At that moment, Gehry consented.

GEHRY'S WILLINGNESS TO DESIGN the music pavilion and bridge was, according to James Feldstein, "the defining moment" in the creation and evolution of Millennium Park. Together, the pavilion, lawn, and bridge comprised the largest and most visible enhancements of the park. Gehry's presence made Millennium Park a singular attraction to artists and private-sector donors alike. Almost overnight, Chicago's Millennium Park was transformed from a transportation and infrastructure project into "a world-class cultural attraction that no other city has," in the words of Richard Daley.[37] John Bryan, with a little help, had hit the moon.

Chapter 7

THE CULTURE BROKER

The introduction of Frank Gehry into the Millennium Park project generated a series of unforeseeable reactions. The first casualty was the timetable. Mayor Daley enjoined Bryan and Millennium Park officials to put construction on a "fast track"—to begin building before engineering and construction plans were fully complete. This, Daley believed, was the only way to open the park in time for the millennium. Gehry, however, was committed to a variety of other projects, and insisted that he could not begin work on the pavilion until July 1999, six months in the future. Uhlir and Feldstein tried to persuade Gehry to accelerate his plans, but "to Frank's credit," remembered Uhlir, "he said no."[1] The long-term aesthetic benefits of Gehry's decision were soon overtaken by the short-term detriments—Millennium Park would not be completed in time to celebrate passage of the millennium.

Gehry's presence also affected the debate over art. In the fall of 1998, after much discussion, Millennium Park officials invited artists Jeff Koons and Anish Kapoor to submit proposals for sculptures in the park. Art committee members were particularly enthusiastic about Koons, in part because of his recent work *Puppy*, a forty-foot topiary display in front of Gehry's Guggenheim Museum in Bilbao, Spain. Some considered Koons, in fact, to be the committee's favorite.[2] Koons was asked to submit a proposal for the central plaza area of Millennium Park.

Much of Koons's previous work explored the relationship between popular kitsch and high art, particularly the impact of commercial products on artistic production. His Millennium Park proposal was no less controversial: a 150-foot tower built with a variety of materials, including his child's toys. The centerpiece of the tower was a water slide that provided access for pedestrians to climb up and slide down. One committee member described the sculpture as "a very exciting, irreverent, monstrosity of a piece," words that Koons himself might use to describe the work. "It wasn't my favorite piece," admitted committee member Richard Gray, "but I was intrigued with it." Chicago's public art director Michael Lash admitted the design was playful and, like many of Koons's works, tongue-in-cheek. "It was," he added, "nuts."[3]

Others were less infatuated. "I remember Cindy Pritzker walking out of the meet-

You try to look for one single figure who is going to define what Chicago is like at the turn of the millennium and . . . certainly John Bryan's name has to be there in so many ways.

DONNA LAPIETRA

ing," recounted John Bryan, and bluntly proclaiming, "I don't like it." More significantly, recalled Marshall Field V, Richard Daley did not like it.[4]

The Koons sculpture also presented significant logistical problems. The first was size. The proposed 150-foot structure towered over everything in the park. Trees, historically the tallest objects in Grant Park, stood between 35 and 45 feet in height. Committee members worried that the sculpture recognized no sense of scale. A second concern was nature. Ice in winter and birds in the summer, observers feared, would present continual, never-ending maintenance problems. Finally, Koons envisioned the sculpture as interactive, allowing people to climb and slide down parts of it. Critics charged that such a design was, at best, inaccessible to anyone with a disability. At worst, it invited suicides.[5]

For Koons, this did not matter. He envisioned the sculpture as a defining symbol of Chicago. "It's going to be the St. Louis Arch of Chicago," he told the committee, "an instant landmark." But committee members were unconvinced; eventually they rejected Koons's design.[6]

The reaction to Anish Kapoor proved less controversial. In December 1998, Kapoor came to Chicago to reveal his proposal for the garden in the southeast portion of the park, his first public sculpture in the United States. He presented a plan for a gleaming, 150-ton, 60-foot-long and 30-foot-high elliptical sculpture. Some described it as a kidney or jelly bean, others as a drop of mercury. Kapoor intended the sculpture to reflect the sky, the city's skyscrapers, and pedestrians in the park who would be able to walk under it. The sculpture was so large that engineers would have to redesign the parking garage to accommodate the sculpture's weight.[7]

Daley was much more impressed with this proposal. He proclaimed Kapoor's design to be a "great catch" for Chicago and predicted it might rival the fame of the Picasso sculpture outside the Richard J. Daley Center. In May 1999, Kapoor signed an agreement to design the unnamed piece for Millennium Park.[8]

Bryan and the Millennium Park committees originally intended to locate Kapoor's sculpture in the garden. Planners envisioned that pedestrians would enter the garden and be confronted with a spellbinding sculpture. Bryan, in particular, envisioned the garden as a "destination site," a place so unique or spectacular that it would attract visitors by itself. "All great cities have parks that are unforgettable to anyone who has ever visited them," explained Bryan's assistant Judith Paulus. The Millennium Park garden was to be one such breathtaking site.[9]

But several garden committee members began expressing reservations with the Nevins-designed garden. Some feared that with Kapoor's sculpture in Nevins's garden that portion of the park was "too confusing," that the space contained an overabundance of artistic elements. Others simply felt that Kapoor's sculpture dominated the garden. What precisely was the relationship between the garden and Kapoor's sculpture? How did Kapoor's sculpture relate to the fauna of the garden? Could a traditional garden "house" such an untraditional sculpture as Kapoor's? These reservations grew more prominent when Frank Gehry, who began designing the music pavilion and pedestrian bridge in July 1999, expressed reservations with the Nevins-designed garden. Most important, according to John Bryan, Shirley Ryan grew disenchanted with the notion of a simple garden because "she thought that a garden in that spot was not permanent enough."[10]

Various Millennium Park committee members increasingly recognized that Gehry's music pavilion design changed the dynamics of other enhancements. Specifically, the garden, Kapoor's sculpture, and Koons's proposal conflicted with elements of Gehry's pavilion. "It just didn't work," believed Michael Lash, in large part because Gehry's music pavilion was seen by other committee members as "a giant piece of sculpture."[11] Why have two more giant pieces of sculpture in such close proximity?

Bryan concluded that the situation was, in his words, "a mess." In April 2000, he contacted Patrick Ryan and expressed these reservations. Bryan suggested starting over. Ryan agreed, and with Bryan's advice, withdrew his financial commitment to the garden.[12]

Bryan and his committee then made a bold change. For aesthetic and economic reasons, the committee not only elected to eliminate Koons's proposed design, but moved Kapoor's sculpture to the site originally targeted for Koons's work. This transformed the garden into a distinct and separate entity. Without the presence of a monumental sculpture, the garden space became, according to one committee member, an "avenue for dialogue between the Art Institute wing, the Gehry [music pavilion] and the Kapoor sculpture in the nearby plaza."[13]

This change was also attractive to Bryan for another reason. As president of the Art Institute's board of trustees, Bryan was well aware of that institution's physical expansion plans along Monroe Street over the Illinois Central tracks, directly across from the Millennium Park garden site. The Art Institute had commissioned the Italian architect Renzo Piano to design its new northern wing, which would now face Frank Gehry's music pavilion—two Pritzker Prize–winning architects in dialogue with each other across Monroe Street. In between was the Millennium Park garden. Bryan now had to find a way to attract not only a leading landscape architect, but an innovative design and a new sponsor.

Bryan and garden committee members elected to sponsor an international competition. In June 2000, under the sponsorship of the Richard H. Driehaus Foundation, Millennium Park officials invited a select group of seventeen landscape architects, garden designers, and planning firms to submit proposals for a garden. The competition prospectus prepared by Ed Uhlir asked participants to create a year-round garden with plants not found in other Chicago gardens. The final design had to accommodate large crowds after concerts, small ones on a Sunday morning, and comply with the Americans with Disabilities Act. In some way, the garden had to acknowledge the surrounding environment of Grant Park. But for Bryan, the most important requirement was "that the garden be a destination garden, that you want to spend time there because it would be educational for you." Bryan then named a jury composed of design professionals and civic leaders.[14]

GEHRY'S ENTRANCE into the project also transformed personal relationships. James Feldstein and Ed Uhlir noted that initially Gehry seemed determined to participate only at the invitation of Adrian Smith, the designer of the park's original master plan. The two architects had met a decade earlier at a symposium sponsored by the Central Area Committee of Chicago on the proposed 1992 World's Fair. SOM and Smith later worked with Gehry on the Guggenheim Museum in Bilbao, Spain. Gehry, consequently, did not want to offend Smith.[15] "You solve the Adrian thing," Gehry instructed the Millennium Park representatives. "I'm not going to enter this and take a job away from this guy." Gehry added, "Adrian is a very special architect. We don't need to fight amongst ourselves." Gehry later acknowledged that Smith was "blindsided," but "I had nothing to do with it." Gehry contacted Smith to reconcile the situation, but admitted, "I'm sure he wasn't happy about it."[16]

John Bryan minimized the tension that emerged between Smith and Gehry. Smith had reservations about Gehry's design because it was such "a strong statement," believed Bryan, and included the lawn, bridge, and bandshell. But Bryan complimented Smith's willingness to cooperate and let Gehry take over. "Adrian was marvelous in the final analysis because he did agree and they worked very well together."[17]

Smith, however, had a different interpretation. Uhlir and Feldstein, he believed, were hell-bent on attracting Gehry to the project. When Gehry said he wanted to do the entire oval and not simply the music pavilion, the Millennium Park representatives agreed. Smith acknowledged that Gehry had said he did not want "to step on Adrian's toes," and initially expressed an interest in collaborating. But Smith remained skeptical. "Gehry doesn't work together with other architects," he contended. Gehry "does what he thinks is right and that's it." Gehry reportedly refused to participate if Smith objected. "When I heard about it, I told him I was unhappy," recounted Smith. "And he said, 'well, too bad.'" Smith admitted that Gehry's decision affected their rapport: "It's a much cooler relationship now than it was before."[18]

Gehry had other reasons for accepting the Millennium Park commission. Professionally, Gehry considered Chicago to be "the best architectural city in America." "The body language of the city is more in the spirit of Paris" than any other U.S. city, he argued, and the city's physical relationship to Lake Michigan made it "probably the best American city." Gehry was particularly fascinated by buildings with unique features—the Tribune Tower, Marina City, and the designs of Mies van der Rohe.[19]

Gehry's interest in Chicago surfaced in 1980 when he joined a group of architects led by Stanley Tigerman, Stuart Cohen, and Laurence Booth who called themselves the "Chicago 7" in organizing an international exhibition based on the premise of restaging the Chicago Tribune Tower competition of 1922. Gehry's contribution was based on a vision that Chicago would eventually be demolished, and that its citizens would move to the wilderness, turning the city "into a music park in the middle of nowhere." His sketch depicted an uninhabited tower of solid concrete topped by an American eagle, a symbol that would appeal to a right-wing newspaper like the *Tribune*.[20]

But Gehry also admitted a sentimental interest in the city. As a boy, the architect occasionally accompanied his father to the Mills Novelty Company on Fullerton Avenue when he came to Chicago on business. "You have these memories of your parents and it was one of them, the most important bonding thing I had with him because we didn't have that much time together," Gehry recounted. "Whenever I went to Chicago it reminded me of that."[21]

But the conflict between Smith and Gehry was more than just personal. The introduction of Gehry into Millennium Park also reflected conflicting visions of architecture and planning at the turn of the millennium. Adrian Smith subscribed to a vision first articulated by Daniel Burnham and then implemented by Edward Bennett: Grant Park should be a formal, classical space, reflective of the beaux arts ideal that inspired much of early twentieth-century architecture. This view remained a guiding principle as Grant Park grew and developed throughout the twentieth century. In 1968, the consulting firm of Johnson, Johnson & Roy argued that the park "is the only area along the lakefront which can appropriately be formal and grand. The park expresses dignity and quiet repose." Smith and, initially, mayor Richard M. Daley expected any expansion of Grant Park to remain loyal to the beaux arts form popularized by Burnham and Bennett.[22]

Daley was especially worried about the impact of Gehry in the park. Early in 1999, the Pritzker family invited Gehry and Daley to dinner in Chicago. Near the end of the evening, Tom Pritzker pulled the mayor and architect aside, hoping to get them more acquainted with each other. Daley issued a friendly challenge: "I know what you're going to build. I can design it myself. It's going to be one of these." Daley raised his hand in the shape of a C. "Why do I need such a fancy architect to build one of these?" Gehry chuckled and promised the mayor he would design something "a little more inspirational than that."[23]

Daley was also apprehensive about Gehry's bridge design. "He found it too bold and too dramatic," admitted one Millennium Park planner. In retrospect, banker and Millennium Park planner Richard Thomas suspected that Daley worried that the pavilion and bridge together had "too much Gehry influence" in the park. Thomas remembered discussions in which city and Millennium Park officials wondered if indeed the bridge was too unconventional. Some suggested "it should be toned down a bit because it's not going to be the Frank Gehry Park." After much discussion and debate, however, Millennium Park and city officials relented. "Frank Gehry was probably the foremost architect in the world," Thomas concluded, "and we felt very fortunate to get him."[24]

Gehry later admitted that the bridge, when viewed from above, was "pretty pushy." But he quickly added that when seen from eye level or on the ground, the curving, snake-like form disappeared. Gehry personally demonstrated this to Daley over coffee. "We had a knife on the table," remembered Gehry. "I flipped it and showed it to him with the blade like that. Then I said, 'Look what happens when you turn it.' That seemed acceptable to him and I thought he was okay with it." Gehry later learned that Daley was less convinced.[25]

Daley's reservations about the bridge were tied to other parts of the Gehry design, particularly the park's acoustics. "The bridge I questioned because I wanted to make sure the sound system worked," Daley later explained. The mayor worried that without a good sound system, the outdoor pavilion (and perhaps Millennium Park) would be considered a failure. "The bridge is just another sideshow," believed Daley. "The whole key was the theater and not the bridge."[26]

But, Gehry later complained, Daley never expressed reservations about the bandshell. The architect later surmised that the tension with Daley originated, in part, from the mayor's traditional view of Grant Park. Daley envisioned something akin to Bennett's beaux arts design from the early twentieth century. "I think Millennium Park became a modernist, more twenty-first-century image than what he wanted," Gehry speculated. "I suspect now, after the fact, that he probably didn't like it, that he has a more traditional taste than that."[27]

Bryan's avant-garde vision violated the "ethos" of Grant Park in the minds of Adrian Smith and other traditionalists. Millennium Park replaced the Burnham and Bennett aesthetic with "a sort of sculpture gallery extravaganza," Smith complained. Why, for example, were the most creative elements segregated together in one small part of the park? "I think that it would have been more successful had it been spread around throughout the park instead of having a $5 [later 20] million sculpture by Anish Kapoor and $50 [later 60] million band shell and a bridge all located in that area," insisted Smith. Much like Burnham and Bennett, the architect envisioned Grant Park as a coherent whole, a civic center devoted to classicism and civic unity.[28]

Smith also faulted Bryan's fundraising strategy as poor urban planning. Bryan, in his effort to incorporate as many views and opinions as possible, invited a wide array of individuals to participate in various committees and subcommittees. Marshall Field V later remembered some committee meetings with as many as forty people in attendance. Smith criticized this planning-by-committee strategy because Bryan linked fundraising to design. "In most projects, there is a fundraising effort and the fundraisers, as individuals, are not involved in the selection of the pieces and the selection of the architecture," insisted Smith. Their role "is basically to fund something."[29]

Bryan's defenders, however, believed that Smith's SOM plan was too wedded to the Burnham and Bennett vision of Chicago. Ed Uhlir, for example, explained that the Grant Park Design Guidelines adopted in 1992 identified the Lakefront Gardens site as one of the few places in the park that allowed for designers to break out of the beaux arts tradition because Bennett assumed the site would always remain an open cut for the railroad. Succeeding planners and park officials made similar assumptions.[30]

Gehry and his team of architects concurred. The beaux arts style was "something that's really foreign to us," admitted Gehry's partner and architect Craig Webb. "It's looking to the past rather than the future." In Webb's opinion, Chicago possessed so many beaux arts structures that adopting that style would result only in their blending and camouflaging the architecture. Philosophically, added Webb, Gehry and this team not only wanted to create something "beautiful, that people were going to enjoy," but hoped to encourage citizens "to look at it and ask themselves questions about what architecture is about."[31]

Other Millennium Park planners believed the park represented the ideal opportunity not to simply extend the beaux arts design, but to build upon it. "Paris on the Lake is a wonderful place to be and live," summarized one planner, "but I don't know that Burnham would be speaking for the twenty-first century." The beaux arts interpretation of Grant Park spoke to a nineteenth-century aesthetic that prioritized French and English formal garden designs at the expense of the avant-garde.[32] Other parts of Chicago—the Wacker Drive restoration, elements of Michigan Avenue—followed this model. Millennium Park offered an opportunity to develop a more original design.[33]

Whatever reservations Daley had, Gehry eventually persuaded him that they were unfounded. When Gehry's pavilion and bridge design was publicly displayed for the first time, Daley described it as "a good statement" that showed Chicago was "not caught in the past." The mayor, Richard Gray believes, does not keep his head in the sand: "He is able to be moved on occasion."[34]

In retrospect, Burnham's plan was irrelevant. The *Plan of Chicago* emphasized roads, both rail and vehicular, along with a vision of transforming Chicago into an American vision of Paris. More appropriate was architect Peter Wight's observation in 1895 that any new lakefront park should depart in both character and form from other city parks. "It is not simply that the city needs another park," insisted Wight, "it needs another sort of park." The waterfront location presented a unique opportunity to create a civic and cultural center, one that in Wight's words should not be squandered. "Here art should predominate over nature."[35]

A century later, John Bryan assumed a similar position. Grant Park did not need another Burnhamesque, beaux arts design; rather, the space demanded something of an entirely different character, to use Wight's words. Bryan, in rejecting the classical themes found throughout Grant Park, was about to do something entirely different.

FRANK GEHRY'S WILLINGNESS to participate in Millennium Park made John Bryan's job easier. More important, Bryan exploited a variety of corporate and cultural networks he had developed during his quarter-century residence in Chicago. In multiple ways, Bryan impressed his global, corporate peers after his arrival to Chicago in the 1970s. In a short time, he was elected to a variety of high-profile leadership positions: chairman of the business advisors council of the Chicago Urban League; chairman of Chicago Council on Foreign Relations; chairman of the board of directors of the Grocery Manufacturers of America; vice chairman of the Business Council; cochairman of the World Economic Forum's annual meetings in 1994, 1997, and 2000; chairman of the board of directors of the World Business Chicago; and president of the Economic Club of Chicago. He was also a member of the policy committee of the Business Roundtable, the Trilateral Commission, and the Commercial Club of Chicago.[36] By 1998, John Bryan knew a lot of chief executives.

While efforts to recruit Gehry were underway during 1998, Bryan was busy introducing the Millennium Park project to Chicago's corporate and philanthropic elites. On June 16, 1998, Bryan organized a meeting with his Blue Ribbon Committee and many of Chicago's leading corporate and philanthropic leaders: Jerry Choate of Allstate, Richard Notebaert of Ameritech, Edgar Jannotta of William Blair & Company, Bruce Newman of the Chicago Community Trust, Richard Thomas and Verne Istock of First Chicago, John Schmidt of Mayer, Brown & Platt, Gen. Neil Creighton of the McCormick Tribune Foundation and others. Helping Bryan explain the project was Chicago transportation commissioner Thomas Walker, McDonough Associates senior vice president Bernard Ford, and Skidmore, Owings & Merrill architect Leigh Breslau.[37]

After each made brief presentations, Bryan made his pitch. Millennium Park, he argued, represented a unique cooperative opportunity—the private sector had never worked in conjunction with elected and public officials to design and build a park of this magnitude. Millennium Park would, if properly supported, represent a cultural statement for Chicago at the turn of the century. In Gilded Age Chicago, the city's elites had created the cultural institutions that defined the city for a century: the Chicago Symphony Orchestra, the Art Institute of Chicago, and the Chicago Public Library. Millennium Park could do the same a century later. This was, in Bryan's words, "the opportunity of a lifetime."[38]

Bryan explained that Daley wanted a simple campaign: recruit and accept only large gifts of $1 million. In return, the private sector would enjoy the responsibility of designing the creative additions to the above-garage park. Bryan and the park's architects believed eight to ten enhancements offered unique design opportunities: several pieces of public sculpture, an ice skating rink and plaza, a water fountain, the restored peristyle and surrounding square, the promenade, a garden, a bridge, and a music pavilion. But these major enhancements demanded donations considerably larger than $1 million. Here Bryan revealed a specific strategy: invite a select group of families and institutions with long, historic ties to Chicago to support one of the major enhancements in the park. More important, the enhancements offered a naming opportunity in return for a gift in excess of $3 million. In 1999, Bryan's labors started to pay off.

On February 9, 1999, the Robert R. McCormick Tribune Foundation signed an agreement to support an ice skating rink and plaza with a $5 million gift.[39] Established in 1955 upon the death of Colonel Robert R. McCormick, the longtime editor and publisher of the *Chicago Tribune*, the charitable trust's assets of $1.8 billion made it one of the two largest foundations in Illinois (see appendix 10). More important for Bryan was the venerable McCormick name. Colonel McCormick, as he called himself, was more than just a major figure in twentieth-century American journalism; his name went back deep into the nineteenth century when Cyrus McCormick migrated to the city from Virginia to build a reaper and agricultural machine factory that grew into International Harvester Corporation (now Navistar). Equally symbolic, it was Colonel McCormick who transformed the Tribune Company from a single newspaper into a global media organization of newspapers, radio and TV stations, and newsprint factories.[40]

Bryan also set his eyes on a friend across the street from the Tribune Tower. William Wrigley, the chief executive officer of the William Wrigley, Jr., Company, possessed a name and a company that had been a Chicago fixture for over a century. In certain ways, the family embodied the "big shoulders" and "rags-to-riches" legends popular among Chicagoans. William Wrigley, Jr., arrived in Chicago in 1891, only twenty-nine years old with a mere $32 in his pocket. But Wrigley possessed an enthusiastic personality, a high level of energy, and great talent as a salesman. He started out selling soap, and then moved to baking powder. One day, Wrigley began offering free chewing gum with each can of baking powder. When the gum proved more popular than the baking soda, the William Wrigley, Jr., Company became a chewing gum manufacturer. Success came quickly and proved long-lasting. Wrigley and his immediate successors quickly made the company into a global enterprise, opening factories in Canada (1910), Australia (1915), Great Britain (1927), and New Zealand (1939). For decades, the Wrigley Company was known as "the General Motors of the gum industry," controlling as much as two-thirds of the total gum market into the 1970s.[41]

For over a century, the company remained one of the best known in Chicago, in part because of the beloved and prominently located Wrigley Building on North Michigan Avenue and the Chicago River. The family also retained a prominent role as four generations of Wrigleys led the company. William Wrigley, Jr., founded the company and led its development for over three decades before he was succeeded by Philip K. Wrigley in 1925. P. K., as he was known, was a prominent figure in Chicago, in part because of his ownership of the Chicago Cubs. After more than thirty-five years at the helm, Phil Wrigley ceded control to his son William in 1961. The sudden deaths of William's parents in 1977 subjected their estate to federal and state inheritance taxes, and forced him to sell the Cubs to his neighbor on the other side of Michigan Avenue, the *Chicago Tribune*, in 1981.[42]

William Wrigley was considered one of the most private of Chicago's major business figures. Refusing to be "just a name on a letterhead," he involved himself only in organi-

7.2. The earliest renderings of the peristyle differed little from the later design except for the number of columns.

7.3. This computer-generated image of the peristyle envisioned a Michigan Avenue with no skyscrapers.

7.4. A computer-generated image of the peristyle at night.

7.3 | 7.4

zations in which he took a sincere interest. Lucky for Bryan, he knew the reclusive Wrigley through the Grocery Manufacturers of America, the leading trade association of food, beverage, and consumer product companies, for which Bryan briefly served as chairman in 1984–1985. Bryan and Wrigley eventually befriended each other, entertaining their families at their respective North Shore and Lake Geneva homes.[43] Bryan appealed to Wrigley's century-old Chicago legacy, and made a bold suggestion to Wrigley: sponsor the peristyle and the surrounding square in the northwest corner of Millennium Park.

The revised Millennium Park plan envisioned the peristyle as one gateway into the park. Bryan also considered the structure to be an ideal way to commemorate donors, while retaining a link to Grant Park's classical and beaux arts origins.[44] Bryan also believed that the peristyle represented a historic link to Chicago's past. What better way to commemorate that history than to find a donor with a long-time presence in Chicago such as William Wrigley?

Wrigley never had the opportunity to decide. On March 8, 1999, he died suddenly at age sixty-six from complications due to pneumonia. But again, fortune cast its spell on Bryan: William Wrigley, Jr., was immediately named successor to his father. The new CEO had known Bryan since he was a youngster and shared his father's respect for him. The younger Wrigley agreed with Bryan: "This was a great space with a little bit of a reminder of the Wrigley Building." In one of his earliest decisions as the new chief executive, Wrigley elected to contribute $5 million to the project. The donation was the single largest gift ever given by the Wrigley Foundation.[45]

Then on April 27, 1999, mayor Richard Daley announced that the Pritzker Foundation would donate $15 million to pay for a Frank Gehry–designed bandshell for Millennium Park. The Pritzker name might not have been as instantly recognizable among Chicagoans as McCormick or Wrigley, but it was no less influential. Abram Nicholas (A. N.) Pritzker, the son of a penniless Russian Jewish immigrant who arrived in Chicago in 1881, graduated from Harvard Law School and founded the successful law firm of Pritzker & Pritzker in the early twentieth century. A. N. Pritzker proved to be a farsighted businessman and investor, reportedly devising leveraged buyouts in the 1930s before the term was even invented. By the time he died in 1986, his family's wealth had grown from $250,000 in the 1920s to an estimated $2 billion.[46]

A. N. Pritzker's sons Jay and Robert further expanded the family's financial empire. After World War II, they bought small and sometimes troubled companies, reorganizing them at more profitable levels. In 1964, when the Pritzker companies combined with the Marmon-Herrington Company, they became the Marmon Group, a diversified corporation with interests (at various times) in Braniff Airlines, *McCall's* magazine, Levitz Furniture, Hammond organs, Ticketmaster, Royal Caribbean Cruises and casinos in Las Vegas, Lake Tahoe, and Atlantic City. By 2003, Marmon was the nineteenth-largest privately held company in the United States, with revenues in excess of $5.5 billion.[47]

The Pritzker brothers' most famous purchase, however, occurred while eating breakfast at Fat Eddie's coffee shop at Los Angeles International Airport in 1957. Jay noticed that the restaurant was unusually busy, and the Hyatt Von Dehn hotel (named for its then owner) in which it was located had no vacancies. The Pritzker brothers recognized that business executives were using hotels located near airports with growing frequency, so they made a $2.2 million offer to buy it on a napkin. By 1998, the Hyatt Hotels Corporation generated revenues of $3 billion with 182 hotels and 34 under construction. By then, *Forbes* magazine estimated the net worth of the Pritzker family was $13.5 billion, making them the richest Chicago-area residents.[48]

Bryan also contacted Lester Crown, the paterfamilias of the Crown and Goodman families, in hopes he would subsidize a major enhancement within Millennium Park. Like the Pritzkers, the Crowns were descendants of Russian Jews who migrated to Chicago in the late nineteenth century. With a small $20,000 investment, Lester Crown's

7.5. Frank Gehry at the announcement of the Pritzker Foundation gift of $15 to Millennium Park.

father, Colonel Henry Crown, founded a small sand-and-gravel operation he called Material Service Corporation in 1919. He spun the company into a giant operation after the two world wars, and eventually expanded into coal mining, farming, real estate, recreation, trucking, and barge and railroad lines. Crown was particularly close to mayor Richard J. Daley and the Democratic Party organization, even serving on several city planning and building commissions. Like his contemporary A. N. Pritzker, Henry Crown was adept at investing in and reorganizing poorly run enterprises, often selling his interest in smaller companies for stakes in larger concerns, most notably General Dynamics and the Chicago, Rock Island and Pacific Railroad. Crown went on to play a key role in helping Conrad Hilton purchase the Stevens Hotel and the Palmer House in Chicago and the Waldorf-Astoria in New York. He partnered with William Zeckendorf and Philip Klutznick on real estate deals in New York and Chicago, helping the latter finance or construct Park Forest, Water Tower Place, and the shopping centers at River Oaks, Oakbrook, and Old Orchard. From 1951 to 1961, Henry Crown owned the Empire State Building in New York City.[49]

Bryan appealed to the Crowns and Pritzkers not simply because of their wealth, but rather because of their long-time involvement in Chicago culture and philanthropy. Crown and Pritzker family members over the years had served as trustees, directors, fundraisers, and patrons of Chicago's leading cultural and educational institutions. The financial generosity of both families was and remains visible throughout the Chicago region: the Henry Crown Sports Pavilion at Northwestern, the Henry Crown Field House at the University of Chicago, the Henry Crown Space Center at the Museum of Science and Industry, the Ida & Arie Crown Theater at the McCormick Center, the Pritzker School of Medicine at the University of Chicago, the Pritzker Children's Zoo at the Lincoln Park Zoo, the Pritzker Institute of Medical Engineering at the Illinois Institute of Technology, the Pritzker Legal Research Center at Northwestern's School of Law. Both families subsidized wings or galleries in the Art Institute. Less visible but equally important were annual gifts in excess of $100,000 for general operating costs of institutions like the Field Museum, the Rehabilitation Institute of Chicago, the Chicago Public Library, the Shedd Aquarium, the Lincoln Park Zoo, and other leading Chicago nonprofit organizations. In the final quarter of the twentieth century, both families literally gave away more than $100 million. And in December 1999, the Crown family agreed to donate $10 million in support of a "water feature" or fountain in Millennium Park.[50]

In only twenty-one months after John Bryan first learned of plans to construct a garage and park over the former rail yard in Grant Park, he had raised $35 million in four charitable gifts. At the same time, Bryan made inroads in the corporate community. In October 1999, Ameritech CEO Richard Notebaert agreed to donate $3 million for the plaza that would eventually support a sculpture by Anish Kapoor. Two months later, Bryan received an early Christmas present: a $5 million donation from BP Amoco to construct the pedestrian bridge designed by Frank Gehry. Finally, in October 2000, Bank One, the successor firm to the First National Bank of Chicago and the last remaining major commercial bank

TABLE 3. A SAMPLING OF PRITZKER FAMILY PHILANTHROPY

STRUCTURE OR INSTITUTION	LOCATION	YEAR OF GIFT	ESTIMATED VALUE OF GIFT
Pritzker School of Medicine	University of Chicago	1968	$12 million
Nancy Friend Pritzker Laboratory	Stanford University	1977	
Pritzker Prize in Architecture		1979	
Pritzker Wing	Art Institute of Chicago		
Jack N. Pritzker Professorship	Northwestern University	1987	$1 million
Pritzker Children's Zoo	Lincoln Park Zoo	1988	
Pritzker Auditorium	Northwestern University Memorial Hospital		
Pritzker Research Library	Children's Memorial Hospital, Chicago		
Pritzker Playspace	Chicago Children's Museum		
Pritzker Laboratory for Molecular Systematics and Evolution	Field Museum of Natural History		
Illinois Institute of Technology	S. State Street Chicago	1998	$60 million
Pritzker Institute of Medical Engineering	Illinois Institute of Technology		
Pritzker Legal Research Center (Library)	Northwestern University School of Law	1999	$10 million
Pritzker Gallery of Cosmology	Adler Planetarium	1999	
Jay Pritzker Pavilion	Millennium Park	2000	$15 million
Pritzker Director	Museum of Contemporary Art	2001	$3 million
University of Chicago	Hyde Park, Chicago	2002	$30 million
Pritzker Military Library	610 N. Fairbanks Ct., Chicago 2002		
A. N. Pritzker School	2009 W. Schiller, Chicago		
Asian Studies Program	University of Chicago		
Law School	University of Chicago		
Providence-St. Mel School	West Side, Chicago		$4 million
Holocaust Memorial Foundation of Illinois	Skokie, Ill.		$1 million
Waldorf School movement			$17 million

SOURCES: *CT*, 6 June 2002; *New York Times*, 11 Dec. 2002; *Chicago Magazine*, Dec. 2002, p. 116; *Northwestern Observer*, 1997–98.

headquartered in Chicago, informally agreed to fund the promenade for $5 million.[51]

Wittingly or not, Bryan was now Chicago's culture broker. Like Eli Broad in Los Angeles or Jerry I. Speyer in New York, Bryan was the galvanizing force in bringing Chicago's philanthropic, cultural, and political establishments together in the pursuit of common, agreed-upon projects. Not since the banker and Board of Trade president Charles

TABLE 4. A SAMPLING OF CROWN FAMILY PHILANTHROPY

STRUCTURE	LOCATION	YEAR OF GIFT
Ida Crown Jewish Academy	Chicago	1942
Arie Crown Hebrew Day School	Skokie, Ill	1943
Rebecca Crown Administration Building	Northwestern University	1961
Ida Crown Natatorium, Eckhart Park	Chicago	
Henry Crown Gallery	Art Institute of Chicago	
Crown Family Room, Chicago Historical Society	Chicago	
Henry Crown Sports Pavilion	Northwestern University	
Rebecca Crown Center	Northwestern University	1961
Ida & Arie Crown Theater	McCormick Center	1971
Henry Crown Field House (renovation)	University of Chicago	1975
Robert Crown Center and Ice Rink	Evanston, Illinois	1973
Edward Crown Center for the Humanities	Loyola University Chicago	1984
Henry Crown Space Center	Museum of Science & Industry	1985
Henry Crown Symphony Hall	Jerusalem	1986
Professor in Jewish-Christian Studies	University of Notre Dame	1990
Covenant Foundation	Chicago	1990
Crown Gallery Children's Museum	Chicago	1990
Crown Studios, WTTW-TV	Chicago	1993
Renee Schine Crown Special Care Nursery	Northwestern Memorial Hospital	1998
Access Living Independent Living Center	Chicago	1998, 2003
Aspen Institute-Henry Crown Scholars	Aspen, Colorado	1999
Rush Medical Center Peritoneal Care Unit	Chicago	2003
Collegiate Scholars Program	University of Chicago	2003
Crown Fountain	Millennium Park	2004

SOURCES: Petrakis and Weber, *Henry Crown*, 2:66; e-mail correspondence, Susan Crown to Timothy Gilfoyle, 29 Oct. 2004; Maria Emma Smith to Timothy Gilfoyle, 1 Dec. 2004, in author's possession.

NOTE: The Crown Foundation rarely reveals the value of individual gifts.

Hutchinson, who played critical roles in building the Art Institute, the Field Museum, the Symphony, and the University of Chicago from 1880 to 1924, had Chicago witnessed such a successful and inspirational cultural diplomat. In less than three years, Bryan successfully recruited leading Chicago families—the Pritzkers, Crowns, and Wrigleys—to support major enhancements in the park. Certain corporations long identified with Chicago—BP Amoco, Bank One, Ameritech, and the McCormick Tribune Foundation—were committed. Bryan served as the middleman between the various committees and

TABLE 5. MAJOR MILLENNIUM PARK ENHANCEMENTS AND COMPONENTS

ENHANCEMENT	ARTIST / DESIGNER	DONOR	CONTRIBUTION
Theater	Thomas Beeby	Irving & Joan Harris	$39 million[a]
Music pavilion	Frank O. Gehry	Pritzker Foundation	$15 million
Fountain	Jaume Plensa, Krueck & Sexton	Crown Foundation	$10 million
Garden	Kathryn Gustafson, Piet Oudolf, Robert Israel	Ann Lurie	$10 million
Peristyle & square	O'Donnell Wicklund Pigozzi & Peterson (OWP&P)	Wm. Wrigley, Jr., Foundation	$5 million
Skating rink/plaza	OWP&P; Skidmore, Owings & Merrill (SOM)	Robert R. McCormick Tribune Fnd.	$5 million
Promenade	McDonough Associates	Bank One Foundation	$5 million
Pedestrian bridge	Frank O. Gehry	BP America, Inc.	$5 million
Sculpture & plaza	Anish Kapoor, McDonough Associates, Terry Guen	SBC Corporation[b]	$3 million
Pavilions	Thomas Beeby, Renzo Piano	Exelon	$5 million
Terraces	Harley Ellis	Boeing	$5 million
Bike station	OWP&P, David Steele of Muller & Muller	None	
Original master plan	SOM		
Overall landscape	Carol J. H. Yetkin		
Park infrastructure	McDonough Associates		
Underground garage	McDonough Associates		
Grant Park North Garage	Teng & Associates		

SOURCE: "Chicago's Millennium Park" Promotional Brochure, June 2003; *Chicago Tribune*, 15 July 2004, sec. 7, pp. 8–9.

[a]Includes a $15 million gift and $24 million loan.

[b]Original gift was made by the Ameritech Foundation.

the mayor on one side and the major donors on the other. The wealthiest donors, said Millennium Park executive committee member Marshall Field V, "talk to John [Bryan] and John talks to us."[52]

These six gifts—totaling $48 million—were only the beginning of the story, however. By January 2001, Bryan and his Millennium Park committee of fundraisers had generated $85 million in donations, nearly three times Daley's original $30 million goal. But Bryan had just begun; he now promised the mayor he would raise $125 million.[5]

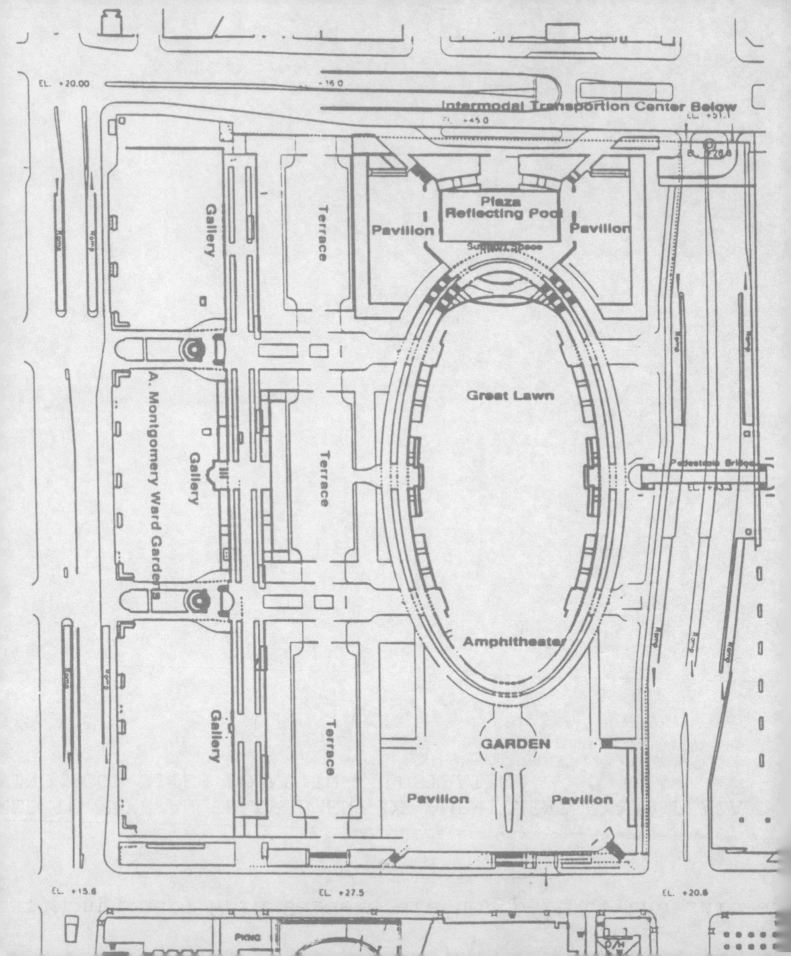

Chapter 8

A THEATER IN THE PARK

John Bryan's unofficial role as Chicago's culture broker involved more than just raising money and recruiting world-renowned artists. At a planning committee meeting with representatives from Skidmore, Owings and Merrill in September 1998, Bryan was joined by fundraisers James Feldstein and Marshall Field V, and project manager Ed Uhlir. Here, for the first time, the fundraising triumvirate learned of the small, 300-seat theater planned for the north end of Millennium Park. Bryan and other Millennium Park officials had given the theater little, if any, thought up to this point. The underground structure was not visible in the early design drawings of the park, and Skidmore's master plan included no specific program for the theater.[1]

Over the years, Feldstein and Bryan had worked on behalf of a variety of nonprofit cultural institutions to raise money and attract patrons. One was the Music and Dance Theater of Chicago, a little-known consortium of twelve small and midsize performing arts companies. Feldstein himself had already helped the organization raise nearly $20 million for a new theater. Yet the consortium had failed to locate a suitable site to build such a structure. Feldstein leaned over to Bryan and whispered in his ear: "Why are we talking about a 300-seat theater with no program? Why don't we see if the Music and Dance Theater can fit there?"[2]

The germinating seed for a music and dance venue was sown not with Millennium Park, but two decades earlier. By the late 1970s, Chicago's performing arts enthusiasts concluded that the city lacked a moderate-sized theater of 1,000 to 2,200 seats for mid-level performing arts companies. Spoken theater generally produced and performed shows for two to six weeks in large theaters with capacities in excess of 3,000. Upon closing, another play replaced it. By contrast, music and dance companies preferred shorter productions in smaller theaters with fewer performers. Music and dance companies were also organized differently, experienced greater turnover, and staged performances only two to four nights a week for periods of less than two weeks. They also toured more. Polk Bros. Foundation president Sandra Guthman aptly summarized the impact of these conditions: "None of them could individually afford their own space."[3]

The most enthusiastic supporters of music and dance in Chicago sought to remedy

The performing arts should be developed more extensively via open music / theater bowls and even a center of enclosed theaters.

JOHNSON, JOHNSON & ROY, 1968

8.1. A close-up of the amphitheater area from the Conceptual Site Plan in the Chicago Plan Commission's 1998 report.

this. In 1978, for example, a group tried to acquire the abandoned Harris and Selwyn theaters on North Dearborn Street. Proponents of the purchase envisioned one theater as a "step-up theater" for small companies and the other as a venue for opera and other performing companies. The effort, however, failed to generate adequate support from the arts and business communities. A second attempt came when Bernard Weissbourd of Metropolitan Structures offered to donate land in the new Illinois Center north of Randolph Street and east of Michigan Avenue to the Chicago Opera Theater. But that proposal also failed to materialize.[4]

In the mid-1980s, the Chicago Opera Theater attempted to purchase the Fine Arts Building at 410 South Michigan Avenue. Joan Harris, president of the organization, envisioned restoring the 1,200-seat Studebaker Theater and the 400-seat World Playhouse, as well as converting some offices for use by Hubbard Street Dance, Chamber Music Chicago, the Chicago Opera Theater, and violin merchants. The rest of the office space was to be converted to residential condominiums. Harris, however, concluded that the building was overpriced, and the plan was abandoned. A few years later, an attempt to purchase the Athenaeum Theater at 2900 North Southport Avenue also proved fruitless.[5]

By this point, Joan Harris had emerged as the leading proponent of finding a midsize music and dance venue in Chicago. Harris was president or board chair of the Chicago Opera Theater between 1977 and 1987. Then in 1987, mayor Harold Washington named her commissioner of cultural affairs. In short time, the *Tribune* identified Harris as one of the ten most powerful women in Chicago and the city's leading liaison and promoter of cultural activities. But in 1989, after her reappointment by the newly elected Richard M. Daley, Harris confronted her new boss by opposing budget cuts for community arts groups and objecting to Daley's plan to lease the old Chicago Public Library Building to the Museum of Contemporary Art. Harris was ultimately forced to resign.[6]

But the defeat was short-term. In 1990, she was appointed to the President's Commission on the National Endowment for the Arts, and later served as president of the Illinois Arts Alliance and chairman of the board of trustees of the Aspen Music Festival and School. She also continued her board associations with the Chicago Symphony Orchestra, the Smart Museum of Art at the University of Chicago, and the American Symphony Orchestra League.[7]

By the late 1980s, the absence of adequate physical spaces for cultural organizations in Chicago was an increasing concern. One independent policy study in 1987 concluded that both central city and suburban Chicago lacked affordable practice, performance, exhibition, and studio spaces.[8] These problems were magnified, believed Sandra Guthman, because music and dance groups lacked the capital and borrowing power to acquire their own performance space.[9]

In 1991, Harris received a call from Bruce Newman of the Chicago Community Trust. "The Trust had been receiving proposals from small and medium sized arts companies for years," remembered Harris, "and the complaint that many of them continued to have is that they had no performing space." Newman asked Harris if she was willing to try again.[10]

But this time, Newman and Harris pursued a different strategy. By now, Harris realized that small arts organizations had no business working with real estate. Her earlier efforts, she admitted in retrospect, were "simply the result of desperation." This time, five foundations—the Chicago Community Trust, the Harris Foundation, the Polk Bros. Foundation, the MacArthur Foundation, and the Field Foundation—were joined by a grant from the Sara Lee Corporation (headed by John Bryan).[11] The mission was to organize a coalition of foundations to find or create a theater space for the midsize performing companies.

The foundations conducted several surveys. One explored every unused or underused theater within several miles of the Loop as a potential site. Another examined all the music and dance companies in Chicago, determining which ones shared the same needs. In the end, nine companies were so identified. They combined their limited resources and established a nonprofit corporation. Within a few years, three more companies joined. Thus was born the Music and Dance Theater of Chicago (MDTC).[12]

The twelve founding companies represented the wide range of diverse cultural institutions that emerged in Chicago in the final decades of the twentieth century: Ballet Chicago (1987), Chicago Opera Theater (1974), Chicago Sinfonietta (1988), the Dance Center of Columbia College Chicago (1969), Hubbard Street Dance (1977), the Joffrey Ballet (1957), the Lyric Opera Center for American Artists (1974), the Mexican Fine Arts Center Museum (1987), the Muntu Dance Theater of Chicago (1972), the Music of the Baroque (1972), the Old Town School of Folk Music (1957), and Performing Arts Chicago (1959).[13]

In retrospect, the establishment of the MDTC might be interpreted as the onset of a theater revival. Within a few years, ten new theaters had opened, including the renovations of the Harris and Selwyn theaters as the new Goodman Theatre ($45 million) in 2000, the Ford Oriental ($32 million) in 1998, and the Cadillac Palace ($20 million) in 1999, as well as the openings of the $23 million Shakespeare Theater (1999) at Navy Pier and the Lookingglass Theatre (2003) at the Water Tower Pumping Station. By 2001, as many as 140 performances were available some weekends. One artistic director noted how Chicago, historically an importer of productions and an exporter of talent, was entering a new era. "Now, Chicago shows and companies go everywhere and talent is flocking in."[14]

But in the early 1990s, Chicago's theatrical landscape did not look so promising. "I knew we needed a good, midsize theater," believed Harris. "Try as I did, working with other arts groups, I couldn't get the idea going."[15] She viewed the MDTC as a last-ditch effort to find a suitable performance space in Chicago.

Harris was named president of the new organization, and was joined by Sandra Guthman, who became chair of the board. Guthman, a former IBM executive and president of the Polk Brothers Foundation, was long involved in supporting cultural programs throughout Chicago and had taken a keen interest in finding a performance venue for small music and dance groups. She and other foundation leaders were concerned about the financial health of many of the performing groups they supported. Inadequate revenue streams made the companies overly dependent on the benevolence of private foun-

8.2. Thomas Beeby.

8.3. Beeby's early design for the Music and Dance Theater of Chicago on Columbus Drive, north of the Chicago River.

dations. Guthman and others increasingly believed that the best solution was to find or create a suitable and affordable performance space. In Guthman's word, it would be better to "teach them to fish rather than give them fish."[16]

The newly formed MDTC then organized an architectural competition to design a theater specific to their interests. Thomas Beeby of Hammond Beeby Rupert Ainge, best known for the Rice Building at the Art Institute (1988) and the Harold Washington Library Center (1991), emerged as the winner. The MDTC then hired James Feldstein as a fundraising consultant, who helped the group raise $20 million. And in 1995, the MDTC purchased land north of the Chicago River and east of Michigan Avenue.[17]

Complications from an adjoining landlord, however, forced them to abandon the site. After six years of fundraising, securing an architect, finding a location, and developing an architectural plan, the MDTC was back to square one. "We were left with the project and no land," remembers Harris. At this point, a number of other sites were offered, including one near the University of Illinois in Chicago, but MDTC officials were unenthusiastic. They believed a downtown site was a prerequisite to attracting patrons.[18] After more than two decades of trying to build a suitable theater, Harris was discouraged. "We were about ready to fold up," she admits, "when one of these strange turns of fate occurred."[19]

The strange turn took place at a Millennium Park planning meeting on September 21, 1998, when James Feldstein, sitting next to John Bryan and Marshall Field V, proposed locating the MDTC in the site reserved for a small, three-hundred-seat theater in the SOM plan. Bryan jumped at the idea. He was well aware of the MDTC. Indeed, he was instrumental in getting Sara Lee to donate $1 million to their campaign. He knew about Beeby's design. Bryan believed all parties could potentially save money, and most important, "it was absolutely a stunning, superb site."[20]

Millennium Park project manager Ed Uhlir immediately went back to his office and contacted Beeby. At this point, Beeby had worked on the design for nearly a decade and had little hope that the project would ever be built. Uhlir's decision to call Beeby first was deliberate; he feared that prematurely contacting anyone at MDTC would needlessly inflate their hopes. He recognized Millennium Park represented "the last gasp" for the MDTC.[21]

Beeby picked up the phone. "I was amazed," he later admitted. "First of all, I didn't know anything about Millennium Park, which was sort of unknown."[22] Uhlir explained the project and gave Beeby the precise structural specifications for the space between the back of the music pavilion and Randolph Street. The architect sat down and spent the week examining them. The following Monday he called Uhlir and voiced the magic words: "I can make it fit."[23]

The theater more than just fit into the space, Beeby later explained. "All the pieces that they [Millennium Park] were missing, we had," and vice versa, he observed. The music pavilion needed more space for rehearsal and dressing rooms; the MDTC included both. A new indoor theater in Millennium Park required attracting a constituency and raising a large sum of money; the MDTC had both, including almost $20 million. The music pavilion's primary season would be during the three summer months, a time when the MDTC companies were touring or preparing for the fall and winter seasons. In fact, the primary seasons for the MDTC extended from September to May, a period when the music pavilion and lawn would not be utilized. "So when we were down, they were up," according to Beeby, "and when they were up, we were down."[24]

Sandra Guthman concurred, admitting that "we never had a clue what we were going to do with the theater in June, July, and August because none of our twelve groups want it." The MDTC always envisioned a nine-month schedule from September through May. Fortuitously, in Millennium Park, the Grant Park Music Festival would assume control in the summer months, thereby paying 25 percent of the theater's operating costs. "There was an enormous economic benefit by having us go in there," Beeby said.[25]

The plan also included another advantage: locating the facade of the MDTC on upper Randolph Street effectively extended Chicago's revived downtown theatrical district farther east along Randolph Street. Four blocks west stood the relocated Goodman Theatre in the renovated Harris and Selwyn theaters. A pedestrian walking east on Randolph would see the Ford Oriental, the Cadillac Palace, the Storefront Theater, the Chicago Theater, and the Chicago Cultural Center. The Music and Dance Theater would serve as the easternmost bookend to this new theatrical streetscape in the Loop.

Even more than the successful recruiting of Frank Gehry to design Millennium Park's music pavilion, the introduction of the Music and Dance Theater transformed Millennium Park into a cultural center. In some respects, this made good planning sense. Grant Park was never a pastoral oasis like other famous urban parks such as Manhattan's Cen-

8.4. Jack Guthman.

tral Park, Brooklyn's Prospect Park, or San Francisco's Golden Gate Park. The presence of the Fine Arts Building (1886), the Auditorium (1889), the Art Institute (1892), the Public Library (1897), Orchestra Hall (1904), the Field Museum of Natural History (1919), the Shedd Aquarium (1929) and the Adler Planetarium (1930) embodied Grant Park's evolution as Chicago's civic center. The historian Carl Condit even dubbed this combination of structures in and around Grant Park as "the largest, oldest, and architecturally most impressive 'cultural center' in the United States."[26] The MDTC would now join this cultural roster.

Harris and Guthman were stunned when they learned of the proposal. "It was clearly the best location we had ever considered," acknowledged Guthman. "It was sort of like having Cupid dropping out of the sky into your arms."[27]

But Cupid is a fickle god. Beeby's original design proved to be too tall, stretching fifty feet above the Randolph Street level. Ed Uhlir and MDTC representatives worried that the height could generate a lawsuit based on the Montgomery Ward court decisions and stop the construction. Joan Harris then sought help from an unusual source: Sandra Guthman's husband, Jack.[28]

Jack Guthman was, by some measures, an unconventional choice to represent the city of Chicago and Millennium Park. Formerly a partner at Sidley & Austin who had moved to Shefsky & Froelich in 1994, Guthman was considered one of Chicago's leading real estate attorneys. *Crain's Chicago Business* even dubbed him "Mr. Insider" for his ability to negotiate the city's complicated and sometimes contradictory real estate regulatory process. Opponents like attorney Reuben Hedlund described him as "a gladiator" and an arch defender of the property rights of developers and large real estate interests.[29] Guthman openly disdained the nicknames, but he indeed regularly represented private-sector clients like the Central Michigan Avenue Association, noted for their opposition to creating a landmark district along Michigan Avenue from Randolph Street to 11th Street.[30]

Guthman himself admitted that working on behalf of the public sector was an unusual task. "I got up and said, 'My name is Jack Guthman and I'm here representing the City of Chicago and Millennium Park.' I expect everybody fainted."[31]

Upon assuming the assignment, Guthman raised two potential problems. First, the original plan approved by the Chicago Plan Commission in 1998 did not include the MDTC on the site; this, feared Guthman, was an invitation for a lawsuit. In fact, Guthman discovered that there was no suggestion of a building of this nature in the planned development ordinance which governed the site. Working with Uhlir, Guthman suggested amending the plan administratively. That tactic was rejected by the Chicago Department of Planning, forcing Millennium Park, Inc., to come up with a new development plan.[32]

Guthman's second worry was more serious: the Montgomery Ward cases. Guthman proposed an innovative tactic. While most Chicagoans considered the Montgomery Ward cases to be a barrier to park development, Guthman believed the court decisions were "a road map" to building in the park. Guthman's road map was *Ward I*, the 1897 lawsuit that allowed building in the park as long as abutting landowners approved, a procedure that was followed in 1891 for the construction of the Art Institute in what was then Lake Front Park. Guthman went to the Art Institute archives, found the consent form used more than a century earlier, and used that for the Millennium Park waiver. "We did not change a word," emphasized Guthman.[33]

In order to gain landlord and city approval, Beeby was nevertheless forced to revise the theater's plan. Originally, he hoped to keep as much of his design as possible, but certain civic groups—Friends of the Parks, the Grant Park Advisory Council, the Friends of Downtown, and others—argued that Beeby's structure was too tall and violated the spirit of the Montgomery Ward cases.[34] Guthman was especially irritated by one civic group. "Friends of the Parks seems to make its living on opposing good things for the public because they don't believe in people using the parks," charged Guthman. "They believe in parks without a lot of activity. I'm overstating that, but only slightly."[35]

In fact, Friends of the Parks liked the Music and Dance structure because it was underground and occupied a small footprint. They requested only that Beeby lower the height of the building.[36] Beeby complied, scaling the height to less than forty feet. On March 11, 1999, Uhlir presented the revised plan to the Chicago Plan Commission, this time with the support of various civic groups.[37]

In the meantime, Uhlir labored to gather approval from surrounding landlords. Along with Joyce Moffatt, the general manager of MDTC, and city attorney John McDonough, Uhlir went from building to building, making presentations to all fifteen landlords surrounding Millennium Park, explaining the project, and persuading each to sign a consent form.[38]

Guthman, however, feared such consent waivers were insufficient. He advised Millennium Park and MDTC officials that no bond lawyer would offer a favorable opinion on the development of Millennium Park without a court case validating the process. Guthman had a solution: a lawsuit.[39]

Guthman proposed identifying one or more residential property owners on the edge of the park who had not consented and encouraging them to file a lawsuit.[40] Guthman found John and Mildred Boaz of 360 East Randolph Drive, a large condominium complex at the north end of Grant Park overlooking Daley Bicentennial Plaza. On April 5, 1999, the Boazes sued on behalf of other condominium owners residing along the northern edge of the park. John Boaz was on the board of the Illinois Council of Orchestras and a supporter of the Symphony Orchestra Institute, a group devoted to preserving and improving the effectiveness of symphony orchestra organizations.[41] Along with his wife, he argued that any building exceeding five feet in height violated not only the Montgomery Ward decisions, but the covenant associated with the Fort Dearborn Addition that the lakefront area remain "open, clear and free."[42]

A few days later, Guthman received a phone call from Daley advisor Ed Bedore. "You know, frankly the Mayor is not happy about having a lawsuit brought on this," Bedore complained.

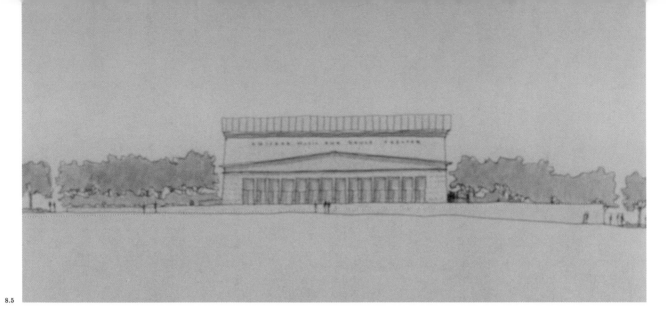

8.5

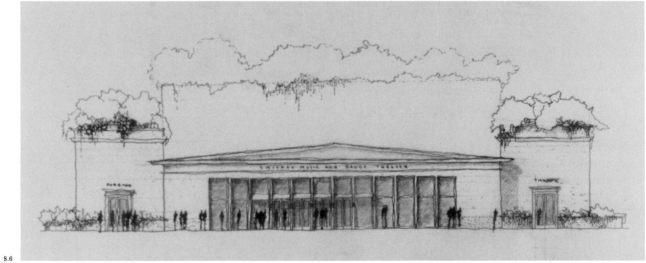

8.6

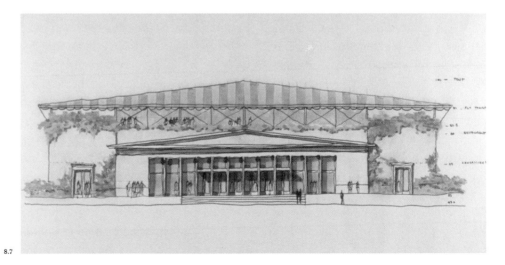

8.7

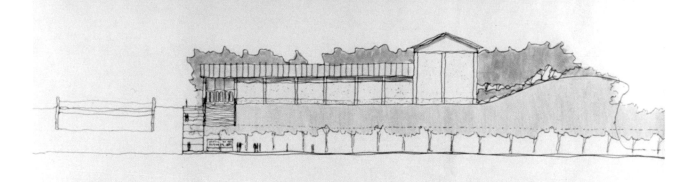

8.8

Guthman stoked Bedore's ego. "You're a very thoughtful guy in the area of public finance," said Guthman. "I think if you explain to the Mayor that, in order to get a bond opinion, you're going to have to have something more than my view of this and some consents. You're going to need to have a court opinion which ratifies the approach to overcoming the Montgomery Ward cases."[43]

Nine months later, Guthman was vindicated. On January 14, 2000, Judge Albert Green dismissed the Boaz complaint, finding that property owners along Randolph Street had no additional rights and that the consents were sufficient. The Music and Dance Theater was not in violation of the Montgomery Ward restrictions.[44]

MDTC, however, faced one more major hurdle: money. Upon accepting the invitation to build in Millennium Park, MDTC's fundraising campaign led by attorney James Alexander had raised nearly $20 million. But changes in the theater's design as well as escalating construction costs demanded more financing. Initial estimates concluded that the theater needed at least $35 million; some later worried that the ultimate price tag might reach $60 million.[45] Equally worrisome to Millennium Park, Inc., officials was that MDTC's revived campaign would generate confusion. "We didn't want to be going to the same donors because we didn't think they'd understand why a theater going in the park was different from the park," remembered Marshall Field.[46]

These increased costs also generated dissent among certain MDTC companies. Performing Arts Chicago and the Chicago Opera Theater officials, for example, complained that delays hurt their fundraising and cash flow, particularly after the MDTC failed to open in February 2002 as promised. Susan Lipman, executive director of Performing Arts Chicago, further predicted that MDTC would be too expensive. Others, like Gail Kalver, executive director of Hubbard Street Dance, were more pragmatic: "We're not happy about the delays, but we have been gypsies for twenty-five years, so we are used to living with frustration."[47]

Some of the companies did not believe that the new theater would solve all their problems. Chicago Opera Theater, for example, expected to book no more than 10 percent

8.5, 8.6. The initial renderings of the Beeby's Music and Dance Theater for Millennium Park in October and November, 1998.

8.7. Beeby included a plan with an open-air rooftop terrace above the underground theater.

8.8. The side view of Beeby's early plan revealed that the theater was to be taller than the outdoor music pavilion.

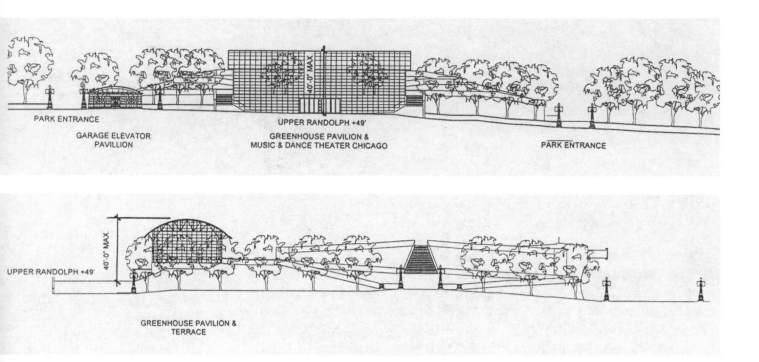

PARK ENTRANCE

GARAGE ELEVATOR
PAVILLION

UPPER RANDOLPH +49'

GREENHOUSE PAVILION &
MUSIC & DANCE THEATER CHICAGO

PARK ENTRANCE

UPPER RANDOLPH +49'

GREENHOUSE PAVILION &
TERRACE

8.9. Beeby's revised theater with a "Greenhouse Pavilion" extended only thirty-nine to forty feet in height.

8.10. Beeby's "Greenhouse Pavilion and Terrace" design in March 1999 did not anticipate the massive music pavilion Frank Gehry proposed several months later.

of their attractions at MDTC. Performing Arts Chicago, the Joffrey Ballet, and Hubbard Street promised not to abandon their current venues. Other groups waited to see how the theater looked and what its costs would be. Frank Solari of the Athenaeum believed most of the groups lacked the funds to pay for the space, arguing that the MDTC would cost as much per day as the Athenaeum charged per week.[48]

But many of these problems were endemic to the American performing arts landscape. In 2001, the Pew Charitable Trusts issued a national report warning that midsize cultural organizations—those with budgets between $650,000 and $9 million—would face the greatest financial strain in ensuing years. Escalating costs, combined with declining audiences in opera and ballet, placed local and regional arts groups in a state of fiscal uncertainty.[49] The challenges confronting MDTC affiliates were hardly unique to Chicago.

In the face of such criticisms, Marshall Field and Sandra Guthman nevertheless developed a plan: "They would give me about a dozen names that they felt were their prime customers," Field explained. They approached the select group, and promised they could split their gift: half would go to the theater and half would go to the park, and they would still be considered a Millennium Park Founder. In the end, sixteen donors split their million-dollar contributions between Millennium Park and MDTC.[50]

But even as Guthman, Field, and other MDTC fundraisers surpassed $45 million in private contributions (on their way to over $62 million), some remained skeptical. "We encountered tremendous difficulty in obtaining letters of credit from a consortium of banks," claimed James Alexander. Chicago's financial institutions were loath to invest in the project, in part because the theater lacked a long fundraising history. "We got really close a couple of times, but we never were able to get the banks to sign off on the letter of credit," Alexander remembered.[51]

Then on February 4, 2002, Irving and Joan Harris made a stunning announcement: the couple agreed not only to donate $15 million to the Music and Dance Theater, but also to provide a $24 million construction loan to jump-start the project. "I think Irving just got disgusted [with the banks]," John Bryan later explained. Of the $15 million gift, $11 million was a challenge grant, requiring MDTC to raise one-and-a-half times that amount, or $16.5 million, by 2004. It was the largest single monetary gift ever to a performing arts organization in Chicago.[52]

For those who knew the Harrises, the gift was no surprise. A passionate advocate of early childhood development programs, Irving B. Harris was one of the nation's leading philanthropists during the final three decades of the twentieth century. He was instrumental in establishing the Erikson Institute for training teachers in child development, the Ounce of Prevention Fund for developing programs to prevent family dysfunction, the Beethoven Project, and Family Focus, all of which served as models for programs across the country such as Early Head Start. Harris also served on the National Commission on Children and the Carnegie Corporation of New York's Task Force on Meeting the Needs of Young Children. For a time, he chaired WTTW, Chicago's public television station. His bequests established the Irving B. Harris School for Public Policy Studies at the University of Chicago and the Neison and Irving Harris Building of the Yale University Child Study Center.[53]

With the money in hand, the city of Chicago gave MDTC an annual one dollar lease to operate the theater on the city-owned land for nine months while the city retained usage

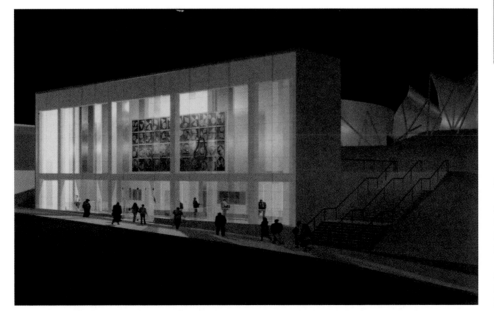

8.11. Irving B. Harris.

8.12. Joan Harris, Joyce Moffatt, and Sandra Guthman at the groundbreaking ceremony for the Music and Dance Theater.

8.13. The final design of Thomas Beeby's Harris Theater for Music and Dance.

rights for three summer months. Two days after the Harrises' announcement, MDTC officials broke ground for the new theater.[54]

The Harris Theater, after nearly two decades of planning and fundraising, opened on November 8, 2003.[55] The final cost of $52.7 million proved to be lower than the anticipated $60 million.[56] And having raised over $62 million, the MDTC possessed a substantial $10 million endowment. Situated along Randolph Street and mostly underground, the five-story facility was named the Joan W. and Irving B. Harris Theater for Music and Dance.[57] Chicago's newest theatrical venue shared dressing, storage, and practice rooms with its immediate neighbor, the Jay Pritzker Pavilion. Perhaps this was a poetic coincidence: in the final decade of the twentieth century and into the new millennium, the Harris and Pritzker families were neighbors in the same East Lake Shore Drive apartment building.

Chapter 9

THE MODERN MEDICIS

Who were the donors or "founders" of Millennium Park, the "modern day Medicis" in the words of Donna LaPietra?[1] While John Bryan developed a strategy to recruit families, corporations, and foundations with historic ties to Chicago, the body of founders reflected much more. In addition to institutions and families long a part of Chicago's economic history, Bryan and his team of fundraisers attracted more recent arrivals representing the "new economy" at the turn of the twenty-first century.[2] The diversity of donating individuals, families, corporations, and foundations mirrored the complexity of Chicago's metropolitan economy and philanthropic sector. Most significantly, Millennium Park was at once a product of the inexorable forces of globalization and a reflection of the impact of those forces on local businesses and politics.

Few fundraising campaigns in Chicago history generated such enthusiasm and wide support from the region's wealthiest citizens as Millennium Park. Bryan successfully attracted more than two-thirds (15 of 21) of the Illinois residents identified from 1998 to 2003 in the list of the 400 richest Americans by *Forbes* magazine, the so-called Forbes 400.[3] Significantly, the commercial backgrounds of the donors reflected three key economic trends in Chicago at the turn of the millennium. First, Chicago had evolved from an industrial and commercial metropolis to an urban economy structured around the provision of diverse services.[4] Second, while service-sector activity dominated the metropolitan economy, corporations devoted to industrial production remained a key component to the region's economic profile. And third, Chicago's economy and cultural institutions were heavily shaped—maybe even dependent upon—the largely uncontrollable forces of globalization. All three of these developments were embodied in Millennium Park.

The wealth of approximately 70 percent of Millennium Park's 115 donors originated in banking, finance, real estate, and other service-oriented activities. This is hardly a surprising trend, since roughly two-thirds of all Chicago workers in 2000 were engaged in some service-related occupation. The most significant group within the service economy was primarily engaged in finance, insurance, and real estate (FIRE). Over one-third of the donors (36 percent) were exclusively involved with that sector, while another twelve possessed wealth that combined finance and service-sector work with industrial activity,

TABLE 6. MILLENNIUM PARK FOUNDERS

INDIVIDUAL GIFTS (75 TOTAL)	AFFILIATED INSTITUTIONS	TYPE OF WEALTH OR BUSINESS
Anonymous		
Barbara and James F. Bere	Borg-Warner Corporation	Industry
Naomi T. and Robert C. Borwell		Finance
Suzann and Gary Brinson	UBS Brinson	Finance
Neville and John Bryan	Sara Lee Corporation	Food processing & industry (apparel)
Gilda and Henry Buchbinder Family	Ardoco, Inc. & Henry M. Buchbinder Trust	Industry
Kay and Matthew Bucksbaum	General Growth Properties, Inc.	Real estate
Rosemarie and Dean L. Buntrock	Waste Management, Inc.	Industry
The Clinton Family	The Clinton Companies	Real estate
Gary and Francie Comer	Lands' End (founder)	Retail
The Crown Family	Material Service Corporation/ Henry Crown and Company	Industry/ Finance & real estate
Judy and Jamie Dimon	Bank One	Finance
Sue and Wes Dixon	G. D. Searle & Co.	Medical products
Richard H. Driehaus	Driehaus Capital Management	Finance
Janet and Craig Duchossois	Duchossois Industries, Inc. & Arlington International Raceway	Industry & entertainment
Deborah and Bruce Duncan	Equity Residential Properties Trust	Real estate
Andrew "Flip" and Veronica Filipowski Family	DivineInterventures & Platinum Technology International, Inc.	Technology
Ginny and Peter Foreman Family	Sirius Corporation/Harris Associates	Finance
Linda and Bill Gantz	Ovation Pharmaceuticals	Medical products
Glasser and Rosenthal Family	GATX Corporation (James Glasser)	Finance
Anne and Howard Gottlieb	Glenwood Trust Corp.	Real estate
William B. Graham	Baxter International, Inc.	Medical products
Perry and Marty Granoff	Valdor Corporation (N.J.)	Finance & industry
Joyce and Avrum Gray & Family	G-Bar Limited Partnership & Alloy Consolidated Industries	Finance & industry
Anne and Kenneth Griffin	Citadel Investment Group	Finance
Sandra and Jack Guthman	Polk Bros. Foundation & Shefsky & Froelich Ltd.	Retail & law
Bette and Neison Harris	Standard Shares/Pittway Corp.	Finance & industry
Joan W. and Irving B. Harris	Pittway Corp.	Finance & industry
Natalie and Ben W. Heineman	Northwest Industries & Ben W. Heineman, Sr., Enterprises	Industry & finance
Blair Hull and Family	The Hull Group	Finance
Judy and Verne Istock	Bank One Corp.	Finance

TABLE 6. MILLENNIUM PARK FOUNDERS *(continued)*

INDIVIDUAL GIFTS (75 TOTAL)	AFFILIATED INSTITUTIONS	TYPE OF WEALTH OR BUSINESS
Debby and Ned Jannotta	William Blair & Co., LLC	Finance
Gretchen and Jay Jordan	The Jordan Company & Jordan Industries	Finance & industry
Dolores Kohl Kaplan and Morris A. Kaplan	Mayer and Morris Kaplan Family Foundation	Industry
Lindy and Michael Keiser	Recycled Paper Greetings, Inc.	Industry
Connie and Dennis Keller	DeVry, Inc.	Retail
Rebecca and Lester Knight Family	RoundTable Healthcare Partners & Allegiance Corp.	Medical products
Janet, Michael, and Rob Krasny	CDW Computers	Retail
Kay and Fred Krehbiel	Molex	Industry
Posy and John Krehbiel	Molex	Industry
Bill Kurtis and Donna LaPietra	Kurtis Productions	Communications
Lavin and Bernick Family	Alberto Culver Co.	Industry
Carol and Larry Levy	Levy Restaurants	entertainment & real estate
Loucks Family	Baxter International, Inc.	Medical products
Ann Lurie	Lurie Investments	Real estate
Martha and John Mabie	Mid-Continent Capital LLC	Finance
Mary and Robert C. McCormack	Trident Capital	Finance
Newton N. and Josephine Baskin Minow	Sidley Austin Brown & Wood LLP	Law
Janet and Richard Morrow	Amoco Corporation	Energy (oil)
Muriel Kallis Newman and son Glenn Steinberg		Real estate
John D. and Alexandra C. Nichols	Illinois Tool Works/Marmon Group	Industry
Ellen and Jim O'Connor	Commonwealth Edison/Exelon	Energy
Cathy and Bill Osborn	Northern Trust Company	Finance
Suzie and Jim Otterbeck	Verizon Communications & OnePoint Communications	Communications
Sarah and Peer Pedersen	Pedersen & Houpt	Law
Port, Washlow, and Errant Family	Lawson Products	Industry
Eleanor and William Wood Prince	Prince Charitable Trust	Finance & industry
Pritzker Family	Marmon Group & Hyatt Corporation	Finance, industry & real estate
Diana and Bruce Rauner	GTCR Golden Rauner LLC	Finance
Patrick G. and Shirley W. Ryan Family	Aon Corporation	Insurance
Chris and Ted Schwartz	APAC Customer Services	Communications
Dan Searle	G. D. Searle & Co.	Medical products
Sally and Bill Searle	G. D. Searle & Co.	Medical products

TABLE 6. MILLENNIUM PARK FOUNDERS *(continued)*

INDIVIDUAL GIFTS (75 TOTAL)	AFFILIATED INSTITUTIONS	TYPE OF WEALTH OR BUSINESS
Stephanie and Bill Sick	American National Can Corp. & MetaSolv Software/Signature Capital	Finance & industry
Alice and Frank Slezak Family		
Lois and Harrison Steans	Financial Investments Corporation	Finance
Stone Family	Smurfit-Stone Corp.	Industry
The Stuart Family	Quaker Oats	
Helen and Richard Thomas	First National Bank of Chicago	Finance
Howard J. and Paula Miller Trienens	Sidley Austin Brown & Wood LLP	Law
Oprah Winfrey	Harpo	Entertainment & communications
Vivian and Alexander Wislow	U.S. Equities Realty	Real estate
Helen and Sam Zell	Equity Residential Properties Trust	Real estate
Lisa W. and James J. Zenni, Jr.	Black Diamond Capital Management	Finance

CORPORATIONS (25 TOTAL)		TYPE OF WEALTH OR BUSINESS
Abbott Laboratories		Medical products
The Allstate Corporation		Insurance
Arthur Andersen		Accounting
Aon Corporation		Insurance
Ariel Mutual Funds		Finance
Baxter International		Medical products
The Boeing Company		Industry
BP America, Inc.		Energy (oil)
Chase (original gift from Bank One)		Finance
CNA Foundation		Insurance
Deloitte		Accounting
Exelon		Energy (utility)
Goldman, Sachs and Co.		Finance
Harris Bank		Finance
JMB Realty Corporation		Real estate
LaSalle Bank		Finance
McDonald's Corporation		Food service
Northern Trust Company		Finance

TABLE 6. MILLENNIUM PARK FOUNDERS *(continued)*

CORPORATIONS (25 TOTAL)	TYPE OF WEALTH OR BUSINESS
PricewaterhouseCoopers LLP	Accounting
Sara Lee Corporation	Food processing & industry (apparel)
SBC (original gift from Ameritech)	Communications
The Sears-Roebuck Foundation	Retail
Target	Retail
UBS	Finance
Wm. Wrigley Jr. Company Foundation	Food processing

FOUNDATIONS/TRUSTS (15 TOTAL)	LEADERS	TYPE OF WEALTH OR BUSINESS
Cooper Family Foundation	Lana & Dick Cooper	Finance
Marshall and Jamee Field Family Fund	Marshall Field V	Retail, finance & communications
Lloyd A. Fry Foundation	Howard M. McCue III	Industry (roofing)
J. Ira and Nicki Harris Family Foundation	J. Ira and Nicki Harris	Finance
Kovler Family Foundation	Jonathan Kovler	Retail
Ann and Robert H. Lurie Foundation	Ann Lurie	Real estate
The Francis L. Lederer Foundation		Medicine
John D. and Catherine T. MacArthur Foundation	Jonathan Fanton and Adele Simmons	Insurance & real estate
Robert R. McCormick Tribune Foundation	Neil Creighton	Communications
Elizabeth Morse & Elizabeth Morse Genius Charitable Trusts	James L. Alexander	Industry & real estate
Polk Bros. Foundation	Sandra Guthman	Retail (Polk Bros.)
The Regenstein Foundation	Susan Regenstein Frank	Industry
Dr. Scholl Foundation	Pamela Scholl	Industry
The Searle Funds of the Chicago Community Trust	Donald Stewart	Medical products (G. D. Searle)
The Siragusa Foundation	John Siragusa	Industry (Admiral)

SOURCE: "Millennium Park: Founders as of June 2005."

most notably the Crown and Pritzker families. When those donors are combined with those involved in the FIRE sector, the figure increases to 46 percent (see appendix 6).[5] Although the FIRE sector of the economy employed only 12 percent of the metropolitan workforce at the millennium, they represented more than three times that percentage among the donors.[6]

The dominance of finance, insurance, and real estate among the founders was magnified when compared to other donors whose wealth was derived from service-related activities. Only eighteen more donors (16 percent) were engaged in businesses related to law, accounting, medicine, entertainment, and communications. Even fewer—eleven donors (10 percent)—possessed wealth that originated with retail services, two of which no longer existed except as nonprofit foundations (Polk Bros. and Kovler).

Equally important, the Millennium Park founders illustrated the ongoing importance of manufacturing in the Chicago economy. The wealth of thirty-three companies, foundations, and individuals (29 percent) originated exclusively from some form of industrial activity, broadly defined to include manufacturing, food processing, medical products, and energy production. When donors involved in both industry and other service-oriented activity were considered, the percentage increased to forty, a figure considerably greater than the 15 percent of workers in metropolitan Chicago employed in manufacturing in 2000.[7]

Millennium Park reflected Chicago's rich industrial history with donations from leading Chicago enterprises or their executive officers: Sara Lee, Molex, William Wrigley, Jr., Company, BP Amoco, Illinois Tool Works, Borg-Warner, and Baxter International, for example. But the historic importance of manufacturing was further reflected by donors originating from Chicago's industrial past. The Kaplan family once owned the Sealy Mattress Company. The Lloyd A. Fry Foundation was created from the wealth of a roofing shingle business. The Siragusa Foundation evolved out of the Admiral Corporation. The Searle donations by individual family members and the Chicago Community Trust originated from the pharmaceutical giant G. D. Searle & Co. The Prince family and the Prince Charitable Trust originated with Frederick Henry Prince, an early owner of the Union Stock Yards.[8] While none of these industrial enterprises exist in their once-dominant form, their family-named foundations remain a significant presence in Chicago philanthropy.

While Chicago does not command the economic power of "global cities" such as New York, London, and Tokyo, the Millennium Park donors exemplify Chicago's stake in the global economy. All the corporate donors and nearly all the donors with wealth originating in finance, insurance, or real estate were tied to global markets of one sort or another. Even among the industrial companies and enterprises, the overwhelming majority were engaged in providing services or manufacturing products for a global market. The Marmon Group included more than 300 production facilities in over 40 countries.[9] Molex's 50 factories operated in 21 countries.[10] Baxter had nearly 70 manufacturing facilities in over 20 countries.[11] Illinois Tool Works employed more than 45,000 workers in more than 600 business units in over 40 countries.[12] The Wrigley Company sold products in more than 150 countries.[13]

A comparison of the leading public corporations and private companies headquartered or engaged in significant business in metropolitan Chicago illustrates the importance of the global economy to the Millennium Park founders. Bryan and his committee of fundraisers persuaded eleven of the twenty-five Chicago-area Fortune 500 public corporations to contribute to Millennium Park, as well as fourteen individuals associated with such firms.[14] Bryan was even more successful with public companies included in Fortune's Global 500, generally considered the largest such enterprises in the world. Sixteen of those corporations had a significant presence in Chicago, twelve (75 percent) of which contributed $1 million or more to build Millennium Park (see appendixes 7 and 8). Perhaps most impressive was Bryan's talent for attracting donations from four global, public corporations headquartered outside Chicago: BP (London), SBC Communications (San Antonio), UBS (Zurich), and Goldman Sachs (New York) (although BP and SBC originally contributed as Chicago-headquartered Amoco and Ameritech, respectively).[15]

By contrast, Bryan never generated similar levels of contributions among private companies. Only eight of forty-one Chicago-area private companies listed in the Forbes 500, or families affiliated with such companies, contributed to Millennium Park. Some of these participants were, in fact, part of larger family financial empires, notably the Marmon Group and H Holding Group (Hyatt Hotels) of the Pritzker family, and CC Industries, an automobile and truck parts manufacturing enterprise controlled by the Crown family. Significantly, the three top private companies Bryan persuaded to donate—PricewaterhouseCoopers, Deloitte Touche, and Andersen—were accounting or business services companies that serviced large, multinational corporations.

This is attributable to several factors. The forty-one private companies in metropolitan Chicago identified in the Forbes 500 enjoyed much lower annual revenues. Whereas Ace Hardware, the twenty-fifth-largest Chicago-area public corporation in 2000, reported revenues in excess of $2.9 billion, only six private companies matched or exceeded such income. Excluding New York-based Deloitte Touche and PricewaterhouseCoopers further emphasizes the limited amount of private, noncorporate capital available for philanthropy. Furthermore, while certain products offered by these concerns were global in their reach—chemical manufacturing by ChemCentral, legal services by Baker and McKenzie, metal products by Amsted Industries, Beanie Babies by Ty—these companies were more often focused on local, regional, or national markets: the construction firms of the Walsh Group and Pepper Companies; regional distributors like Reyes Holding, Coca-Cola Bottling of Chicago, Eby-Brown, Specialty Foods and Wirtz; retail outlets like White Hen Pantry and Lighthouse (controlled by Clark Retail Enterprises).[16]

Bryan's inability to recruit more donations from private companies, however, did not detract from his fundraising achievement. Indeed, it was magnified when compared to other cities. In raising private support for Disney Concert Hall in Los Angeles, for example, Eli Broad failed to attract donations from sixteen of Los Angeles County's eighteen Forbes 400 billionaires. The lion's share of support, once the Disney family contributions were excluded, came from sixty-one individuals who gave $1 million or more, and a loose coalition of local foundations, banks, oil companies, utilities, and others, including two companies that were swallowed up in mergers after making their gifts.[17] In

Seattle, the $118.1 million Benaroya Hall (1998) relied on twenty-five donors who gave $1 million or more, led by the Benaroya family, which gave $15 million. Philadelphia's $265 million Kimmel Center for the Performing Arts (2001) attracted only forty-three $1 million-plus donors, led by Sidney Kimmel's $35 million gift.[18] While the Kimmel Center, like Millennium Park, billed itself as "a unique public-private partnership," in the words of Willard G. Rouse III, the project benefited from large contributions from the commonwealth of Pennsylvania, under governor Tom Ridge, and the city of Philadelphia, under mayors Ed Rendell and John Street.[19]

In sum, Millennium Park embodied Chicago's relationship to and dependency upon the global economy. The overwhelming majority of donors either manufactured products throughout the world or provided services with a global reach. Few were from those areas of businesses which tend to be regional or local in their markets: real estate and commercial developers and managers, commodities brokers and traders, construction and engineering companies, trucking and transportation concerns, advertising firms, groceries, food and beverage distributors, printers and publishers, or restaurant services.

More important than Bryan's corporate connections were his relationships in Chicago's cultural and philanthropic universe. Bryan chaired the board of directors of Americans United to Save the Arts and Humanities and the National Trust for Historic Preservation, and was a member of the President's committee on the Arts and the Humanities.[20] In Chicago, Bryan served on the boards or fundraised for five of Chicago's most prestigious nonprofit institutions: the Chicago Symphony Orchestra, the Lyric Opera of Chicago, the University of Chicago, Rush Presbyterian–St. Luke's Medical Center, and the Art Institute of Chicago.[21] Bryan effectively capitalized on the connections and relationships he fostered in three decades of service to these institutions.

Most important were the networks Bryan developed during the $100 million development campaign for the Chicago Symphony and Lyric Opera. In both that campaign and the one for Millennium Park, the Sara Lee executive established a "blue ribbon committee" of civic and corporate leaders to jump-start the initial support. Bryan also recognized that Chicago's cultural institutions were in the midst of a fundraising renaissance. From 1989 to 1999, fifteen of Chicago's major nonprofit institutions raised nearly $1 billion. In addition to the Symphony and the Lyric, the Museum of Science and Industry, the Field Museum of Natural History, and the Art Institute raised in excess of $100 million each. This was no small feat; Chicago's cultural institutions grew and expanded at the very moment that national giving declined. In other cities, like Cleveland, Detroit, and Philadelphia, leading museums nearly closed and needed bailout campaigns to keep their doors open.[22]

Bryan's network of philanthropic service proved to be a key element in generating support for Millennium Park. While Bryan knew some donors through service on corporate boards—Newton and Josephine Minow (Sara Lee), Verne Istock (First Chicago), Richard Thomas (First Chicago), and Patrick Ryan (First Chicago)—many others he met through his civic activity and philanthropy. Bryan knew at least twenty-five individual donors from serving as a Chicago Symphony Orchestra trustee (fourteen more served on the Lyric board),[23] while twenty-three donors and representatives from six corporate and foundation donors served as Art Institute trustees. At least another nine donors volunteered on various Art Institute committees. Some donors—Wes Dixon, Marshall Field, Cindy Pritzker, Dan Searle, and William Wood Prince—had worked with Bryan as far back as 1985.[24]

In certain respects, Millennium Park's donor group illustrates how Chicago's nonprofit, philanthropic world is organized like a series of interlocking directorships. In addition to the large, overlapping numbers involved in the Art Institute and Symphony, at least thirty-six were trustees of the University of Chicago or Northwestern University,[25] eleven were trustees at the Museum of Contemporary Art,[26] and forty-eight were members of the Commercial Club of Chicago. Every corporation that contributed to Millennium Park included a member of the Commercial Club. Only four of the major foundations had no representation in the organization.[27]

Collectively, the donors displayed a long and ongoing commitment to Chicago's artistic, educational, and cultural institutions. In addition to serving as directors or trustees of numerous cultural institutions, most of the donors gave millions of dollars over the years to many Chicago institutions. In one year alone, for example, twenty-nine donated more than $1,000 each to the Chicago Humanities Festival.[28] Because of their lifelong devotion to building cultural institutions in the United States, six donors had been elected to the American Academy of Arts & Sciences.[29]

Equally important, Bryan knew many of the donors personally: Debby and Ned Jannotta, Ira Harris, Ben Heineman, Vernon Loucks, Martha and John Mabie, Eleanor and William Wood Prince, and Oprah Winfrey. James Zennie was a neighbor in Lake Forest, while Jim and Suzie Otterbeck (Verizon Communications) were friends of Bryan's daughter Margaret French.[30] Perry and Marty Granoff were personal friends of Bryan from New York: "I just told him to give me $1 million and he gave me $1 million," Bryan explained.[31] Out of 115 known donors, Bryan knew more than half in a personal, professional or civic capacity.[32]

Bryan's fundraising acumen impressed even his corporate peers. Former CEOs Richard Thomas and James O'Connor each noted that most people despise fundraising. But Bryan was different; simply put, claimed O'Connor, "John Bryan is not afraid to ask for money."[33] Others, like Bryan's cochair in the campaign, Donna LaPietra, raved: "It's wonderful to work with a man who thinks that raising $30 million is a very easy job."[34]

Marshall Field V, long on experience at fundraising for Chicago nonprofit organizations, expressed surprise over "the broad swath" of contributors. In previous campaigns for the Lincoln Park Zoo or the Art Institute, Field remembered identifying certain patrons to ask for major contributions. "You don't go to everybody," he explained. But for Millennium Park, virtually all Chicago institutions and families were approached. "That for me was new," claimed Field. Even more astounding was the response: no more than 20 percent of the approximately 120 individuals and corporations approached decided against contributing to the building of Millennium Park.[35] Bryan, proclaimed Wrigley Company Foundation president William Piet, "was probably the only one that could have carried this off."[36]

Equally significant was Bryan's capacity to overcome any partisan political divisions between Democrats and Republicans. Bryan was and remains an active member of the Democratic Party. He was an early supporter of Bill Clinton's presidential campaign in 1992 and helped organize corporate support for Clinton in Chicago. Upon Clinton's election, rumors floated around Chicago that Bryan was under consideration for a cabinet position as U.S. secretary of commerce.[37] Bryan's Democratic proclivities alienated few potential donors—Republican supporters outnumbered Democrats by a rough ratio of three to two.[38] If the Millennium Park donors represented an important element of Chicago's global elite, it was an elite in which partisan political divisions were less important than supporting a large and expensive cultural project that promised to enhance Chicago's international visibility and reputation.

Bryan's ability to minimize partisan, political conflict was also related, in part, to Chicago's economic health. A Brookings Institution report in 2000 revealed that Chicago and New York were the only American metropolitan areas where the majority of commercial and office space was located in the central downtown core.[39] In certain regards, Chicago enjoys advantages found in other global cities: a center for finance and related business services such as insurance, real estate, accounting, and law; a concentrated location for these services; and a market for the innovations produced by the financial and service sectors.[40] For businesses devoted to finance, insurance, real estate, law, accounting, engineering, and management services, Millennium Park presented an attractive investment toward improving both the value of downtown real estate and the quality of life in the Loop and vicinity.

The donor list also displayed a paradox of the global economy: a more globalized economy generates more concentration and agglomeration of central functions to a few cities, resulting in the disappearance of certain once-dominant firms. After making their million-dollar commitment, several corporate donors were purchased by competitors and no longer exist: Bank One became part of J. P. Morgan Chase, headquartered in New York; Amoco became part of British Petroleum; and Ameritech merged with SBC in Texas. Another—Arthur Andersen—was rocked by the accounting scandal involving the Enron Corporation and was reduced to a fraction of its original size. Significantly, both Harris Bank and LaSalle Bank were subsidiaries of larger, foreign-based financial institutions (the Bank of Montreal and ABN Amro of the Netherlands, respectively). Millennium Park was not simply a product of the forces associated with globalization, but a reflection of the impact of globalization on local business and politics.

These global conglomerations were replicated elsewhere in Chicago's metropolitan economy. The Chicago Board of Trade, once the world's biggest futures exchange, ranked fourth or fifth at the time of Millennium Park's opening. During the 1990s, Marshall Field's department store was swallowed up by Target Corporation of Minneapolis, Morton Salt by Rohm & Haas, Helene Curtis by Unilever, and Quaker Oats by Pepsi. Advertising agency Leo Burnett became a unit of the Publicis Group of France. Banking, the once defining activity of LaSalle Street, no longer defined that thoroughfare. Northern Trust, specializing in asset management, was the only sizable bank headquartered in Chicago.[41]

Bryan recognized that this pattern of mergers and acquisitions influenced Millennium Park fundraising. During an earlier period, institutions like the Board of Trade, Morton Salt, Leo Burnett, and Quaker Oats most likely would have participated. Kraft Foods Incorporated—the largest food company in the United States and based in the Chicago region—illustrated this point. Bryan solicited Kraft officials, but was rebuffed primarily because the company was owned by Philip Morris in New York. "We didn't get them in the Lyric Opera campaign, and we didn't get them in this," lamented Bryan. Since the philanthropic purse strings were controlled in New York, million-dollar gifts were simply too large for local representatives to approve. "It really makes a difference where the headquarters are," observed Bryan.[42]

Some worried about the philanthropic implications of this globalization. Field Museum president John McCarter, for example, expressed concern about the exodus of corporate offices. Great pockets of private wealth existed in the Chicago area, admitted McCarter, but he wondered, "is there really enough here to enable these institutions to flourish?" For McCarter and other cultural leaders, the question was complicated by how far and how much they would have to "reach outside the Chicago footprint" in their search for financial support to fulfill their missions.[43]

Bryan also admitted that the campaign for Millennium Park occurred at the opportune moment. The United States economy was nearing the end of the single longest expansion in the country's history. From 1980 to 2004, Chicago's economy added 1 million jobs, while the Dow Jones Industrial Average rose eightfold. During the 1990s, the city's gross regional product grew nearly 34 percent to $335 billion, outpacing the larger metropolitan economies of New York and Los Angeles (which grew at rates of 22 and 7 percent, respectively). Metropolitan Chicago's gross regional product of $350 billion by 2002 ranked eighteenth in the world, ahead of Russia, Taiwan, and Switzerland.[44]

Evidence of this economic strength was the 50 percent growth in family foundations created in Illinois from 1993 to 1996, something Bryan was well informed about from his own corporate and fundraising experiences. Nationwide, the number of family foundations rose from 18,276 in 1998 to more than 29,400 in 2002, a 61 percent increase. These family foundations represented more than half of all independent foundations and accounted for similar shares of independent foundations' giving, assets, and new gifts and bequests from donors.[45] By the end of the campaign, Bryan had generated grants from 18 of the top 50 foundations in Illinois, including the three largest in Chicago: the John D. and Catherine T. MacArthur Foundation, the Robert R. McCormick Tribune Foundation, and Chicago Community Trust (see appendix 10).[46]

All of this changed by 2002. The nation's longest economic expansion in history was over. The stock market was in decline. And the Illinois economy was in the doldrums, occupying the lowest quintile of domestic growth among the fifty U.S. states. Over the ensuing year, numerous cultural institutions projected budget deficits: the Lyric Opera ($1 million), the Chicago Symphony Orchestra ($4–5 million), the San Francisco Opera ($9–10 million), and others. Bryan admitted he was a lucky man. If the campaign had been launched after the year 2000, he never would have raised the money.[47]

Chapter 10

CONFLICT AND CONTROVERSY

John Bryan undoubtedly shared Daniel Burnham's philosophy to "make no small plans." But Mies van der Rohe liked to remind architects and planners that "God is in the details," and the details surrounding Millennium Park's cost generated media controversy and public recrimination. In fact, they transformed the public debate on Millennium Park.

On Sunday, August 5, 2001, the Chicago *Tribune* headline blared: "Millennium Park flounders as deadlines, budget blown." Journalists Andrew Martin and Laurie Cohen stated that Millennium Park was not only late in completion and vastly over budget, but had become "an expensive public-works debacle" characterized by "haphazard planning, design snafus and cronyism."[1]

On the face of it, such criticism was hardly unprecedented. For some, this was "business as usual," a reflection of Chicago's tradition of construction cost overruns. The Thompson State of Illinois Center (1985), for example, was expected to cost $75 million to $83 million; the final price was $173 million. Similarly, the first McCormick Place expansion from 1984 to 1986 opened late and $60 million over the initial budget estimate of $252 million.[2]

But with Millennium Park, charges of nepotism and municipal malfeasance more than dogged the Daley administration over the next three years; they shaped much of the public's perception of the project prior to completion in 2004. On January 13, 2002, for example, another Sunday *Tribune* headline proclaimed "Millennium Park Fund Fails." Reporters complained that Daley promised that Millennium Park would be built without any property tax money; yet, the *Tribune* argued, the Central Loop Tax Increment Fund [TIF] was just that—a property tax. Worse yet, the project's original price tag of $150 million had ballooned to $370 million.[3] Others, like David Roeder, described Millennium Park as "the biggest boondoggle of the Daley administration." Journalist Steve Rhodes, employing the moniker most often associated with McCormick Center, now lumped Millennium Park and the renovated Soldier Field as "the so-called Mistakes by the Lake." Civic groups like the Metropolitan Tenants Organization complained that TIF funds were intended to redevelop "blighted" areas, not benefit well-to-do downtown luxury apartment dwellers and condominium owners.[4]

The most piercing attack came one month before Millennium Park opened. A *Tribune* editorial on June 17, 2004, complained that Daley failed to address corruption with the same enthusiasm as school reform, downtown redevelopment, or economic growth. "We don't have a federal secretary of integrity to come into town and tell the rest of the nation that Chicago is one of the most corrupt cities in America," editorialized the *Tribune*, "if not the most corrupt city in America." Three days before Millennium Park opened, the *New York Times* featured a national report on the project, while quoting the *Tribune* editorial. For better or worse, the Millennium Park project now symbolized the inspirational vision and "I Will" forbearance of mayor Richard M. Daley, and what critics described as the underside of his legacy.[5]

Daley fumed at these charges. They even clouded his judgment. Two weeks after the initial *Tribune* story in 2001, the mayor blamed Frank Gehry. "We are still waiting for Frank Gehry's design," he told reporters at the Lane Technical High School graduation. "He has to get going and be committed on that. The longer he delays, his contract keeps going up, and that has been the problem."[6]

Upon hearing Daley's allegations, Gehry and his associates were livid. Not only had they submitted the drawings a year earlier, but they were nearly finished with the bridge drawings. "It's conventional illiteracy to blame the architect for all cost overruns," Gehry later complained. Gehry's team of architects more than just completed the music pavilion drawings on time; according to one Millennium Park official, they speeded up the process to accommodate the project's timetable.[7]

Two years later, the incident remained a sore point for Gehry. The architect recounted how he invited Daley to his studio and went over the pavilion and bridge designs with the mayor during the 2000 Democratic Party convention in Los Angeles. Daley never hinted at any displeasure. "For him to say that seemed . . ." Gehry never finished his sentence. "He has never apologized really. I guess mayors don't apologize."[8]

Gehry's irritation was magnified by a larger concern. In the United States, he complained, "the culture is that if anything goes wrong you blame the architect. The costs go up, you blame the architect. The schedule goes wrong, you blame the architect. If your wife gets sick, you blame the architect. There's war in Iraq, you blame the architect." Architects simply present an easy target because their work is so visible. "I don't know why we put up with it. . . . Ungrateful bastards."[9]

Richard Daley probably wondered how such a visionary public project with an unprecedented number of renowned, international artists and inspirational designs had come to such an impasse. Here was a project that cost the average Chicago resident virtually nothing; yet, he was now being lumped with ghosts of Chicago's corruption-plagued past.

Two words best explained this: fast track. Daley wanted Millennium Park and he wanted it quick. Early in 1998, he instructed city contractors and officials to complete the project in time to celebrate the new millennium in the year 2000. This required putting the project on a "fast track," a construction industry term employed when building starts before the ultimate design specifications are finalized. Instead, detailed drawings are completed in phases as the project moves forward.[10] On May 14, 1998, six weeks after Daley publicly announced the project, the Chicago Plan Commission approved the Lakefront Millennium Project.[11] A week later, the Chicago City Council approved plans to float $150 million in bonds. The Chicago Department of Transportation was named to oversee the project.[12]

Then the problems began. The city quickly awarded a $6 million design contract—some labeled it the largest "no-bid contract" in city history—to Lakefront Millennium Managers, a team of local firms led by McDonough & Associates (engineering), and twelve subcontractors, including Kenny Construction and SOM.[13] Some charged that the contract was "cronyism"—that James McDonough benefited from his relationship with Daley advisor Ed Bedore. Many years earlier, McDonough had been commissioner of the Department of Streets and Sanitation while Bedore was budget director during the administration of Richard J. Daley in the 1960s.[14] McDonough was on the job for eight months before a construction manager was hired to keep tabs on Millennium Park for the city, normally the first hired in such a complex project.[15] Most important, construction began in September 1998, long before anyone knew what was going to be in the park on top of the garage.

Six months later, in March 1999, the project looked very different. Park planners returned to the Chicago Plan Commission and submitted a revised plan with nine significant changes in the park's design and configuration:

1   The rebuilding of the Grant Park North Garage was incorporated into the project. The garage was in such deteriorating condition (temporary timber beams were supporting certain parts of it) that the entire structure needed to be rebuilt.[16]

2   The Montgomery Ward Gardens above the Grant Park North Garage were added to Millennium Park, thereby increasing the project's acreage nearly 50 percent, from 16.5 to 24.5 acres.

3   The two entrances and two exit ramps to the Grant Park North Garage on Michigan Avenue between Washington and Madison Streets were consolidated and moved to the center of Michigan Avenue.

4   The Music and Dance Theater was added to Millennium Park, resulting in the elimination of six pavilions and kiosks (totaling 13,300 square feet) and the addition of a 5,000-square-foot entrance for the theater along Randolph Street.

5   Since most of the 1,500-seat Music and Dance Theater was below the surface grade of the park, the city lost 300 parking spaces, from 4,600 to 4,300 (2,500 beneath Millennium Park and 1,800 beneath Grant Park North Garage).

6   At the suggestion of project director Ed Uhlir, the ice rink and plaza fronting Randolph Street were relocated to a more accessible location on Michigan Avenue.[17]

7   The proposed outdoor amphitheater was eliminated in order to increase the capacity of the Great Lawn.

8   An under-plaza-level commuter bike facility was added in the northeast corner of the park.

9   A variety of retaining walls and stairways were eliminated throughout the park, while additional ramps to improve pedestrian access were introduced.[18]

{ OVER }

10.1. The Conceptual Site Plan approved by the Chicago Plan Commission on May 14, 1998, was limited to only 16 acres and was modest in scope.

10.2. By contrast, the revised plan submitted to and accepted by the commission in March 1999 incorporated A. Montgomery Ward Gardens, relocated the skating rink, and introduced the Music and Dance Theater into the project.

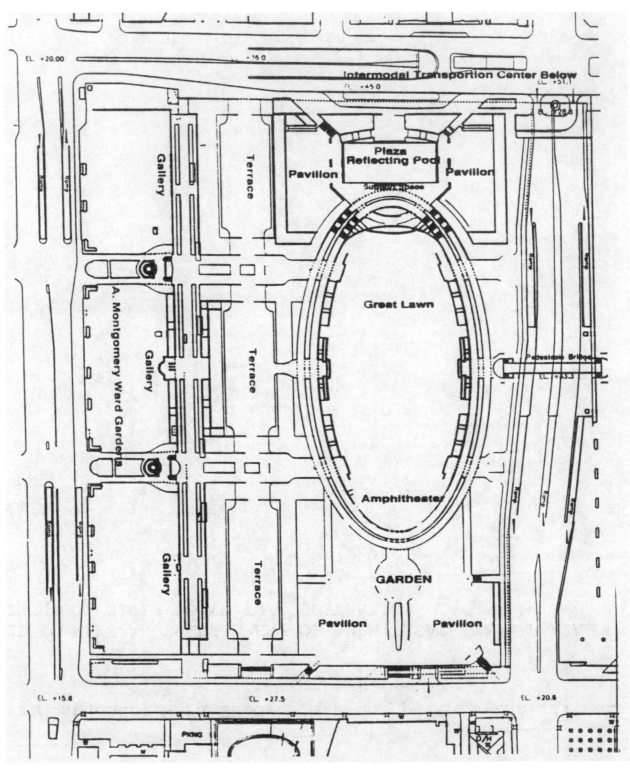

10.1

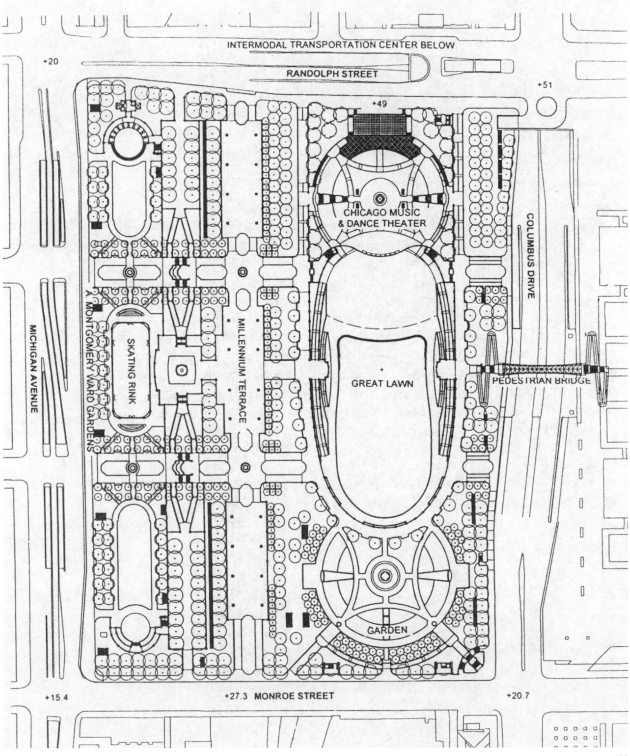

INTERMODAL TRANSPORTATION CENTER BELOW

RANDOLPH STREET

+20

+51

+49

CHICAGO MUSIC & DANCE THEATER

COLUMBUS DRIVE

MICHIGAN AVENUE

A MONTGOMERY WARD GARDENS

SKATING RINK

MILLENNIUM TERRACE

GREAT LAWN

PEDESTRIAN BRIDGE

GARDEN

+15.4

+27.3 MONROE STREET

+20.7

10.2

By September 1998, when Ed Uhlir became project director, these changes were already complicating budget issues. Uhlir quickly realized that the SOM master plan was expensive. The decorative fixtures and granite surfaces, in particular, increased the cost. Disagreements between Millennium Park officials and SOM regarding design and costs were so strained that the architectural firm of O'Donnell Wicklund Pigozzi & Peterson was awarded the contracts to design the peristyle and ice skating rink. At one point, Uhlir handed a copy of the plan to one consultant with the orders to "cut as much money out of this as you can without compromising the design intent."[19]

But the private-sector donor group led by John Bryan was simultaneously working in a contrary direction. Relying upon a budget associated with SOM's original master plan, Bryan assumed that the city would pay a certain amount for infrastructures. If he raised anything above the $30 million from donors, that "excess money" could be applied to other enhancements that were more expensive than originally anticipated. Complicating matters, many of the initial cost projections for the enhancements were too low. "I had to convince them that they needed more than $1 million for the ice skating rink," remembers Ed Uhlir, "that we needed $3.5 million out of the $5 million donation they got from McCormick [Tribune Foundation] and they could take that $1.5 million and apply it to something else because *that* was the real cost of building an ice skating rink." The initial estimates that SOM provided, added Uhlir, "were difficult to overcome [to] convince John Bryan and others that the city wasn't inflating costs."[20]

In essence, no one clearly or precisely defined what a private-sector donation would cover and what parts of the underground infrastructure were the purview of the city. Municipal authorities recognized their responsibility to construct the underground garage; but if a 110-ton sculpture were plopped on top, who paid for the added structural support? Or if a cantilevered, steel music pavilion were incorporated into the park, who was responsible for strengthening underground caissons? If the fountain needed underground rooms for infrastructure, who compensated the city for the lost parking spaces and revenue? No one had ready answers.

At the same time, Uhlir had to find a way to ensure that the project remained on the fast track with a completion date in the year 2000, a hasty process that inevitably generated inflated costs. In his discussions with Bryan and his fundraising team, Uhlir realized that certain enhancements were going to be added to the park, most of which would be subsidized by the private sector. Uhlir, in effect, faced an impossible task: cut costs, speed up the project, and then add expensive amenities to the park.

Over the ensuing three years, Uhlir was confronted with some mammoth enhancements. The music pavilion, initially expected to cost $10 million in 1998, grew in cost when the pavilion foundation had to be strengthened to accommodate the addition of Gehry's steel-constructed, cantilevered proscenium and headdress. In January 2000, workers built seventeen additional caissons to support the Gehry structure. Three months later, they had to cut off the tops of other caissons to accommodate more changes.[21] In the end, the music pavilion's cost exceeded $60 million.[22]

Similarly, public sculpture in the park was originally budgeted at $600,000.[23] In 2000, engineers realized that the weight of Anish Kapoor's sculpture required additional underground bracing. That meant going back and shoring up the foundations in the garage. The 60-ton sculpture eventually grew to 110 tons, necessitating more support columns and walls underneath. The final cost was in excess of $20 million.[24]

Some of these problems were simply unavoidable. Gehry and his partners warned Uhlir and Bryan that it was impossible to build the music pavilion for only $15 million. According to Craig Webb, "we told the clients that the budget that they were proposing was inadequate to meet the expectations of what they were asking us to do." A more realistic figure was $45 million. "We try to meet budgets, but usually, if we think we can't, we'll tell people," claimed Gehry. Before construction ever begins, the architect explained, they price the project. But too often, lamented Gehry, clients urge him to proceed and "see what comes out."[25]

The changes above ground wreaked havoc underneath. The parking garage and bridge over the Metra tracks were originally expected to cost $66 million. In 1999, only two firms submitted bids, and the lower one from Harston/Schwendener (H/S) was 20 percent over the city's estimate. Rather than rebid the project, the city negotiated with H/S to do it for $72 million.[26]

The garage was also a complicated piece of engineering. In order to allow commuter trains to continue running, McDonough engineers designed and built caissons between railroad tracks. Another difficulty was that the new electrical system had to be constructed before demolishing the old one. Engineers then built a 1,200-foot, underground, bridgelike steel structure running from Randolph Street on the north to Monroe Street on the south, and spanning 120 feet from east to west. All the beams were designed with an arch, known as a camber, that flattened from the weight of park's stone and soil on top.[27] "I don't know anywhere else in the country where they were able to accomplish an engineering-type project that would actually span such a width and allow a commuter station to remain functioning twenty-four hours a day," project director Michael Hannemann later reported. "I actually got calls from people in New York and Philadelphia" asking how Chicago did it.[28]

But the rapidly changing park design above ground eventually generated problems with the garage construction. In November 1998, one month after building began, project engineers issued new designs for all the caissons, calling for more and bigger structures that added months to the job. The pattern continued: in less than a year, the city issued over 1,000 design revisions, forcing Harston/Schwendener to incur ever-increasing costs. After the contractor asked for $58 million to compensate for the changes, the city fired the firm in June 2000 for "arbitrary work-week reductions" and "schedule slippage." A month later, Daley administration officials shifted control from the Chicago Department of Transportation to the Public Building Commission, which in turn replaced Lakefront Millennium Managers with another construction management firm. Almost immediately, G. M. Harston sued the city in federal court.[29]

Harston's attorneys later claimed in a brief filed in U.S. District Court that Harston officials secretly tape-recorded five city officials at the June 1, 2000, meeting, including Stan Kaderbek, a deputy commissioner in the city's Department of Transportation and a former supervisor on the Millennium Park project. "We will compensate you for every dollar you have spent . . . with markup and profit," Kaderbek reportedly promised. Kaderbek flatly denied making such a commitment.[30]

Media reports claimed that the change did not staunch the fiscal bleeding. The joint venture contractor (Walsh Construction and II in One Contractors) that replaced Harston/Schwendener received $21 million, 40 percent over the original bid.[31]

While these charges remained unproven and subject to court action when Millennium Park opened in 2004, other problems were documented. The caisson contract, for example, reportedly went 150 percent over budget. Estimators allegedly failed to accurately calculate the amount of cement necessary for the "bells" or upper supports in the garage columns, which led to the added expense.[32] When the garage was nearly completed, contractors discovered columns cracking because they were too rigid to allow for movement of the concrete floors. McDonough took the blame for the design error and paid about $1 million to repair about 10 percent of the garage's columns.[33]

Adding fuel to the media fire was the slow growth of garage revenues. In the first year of operation, the garage revenues failed to meet predictions. The parking facility needed $725,868 in monthly income to cover debt payments (or $8.7 million annually). The best month was December 2001, when income totaled $349,576.[34] Only by the end of 2002, with 2,181 spaces (down from 2,500 at start of project) finally completed and available, did the net Millennium Park garage revenue for 2002 surpass $4 million. Yet the $7.5 million collected in 2004 still failed to cover bond payments, forcing the city to dip into a reserve fund.[35]

Millennium Park officials recognized that the changing dynamics of the park plan were the cause of the ballooning budget. "The change orders, once we decided to shoot [for] the moon, were huge," admitted executive committee member Marshall Field V. The city, Field added, was "taking a licking for something that really isn't a hundred percent their fault." Richard Thomas, another committee member, agreed that Daley was blamed for developments that were beyond his control. "We did not plan as astutely as we should have," Thomas conceded, primarily because the project expanded in scope. Attorney Jack Guthman willingly conceded that the failure of the fast-track process was a legitimate criticism, but hardly corruption. Daley "had a vision," believed Guthman. "You take risks sometimes. There's nothing nefarious about that."[36]

To help offset some of the escalating costs, Millennium Park and city officials arrived at what Ed Uhlir called an "educated guess"—$5.4 million—which the private donors contributed for "base park improvements." These included the added costs related to the music pavilion, Kapoor's sculpture, the peristyle structure, and the underground supports for the garden.[37]

Skidmore, Owings and Merrill's Adrian Smith blamed Bryan's fundraising strategy for the ever-escalating Millennium Park budget. Dividing up the enhancements and giving donors so much control "was a terrible move," charged Smith. "It broke up the continuity of the master plan and it created enormous cost overruns." Smith remembered warning Bryan, "John, you need to give budgets before you go out and have a competition on a piece here or there. You need to tell the artist or the landscaper or the architect what the budget is and you have to meet that budget." Smith believed that when Bryan refused to do that, the construction bids proved to be more expensive. "If he identified a $5 million project, the piece ended up at $15 million, and in many cases, much higher than that," complained Smith. "Fifteen million was set aside for that band shell and Frank's scheme was in excess of $50 million, just for the bandshell."[38]

Frank Gehry and his associates considered the fast-track pace of design and construction a major problem from inception. The initial time frame was simply too ambitious. In December 1998, Uhlir and Feldstein asked if Gehry could complete a design in time for the millennium. The architect was aghast. "Gee, I can't possibly get it done," he exclaimed. "Even in L.A. you couldn't get it done, and in Chicago you certainly couldn't." But Feldstein and Uhlir were so determined to secure Gehry's participation that they gave him the time he needed. Gehry believed he could complete the project by 2001 (and he ultimately did).[39]

Under the pressured circumstances, Gehry and his team of architects moved with great dispatch. They "worked extremely quickly to get this thing done within the time schedule, and that's why this notion that they delayed this project is just not right," believed Millennium Park official James Feldstein. "Not only did they not delay it, but they expedited their part of it."[40]

The growing Millennium Park budget grew more controversial because of a series of projected municipal budget deficits. In August 2003, Daley administration officials feared a potential $116 million budget shortfall in 2004 and threatened to decrease the city workforce to bridge the revenue gap. The projected deficit in the $4.7 billion budget was virtually identical to 2003 estimates, and the city had to resort to "aggressive management and creative cost savings" with no serious consideration of raising taxes or reducing services to residents. While the city made significant cuts through retirements and attrition in 2002, the 2004 budget required "inevitable layoffs," according to budget director William Abolt. Indeed, Daley's administration eliminated 1,000 positions annually in 2001 and 2002.[41]

Others complained about the city's resort to the Central Loop TIF. While TIF funds were technically not "neighborhood taxes," the yearly increment contributed by Loop taxpayers (over $30 million annually since 1994) diverted revenues that could have been distributed to other, needier neighborhoods or services. Furthermore, by shifting Central Loop TIF funds to Millennium Park, the potential amount of surplus money available when the fund expired in 2007 was "seriously reduced," according to the Neighborhood Capital Budget Group.[42]

Finally, city officials were often less than forthcoming on many of the financial details on Millennium Park. In part, this was a product of "donor privacy"—an unwilling-ness to release details on the private gifts for fear that donors or potential donors would be discouraged from contributing to the project. But some officials behaved as if the city had something to hide. Uhlir remembered *Tribune* reporter Andrew Martin confronting him after a public presentation. Uhlir invited him to contact him the next day. But when Martin telephoned, Uhlir gave him the bad news: "You've got to go through the press office." According to Uhlir, city officials "thought it was better to have a central source identify the appropriate spokesperson."[43]

While such behavior generated media suspicion and legitimate public policy ques-tions, news coverage suffered from inaccuracies and sometimes exaggeration. The *Tribune's* August 2001, front-page story, for example, correctly identified dubious con-struction practices on the part of the Daley administration, but suffered from numer-ous errors regarding design. Reporters Andrew Martin and Laurie Cohen, for example, argued that a paved grand promenade (eventually Chase Promenade) was scrapped for a simple sod covering. In fact, the paving of the three-block long promenade was ini-tially supposed to be gravel like Buckingham Fountain Plaza, and grass was a temporary design material. Concrete was later substituted as a donor enhancement, making the promenade better suited for special events. The work, however, could not be completed until the Anish Kapoor sculpture was installed.[44]

The *Tribune* also reported that plans to slope the great lawn were cut for budgetary reasons, making the expanse so flat "that most concertgoers would be unable to see the stage." In reality, the slope, while not as steep as Frank Gehry desired, was more gradual in order to accommodate people with disabilities and allow other lawn-related activities. The journalists also alleged that the fountain lacked a donor, even though the Crown family had agreed in December 1999 to fund a water project in Millennium Park. A month later, Jaume Plensa arrived in Chicago and presented his ultimately successful proposal to the Crown family.[45]

The *Tribune* even belittled the Daley administration's argument that Millennium Park's cost increased when the reconstruction of the Grant Park North Garage was incor-porated into the project. The "claim is hard to defend because contract documents show the park's boundaries have always included the Ward gardens," they argued. Yet publicly released initial plans for the "Lakefront Millennium Project" included only the 16.5 acres from Columbus Drive to and above the Illinois Central Railroad tracks. A. Montgomery Ward Gardens "will continue to be used for recreation, temporary art, and small scale performances," claimed the first published Lakefront Millennium Project newsletter. The *Tribune's* Blair Kamin even described the 16-acre site in his initial review of the project.[46]

The *Tribune's* charges of corruption and cronyism resonated with some, because similar accusations plagued the Daley administration in regard to the city's bidding process. Cleanup contracts to the Duff family's Windy City Maintenance company from 1990 to 1999; the city's hired-truck program; overcharging for automobile towing by En-vironmental Auto Removal; the O'Hare concession licenses to bookseller W. H. Smith,

10.3 | 10.4

McDonalds, and a duty-free shop operator; and the fencing contract to G. F. Structures owned by Richard Crandall pointed to municipal malfeasance within Daley's City Hall.[47] Daley himself took responsibility for some of this.

Yet these examples paled when compared to those in other cities. In 1994, for example, Orange County, California, became the largest municipality in the United States ever to declare bankruptcy after the county treasurer lost $1.7 billion of taxpayer money when he invested in questionable Wall Street securities. Farther south, San Diego suffered from what one observer described as "a thoroughly corrupt [political] community" at the turn of the millennium. Indicted city council members, a public employees' pension fund found to be $1.2 billion in the red, and federal investigations of municipal financial statements pushed that city to the verge of bankruptcy. San Diego, wrote one local observer, was an "open sewer" of corruption and mismanagement. By some accounts, Chicago at the turn of the millennium was less corrupt, especially compared with the period before 1990, when organized crime controlled election and judicial officials. "They knew who they could kill and get away with it," according to convicted mob insider Robert Cooley. Charges that Daley's Chicago was "the most corrupt city in America" seemed more hyperbole than fact.[48]

The sea of negative media coverage of "cost overruns" ignored the source of the problem: the enhancements, or more precisely, new enhancements. The enlarged and dramatically changed designs, spurred by Bryan and his fundraising team, more accurately represented new costs, not cost overruns. A careful examination of the final price tag of Millennium Park shows that the Daley administration, while failing to stay within the original $120 million budget, ultimately spent nearly $269 million for the garage and supporting structure underneath the park, 124 percent over the original estimate.

By contrast, the private sector's decision to "shoot for the moon" and attract world-renowned artists and architects transformed the above-ground budget. Excepting the ice rink, every enhancement was 130 percent or more over the original estimated cost: the peristyle jumped in price from $2 million to $5 million, the sculpture from $5 million

10.3. SOM's initial Lakefront Millennium Park plans included only the 16.5 acres east of Montgomery Ward Gardens.

10.4. The July 1998 issue of *Notes: The Newsletter of the Lakefront Millennium Project* stated that A. Montgomery Ward Gardens "will continue to be used for recreation, temporary art, and small scale performances."

(or $600,000 according to Ed Bedore) to $20 million, the bridge from $5 million to $14.5 million, the garden from $2 million to $13.2 million, and the fountain from $2 million to $17 million. The donors' group increased the endowment from $7 million to $25 million. The addition of the Harris Theater added still another $62 million. Together, the more expensive enhancements alone generated an additional $180 million in costs. In the end, the private sector's $222 million contribution exceeded the original goal of $30 million by 640 percent (see tables 7 and 8).

"Reporters look at the budget and say it's a project out of control," complained Uhlir, "but in reality it's a completely different project—it's bigger and has many more expensive elements which were not calculated in the initial projections."[49] Uhlir pointed out that much of the criticism was old news. "I thought they were just rehashing stories that we'd already been through," he remembered. By 2001, "the city's contribution was still $220 [million], the same as it was a year ago." Indeed, city officials were well aware of the escalating costs early in the project. In the spring of 1999, for example, the city issued $33 million of additional bonds. In June 1999, the bond announcement projected Millennium Park's cost at $234 million. Then in May 2000, the Daley administration took $35 million from the Central Loop TIF, and then another $50 million in 2002. By the end of that year, a total of $95 million from the Central Loop TIF fund was allocated for Millennium Park, according to the Chicago Capital Improvement Plan.[50] In private conversations by the end of 2000, John Bryan accurately predicted that the total cost of the park would be between $400 million and $500 million.

Others complained that much of the media's criticism was short-sighted and failed to consider the larger picture. Randy Mehrberg, a former park district counsel, believed cost increases were no surprise. The original $150 million park was simply "going to be a parking structure with some grass," he pointed out. Architect Laurence Booth reiterated the same: "It changed scope several times, and when that happens you always go over the budget. You decide you're going to build A and you end up building Z, and Z has more to it than A." Booth believed much of the criticism was small-minded and ignored the foresight of Daley and Bryan's collaboration. "The fact that it's over the budget—so what? Maybe it was behind schedule—so what? It's a big deal and it's ambitious."[51]

City officials insisted that Millennium Park would give "added luster to nearby commercial properties, particularly those for overseas investors," thus enhancing the city's tax coffers in the years ahead. Local developers echoed these predictions. Richard Hanson, the lead builder for the Heritage at Millennium Park, a 356-condominium complex overlooking Millennium Park under construction at Wabash and Randolph when the park opened in July 2004, argued that his project added $5 million in new tax revenues to the city. Not only did the park represent "a grand plan," insisted Hanson, but it "was the single biggest factor to take the risk and build something in the Loop." More significant, Millennium Park stimulated additional downtown real estate development. Projects such as 340 on the Park, a 62-story, 343-unit high-rise on Randolph Street by LR Development, and another at 1000 South Michigan Avenue, were started "because of

TABLE 7. PRIVATE-SECTOR ENHANCEMENTS, BUDGET AND COSTS, 1998-2004 (IN $MILLIONS)

	1998	MAY 1999	JUNE 1999	2001	2003	FINAL COST
Total for public and private-sector contributions	150	200[a]	233.85	320[b]	410[c]	484[d]

ENHANCEMENT	MARCH 1998	MAY 1999[e]	FINAL COST[f]
Total	30	69	216.9
Endowment	7	30	25
Music & dance theater (Harris Theater)		36	60[g]
Music pavilion (Jay Pritzker Pavilion)	10	4.5[h]	34.9[i]
Monroe Garden (Lurie Garden)	2	2	13.2
Randolph Garden	2	2	
Public art (*Cloud Gate*)	5–6	5	20[j]
Pavilions (later Exelon Pavilions)			7
Rink (McCormick Tribune Plaza)			3.2
Peristyle (Wrigley Square)	2?	2	5
Fountain (Crown Fountain)	2?	2	17
Bridge (BP Bridge)		5	14.5
Finance cost		6	
Promenade tent system		1	4[k]
Signage		1	
Portable music shell		3	
Bike station		1.5	3.1
Art Institute tunnel		1.5	
Butler Field restoration		3	
Base park improvements			5.4[l]
Sound system enhancements			2.5
Miscellaneous[m]			2.1

[a]Figure based on February 1999 "Approximate Total Cost" table, cited in online *CT*, 23 July 2004, based on City of Chicago, Public Building Commission and Millennium Park, Inc.

[b]Figure based on August 2001 "Approximate Total Cost" table, cited in online *CT*, 23 July 2004, based on City of Chicago, Public Building Commission and Millennium Park, Inc.

[c]Figure based on December 2002 "Approximate Total Cost" table, cited in online *CT*, 23 July 2004, based on City of Chicago, Public Building Commission and Millennium Park, Inc.

[d]This figure exceeds the publicized $475 million because of the additional $9 million added for *Cloud Gate*, which in July 2004 was estimated to cost $11.5 million.

[e]Figures based on "Millennium Park Costs," memo dated 11 May 1999.

[f]Figures based on John Bryan, "Chicago's Millennium Park," Speech at the University of Chicago, 10 Sept. 2003; *CST*, 15 July 2004.

[g]This figure includes the $52.7 million for the cost of construction and $7.3 million for an endowment.

[h]The $4.5 million figure is an incomplete calculation that included only the fees paid to Gehry Associates.

[i]Includes trellis and ribbons ($31.0 million), sound enhancement system ($2.5 million), and seating ($490,000); does not include $25.4 million contribution from the city.

[j]E-mail communication with Rob Omori, 11 January 2006.

[k]Chase Promenade.

[l]This included added costs related to the pavilion, Kapoor's sculpture, the extra structure for the peristyle, and the garden. See Uhlir interview no. 2.

[m]Includes fixed seating ($490,000), demountable fence ($750,000), midlevel terraces ($600,000), graphics ($200,000), furnishings ($100,000).

TABLE 8. RISING COSTS OF ENHANCEMENTS, 1998–2005 (IN $MILLION)

STRUCTURE	ORIGINAL ESTIMATED COST[a]	FINAL COST	DIFFERENCE	INCREASE (%)
Pavilion[b]	10	60	50	500
Theater	0	60	60	
Public Art	5	20[c]	15	300
Bridge	5	14.5	9.5	190
Garden	2	13.2	11.2	560
Fountain	2	17	15	750
Peristyle	2	5	3	150
Ice Rink	2	3.2	1.2	60
Endowment	7	25	18	257
Totals	35	217.9	182.9	523

[a]Figures based on "Millennium Park Costs," memo dated 11 May 1999.

[b]The $60 million final cost is a rounded total of the $34.89 million contribution from the private sector ($31.9 for the trellis and headdress, $2.5 million for the sound enhancement system, and $490,000 for the seating) and $25.4 million from the city.

[c]E-mail communication with Rob Omori, 11 January 2006.

the park," believed Hanson. He had "no doubt" the new tax revenues from the Heritage and other nearby projects would eventually cover the city's TIF expenditures. In less than twenty years, the tax revenues from the Heritage alone would cover the TIF subsidy for Millennium Park.[52]

City officials probably wondered why critics singled out Millennium Park from other Central Loop TIF-funded projects. Between 1998 and 2000, the TIF spent nearly $20 million on four residential tower conversions, including the Fisher Building and the American Youth Hostel. Five hotel projects received over $25 million after 1986. Most expensive were the various TIF subsidies totaling $59 million to the Chicago, Goodman, Oriental, and Palace theaters from 1985 to 2000 to create a downtown entertainment district.[53] Few complained that these expensive residences, hotels, and theaters "seriously reduced" the future surpluses that would be available when the fund expired in 2007. Compared with these largely private and profit-driven projects, Millennium Park's expenditures hardly seemed outlandish.

Few critics acknowledged hidden savings. Ed Bedore, for example, pointed out that inclusion of the Grant Park North Garage represented an enormous savings to taxpayers. Not only did the wall of the severely deteriorating North Garage abut the new garage of Millennium Park, but the air ducts and other infrastructures for the older garage were in part of Millennium Park. Within three years, the entire North Garage would have been replaced, possibly forcing the city to dig up Wrigley Square, McCormick Tribune Plaza, and the *Crown Fountain*. Not only did the city save on the inevitable reconstruction of the North Garage, but they avoided the embarrassing and expensive reconstruction of the western side of Millennium Park.[54]

For all these reasons, the expanding Millennium Park budget was not an "overrun" to Daley, Bryan, and Millennium Park supporters. "It is exactly the opposite," retorted Bryan. "What happened was that the resources became available, practically all from the private sector, to let us do something that is of extraordinary quality and high level of design."[55] The project would inevitably enhance the visibility and reputation of Chicago.

In a letter to major donors and founders of Millennium Park, John Bryan and members of the Millennium Park Executive Committee criticized the *Tribune* and the *Sun-Times* for ignoring how garage expansion and the redesign of the park from the initial plans in 1998 resulted in "obviously" higher costs and a different construction schedule. Bryan reminded donors that Millennium Park was "a work in progress and the final design will bear very little resemblance to the original 1998 concept." Because the goal was to develop a world class design with leading artists and architects "for the long-term benefit of all Chicagoans," construction delays made little difference. "We are philosophical enough to know," lamented Bryan, "that this kind of publicity goes with the territory."[56]

Some historical evidence supported Bryan's view. In 1957, for example, when Danish architect Jorn Utzon was named to design the Sydney Opera House, authorities estimated the facility would take four years and $7 million to build. The opera house did not open until 1973 and cost $102 million, twelve years late and fourteen times more than the original estimated cost. Like Millennium Park, the project suffered from "fast-track construction"—building began before Utzon completed design drawings. The Sydney Opera House is now an international icon, and with an average of three thousand events and two million spectators annually, the busiest performing arts center in the world. The structure is, for some tourists, the only reason to visit Sydney.[57]

More important, the media's focus on cost overruns diverted public attention from the unique qualities of the private fundraising efforts. The $173.5 million raised in private donations for a public park ($235.5 million if the Music and Dance Theater contribution is included) was a rare event. By comparison, when Lillian Disney donated $50 million for the construction of Walt Disney Concert Hall in 1987, she and city officials hoped private fundraising would generate another $60 million for the $110 million project. In 1992, the city of Los Angeles began fast-tracked construction on an underground garage, the fees from which would help subsidize the project. In 1994, however, when the necessary private funds were still not forthcoming from the city's philanthropic and corporate communities, the project halted. Only in 1999, under the leadership of businessman and philanthropist Eli Broad and a new price tag of $275 million, did construction resume.[58]

By contrast, the city of Milwaukee avoided the pitfalls of Los Angeles. In 1993, the city's Museum of Art released modest plans for an $8 million to $10 million addition. But after Spanish architect Santiago Calatrava was recruited in 1995 to design his first building in the United States, he suggested enlarging the project by at least one-third; the budget grew to $35 million. Fundraiser Jack Pelisek generated $30 million in only nine months. Eventually, twenty-three donors gave gifts of $1 million or more. Upon opening in October 2001, Calatrava's design with its signature Burke Brise Soleil brought

TABLE 9. A COMPARISON OF RECENTLY CONSTRUCTED CULTURAL CENTERS

VENUE	YEAR PROPOSED	ESTIMATED COST ($MILLIONS)	YEAR COMPLETED	YEARS TO BUILD	FINAL COST ($MILLIONS)
Sydney Opera House	1957	7	1973	16	102
Meyerson Symphony Center, Dallas	1982	47.7	1989	7	81.5 or 157
New Jersey Performing Arts Center, Newark	1987[a]		1997	10	187
Museum of Art addition, Milwaukee	1993	10	2001	8	120
Benaroya Hall, Seattle	1995	118	1998	3	118
Millennium Dome, London	1997	525[b]	2000	3	1,200[b]
Kimmel Center for the Performing Arts, Philadelphia	1998	245	2001	3	265
Disney Concert Hall, Los Angeles,	1987	110 (plus garage)	2003	16	384 (includes $110 million garage)
Millennium Park, Chicago	1998	150	2004	6	475
Music Center at Strathmore, North Bethesda, Maryland	2001	68	2005	4	98.6
Performing Arts Center, Miami, Florida	2001	255	2006?	5?	412[b]

SOURCES: Laurie Shulman, *The Meyerson Symphony Center: Building a Dream* (Denton, Tex., 2000), 142, 150, 269–70, 345; Deborah Wilk, "Winged Victory," *Chicago Magazine*, Sept. 2003; "A New Museum," *Milwaukee Journal Sentinel*, 7 Oct. 2001 ($100 million cost); *New York Times*, 8 May 2003; *The Richard B. Fisher Center for the Performing Arts at Bard College* (pamphlet, 2003); "The Sydney Opera House," at http://www.anzac.com/aust/nsw/soh.html; http://www.bizjournals.com/seattle/stories/1998/11/16/newscolumn3.html; http://www.kimmelcenter.org/news/item.php?item=2001-03-20; *Dance Magazine*, Dec. 1999 (Royal Opera House), at: http://www.findarticles.com/p/articles/mi_m1083/is_12_73/ai_58050360; *Washington Post*, 3 Feb. 2005 (Strathmore); *Washington Times*, 5 Feb. 2005 (Strathmore) http://www.miamidade.gov/pac/synopsis.htm; http://www.miamitodaynews.com/news/040311/story1.shtml; Fred Tasker, "Commission to decide on who will run PAC," *Miami Herald*, 27 July 2004, at: http://www.miami.com/mld/miamiherald/entertainment/9250261.htm

[a]1993 construction.　　[b]Approximation.

international acclaim to the city. By then, the cost had risen to $120 million, more than tenfold the initial projection.[59] Similar stories were repeated about cultural centers constructed in Dallas, Miami, and Newark during the 1990s (see table 9).[60]

IN 2002, BRYAN PREDICTED that the increased costs and use of TIF funds will represent "the biggest part of trivia" twenty years from now.[61] Only time will tell. But the completion of the park did resolve some earlier tensions. The disagreements between Richard Daley and Frank Gehry were eventually seen as "constructive tension," in the words of Thomas Pritzker. Richard Daley never formally apologized to Frank Gehry; perhaps it was unnecessary. In extemporaneous remarks at the dedication dinner for the BP Bridge in the Jay Pritzker Pavilion on May 22, 2004, Frank Gehry declared that Richard M. Daley was "the most extraordinary mayor in the world."[62]

Chapter 11

DEFINING ART

The media's attention on the escalating costs of Millennium Park deflected attention from two of the most problematic elements in the park's creation: finding a sponsor for the garden and the unprecedented height of Frank Gehry's music pavilion.

Early in 1999, Patrick and Shirley Ryan elected not to support the Millennium Park garden. John Bryan was disappointed, both because the Ryans' tentative commitment was the first major gift he had secured for the park, and because the Ryans were close personal friends. For the next three years, Bryan pursued an up-and-down adventure in search of a new garden sponsor. Ironically, when the Chicago *Tribune* published its indicting, front-page story on Millennium Park in August 2001, reporters claimed that Bryan had found no donor for the fountain. In fact, the Crown family had agreed to fund such a project in Millennium Park in December 1999.[1] It was the garden that lacked a benefactor.

But Bryan was not easily discouraged; out of this failure, he reached for a better alternative: an international competition. On July 17, 2000, Millennium Park, Inc., with the sponsorship of the Richard H. Driehaus Foundation, issued invitations with a $10,000 honorarium to seventeen selected landscape architects, garden designers, and planning firms to submit proposals for a garden. The challenge described by the prospectus was daunting: to provide for a changing and "extraordinary flora display" all year-round, thereby accommodating Richard Daley's wish for a year-round park; to include plants not found in other Chicago gardens; to be flexible enough to accommodate large crowds after concerts and small ones on a Sunday morning; to comply with the Americans with Disabilities Act; and to fit into the surrounding environment of Grant Park, including the new enhancements in Millennium Park. In the end, eleven projects were submitted and judged.[2]

The winning proposal was the Shoulder Garden, designed by the international team of Kathryn Gustafson from Paris and Seattle, Piet Oudolf from the Netherlands, and Robert Israel of Los Angeles. Garden critics raved about the design; the jury described it as "bold, intellectual, daring, cutting edge." Equally impressive, the Shoulder Garden combined Gustafson's expertise in landscape design and spatial structure, Oudolf's on horticulture, and Israel's on theater lighting.[3]

Despite the critical acclaim of the Shoulder Garden design, Bryan and his commit-

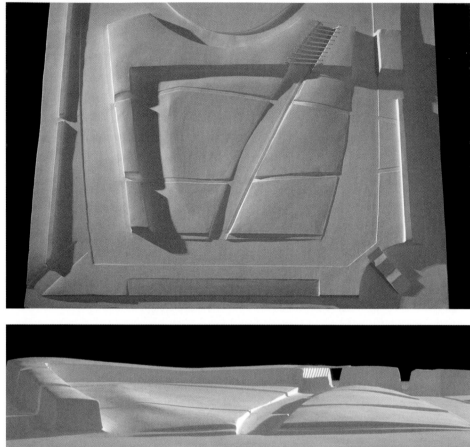

11.1, 11.2. Early models of *The Shoulder Garden* design.

11.1

11.2

tee of fundraisers were frustrated in finding a suitable sponsor. Part of the problem, admitted Bryan, was "we had a more ambitious garden than we had before." Whereas other enhancements, such as the peristyle, the skating rink, the promenade, and the pedestrian bridge, were estimated to cost about $5 million, Bryan realized he needed a gift twice that amount for the garden.[4] Like the other enhancements, Bryan's ambitious vision proved more expensive than originally planned.

Over the next several years, Bryan approached a number of potential sponsors. "I had it sold to Allstate [Insurance Company] for about six months," recounted Bryan, "and then they backed out, so we had to start over." Bryan then entertained Jules and Maggie Knapp with the possibility of making the garden a memorial to their deceased daughter. Finally, Bryan arranged a lunch with Cindy Pritzker and the philanthropist Ann Lurie. Trained as a pediatric nurse, Lurie was president of the Ann and Robert H. Lurie Foundation, an institution she created in the wake of her husband's premature death in 1990. "We didn't talk about the garden," Bryan remembered. "We talked mostly about her work in Kenya."[5]

But Lurie was interested in Millennium Park. After several additional discussions, Bryan arranged a meeting with Kathryn Gustafson and Lurie. "She never said no," Bryan remarked, and in May 2003, Bryan secured a verbal promise from Lurie to provide a $10 million endowment for the garden.[6]

The Lurie name was not as well known in Chicago as Pritzker or Crown, but Ann Lurie was arguably just as generous with her wealth. Her husband, Robert Lurie, had run Equity Group Investments with Sam Zell during the 1970s and 1980s, during which time Ann had raised six children. After Robert's unexpected death, Ann Lurie became an internationally known humanitarian and philanthropist, giving away over $144 million by 2004. At the University of Michigan, her husband's alma mater, she subsidized the construction of the Robert H. Lurie Engineering Center, the Ann and Robert H. Lurie Tower, the Samuel Zell and Robert H. Lurie Institute for Entrepreneurial Studies, and a new biomedical engineering facility. In Chicago, Lurie endowed the Robert H. Lurie Comprehensive Cancer Center of Northwestern University, funded the completion of the center's new outpatient unit, and provided the lead gift for the Robert H. Lurie Medical Research Center on the Feinberg School of Medicine campus. Lurie's additional gifts to Chicago include cornerstone funding for the Greater Chicago Food Depository Capital

TABLE 10. A SAMPLING OF LURIE FAMILY PHILANTHROPY

STRUCTURE OR INSTITUTION	LOCATION	YEAR OF GIFT	ESTIMATED VALUE OF GIFT
Robert H. Lurie Cancer Center	Northwestern University	1992	$12 million[a]
Robert H. Lurie Engineering Center[b]	University of Michigan	1993	$12 million
Ann & Robert Lurie Tower[b]	University of Michigan	1993	
Marion Elizabeth Blue Endowed Professor of Children and Families[b]	University of Michigan		
Giza Plateau Mapping Project[c]	Egypt	1997–1999	
Sam Zell & Robert Lurie School of Entrepreneurship	University of Michigan	1999	$5 million[b]
Diana, Princess of Wales, Professor of Cancer Research	Northwestern University		$1 million[d]
Greater Chicago Food Depository	Chicago	2001	$5 million[d,e]
Robert H. Lurie Medical Research Center	Northwestern University	2001	$40 million[f]
College of Engineering[g]	University of Michigan	2002	$25 million
Music and Dance Theater	Chicago	2003?	$1 million[e]
Millennium Park	Chicago	2004	$10 million

[a]*Crain's Chicago Business*, 6 Sept. 2004.   [b]*University of Michigan Record*, 19 July 1999, at: http://www.umich.edu/~urecord/9899/Jul19_99/3.htm.
[c]http://www.fas.harvard.edu/~aera/Giza_Pages/Aeragram_Pages/AERAG3_1/LurieGrant.html.
[d]http://www.suntimes.com/special_sections/powerful_women/philanthropy_lurie.html.
[e]http://philanthropy.com/free/articles/v15/i09/09002401.htm.   [f]http://www.feinberg.northwestern.edu/about/lurie_building.htm.
[g]*University of Michigan Record*, 22 July 2002, at: http://www.umich.edu/~urecord/0102/Jul22_02/2.htm.

11.3. Ann Lurie and her children dedicating Lurie Garden, with Richard M. Daley and John Bryan standing in the rear.

Campaign, along with a major gift to the Joan and Irving Harris Music and Dance Theater. In Africa, she funded the construction of twenty rural schools in Ethiopia, and conceived of and implemented AIDS Village Clinics, Inc., in Kenya. In 2003, Lurie ranked among the top fifty philanthropists in the United States.[7]

On August 25, 2003, Lurie made her sponsorship of Millennium Park's garden official.[8] Not only was the Lurie donation the last major gift Bryan secured; it meant that Millennium Park, Inc., had sponsors for every major enhancement in the park.

BY FOCUSING ON CONFLICTS concerning the escalating costs of Millennium Park, the media, planners, and even city officials ignored what was perhaps the most important event in the park's ever-evolving design. On December 9, 1999, Millennium Park project manager Ed Uhlir presented Frank Gehry's music pavilion design to the City's Public Art Committee. Uhlir's presentation was unusual. The Public Art Committee's primary responsibility was to evaluate "Percent for Art" projects—public art commissioned for new or renovated municipal buildings. While the committee could reject donations from a patron, the art in Millennium Park did not fall under their purview, since the projects were completely funded by private donors.[9] Few people were aware of the hearing at the time; no minutes remain documenting the discussion. But Uhlir recognized, unbeknownst to anyone else, the gravity of the meeting: Frank Gehry's pavilion design violated the Montgomery Ward height restrictions in Grant Park.

Uhlir had recently completed the public approval process for the Music and Dance Theater, a structure that not only adjoined Gehry's music pavilion, but shared the same loading dock and storage areas. Objections by various civic groups compelled Music and Dance Theater architect Thomas Beeby to cut the height of the Randolph Street facade and entrance. Indeed, at that moment the litigation that challenged the city's right to permit the construction of the forty-foot theater facade was moving through the courts. Uhlir did not want to risk another lawsuit.[10]

The Music and Dance Theater approval process made Uhlir ever-more aware that numerous historical and legal precedents existed for rejecting the Gehry-designed music pavilion. For much of the twentieth century, Grant Park music pavilion proposals foundered because their heights violated the Montgomery Ward restrictions prohibiting permanent structures in the park without landlord approval. Pavilions designed by Richard Bennett on behalf of the Montgomery Ward Foundation and the Chicago Park District in 1962, and Gene Summers for the Chicago Park District in 1972 were rejected because those structure were deemed too high. So rigid were these restrictions that when Colonel Henry Crown suggested building a Grant Park ice skating rink with a simple protective roof in the early 1960s, park district officials rejected the idea because of the Montgomery Ward height injunction.[11]

When acoustician Rick Talaske was chosen to design the sound system in 1998, he remembered that the height of the pavilion was the critical issue. "The key thing that we were dealing with, even with SOM, was the ceiling height within the stage enclosure,"

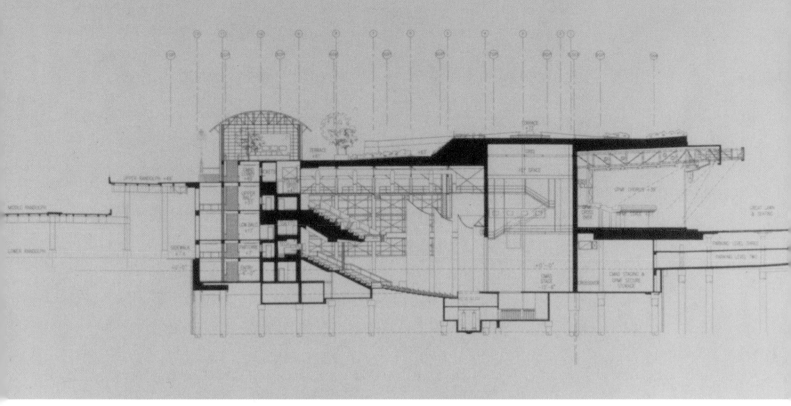

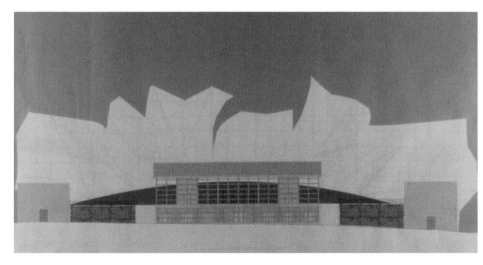

11.4
11.5

11.4. One of Thomas Beeby's early renderings for the Music and Dance Theater illustrates how Millennium Park officials sought to keep the height of the music pavilion below that of the theater.

11.5. Frank Gehry's exuberant design towered over the Harris Theater.

remembered Talaske. City officials insisted that there were limits on how high a structure could be in Grant Park. Talaske argued that he needed another fifteen feet of ceiling height to create a proper acoustic environment on stage. "Everybody at that time was saying, no, we can't do it," Talaske later recounted.

When Gehry finally revealed his pavilion design to the public in November 1999, Ed Uhlir knew he had a problem. The height of the pavilion stage approximated that of the Harris Theater to the rear, but the prominent metal ribbons that cantilevered out over the audience and extended upward reached a height of 130 feet. By comparison, the rejected proposals of Richard Bennett and Gene Summers forty and thirty years earlier extended only 29 and 59 feet, respectively.[12]

"I knew it could be an issue," Uhlir later acknowledged. But he devised an ingenious solution. He was well aware that the Illinois Supreme Court had indicated, without actually ruling on the matter, that certain structures necessary to the proper use of Grant Park are not "buildings." These include shelters to provide protection during storms, band stands, lavatories, and similar support structures.[13] With this caveat in mind, Uhlir determined that Gehry's bandshell—specifically the curving ribbons of stainless steel above the proscenium reaching more than 130 feet in some parts—was not a physical structure or a building. Rather, it was a piece of art. "It's really a piece of sculpture because it doesn't serve any functional purpose and it doesn't enclose space," claimed Uhlir. He admitted that if the cantilevered metal ribbons were defined as a "structure," the pavilion was indeed in violation of the park's height limitations. But that portion of the pavilion "really isn't a building," Uhlir insisted. "It's just a sculptural element."[14]

Rick Talaske remembered that when Gehry was introduced into the park, attitudes changed. The architect quickly joined Talaske and insisted more ceiling height was necessary. "He wanted it from a visual perspective; we wanted it from an acoustics perspective," remembered Talaske. Lo and behold, "the powers that be in Chicago determined that it wasn't a structure, that it's a piece of sculpture, and somehow they were able to move past those restrictions," remembered Talaske.[15]

What happened was that Ed Uhlir astutely managed Chicago's complicated planning process. After the Millennium Park plan was revised with the Gehry-designed pavilion, Uhlir and Millennium Park officials did not seek the Plan Commission's endorsement. Such approval was too time-consuming. Instead, they went through the staff of the Plan Commission. Since the SOM plan was approved through an open public hearing with considerable public debate and input, little more was required, according to Uhlir. "All we did at that meeting was say, we're negotiating with Frank Gehry now, and we do not have a design for the pavilion, but we will be hiring Frank Gehry to do it. We did not promise to come back to the Plan Commission." No Plan Commission official ever requested another hearing. Instead, Uhlir obtained a favorable administrative review from the Department of Planning concurring that the design was "consistent with the original plan." With that approval, the Gehry design went forward.[16]

Critics might argue that Uhlir and Millennium Park officials usurped the public approval process. In fact, Uhlir followed the same procedure of Plan Commission staff approval on other design changes in Millennium Park: the height revisions for the Music and Dance Theater, various changes in the garage, and several small service pavilions that were later added and approved.[17]

Furthermore, Uhlir went out of his way to appeal to potential critics. When Gehry's pavilion design was announced, Millennium Park officials hid nothing from the public; indeed, they encouraged criticism. Uhlir pointed out that "we invited everyone: planning commissioners, the civics, they were all there. We asked them for comments."[18]

To cover all possible bases, Uhlir even brought the design before the city's Public Art Committee late in 1999, a month after Gehry's pavilion design was made public. Since this project was technically beyond the committee's purview, Uhlir was trying to obtain some kind of public blessing. "Since this was totally funded by private donors," Uhlir recounted, Millennium Park projects did not require committee approval. "We were just getting unofficial endorsement," he declared.[19] The committee agreed that the decorative elements above the proscenium were not "structures" but "art," thereby complying with the Montgomery Ward restrictions.[20] "They loved it," Uhlir added, and "supported it unanimously."[21]

Did Uhlir ever worry that at some point in this ill-defined approval process somebody might object, arguing that the massive, 130-foot Gehry design was a structure or a building and deserved at least a full, public open hearing before the Plan Commission, if not the approval of the surrounding property owners?

"Yes, I was worried about that," admitted Uhlir, but "it was such a spectacular sculpture that no one raised any objections."

Back in Los Angeles, Frank Gehry knew little about this political maneuvering. "I don't know that they necessarily got art," he said after learning about it, "but they got a building."[22] Ed Uhlir might have shuddered upon hearing that.

11.6. Richard Bennett's proposed 29-foot Montgomery Ward Pavilion (1962) and Gene Summers's proposed 59-foot pavilion (1972) were rejected because their height violated the so-called Montgomery Ward height restrictions. Jaume Plensa's 50-foot *Crown Fountain* and Frank Gehry's 130-foot Pritzker Pavilion were exempt from such limitations because they were defined as pieces of art, not buildings or structures.

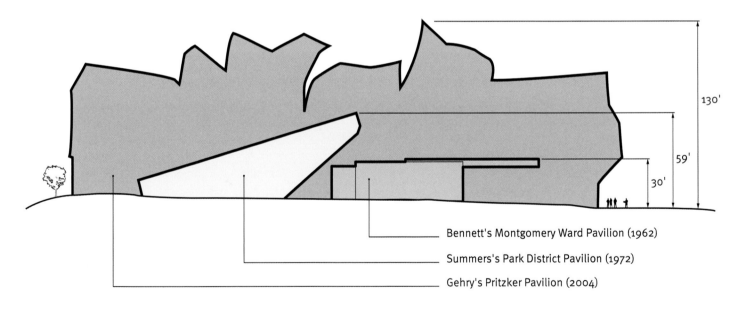

130'

59'

30'

Bennett's Montgomery Ward Pavilion (1962)

Summers's Park District Pavilion (1972)

Gehry's Pritzker Pavilion (2004)

100' - 0"

30' - 0"

11.7 Skyscrapers soar over
Frank Gehry's Pritzker Pavilion,
but the pavilion nevertheless
towers over Grant Park.

11.8. The final plan for Millennium
Park. Compare this map with 4.6, 6.7,
and 10.1.

PART THREE CULTURE

12.1

Chapter 12

CONSTRUCTING MILLENNIUM PARK

12.2

12.3

12.1. The early stages of construction at Wrigley Square and McCormick Tribune Plaza, May 2001. The completion of the Grant Park North Garage in November, 2000—six months ahead of the initial schedule—allowed Millennium Park officials to begin constructing the peristyle and the ice rink/plaza. Note the concrete foundations for the peristyle (left center) and ice rink beginning to take shape (lower right).

12.2. The peristyle emerges. Within the cocoon of scaffolding, the Doric columns of the Millennium Monument slowly appeared in February and March of 2002.

12.3. Peristyle details.

12.4–12.6. The music pavilion is a steel building encased in concrete. The concrete superstructure for the pavilion was complete by the end of 2002. Workers then erected support scaffolding to begin constructing the cantilevered trusses necessary to form the "headdress" of the pavilion.

12.7–12.10. Once the cantilever was firmly anchored, the curved steel frame supports of the headdress were attached during the spring and summer of 2003.

Jay Pritzker Pavilion

Construction of the then-unnamed Millennium Park pavilion began in September, 2001.

12.4

12.5
12.6

12.7
12.8
12.9
12.10

CONSTRUCTING MILLENNIUM PARK JAY PRITZKER PAVILLION : **189**

12.11

12.11. A yellow structural steel back-up, or anchor, for the steel and aluminum panels at the construction site.

12.12. The yellow steel backup before the panels were attached, with the Aon Building in the background.

12.13. Once the backups were in place, steel panels were attached. The panels consist of structural steel beams which support aluminum sandwich panels. Stainless steel plates are finally attached on top of the aluminum panels.

12.14, 12.15. Inside the super-structure of the headdress, pavilion workers had unique vistas down Washington Street

12.16. A rear view of the music pavilion and trellis under construction on November 25, 2003. In the distance on the left is the Petrillo Bandshell, which the Jay Pritzker Pavilion replaced as the home for the Grant Park Music Festival. In the foreground is the Harris Theater for Music and Dance, which had opened only 17 days earlier.

12.16

12.19

12.17. Simultaneous with the pavilion's construction in the spring and summer of 2003, the foundational pylons or piers for the trellis and the bridge's concrete base were completed.

12.18, 12.19. The trellis (supported by scaffolding during construction) is a completely welded structure. In hot weather, the steel expands and increases the size of the trellis. In cold weather, the steel contracts and the trellis shrinks. The concrete floor beneath the trellis became the Great Lawn.

12.20. A trellis and pylon with Michigan Avenue skyscrapers to the rear. Tension from the trellis is transferred to the 24 pylons along the circumference of the Great Lawn, which then transfer the tension underground into the garage.

12.21. Upon completion of the trellis and the installation of the sound system, the Great Lawn was sodded.

12.22. As the pavilion neared completion, the 30-by-50-foot sliding glass doors were installed.

12.23

12.24

12.31 | 12.32

12.23, 12.24. Before Millennium Park officially opened, engineers and designers experimented with different nighttime lighting schemes for the pavilion.

12.25–12.32. A time-lapse view of the construction of the Pritzker Pavilion from 2002 to 2004. Note the triple nine crane needed to carry and move the heavy loads of steel.

12.33. The beginnings of BP Bridge and the concrete berm that blocks traffic noise from the Great Lawn.

12.34. Although Frank Gehry's BP Bridge looks light and airy, most of the bridge is solid concrete.

12.35. The concrete foundation ramp winding its way into Daley Bicentennial Plaza.

12.36. Once the concrete ramps on both sides of Columbus Drive were completed, the metal supports for the steel plates were attached to the bridge.

12.37–12.39. Completion of the concrete ramps allowed workers to attach the steel box girder over Columbus Drive. In November 2003, the two sides of the bridge were united.

BP Bridge

12.33
———
12.35

12.34
———
12.36

12.37

12.38

12.40

12.41

12.42

12.43 | 12.44

12.40, 12.41. With the box girder in place, the underlying steel structure to support the stainless steel panels is attached.

12.42–12.44. The metal skeleton of the bridge's serpentine form took shape by the end of 2003.

12.45. Rebar for the concrete deck of the bridge.

12.45

12.46. Upon completion, only the thick, circular support column in the middle of Columbus Drive hints at the steel and concrete that comprised the bridge's substructure. Gehry wanted the bridge to emerge from both sides of the street, eliminating the need for the support column in the middle of Columbus Drive. But this would have required cantilevering the bridge from two structural positions on opposite sides of the street. Not only was this expensive, it would have necessitated digging up significant portions of both garages. In Daley Bicentennial Plaza, the support structure would have been precisely at the entrance to the Monroe Street Garage.

12.47–12.52. BP Bridge under construction from the fall of 2003 to completion in 2004.

12.47

12.48

12.49

12.52

Cloud Gate

Anish Kapoor's *Cloud Gate* presented distinctive problems. Some worried it would be too hot to touch in the summer, so cold in the winter that your tongue would stick to it. Others worried that Chicago's 100-degree variation in temperatures would weaken and destroy the sculpture over time. Some expressed fears that if the object did not attract graffiti artists, fingerprints would be all over it. The "seamless" surface of the sculpture would require regular and frequent polishing.[1]

Most important, many doubted that such a large, seamless structure was possible. Kapoor asked the eminent architect Sir Norman Foster about creating a "single skin" sculpture. Foster replied that such an idea was probably impossible. But, in Kapoor's words, engineer Ethan Silva of Performance Structures, Inc., "found a way."[2]

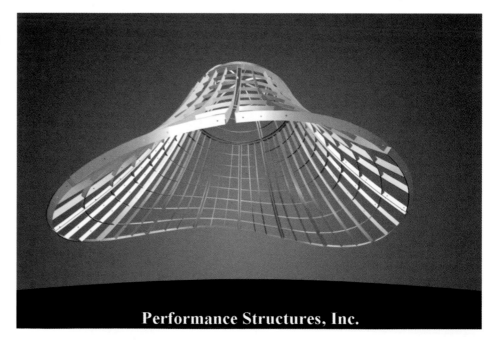

Performance Structures, Inc.

12.56

12.54. The tip of the "omphalos" in Oakland during fabrication. The omphalos is a mirrored indentation that provides multiple reflections of anyone standing below the sculpture and looking up. Millennium Park officials originally envisioned constructing the sculpture in either Scotland or California. As late as August 2003, they planned for the completed design to be transported by ship either through the Panama Canal or the St. Lawrence Seaway. When the dangers grew too significant, they elected to dismantle the nearly completed sculpture in Oakland and reassemble it in Chicago.

12.55. An empty SBC Plaza in June 2003.

12.56, 12.57. In March 2004, workers begin constructing the internal steel skeleton rings and trusses necessary to support the bean-shaped structure. Because the surface will expand and contract according to weather conditions, the skeleton is loosely attached to the skin.

12.57

12.59

12.60

12.61

12.58. The tip of the omphalos and the Aon Building.

12.59–12.62. Construction of *Cloud Gate* began with the omphalos. Panels were then sequentially attached to the internal steel support structure, moving from the "inside" of the sculpture downward to the outermost surface. The panels were 98 percent polished and covered with a white protective film (seen here) before they were sent to Chicago.

12.62

12.63. Kapoor described the inside of *Cloud Gate* as looking like a "medieval ship."

12.64, 12.65. In the spring of 2004, a protective tent was erected around the sculpture. Upon completion of the innermost surface of the sculpture, the most sharply curved panels were installed at the bottom near the ground.

12.66

12.67 | 12.68

12.66. Once the bottom of *Cloud Gate* was intact, the structure looked like a large sombrero. This was the extent of the sculpture previously completed in Oakland, so all the ensuing panels needed to be fitted and ribbed for attachment upon reaching the Millennium Park construction site.

12.67–12.69. Workers install the new panels and begin moving up the outside of the sculpture, swallowing up the internal steel structural support. Silva's team used aerospace technology to bend over 100 steel plates to a precise curvature before welding them together.

12.69

12.70

12.71 | 12.72

12.70. As the sculpture neared completion, workers prepared to attach the tip of the omphalos. Once the outer surface was completely attached and intact, this was the only means of access to the interior of *Cloud Gate*.

12.71, 12.72. The final stages of attaching the panels. Much of *Cloud Gate*'s 110-ton weight is due to the internal steel support. While the inner steel structure was unnecessary for supporting the sculpture upon completion, it was absolutely necessary during the fabrication and construction process. Upon completion, workers disassembled the interior supports from the skin and removed any ferrous material that could rust. Only stainless steel remained.

12.73. Artists and engineers celebrate the attachment of the final panel on the top of *Cloud Gate*. From left to right: Robert Wislow of U.S. Equities Realty, Ethan Silva of Performance Structures, Inc., and the artist, Anish Kapoor.

12.74, 12.75. Although the outer surface of *Cloud Gate* needed to be further welded, grinded, and polished in order to eliminate any visible seams, the protective tent was removed in preparation for the official opening of Millennium Park on July 16, 2004. "I'm interested in a condition of perfection," Kapoor later explained. This required specialized engineering assistance, as the margins of error were very small. To achieve this perfection, this "unreality," he needed the reality of engineering.

12.73

12.74

12.75

Like Kapoor's *Cloud Gate*, Plensa's *Crown Fountain* presented multiple challenges. Could the most sophisticated light-emitting diodes be combined with the most complicated type of water fountain technology? Would water falling from a fifty-foot tower injure people below? Would the "gargoyle" spray harm children? Would the African granite become unbearably hot in the summer? Who would prevent the fountain images from being used for commercial purposes? Would the technology quickly become outdated?

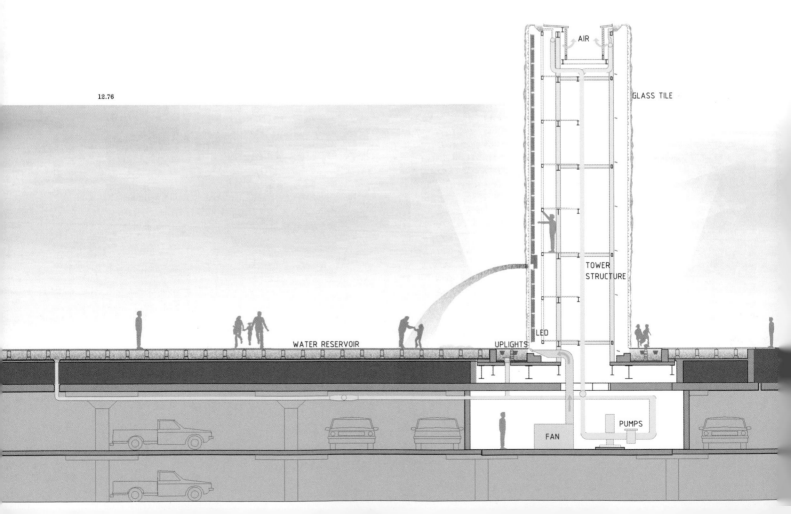

12.76

12.76. A cross-sectional diagram of the *Crown Fountain*. Note the tight configuration of various technologies, which include three separate water systems: (1) the two-foot pool beneath the visible African granite surface, (2) the reservoir at the top of each tower, and (3) the pipe for the gargoyle's mouth. Uplights illuminate the surface in front of the tower. A three-inch space between the back of the glass brick facade and the LED screen allows for cooling air within the tower. The towers contain seven levels of catwalks to allow for maintenance and repair. Virtually all of this is invisible to outside observers.

12.77. Steel mold for the *Crown Fountain*'s glass bricks. Before construction began, Plensa and representatives from U.S. Equities tested a variety of materials and technologies. Eventually, L. E. Smith in Mount Pleasant, Pennsylvania, was commissioned to cast approximately 28,000 specially made, 5″ × 10″ × 2″ "water white" glass bricks. Each brick was 2.5″ to 3″ thick, weighed about 10 pounds, and was cast by hand.

12.78. An early mockup of the glass bricks used in the *Crown Fountain*. Once the bricks were manufactured, they were shipped to Circle Redmont's assembly plant in Melbourne, Florida. There the bricks were placed into a supportive steel frame and cemented in with mortar and silicone, thereby camouflaging the frame. According to *Crown Fountain* designer Jaume Plensa, "The beauty is to keep its transparency as much as possible."

12.79. Testing panel with light-emitting diodes (LED) on the left and a glass brick wall on the right.

12.79

12.80. The builders of the *Crown Fountain* (left to right): Mark Sexton of the architecture firm Krueck and Sexton; Alan Schachtman and Roark Frankel of U.S. Equities Realty, the construction manager for the *Crown Fountain* and *Cloud Gate*, Steve Crown, representing his family; and the artist, Jaume Plensa. They are discussing test panels in the alley behind Krueck and Sexton at 221 West Erie in Chicago in May 2002.

12.81. In order to provide the infrastructure to support the various technologies in the *Crown Fountain*, the city had to relinquish 26 parking spaces in the underground garage.

12.82. Workers begin building the pool's foundation after clearing the site. The skin pool is an illusion. Water enters the pool not from the towers above, but via a hidden, four-foot-deep pool below. Water rises up between the granite blocks.

12.83, 12.84. The frames for the two towers revealed the first outlines of the fountain.

12.83 | 12.84

12.85

12.85. By early 2004, the north tower was complete and the black LED screen installed with no glass protection. In the foreground, a winterized tent was placed over the fountain site to protect workers and allow construction to continue on the pool.

12.86. By April 2004, the water and lighting systems were installed in the south tower. In the foreground, note the exposed pipes in the pool below the tower.

12.87. Plensa observing construction. In the foreground, note the pool's actual two-foot depth and the pedestals which support the granite surface.

12.88–12.90. Once the infrastructure of the towers was complete, workers installed panels of steel frames which contained the glass bricks. Engineers developed a special stainless steel panel grid with the same shape and position of the glass blocks. The grid supports the tower and holds the blocks, but is camouflaged by the silicone and the reflection of the glass. The black covering in the tower is the LED screen. Jaume Plensa and Mark Sexton stand in the foreground of figure 12.90.

12.88

12.89 | 12.90

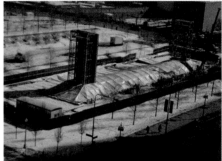

12.91–12.94. Upon completion of the towers, Millennium Park officials experimented with various lighting schemes. Later, faculty and students at the Art Institute photographed and organized the faces for the fountain.

12.95–12.102. A time lapse view of the construction of the *Crown Fountain* from 2003 to 2004.

12.103. The artist and his master-piece: Jaume Plensa in front of the north tower of the *Crown Fountain*.

12.103

12.104

12.106

12.105

12.107

12.104–12.107. Lurie Garden was the final major enhancement constructed in Millennium Park. These views show construction from February 2004 to completion in July 2004. By March 2004, the outline of paths in the "Light Plate" (a section of open prairie, in contrast to the "Dark Plate" of shading trees) was visible. One of Renzo Piano's Exelon Pavilions along Monroe Street was under construction (12.105). By April, the steel scaffolding for the shoulder hedge was under construction (12.106).

12.108. In order to provide contours and elevate the grade of the garden without adding the weight of heavy soil, light, white poly-foam fill was laid on top of the concrete roof of the garage.

12.109, 12.110. A series of elevated platforms of poly-foam fill below the Lurie Garden's surface provided the tilt for the Light Plate. Figure 12.110 reveals the wall of the seam in the background.

12.108

12.109 | 12.210

12.111. The wall of the seam under construction.

12.112. The seam is essentially a concrete ditch (later filled with water) covered with wood. The tall concrete wall is the edge of the Dark Plate.

12.113. The Light Plate under construction. The metal brackets in the foreground support the wooden floor of the seam.

12.114. An aerial view of the completed Millennium Park.

12.111 | 12.112

12.113

12.114

VERMEER IN CHICAGO   THE JAY PRITZKER PAVILION AND BP BRIDGE

No other enhancement in Millennium Park attracted more attention than the $60.3 million Jay Pritzker Music Pavilion designed by California's Frank Gehry. The exterior reflects Gehry's distinctive style: a series of irregular, stainless steel panels wrap the stage, erupting like petals across the top of the proscenium. The sculptured headdress extends ninety to one hundred feet above the stage. The pavilion's dramatic and flowing form made it the identifying structure of Millennium Park upon opening. Gehry described the flamboyant covering as "a bouquet of flowers in the park." The architect wanted this gift to Chicago to be, in his words, "entertaining, something that's festive."[1]

The steel ribbons, however, are more than just decoration. As they cantilever out beyond the stage, supported by twelve custom-designed trusses, the ribbons provide cover for the closest seats, conceal the lighting and catwalks, and reflect sound from the stage down to the audience below. The stage interior is clad in Douglas fir—the same wood Gehry employed in the auditorium of Walt Disney Concert Hall in Los Angeles—and accommodates 120 musicians. A choral terrace holds up to 150 performers. Two massive, fifty-by-thirty-foot sliding glass doors enclose the stage in inclement weather, transforming the stage into an indoor reception area. Backstage, the pavilion shares dressing rooms and storage space with the adjacent indoor, below grade, 1,500-seat Harris Theater.

On the Great Lawn, 4,000 spectators enjoy fixed seats, while an additional 6,000 to 7,000 can lounge on the surrounding lawn. Above the 625- by-325-foot space of the Great Lawn (more than twice the size of a football field) stretches a state-of-the-art, trellised sound system intended to equal the finest indoor music venues.[2]

The close personal relationship between the Pritzker family and Gehry played a key role in persuading the architect to accept the Millennium Park commission. Gehry admitted he owed a great deal to the friendship of the Pritzker family, which began after he won the Pritzker Prize in 1989. "I didn't cash the check for six months and that's how our friendship started," he joked.[3] But Gehry was attracted to the project for its variety of artistic challenges. Millennium Park presented the architect with an opportunity to work with a skyscraper skyline as part of his palette. Chicago, Gehry believes, has the best collection of contemporary architecture of any city in the world.[4] More specifically, the

I think my attitudes about the past are very traditional. You can't ignore history; you can't escape it even if you want to.

FRANK GEHRY (1990)

Grant Park site offered Gehry a chance to demonstrate how a tangible, physical structure captures and reflects an intangible, auditory entity like music. Can the shape of a music venue embody—not just contain—music itself?

As in most Gehry projects, the architect and his team followed an experimental strategy. Gehry rarely approaches his projects with a specific preconception. "I just sort of let it unfold and meet with the people and then try to meet their expectations as best I can," he explains. "We try everything we can think of," points out Gehry's partner and project architect, Craig Webb. They literally play with blocks to come up with a specific form. When someone comes up with an idea, they try it out, put it in the model, and look at it. In the end, according to Webb, "we seldom sit and have long discussions about it." The Gehry team of architects experimented with close to fifty models and sketches for Millennium Park.[5]

Gehry was particularly sensitive to the context of Grant Park. The building walls along Michigan Avenue and Randolph Street effectively created a container, or box. "The park is a void inside this box," pointed out Craig Webb. Gehry's goal was to create something dynamic within the box.[6] Gehry and Webb eventually narrowed their choices to four different models. One was a simple, curving wedge of metal intended to serve as a homage to Mies van der Rohe. "I kind of liked the simple one," Gehry later claimed. "It was cheaper and I would have taken it somewhere."[7] In direct proximity to the modernist designs of the Prudential, Aon, and Blue Cross–Blue Shield buildings along Randolph Street, this seemed to be a contextual solution.

The weakness in the simple Miesian design was threefold. According to Webb, the pavilion had little presence from the audience side—concert goers could see the orchestra but not the proscenium. Second, the pavilion was concealed by the Grant Park tree canopy and would have been hidden within the park landscape. Third and most important, however, was that no one liked it. "There was sort of a violent reaction to it," Gehry admitted. "Oh, God! Don't do that!" The model was rejected by Millennium Park officials because "they wanted a real Frank Gehry, whatever that is," wondered Gehry.[8]

Over time, Gehry's enthusiasm for this tribute to modernism withered. Later, when asked if the simple form would have complemented the modernist buildings along north Randolph Street, Gehry retorted, "Those are horrible buildings. Why try to look like that?" Gehry also recognized that the pavilion would be used only half the year, and that with a capacity of only 10,000 to 11,000, the concerts would be small and restrained. A structure that was "real quiet or laid back," believed Gehry, "would have been anti-climactic."[9]

13.3

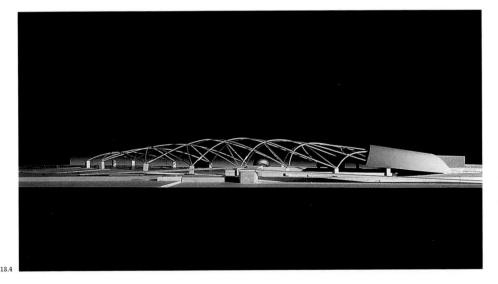

13.4

13.3. Frank Gehry (right) with his friend and pavilion-namesake Jay Pritzker at a reception some time before the latter's death in 1999.

13.4. One of Gehry's models was a homage to the modernism of Mies van der Rohe.

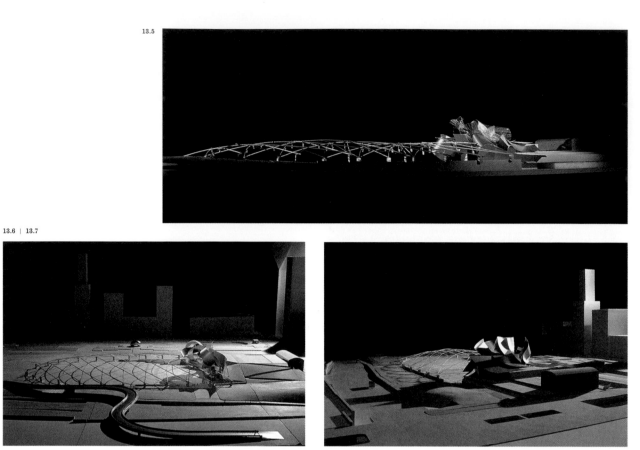

13.5–13.7. Gehry experimented with a variety of pavilion models. One had a simple form, but was constructed with a mesh-like material, making it transparent (13.5). Another included a series of towers and spires (fig. 13.7).

Millennium Park officials were ultimately attracted to the most flamboyant model. "I started playing with the more exuberant solution," Gehry admitted, "which I think is more appropriate for the park." His inspiration came from an unlikely source: Johannes Vermeer. Gehry has long appreciated the art of the seventeenth-century Dutch masters. One day, while working on another project, Gehry approached Craig Webb with a copy of Vermeer's *Woman with a Water Jug*. He pointed to the bright, almost translucent pleats on the woman's shoulder. "We started on this idea inspired by this painting, to make a stainless steel roof that is folded in those very flat pleats, and curving over the top of it," remembered Webb. The challenge was to translate the two-dimensional elements found in Vermeer into the three-dimensional design of the pavilion.[10]

Gehry wanted to create an intimate setting, or in the words of Craig Webb, "the feeling of a space shared with performers." Yet the pavilion was distinctly separated from the audience, whose 4,000 seats number more than the Lyric or Symphony Hall, to say nothing of the additional 6,000 to 7,000 sitting on the lawn. "We started working on a bandshell with curved stainless-steel elements which would surround the concert enclosure," Webb explained. Consequently, the exterior of the Pritzker Pavilion wraps the stage.[11]

But Gehry's search for an intimate setting was partly stymied by timing. When he

13.8. Johannes Vermeer, *Woman with a Water Jug* (1660–1667).

started the pavilion design, the footings for the underground parking garage were already installed. Gehry quickly realized that the sight lines presented problems, because the flat rake of the stage was roughly the same elevation as the rear of the lawn. Gehry suggested raising the lawn's slope, but the cost to "tip" the lawn was a prohibitive $6 million.

A compromise was reached in which the 4,000 permanent seats enjoy good sight lines, while those on the lawn have few unobstructed views.[12] Gehry partly resolved the sight-line problem by enlarging the stage. Past experience with the Hollywood Bowl convinced Gehry that small stages at outdoor venues make the performance spaces look even smaller for those sitting in the rear. Enlarging the stage, he hoped, would give it more presence and intimacy, especially to those sitting on the lawn.[13]

The prominent headdress over the proscenium serves two purposes. While some compare the design to petals, slivers of chocolate, or even Betty Boop's eyelashes, Gehry points out that the shell demanded a certain amount of curvature in order to distribute the sound. Consequently, he extended the pavilion roof over part of the permanent seating, ensuring that sound from the stage would reverberate to the audience below. But Gehry did not stop there; rather he "flipped" up the roof, creating the sculptured, eye-catching mixture of stainless steel petals. And in Gehry's words, "that's the fluff."[14]

But even the fluff is functional. Gehry included a permanent lighting system that throws color washes onto the stainless steel, developed in collaboration with theater consultants and lighting designers Duane Schuler and Robert Shook . The result is a slowly changing rainbow of colors across the decorative headdress panels.[15]

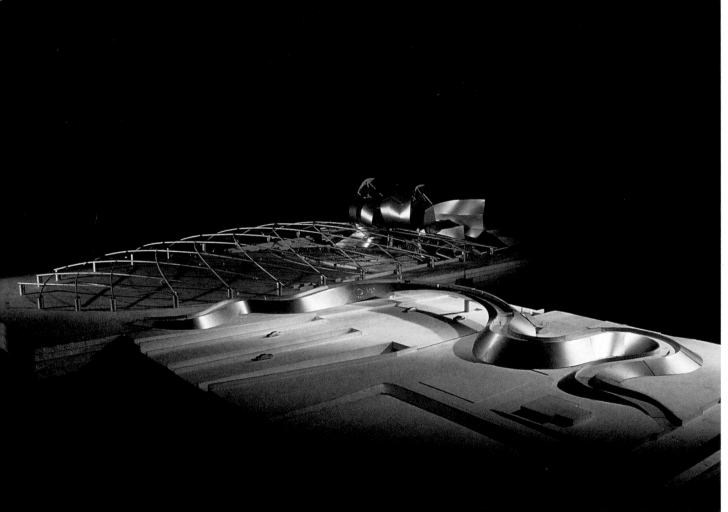

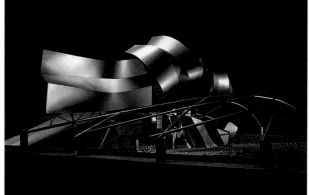

13.9–13.12. Different views of final design models.

Some claim that the Pritzker Pavilion and BP Bridge are derivative, that the bold curves and the sweeping steel mimics other Gehry-designed structures. "Some of my colleagues think this is 'wow' architecture and it shouldn't be 'wow' architecture," Gehry concedes. The artist, charge critics, is simply repeating himself.[16]

Superficially, this is true. The pavilion and bridge reflect Gehry's reputation for stretching, shrinking, and breaking the modern box, for designing structures that appear to explode, for challenging traditional artistic conceptions of perspective and ge-

13.14. Weisman Art Museum, Minneapolis (1990–1993).

13.15. Experience Music Project, Seattle (1995–2000).

13.16. Richard B. Fisher Center for the Performing Arts at Bard College.

13.17. Walt Disney Concert Hall model (1989–2003).

ometry. "Gehry's architectural creations seem to split open and break apart, to burst out of closed containers and shoot off in all linguistic directions," argues one critic. The forms of the pavilion and the bridge indeed conform with Gehry's preference for breaking the rules of architectural symmetry.[17]

This is hardly surprising because it reflects Gehry's distinctive urbanism. "Cities of the present are chaotic. They are a product of democracy," he believes. "Everybody does what they want. They're moving, there are cars moving." Gehry's architecture seeks to unearth a language that relates to that.[18] Consequently, disorder is a persistent theme in his work. "I think you've got to accept that certain things are in process that you can't change, that you can't overwhelm. The chaos of our cities, the randomness of our lives, the unpredictability of where you're going to be ten years from now—all of those things are weighing on us, and yet there is a certain glimmer of control. If you act a certain way and talk a certain way, you're going to draw certain forces to you."[19]

This philosophy informed Gehry's design for the Frederick R. Weisman Art Museum (1993) at the University of Minnesota in Minneapolis; the Experience Music Project (1996) in Seattle; the Guggenheim Museum (1997) in Bilbao, Spain; Richard B. Fisher Center for the Performing Arts (2003) at Bard College in Annandale, New York; and the Walt Disney Concert Hall (2003) in Los Angeles. Like the Pritzker Pavilion and BP Bridge, all of these structures included a variety of curves and swirling lines, and evoke similar qualities: fluidity, continuous motion, sculptural abstraction. All reflect Gehry's affection and affinity for the arts.

The Weisman Art Museum is clad in stainless steel and sits overlooking the Mississippi River, responding to the setting sun and the flowing water with fascinating reflections and ever-changing forms.[20] Like Millennium Park, the sites for the Disney Concert Hall and the Guggenheim Bilbao were derelict urban areas and warehouses chosen for redevelopment, using culture and art to spur gentrification and reinvestment in former industrial or abandoned spaces. Disney Concert Hall, like Millennium Park, was constructed over a municipal garage and plagued by mounting costs.[21]

But the similarities of these structures—their metallic facades, the spectacular and sculptured curves, their musical or artistic purposes—disguise the far more significant differences in Gehry's Millennium Park project. "Does it look like Bilbao?" Gehry inquires. "I don't think it does." But, he concedes, "I've never been able to escape myself."[22]

Gehry is right. The visual and technological impact of Bilbao and Gehry's more recent works overshadows the multiple ways Gehry's Millennium Park project departs from his earlier works. Consider the Experience Music Project. Although the design includes a variety of swirling curves, unconventional shapes, and metallic forms like the Millennium Park pavilion and bridge, EMP "is very raw," in the words of Craig Webb. "I think we left it in a state that is more spontaneous." By contrast, the Millennium Park structure "is more refined and reduced." Similarly, the pavilion and bridge may share the same curved forms, metallic colors, and adjacency to water as the Weisman Art Museum in Minneapolis, but Gehry maintains that the two have little in common. The steel slivers atop the Pritzker Pavilion have a fundamental purpose: "They break up the sound," Gehry insists.[23]

The Pritzker Pavilion and BP Bridge may share curving facades and metallic coloring with earlier Gehry works, but both are much more dynamic pieces of architecture. By Gehry's admission, he became fascinated with incorporating movement into his architecture, specifically the shapes of sails, while working on Walt Disney Concert Hall in Los Angeles. "When you're sailing, the wind catches the sail and it's very tight, and it's a beautiful shape," he believes. "And when it flutters, it has a beautiful quality that was caught in the seventeenth century by Dutch painters." But Gehry felt this was a risky proposition. "I didn't have the guts to do it," he later admitted. "So everything is tight in Disney Hall."[24]

Nothing is tight in the Pritzker Pavilion or BP Bridge. Not only does the facade break out of the proscenium and the bridge flow in unexpected directions; each one simultaneously and distinctively breaks from the traditional urban and architectural forms which surround the pavilion: the 24.5-acre Millennium Park, the classical design of Grant Park, and the historic grid form of Chicago.

Another departure in Gehry's Millennium Park project is that the architect had never designed a structure like the trellis. More than a football field in width and over two football fields in length, the trellis's distinctive dome over the Great Lawn is both a state-of-the-art design and a functional element in distributing the sound. The twenty-two crisscrossing members of the trellis are each only fifteen inches in diameter at the center, making the trellis a light, thin structure. Gehry even suggested employing sail technology and stretching a lightweight fabric over the trellis during rainy weather. "We affectionately call that the *shmattee*" (Yiddish for "rag"), he laughs. The estimated $17 million cost, however, shelved the proposal.[25]

More important, Gehry's music pavilion designs over three decades illustrate better than any other building genre the radical evolution of the architect's oeuvre. From the Merriweather-Post and Concord pavilions to the Hollywood Bowl, Millennium Park, and Disney Concert Hall, Gehry's musical venues look like projects by different architects.[26]

Merriweather-Post Pavilion (1966–1967) was one of four commissions Gehry completed for the famed developer James Rouse in the planned community of Columbia, Maryland. The 3,000-seat open-air amphitheater, covering 35,000 square feet and budgeted at $449,000, was built for and is the summer home of the National Symphony Orchestra. Constructed in only seventy days, the steel, concrete, and wood-sided enclosure is concealed from view unless approached on foot because the site is a natural dish, sloping into the woods of a thirty-five-acre park near Columbia's town center. Although the pavilion retains the intimacy of a smaller structure, some consider it Columbia's most successful architectural structure in terms of function and popularity.[27]

Gehry's Concord Performing Arts Center (1973–1976; now called the Chronicle Pavilion) is a 35,000-square-foot outdoor pavilion at the foothills of California's Mt. Diablo, just west of San Francisco. Since the facility was built to accommodate multiple functions—the Concord Summer Music Festival, theatrical and dance performances, graduation ceremonies, and large concerts—Gehry designed a stage which could be converted into four formats: a traditional proscenium, an arena theater, a thrust stage projecting into the audience, and an intimate theater for six hundred. The structure is a concrete slab slung by a steel-truss roof over a thirty-five-acre crater. Four steel columns, four and a half feet in diameter (for earthquake protection), support twelve trusses and 400,000 square feet of steel decking and two-inch-thick concrete. Some noted that the prominent roof trusses and structural expressions evoked the atelier of Mies van der Rohe.[28]

Gehry's interest in acoustics was prominent in these earlier pavilion designs. At Merriweather-Post, Concord, and the Hollywood Bowl, Gehry worked with acoustical engineer Christopher Jaffe. The most favorably reviewed quality at each was the sound system. At Concord, Gehry and Jaffe designed a unique acoustical moat and orchestra pit sunken underneath and surrounding the stage. At Merriweather-Post, an early and

13.18

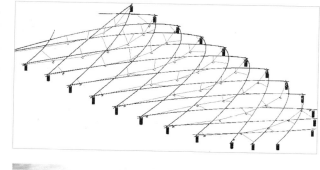

13.19

13.20

13.21

13.22

13.18. Millennium Park trellis model.

13.19. A computer model of the trellis.

13.20. Merriweather-Post Pavilion, in Columbia, Maryland.

13.21, 13.22. Views of Concord Pavilion, in Concord, California.

less technologically sophisticated version of the Millennium Park trellis sound system was employed. Five high-fidelity speakers were mounted in the rear fascia. A tape-delayed system recorded stage sound, and then played it over the loudspeakers, theoretically allowing natural and reinforced sound to arrive at the same instant. The acoustics were considered among the best of outdoor music pavilions. When Merriweather-Post

opened in 1967, Harold Schonberg of the *New York Times* described it as "probably the best-sounding outdoor hall in the United States," adding that the pavilion was "better than most regulation concert halls."[29]

Gehry's attention to sound, however, was most influenced by his renovation work on the Hollywood Bowl. Southern California's premier outdoor concert venue since opening in 1929, by the 1960s it suffered from poor acoustics, attributed to the enlarged seating capacity (up to 18,000), increased air and vehicular traffic, and amplified sound. Spectators in the rear and stage performers alike had a difficult time hearing. Gehry compared the sound to that of a cheap car radio.[30]

From 1970 to 1982, Gehry directed six phases of renovation, finally working with Jaffe and Israeli acoustician Abe Melzer. The final result was a permanent acoustical modification of the existing shell with fiberglass spheres of varying sizes suspended inside the shell to reflect and distribute sound to the orchestra. Conductor Josef Krips was said to have ranked the installation as "the best outdoor enclosure in his experience."[31]

In Millennium Park, Gehry had two acoustic goals: to avoid creating another "Hollywood Bowl like" structure, and to keep the pavilion clear of obtrusive structures. In the initial plan, Gehry faced a "forest of poles" every seventy feet on the Millennium Park lawn. The ornamental poles supported the speaker and lighting systems, but obstructed sight lines, hid the skyline, and generated objections from Mayor Daley. Upon learning that relocating the poles to the perimeter of the lawn was a technical impossibility for distributing sound, Gehry devised a trellis to both span the entire lawn and support the sound system.[32]

At first glance, the trellis appears to be modeled after the double-curved window and lattice over the atrium in Gehry's DG Bank Building in Berlin. Both create shell shapes

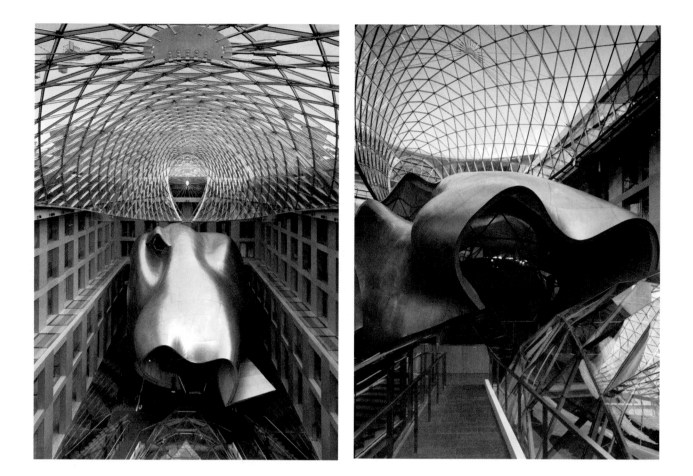

with triangular members woven together like a basket. Both designs are situated within the most important civic spaces in each city: DG Bank is located on Pariser Platz in the shadow of Brandenburg Gate, a space informally known as "Berlin's Front Plaza."[33] Similarly, Millennium Park lies on the northwest corner of Grant Park, Chicago's "front yard."

But Gehry insists the two structures have little in common. The DG Bank lattice functions as a roof and a source of light, whereas the trellis provides an equal distribution of sound while minimizing any intrusion on spectators' sight lines.[34] Furthermore, despite their civic similarity, Gehry recognized that each space called for its own design. Pariser Platz was a public plaza and civic meeting space. For this reason, he wanted, in his words, to "be a good neighbor" by designing an understated facade that, in his words, "would not detract or would not trivialize Brandenburg Gate." Gehry created a structure with a spare vocabulary that was uniform in scale to adjoining structures.[35] The minimalist facade of DG Bank evokes the flat roofs, sheer facades, and lack of decoration identified with modern, international-style buildings. Upon entering the interior atrium, however, visitors witness a visual explosion of translucent curves and colors overhead. Appropriately, Gehry describes the DG Bank as "a mousetrap."[36]

13.26. Richard Talaske and Jonathan Laney.

Gehry relied upon acousticians Rick Talaske and Jonathan Laney to implement his plan for the Pritzker Pavilion. Originally commissioned to design the sound system by SOM in 1998, Talaske and Laney were determined to make Millennium Park an acoustic model for outdoor music venues. Historically, outdoor pavilions can do little to control environmental sounds beyond building simple barriers or berms. Acoustical problems are magnified because an outdoor pavilion cannot replicate the ambient sound bouncing off the interior walls of an enclosed concert hall. "You feel enveloped in the reverberation from the side walls, ceilings, and floor," explains Laney. The concert hall "is very much part of the performance, almost an instrument in itself." Outside, sound-reflecting surfaces are minimal or nonexistent. "For musicians," notes Talaske, "it's like playing in a Victorian funeral home, where all sound is absorbed."[37]

Consequently, most outdoor venues offer sound reinforcement for clarity and amplification. To this, Talaske and Laney added an acoustic enhancement system to provide virtual walls and mask peripheral city noise. The trellis and the attached messenger cable system concentrically distribute fifty-two loudspeakers sixty feet apart and thirty-five feet above the seating area and lawn, effectively creating the sound effects of an interior room outside. Patrons in the audience are never more than fifty or sixty feet away from a speaker. One part of the sound system reinforces the music, creating the volume that brings out musical clarity and detail. Computerized lateral speakers along the perimeter project sound toward the center, providing a "room effect" by delaying the sound so precisely—within milliseconds—that the sound arrives from all directions and creates the illusion that it is reverberating off interior walls.[38] The second part, the distributed reinforcement system, amplifies the sound so listeners can hear detail and clarity. Sound also goes out to what Laney calls the "lobby," the park beyond the lawn, and sound comes back to the performers. A computerized delay system synchronizes sound from different locations at fractionally different intervals. The result is high-quality sound in both the front and back of the trellis.[39]

Talaske also contributed to the shape of the pavilion stage. The unusual curves and angles on the walls are not simply fanciful, decorative Gehry touches; they serve to bolster cross-room sound reflections and thereby enable musicians to hear one another. An orchestral riser system also allows for an acoustically favorable staging for an orchestra. The wood floor, through interconnected parts and resilient materials, transfers more precise vibrations across the stage. Even during loud passages, musicians feel floor vibrations from certain instruments, resulting in a more precise ensemble. The end result is a blending of architecturally and electronically created sound.[40]

The pavilion area is recessed, so many audience members are located ten feet below the adjacent street elevation. The acoustic enhancement system, which delivers sound from the sides and rear of listeners, helps mask peripheral noises. The design allows for connection to broadcast and recording equipment and minimizes weather-related effects on the amplified sound. A portion of the bridge along Columbus Drive also provides a berm that disperses automobile noise. The result, Gehry adds, is that the trellis

13.27

13.28

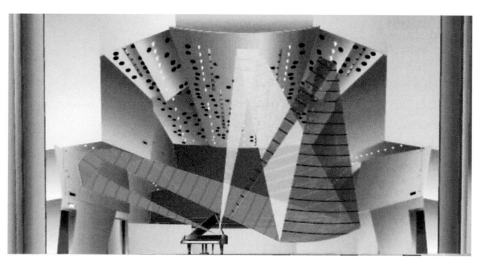

13.29

13.27, 13.28. These diagrams illustrate how the acoustic enhancement system (13.27) directs sound down from the trellis, while the sound reinforcement system (13.28) directs the sound in an angular direction.

13.29. This frontal view of the stage details the movement of sound on stage.

makes the sound "democratic" and thereby "defines the space on the grass as an out-door room."[41]

As a final benefit, the trellis system allows acoustical environments to be changed, depending on the musical needs of performers. Musicians and acousticians can tailor the amount of clarity and reverberation in accordance with the needs of the repertory. Talaske insists that this can be accomplished "even as the music is being played." In short, the trellis's specialized electronics, digital processing, virtual walls, and ceilings will simulate the acoustics of a concert hall. While the system will not eliminate all traffic noise and urban din, the Pritzker Pavilion will have its own "acoustic signature."[42]

THE BP BRIDGE WAS the final distinctive element in Gehry's Millennium Park atelier; it was the only Gehry-designed bridge in the world upon completion. The architect had designed several bridges previously, such as the Pferdeturm USTRA Bridge in Hannover,

13.33. A performance on the Jay Pritzker stage.

Germany (1994–1995), and the Financial Times Millennium Bridge in London (1996), but none was ever constructed. The latter was notable for being a collaboration with sculptor Richard Serra in which a singular curving form served as the bridge.[43]

The BP Bridge was designed after the Pritzker Pavilion. Initial models included a straight bridge with a ramp on the west side leading south and another on the east side leading north, thereby creating a Z shape. This design, however, generated two problems: elevators were needed to conform to the requirements of the Americans with Disabilities Act, and the bridge terminated at the usually empty north end of Daley Bicentennial Plaza. Ed Uhlir and consultant John MacManus encouraged Gehry to redirect pedestrian flow to the middle of the plaza and toward the lake. Gehry also realized that if curves were added to the Z, the bridge would be handicapped-accessible and allow everyone to have the same experience. The ramps were then extended on each side, adding still more curvature and length to the structure; the bridge's 925-foot length is ten times the width of Columbus Avenue below. The brushed stainless steel plates that clad the bridge overlap like scales, further adding to the reptilian form. In time, the Z was transformed into a slithering, snakelike shape.[44]

Gehry's move to transform a simple bridge into a snake is no surprise to those familiar with his earlier work. Gehry's interest in fish-related designs is well known: fish lamps and the truncated fish shape of the Guggenheim Museum in Bilbao are the best-

13.34

13.35

13.36

13.37

13.38

known examples.[45] But Gehry simultaneously experimented with snake forms. Given the design requirements for Millennium Park, the bridge offered Gehry an opportunity to apply a new form to an old structure.

The winding, curving structure, however, was more than just whimsy. The form was functional. The greater number of curves allowed for a more-gentle, 5 percent slope and thereby made the bridge accessible to wheelchair users. The rot-resistant Brazilianwood (pau lope) flooring and the absence of handrails invited pedestrians to wander up to the site. The curvature of the west ramp also allowed for the construction of an earthberm to block or screen noise from Columbus Drive. Finally, when the Lurie Garden design of Kathryn Gustafson was adopted, Gehry altered the terminus of the west ramp to coincide with the garden's seam.[46]

13.39

13.34. Model of the proposed USTRA Bridge.

13.35. Model for the London Millennium Bridge competition.

13.36. Gehry's paper snake lamp (1983–1986).

13.37. Gehry's snake and fish lamp (1983–1986).

13.38. Millennium Park bridge computer model.

13.39. As Richard M. Daley speaks at the dedication of the BP Bridge, Frank Gehry contemplates the first bridge he ever built.

PRITZKER PAVILION AND BP BRIDGE reflect Gehry's distinct urbanism. While Gehry's design breaks with certain historic traditions in Chicago architecture, other elements genuflect to history. For example, Gehry did not completely abandon the SOM design. He kept the pavilion in the same location, as well as the oval shape of the lawn. The overall plan relied on the tree canopy of Grant Park to tie various elements together. "The part visually may be disparate, but all of that is going to be woven together by the tree canopy," insisted Craig Webb, adding that skeptics should consider New York City's Central Park. "There's a lot of disparate elements going on in Central Park, but its all within the trees and it all hooks together."[47]

Gehry also employed the trellis to resolve the conflict between the nineteenth and twentieth centuries. Gehry admits that Grant Park's design was rooted in the nineteenth century, yet Millennium Park "was busting out" with various twenty-first century designs. In order to provide some balance, the columns supporting the trellis were proportioned to echo a nineteenth-century classicism.[48]

For Gehry, Grant Park is comparable to Central Park. "It's the lungs of the city," believes Gehry, "a place where you can breathe." Gehry and his team recognized that the Michigan Avenue facade of high-rises was "an organic piece of urban fabric" developed over decades according to the economics and aesthetics of each era. The skyscraper walls on both Michigan Avenue and Randolph Street represented a powerful vista, demanding a stronger, more dynamic piece of architecture in the music pavilion.[49]

At the same time, Grant Park differs from Central Park in a major way. Chicago's "front yard" presents, according to Craig Webb, "a U-shaped massing of the city with no fourth side." The result is an unusual asymmetry with skyscrapers on two sides, and then the lake "blown out" on the other.[50] Nature sits on one side, congestion on the other.

Most of Gehry's designs before 1990 were concerned with problem solving and small-scale neighborhoods, while his Millennium Park creations take a bolder approach, visually telling residents and sightseers alike that this is a space to visit and inhabit, to play and contemplate. Pritzker Pavilion and the trellis create a new civic space, open and free to an entire city, connecting the citizens of one of the most densely populated American cities with both nature and art. A space occupied for nearly 150 years by railroad tracks, empty freight cars, and parked automobiles is now reserved for pedestrians lounging on grass, listening to music, or daydreaming up at the sky. To the east, BP Bridge offers still another connecting link between the skyscrapers of Michigan Avenue and the natural beauty of Lake Michigan. In more ways than one, the historic railroad trench that separated the man-made chaos of the Loop from the sublime nature of Lake Michigan is transcended.

13.42. Thomas Pritzker, Margo Pritzker, Frank Gehry, Cindy Pritzker, Maggie Daley, Richard M. Daley.

Chapter 14

THE JOAN W. AND IRVING B.
HARRIS THEATER FOR MUSIC AND DANCE

Before a single patron entered the door, or a performer sang or danced across the stage, the Harris Theater was a hit. In 2002, the Chicago Athenaeum, a museum devoted to architecture and design, bestowed an American Architecture Award upon the theater for its economical and innovative design. The structure was one of forty-one projects recognized in the United States that year, only two of which originated from Chicago.[1]

Harris Theater officials like to describe the structure as Swiss watch in a country box.[2] Visitors entering the upper-level Randolph Street entrance are met by a simple, white rectangular concrete lobby made luminous by a facade of windows. Instead of a traditional theater marquee, an enormous stage curtain designed by Louise Nevelson for the Opera Theater of St. Louis's production of *Orpheus and Eurydice* in 1984 dominates the interior wall and is visible through the windows.

The Harris Theater is the end product of a nearly two-decade search by the Music and Dance Theater (MDTC) to construct a state-of-the-art midsize venue. "It seemed like every Christmas I would sit down and redesign a different part of it," remembers the theater's architect Thomas Beeby. The combined frustrations of changing locations and design specifications, Beeby now admits, generated a more creative design.[3] The Harris Theater evolved from an all-steel, above-ground building into a unique, precast concrete structure, most of which is underground. Beeby's partner Gary Ainge pointed out that not only is precast concrete infrequently used in theater structures, but he and Beeby employed the material in totally new and unexpected ways.[4]

Early in the design process, the MDTC companies gave Beeby and Ainge a strict set of guidelines: they wanted a multiuse facility with a chamber designed to accommodate small audiences, who often felt lost in larger theaters that were not filled to capacity; in order to provide good sight lines for dance, the audience had to see the floor; hierarchical seating arrangements with the best seats in boxes and inferior seating in the rear would not be accepted.[5]

These demands were the outgrowth of the inadequacies of other theatrical venues. Staging areas in many theaters were too small for MDTC companies. Most lacked fly

14.1

14.2

14.1. The Harris Theater on Randolph Street.

14.2. Louise Nevelson's stage curtain for *Orpheus and Eurydice* in the theater lobby was purchased by Irving and Joan Harris in 1985 and later donated to the Chicago Public Library. When the library failed to find a suitable location to display it, the Harrises persuaded library officials to loan the curtain permanently to the new theater.

towers and did not provide enough depth, thereby making it difficult to stage opera. Others either lacked an adequate alley to service the facility, or had floor plans too small to include a lobby.

The loading dock was a key issue. MDTC companies needed a facility with a staging area and loading space large enough to allow one company to unload scenery and supplies and begin setting up its production while another company simultaneously occupied the stage, thereby avoiding extra days on the site for which they had to pay rent.[6] Consequently, the loading dock had to be large enough to accommodate two tractor trailers simultaneously and provide enough space for trucks to easily enter and exit on

14.3. Harris Theater's loading dock.

14.4. The Harris Theater's fly space reaches 75 feet above the stage.

lower Randolph Street. "The economics of theaters have a lot to do with how much you have to spend getting in and out," explained Beeby.[7]

Beeby made a variety of changes to address these concerns. First, he designed a fly space reaching seventy-five feet above the stage, with a thirty-foot proscenium and a backstage rigging system with sixty line sets for hanging scenery and lighting. More important, he devised a plan with a staging area in the space between the Harris Theater and the outdoor music pavilion above. A music or dance company can build sets offstage and then roll them directly onto the stage. A large elevator at one end allows companies to lift large pieces from the loading dock at the level of the Harris Theater to the outdoor music pavilion above. Wide hallways allow backstage workers to easily move twelve-foot wardrobe racks throughout the theater. Double acoustic doors and walls separate the two structures and prevent sound in one venue from disturbing performances in the other.[8]

The most noted quality of the Harris Theater is the austere, concrete interior. "When you get to your seat, you expect a hockey game," states architect Laurence Booth, "and instead you get a ballet or an opera." Beeby himself describes the theater as "a concrete box with metal pieces inside." Beeby's goal was to create a theater with high-quality acoustical fidelity and exceptional sight lines for patrons, with easy-to-use facilities for performers. In the auditorium, the interior chamber is divided into two major sections: a 400-seat balcony and a 1,100-seat orchestra. The chamber is an elegant combination of grays and blacks with colored and patterned theater lights projected onto the walls and curtains.[9]

To avoid any sense of hierarchy in the auditorium, Beeby made the main floor one-third of the house, steeply tipping up the back half and making it into the parterre. The design ensues better sight lines for dancing. The wide and deep stage ensures a level of flexibility to accommodate a large ballet performance as well as an intimate duet. In the end, according to Beeby, the seating was "extremely democratic."[10]

The minimalist style and "off-the-shelf" construction continues throughout the interior space. The walls are devoid of applied finishes and composed of 1,750 precast cement panels painted in shades of white, gray, and black. Pipes and other infrastructure

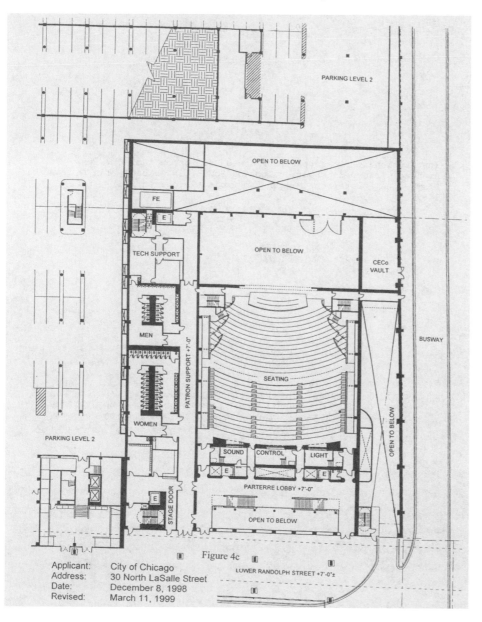

14.5. Lower Randolph Street/parterre–level plan.

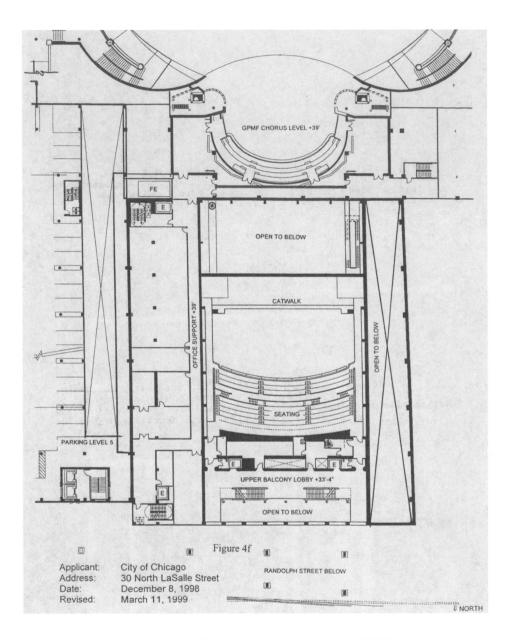

GPMF CHORUS LEVEL +39'

FE

E

OPEN TO BELOW

CATWALK

OFFICE SUPPORT +39'

OPEN TO BELOW

SEATING

PARKING LEVEL 5

E   E

UPPER BALCONY LOBBY +33'-4"

OPEN TO BELOW

E

Figure 4f

Applicant: City of Chicago
Address: 30 North LaSalle Street   RANDOLPH STREET BELOW
Date: December 8, 1998
Revised: March 11, 1999

⇓ NORTH

14.6. Upper balcony–level plan.

are exposed. To prevent visitors from getting lost, the various lobbies are color-coded with lights: white for the upper lobby, yellow for the upper balcony, green for the lower balcony, and blue for the orchestra level. Orange designates "transportation"—stairs and elevators. Beeby describes the theater as "a machine for making music."[11]

To produce the desired acoustics, Beeby included a series of forestage reflectors which direct sound throughout the chamber and ensure undistorted, even sound throughout the entire auditorium. The reflector over the stage also projects sound back to the performers so they can hear each other. Six towers on each side of the stage support light-

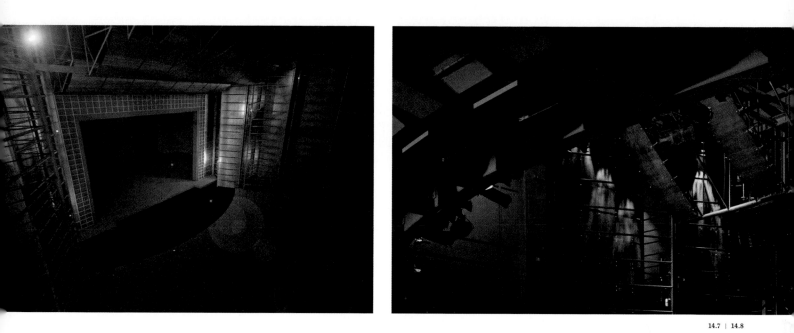

ing and reflectors that move the sound out to the audience. Hoping to eliminate dead spots and echoes in the audience, Beeby designed irregular walls with indentations and grooves on the concrete panels to break up the sound and added acoustic quilting on the balcony walls. The sound thereby moves in different directions across the hall.[12] Early reviews spoke favorably of Beeby's accomplishment. *Chicago Tribune* music critic John von Rhein commended the quality of the sound, comparing it to the Harris Theater's architecture: "bright, clean, direct, unadorned."[13]

Beeby not only accommodated the demands of performers and patrons; external forces were equally influential. The most controversial source of contention was the original height of the theater, to which a variety of civic groups objected. Beeby understood these demands, and even sympathized with them. "The lakefront is a commonly held land in Chicago," he acknowledges, "and the public has a voice in it." Debates over lakefront use have a long and checkered history in Chicago. "It's like an opera in that you sense that it has been played before," muses Beeby. "It's not a new event."[14]

The result was a relatively small rectangular box on Randolph Street. Although the final height of the theater structure was eighty-nine feet, only thirty-eight feet rise above Randolph Street. The remaining four stories, or fifty-one feet, are located below the surface. Furthermore, the Harris's 110-foot-wide facade is only slightly more than the width of four city lots, while its fourteen-foot depth makes it one of the narrowest structures in the park.[15]

Beeby also adapted his design to Gehry's adjacent music pavilion. For Beeby, the trick was to do something that was powerful enough to stand up to Gehry's massive, flamboyant structure, but not compete with it. "I changed the design of the exterior piece so it would be simpler," Beeby admitted. Recognizing that Gehry's music pavilion was a

14.7. Reflectors inside the Harris Theater distribute sound.

14.8. The Harris Theater stage and orchestra-level seating.

"figural" structure, Beeby concluded that his theater need to be a simple backdrop. At one point, the Harris Theater design included a series of curves. When Gehry revealed a pavilion full of curves, however, Beeby responded with a more modest structure in which smaller, elegant pieces defined the space. "I was looking for something that would be different," stated Beeby, "that would be memorable, but not competing with his."[16]

The Harris Theater counters charges that Millennium Park is a venture for Chicago's elite. Joan Harris explains that the facility offers a conscious alternative to the Chicago Symphony, the Art Institute, and the Lyric Opera, the three principal arts institutions in the city. "Each one of them in its own way has been working feverishly to reach out to the greater community, to attract new audiences, to do all kinds of outreach to get to the schools," Harris acknowledges. But as a trustee of the orchestra, she sees firsthand how

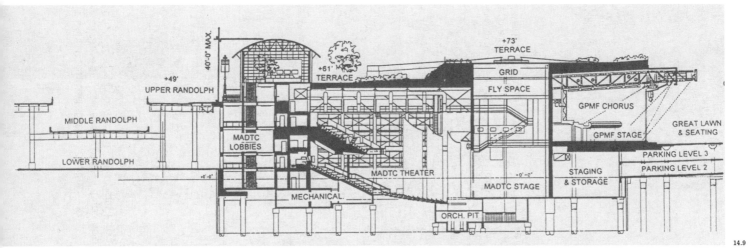

14.9

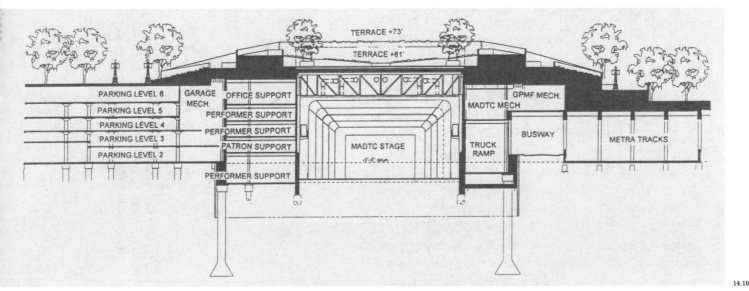

14.10

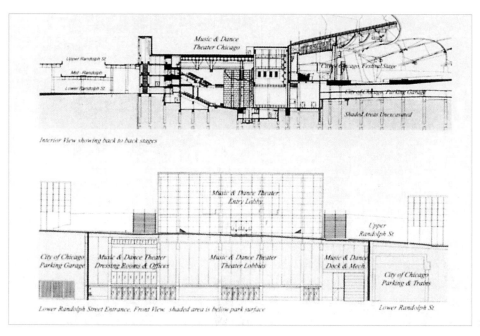

Interior View showing back to back stages

Music & Dance
Theater Chicago

Music & Dance Theater
Entry Lobby

Upper
Randolph St.

City of Chicago
Parking Garage

Music & Dance Theater
Dressing Rooms & Offices

Music & Dance Theater
Theater Lobbies

Music & Dance
Dock & Mech.

City of Chicago
Parking & Trains

Lower Randolph Street Entrance, Front View, shaded area is below park surface

Lower Randolph St.

14.9. An early longitudinal rendering of the Harris Theater looking east. This drawing included a curved roof for the theater and predated Frank Gehry's flamboyant headdress on the music pavilion (right).

14.10. Transverse section of the theater looking south.

14.11. By 2002, these cross-sectional views of the Music and Dance Theater (later Harris) depict the theater's 39-foot-high entry on Randolph Street (below) and Frank Gehry's Pritzker Pavilion (top).

hard it is overcome the social divisions associated with Chicago's elite cultural institutions. "The physical buildings," she believes, "present at least some of the barrier."[17]

By contrast, Beeby's Harris Theater design conveys a different message. "It's plain," insists Harris. "It has no chandeliers and no marble; none of the stuff of old elegance." Harris, Beeby, and MDTC officials consciously sought an architecture that avoided the class and racial ideologies associated with classical and Western styles, creating a space that evoked, in Harris's words, "racial and economic neutrality." In her mind, the MDTC is more than just a cultural institution; it embodies a larger civic project.[18]

The Harris Theater also marked a sharp departure from Beeby's best-known work, the Harold Washington Public Library. According to Beeby, the library presented different problems. "First of all, it was in the Loop, with a site that had everything built out to the street line." Consequently, Beeby felt compelled to build the structure out to the street line. "It was all about walls—facades on streets, which is what nineteenth-century architecture's all about—the architecture of walls," argues Beeby.[19]

The Harris Theater represents something much different. The bulk of the theater is underground; at its lowest point, it is more than twenty feet below the level of nearby Lake Michigan. "Most of the building is actually hidden," admits Beeby. "In the end, I think it's better this way. You go in, and the whole building evolves going down underground." Beeby points out that most theaters have no windows because their form is determined by their interior. Consequently, this creates problems in designing the facades. The Harris Theater avoids this dilemma because 90 percent of the structure is below the surface of the park. "I think it's actually much more interesting than if it was above grade," concludes Beeby.[20]

This "invisibility" and the absence of a traditional facade or box produced an added benefit: a greater emphasis on the interior space. "The space is where the idea is," Beeby emphasizes. "It's all about playing music, and it's not about anything else. It's about a kind of democratic way of thinking about it, where the audience are all equal." In the final analysis, "the engagement between the audience and the stage is the whole thing." Beeby sought a warm, welcoming environment, to move spectators as close to the stage as possible, to foster an intimate relationship with performers on stage. In this theater without traditional hierarchies, Beeby envisioned a venue "to make the audience participate in the performance."[21]

IN 1999, A REPORT commissioned by the New York State Council of the Arts concluded that New York City had no affordable, midsize theater. The lack of such a facility severely restricted the ability of dance and other performing arts companies to build audiences, foster financial stability, fundraise, and market their programs. The result was public ignorance regarding "contemporary dance's ongoing contributions to national and world culture."

Three weeks after the Harris Theater opened in 2003, the *New York Times* was still bemoaning the lack of any midsize theater for dance in New York. The 2,750-seat City Center, with its rich dance history, was unaffordable for many companies. The Metropolitan Opera House (3,718 seats) and the New York State Theater (2,737) were often unavailable because of resident opera and ballet companies. And the 472-seat Joyce Theater lacked the wing and fly space required by many companies.[22]

But in Chicago, Tom Beeby's Harris Theater had solved each of those problems.

Chapter 15

CLOUD GATE

Anish Kapoor's *Cloud Gate* is a mammoth piece of public art. The gleaming, elliptical sculpture is one of the world's largest outdoor sculptures: 110 tons, sixty-six feet long, forty-two feet wide and thirty-three feet high. To accommodate the massive $20 million object, engineers were forced to redesign the underground parking garage and SBC Plaza where it rests. The mirrored finish is forged of a seamless series of 168 highly polished, stainless steel plates, each weighing between 1,000 and 2,000 pounds. The bean-shaped sculpture reflects the sky, the city's skyscrapers, and pedestrians strolling through Millennium Park. The concave opening along the underside invites observers to walk under and around the massive object. Once underneath, viewers' eyes are drawn upward into the twenty-seven-foot-high omphalos, a mirrored indentation providing multiple reflections of those below. According to Kapoor, he wanted the piece to have a classical feel yet at the same time to be very contemporary.[1]

Kapoor is distinguished for his paradoxical sculptures that simultaneously explore physical and psychological themes. He has worked in a variety of mediums: from powdered pigment sculptures and site-specific pieces on walls or floors, to gigantic installations both indoors and out. His inventive and versatile art explores what he considers to be universal metaphysical polarities: being and nonbeing, place and nonplace, and the solid and the intangible.

The sculpture—described variously as a "jelly bean," a "silver bean," a "kidney bean," a "steel kidney," and a "tear drop"—is the first public Kapoor sculpture in the United States. Millennium Park officials were particularly drawn to the artist's original proposal because of its interactive qualities, reflecting the skyline, the clouds, the lake, and individual observers, sometimes simultaneously.[2] Before Kapoor even began constructing *Cloud Gate*, the art dealer and art committee member Richard Gray predicted the sculpture would become a Chicago icon. The changing finish, the multiple reflections, the seemingly evolving shape, and the interactive qualities would make it a magnet for people. The work was, simply put, "going to knock everybody's socks off."[3]

Unlike much of modern art, or even Picasso's *Untitled* work in Daley Civic Center, *Cloud Gate* was envisioned with an identifiable purpose, rooted in the specific context of

I'm not sure I believe in truth as a fixed reality. I think it's always changing and, in our everyday world, it's certainly relative.

ANISH KAPOOR

Grant Park. "This piece hovers between architecture and sculpture," claims Kapoor. "It is a kind of gate, and when completed, three-quarters of its surface will be [reflections of] sky. So it naturally suggested *Cloud Gate*, even though some people will probably still call it *The Bean*."[4]

Like much of Kapoor's art, *Cloud Gate* examines perception. Most explicitly, the sculpture reflects the surrounding landscape. "When you're standing around it, it's picking up the sky and bringing the sky down to you, and then it's actually warping the skyline of what's behind you, and you are also reflected in that," points out Chicago public art committee chair Michael Lash. "You cannot not be in the sculpture."[5]

Born in Bombay, India, in 1954, Kapoor was raised in a household with an Indian Hindu father and an Indian Jewish mother. After attending private schools, he enrolled in an engineering program in Israel, dropped out after six months, and remained in Israel for two years. He eventually migrated to London and attended the Hornsey College of Art (1973–1977) and the Chelsea School of Art (1977–1978).[6] During the 1980s, Kapoor became identified with a group of British sculptors labeled the "new generation" or the "new British sculptors," the successors to Henry Moore and Barbara Hepworth. Kapoor and sculptors like Tony Cragg, Richard Deacon, and Jean-Luc Vilmouth openly reacted against modernism's emphasis on sculpture as autonomous, hermetic, non-referential, and radically abstract. In particular, Kapoor addressed a wider range of issues rather than purely formalist or aesthetic questions. "I don't wish to make sculpture about form," Kapoor revealed in the 1980s, "it doesn't really interest me."[7] Art intended to produce beautiful objects was of little interest to Kapoor. His aesthetic ideal had a much more introspective purpose, "towards an unveiling of some internal state," in his words.[8]

Kapoor's internalism is a key component of his art. "Making art isn't an intellectual or theoretical activity, it's deeply rooted in the psychological—in the self," he says. For Kapoor, art is personal, an ongoing process of self-discovery. At the same time, he emphasizes that his art is not simply biographical, or a detailing of his personal neuroses. Kapoor envisions an art addressing the spiritual and emotional: "I wish to make sculpture about belief, or about passion, about experience, that is, outside of material concern."[9]

Kapoor's *Cloud Gate* reflects themes and issues with which the artist has grappled for the past quarter century. The sculpture, by reflecting the sky, the surrounding skyscrapers, and pedestrians strolling underneath, can be only "seen" or understood in parts, never in its entirety. Viewers, moving from one dimension of the sculpture to another, are in a state of paradox and "in-betweenness." As a disembodied, luminous form, the sculpture reflects a spiritual state, not a physical being.

The name of the work encapsulates Kapoor's purpose. "What I wanted to do was to make a work that would deal with the incredible skyline of Chicago and the open sky and the lake, but then also be a kind of gate," he said in one interview. "The tradition of public sculpture is for the gate, the archway, the square to flow within [the landscape] rather than be an object decorating it." In Millennium Park, Kapoor was motivated to create a work that, in his words, "was drawing in the sky," while "allowing you to enter it like a piece of architecture that was pulling your own reflection into the fulcrum, making a kind of participatory experience."[10]

Kapoor first explored these themes in *1000 Names* (1979–1980). The generic title reflected the artist's belief that the pieces were parts of a larger whole that could never be known in its entirety, but only intuitively grasped in specific cases, in temporary and transient works that had to be reconstructed anew, from powder, for each showing. In these dematerialized, disembodied, luminous forms, Kapoor searched for an art that

15.3. *1000 Names* (1979–1980).

reflected spiritual states, not just physical being. The pieces lacked texture and surface, creating the illusion that they existed only as color and light. Observers were forced, in his words, to "read the inner form in a completely different way." In this way, Kapoor created a sculpture addressing the metaphysical and the mystical. The pigment also expressed a contradiction: the sensuality of the colorful material and the impossibility of touching the piece without disturbing the image.[11]

This theme of ambivalence is repeated in much of Kapoor's work, including *Cloud Gate*. "We are all in exile," he contends, "in a positive sense of cultural ambiguity." Kapoor sees artists in a state of ambiguity in a world full of duality: male/female, East/West, earth/sky. For Kapoor, duality represents the energy of transformation and evolution, generating the conflicts which produce a state of being—internal and external, the superficial and the subterranean, conscious and unconscious.[12]

Kapoor's interest in duality and being evolved into a fascination with voids and emptiness, best exemplified in his series of concaves, spheres, and mirrored pieces. While some critics saw this as a sharp departure from his earlier work in pigment, Kapoor argued that polished surfaces were little different. "In the end it has to do with issues that lie below the material, with the fact that materials are there to make something else possible," he claimed. "That is what interests me."[13] In *Untitled* (1996) and *Turning the World Inside Out II* (1995), Kapoor created works that displayed no images, or only contorted

15.4

15.4. In *Untitled* (1996), Kapoor hung a bronze vortex on a wall with a reflection that seemed to engulf and annul surrounding objects.

15.5, 15.6. *Turning the World Inside Out II* (1995) was a chromium-plated bronze vortex sunk into the floor, which seemed to suck in everything around it like a whirlpool.

15.5
———
15.6

15.7. *Untitled* (1996) in the Kunst-Station St. Peter in Cologne (1996).

images, of the viewer.[14] For Kapoor, the art briefly renders the viewer invisible; thus, in Kapoor's words, "time and space are seemingly absent, at a standstill . . . , in that narrow passage, paradoxically there is a restlessness, an unease."[15]

In 1996–1997, Kapoor took two untitled metallic, spherical, double concave mirrors and placed them within sacred and ritualistic spaces: the Kunst-Station St. Peter in Cologne (1996) and in the Mausoleum am Dom in Graz (1997). Here Kapoor attempted to instigate a dialogue with religious architecture, dissolving the barriers that separate the seemingly insuppressible differences between the sacred and the profane in Graz. By blurring the boundary between the real and the reflected, Kapoor's sculpture, wrote one critic, "enters an inexhaustible dimension" and becomes "a synthesis between the limit and the limitless."[16] This blurring of boundaries would later appear in *Cloud Gate*.

Kapoor pursued these questions again with *Sky Mirror* (2001). The concave stainless steel mirror, twenty feet in diameter and ten tons in weight, reflects the way its surroundings change with the weather, offering each viewer an opportunity to see different images simultaneously. At the same time, no observer shares the same view, thereby allowing each to have an individual response. It is "a hole in space." Much like *Cloud Gate*, passersby can view themselves, the sky, and surrounding buildings in the parabola.[17]

The theme of emptiness is everywhere visible in Kapoor's work. Some contend that his work suggests that the presence of an object can create the illusion that the space is "more empty" than in the absence of an object. The critic Germano Celant argues that Kapoor's art centers around the paradox of the absent body-shadows, gaps, and vacuums.[18] This explains Kapoor's fascination with voids and concaves. Each serves "to make an object which is not an object, to make a hole in the space, to make something which actually does not exist," writes one admirer.[19]

Kapoor's interest in voids and nothingness entered a new phase with a series of massive, metallic spheres. *Turning the World Inside Out* (1995), *Turning the World Upside Down III* (1996), and *Turning the World Upside Down #4* (1998) appeared to be early, miniaturized versions of *Cloud Gate*. The geometric forms in each displayed a higher level of tech-

15.9. *Turning the World Inside Out* (1995).

nological complexity, evidenced by the hollow, concave omphalos on one side and the multireflective, mirrored surface. As viewers approached the omphalos, or indentation, they were visually "scooped" or pulled into it, thereby confusing the distinction between inside and outside. The effect was a colder, more remote, less intimate sensibility. One critic concluded that *Turning the World Inside Out* externalized and reflected reality and simultaneously devoured it.[20] In this fashion, Kapoor continued to grapple with presence and absence, being and nonbeing, place and nonplace, the solid and the intangible.

In the summer of 2003, *Turning the World Inside Out* (1995) was placed in the center of the prehistoric Rollright Stones, erected in Oxfordshire, England, in the Late Neolithic period around 3000 BCE. Just as Kapoor had earlier explored the relationship between sacred and ritualistic spaces at the Kunst-Station St. Peter in Cologne (1996) and in the

15.10

15.10. *Turning the World Upside Down III* (1996).

15.11–15.12. Two views of *Turning the World Upside Down #4* (1998).

Mausoleum am Dom in Graz (1997), here he placed his work within what some considered to be a more ancient portal between the physical and spiritual worlds. The stones, with their worn, rugged surfaces, presented a dramatic foil to the smooth, reflective steel sculpture. For Kapoor, this represented an opportunity to move away from a traditional gallery setting and place his art in a public and historical context. Juxtaposing the modern and the ancient, Kapoor hoped to show that both "have the same intention."[21]

Placing his sculpture within a prehistoric setting also enabled Kapoor to experiment with public art. "I've always detested public sculpture," Kapoor bluntly admits. "For far too long, it seems to me—since the nineteenth century—there has been a loss of purpose." Kapoor questions the propriety of placing "a little jewel" on a lawn, juxtaposed against a monumental building. He wonders: why is the object there? Kapoor believes something more complicated is necessary, something contextual and immediate to the surroundings of the sculpture itself.[22]

The placement of *Turning the World Inside Out* within the Rollright Stones also enabled Kapoor to more explicitly explore gender and sexual ambiguity, as well as notions of the East and the West. For some, the round, womblike shape of the sphere with a vaginal indentation represented the female form. Placing the object in the middle of a circle of upright stones had an unmistakable phallic symbolism.[23] Others contend that Kapoor's significant works after 1981 presented hemispheric cavities and oval or roundish constructions that evoked the female body. The dome is an absolute symbol of the whole, a sacred enclosure and uterus, the locus of the feminine and the Great Mother, an inexhaustible reservoir of psychic and erotic energy, the source and origin of all becoming.[24]

While such Jungian and essentialist ideas of the feminine have generated criticism of Kapoor's work, the artist continually reminds observers that intuited meaning in his (if not all) art is diffuse. The observer, not the artist, infuses meaning and relevance into a work of art, a process that results in multiple interpretations and myriad truths. "A sculpture is like a vessel offered to the viewer to fill with meaning," according to Kapoor. "What makes a good work is the range of these references."[25]

These themes culminate in *Cloud Gate*.[26] How can a public sculpture capture the essence of a space? Can a piece of public art reflect the public realm that surrounds it? *Cloud Gate* answers such questions by scale. *Cloud Gate* is not "big," as some might conclude upon first viewing, but a physical reflection of the open park space, towering human-made structures to the west and north, and the seemingly endless water to the east. Size is simply a product of scale.[27] Compared to the 167-ton *Untitled* by Picasso a few blocks away, Kapoor's work seems small. Just as Gehry's BP Bridge physically connects the human-made skyscrapers of Michigan Avenue and the natural, sublime beauty of Lake Michigan, *Cloud Gate* contextualizes and incorporates this massive landscape into a single reflection.

Cloud Gate creates dramatic and new vistas of Chicago. Observing the sculpture at the steps entering SBC Plaza, viewers simultaneously see the Chicago skyline, Lake Michigan, and themselves. One looks west and sees Lake Michigan to the east. In Kapoor's mind, the traditional sublime drew a viewer's gaze into the distance; in *Cloud Gate*, the sublime now *includes* the viewer.[28]

This changes yet again when the viewer moves beneath *Cloud Gate*. One looks up into the omphalos and all perspective is lost and confused. Viewers see a multiplicity of images, many of which are a bewildering array of themselves. What is "real" and what is reflection? Is this an object or a "hole in space"? What is the form? Where does the object end or begin? Here Kapoor achieves his goal of turning an object into an "un-object," of disarranging the distinction between reality and unreality. All perspective is rendered meaningless; the disoriented viewer stands in a state of ambiguity.

The mixture of scale and interactivity allows Kapoor to introduce multiple vistas and nuanced meanings in *Cloud Gate*. Is the sculpture not so much a "kidney bean" but a "seed"? Is Kapoor providing a symbol of fertility, simultaneously reflecting the generative powers of humankind in both nature (reproduction) and architecture (the building of cities)? How "big" is this "hole in space"? Like his works before 1990, *Cloud Gate* generates an ongoing multilevel, participatory dialogue between the artist and the viewer. As one moves around the sculpture, the hypnotic reflections and even the shape change; it is never one thing in one place. The stationary object is always in transition, continually in a state of flux. Kapoor encourages individuals to "let go," to allow the piece to act upon the viewer. As in many of Kapoor's earlier works, the observation becomes integral to making the work itself. "Not only do you look at it," Kapoor insists, "it looks at you."[29] Literally.

Chapter 16

THE *CROWN FOUNTAIN*

The *Crown Fountain* consists of two rectangular glass brick towers designed by Spanish sculptor Jaume Plensa. Fifty feet tall, 23 feet wide and 16 feet thick, the illuminated towers face one another from either end of a 232-foot-long, 48-foot-wide rectangular reflecting "skin pool." Water cascades down the sides of the towers into the shallow, quarter-inch-deep pool paved in black African granite. The pool and towers not only encourage pedestrians to cross the plaza and "walk on water," but transform the fountain into a downtown piazza and meeting point.[1]

The fountain combines for the first time a variety of technologies. Over one million light-emitting diodes (LED) line the interior of the towers' facades, effectively becoming high-rise television screens. Each one displays mammoth video portraits of approximately one thousand Chicago citizens that change every five minutes. Periodically interspersed between the faces are a variety of nature scenes. After nightfall, the other three sides of the towers display changing colors of orange, red, yellow, green, purple, and white. At timed intervals, the faces on the towers purse their lips and water spouts out, a digital reference to the European, Renaissance-era gargoyles that inspired Plensa.[2]

Historically, public fountains—both monumental and modest—played significant roles in the civic life of European and American communities. Fountains initially served functional needs, namely drinking and washing. But by the Renaissance, European cities had built ornate, highly decorative structures with the most advanced water technologies to express civic pride or celebrate the values of religion, health, purity, wisdom, or youth. Some of these fountains—the *Fontaine des Innocents* (1549) in Paris and Bernini's *Triton Fountain* (1642–1643) in Rome—remain artistic and cultural landmarks.[3]

In the United States, the first fountains appeared early in the nineteenth century in conjunction with municipal water systems. After Philadelphia opened the nation's first public water works in 1801, for example, the Centre [later Penn] Square pump house was adorned with William Rush's fountain sculpture *Water Nymph and Bittern* (c. 1809).[4] By midcentury, city reformers promoted both sidewalk drinking fountains to better serve growing urban populations and monumental fountains like Central Park's *Bethesda Fountain* advertising the values of temperance and health. Early in the twentieth century, Chi-

I am not looking for similarities, but differences, since it is in an understanding of them that the strength of the 21st century lies.

JAUME PLENSA

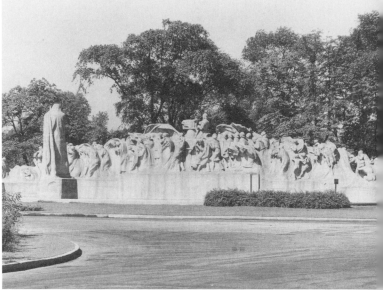

16.2. *Bethesda Fountain* (1873), Central Park, New York City.

16.3. Lorado Taft's *Fountain of Time* (1922).

16.4. Lorado Taft's *Fountain of the Great Lakes* (1914).

16.5. Edward Bennett and Marcel François Loyau's *Buckingham Fountain* (1927).

16.6. Lester Crown.

cago philanthropists built some of the most significant commemorative fountains in the United States: Lorado Taft's *Fountain of the Great Lakes* (1914) outside the Art Institute of Chicago, and Taft's *Fountain of Time* (1922) at the western terminus of the Midway Plaisance celebrated nature and the American alliance with Great Britain, respectively. Edward Bennett and Marcel François Loyau's *Clarence Buckingham Memorial Fountain* was the world's largest decorative fountain upon opening in Grant Park in 1927. Many considered *Buckingham* a technological marvel and the greatest fountain achievement because of its immense size and the height of its soaring water.[5] It remains one of Chicago's most popular attractions.

In December 1999, the Crown family agreed to fund a "water feature" in Millennium Park.[6] In contrast to the funding of other enhancements, where donors provided large financial gifts to support a design chosen and developed in conjunction with various Millennium Park officials, the Crown family was directly involved from the inception of the fountain project. The Crowns explored different water technologies, including the spectacular fountain designs associated with Las Vegas casinos and hotels. They recruited outside advice in the selection of the artist. They sponsored an informal competition among artists they solicited. They were active participants in the evolving design and engineering. "They actually liked the idea that they were going to build it for the people of Chicago," remembered John Bryan. "They are builders after all."[7]

Negotiations between Bryan and members of the Crown family lasted almost a year. "Lester [Crown] and I had to do a little dance," recounted Bryan. "We're great friends, but we had to get it all out." Since the Crowns are active in real estate development, Bryan quickly learned that they were familiar with all aspects of constructing such a project. Eventually, the Crowns and Bryan agreed that Millennium Park, Inc. (the organizational

16.6

entity representing the donors) would "cap" the Crown's cost at $10 million, with the corporation paying for anything in excess up to $17 million. "If it happened to get above that," Bryan stated, "we'd go back to the drawing board and decide whether to build it and how to handle the costs."[8] The final price tag was $17 million.

By the time the Crowns became involved in Millennium Park, Frank Gehry had agreed to design the park's pavilion and bridge. According to Millennium Park fundraiser James Feldstein, "Gehry set a standard, and I think Susan Crown had the same notion as Cindy Pritzker: 'If you folks are serious about doing a fountain, let's do it right.'"[9] In conversations with John Bryan, Crown family members expressed an interest in supporting and developing a design that was reflective of the twenty-first century, not one that simply evoked earlier fountains. "They began to realize, to our good fortune," believed Bryan, "that if they were going to put their name on something, it had to have an originality to it and not be a store-bought fountain."[10]

The Crowns began the selection process with no specific artist or design in mind. Instead, they asked Bob Wislow of U.S. Equities Realty (who later managed the construction of the fountain, music pavilion, bridge, and Anish Kapoor's sculpture) to compile a list of prospective artists and architects. Hoping to attract the most creative proposals possible, the Crowns issued a broad program with minimal restrictions to potential designers. They initially treated the fountain design as a piece of architecture and provided general visual and architectural plans of the park, the space allotted to it, and its relationship to the city.[11]

Although the Crowns were never predisposed to a particular style or artist, the family arrived at a philosophical consensus early in their deliberations. "Lester Crown described it as dreaming something new," remembers gallery director and art collector

Paul Gray, "something for the twenty-first century, something that didn't necessarily look backwards in terms of its physical form." Most important, the Crowns did not want to duplicate contemporary or even historic fountains.[12]

In January 2000, the Crown family narrowed their choices to three individuals: Maya Lin, Robert Venturi, and Jaume Plensa. Each one was invited to Chicago to present a proposal to Crown family members and representatives from the city and Millennium Park.[13] Lin and Venturi were the best known of the three. Lin had first rocketed to fame two decades earlier with her *Vietnam Veterans Memorial* (1982) in Washington, D.C., one of the best-known pieces of public art of the twentieth century. She attracted the interest of the Crowns, in part, because of her fountain design for the *Civil Rights Memorial* (1989) in Montgomery, Alabama. Building on this earlier work, Lin presented a design largely horizontal in form and low in height, a reflection of her dislike for things vertical. By contrast, Venturi, a Pritzker Prize laureate in architecture and coauthor of the classic *Learning from Las Vegas* (1972), proposed a 150-foot-tall fountain with lights arranged and sequenced to look like flowing water, even in the winter.[14]

But the Crowns were most impressed with the least known of the three designers: Jaume Plensa. The Spanish-born artist, ironically, was not included in the original list of prospective artists compiled by Bob Wislow. Upon assembling the list, Wislow sent it to several friends and associates, including the attorney and modern art collector Jack Guthman, who had earlier anchored the city's effort to build the Harris Theater. Guthman contacted Wislow: "Bob, you've left off a terrific young talent from Barcelona." He reminded Wislow that they had both seen Plensa's work at the Jeu de Paume on a recent trip to Paris.

"But does he do fountains?" Wislow asked. Guthman cited Plensa's outdoor work in France, Jerusalem, Stockholm, and elsewhere. Wislow added Plensa to the list.[15]

A few weeks later, Susan Crown visited Wislow's U.S. Equities Realty office to examine nearly a thousand images of public art throughout the world compiled by Wislow. "I spent an afternoon around this huge conference room table and made piles," remembered Crown. But one in particular stood out. "The piece that was overwhelming to me," Crown recounted, "was this light sculpture in Jerusalem." Crown had discovered Jaume Plensa's *Bridge of Light* at Mishkenot Sha'ananim, in Jerusalem, Israel (1998). The flat plaza with a simple hole that is transformed into a powerful beam of light at night impressed Crown. "It's remarkable," she still insists.[16]

Although Plensa's public profile was less visible in the United States, his work was highly regarded in Europe and Asia, where many considered him to be one of the world's leading sculptors. Although he was only forty-four years old, Plensa had had his art displayed in the Galerie Nationale du Jeu de Paume in Paris, the Henry Moore Sculpture Trust in Halifax, England; the Malmö Konsthall in Sweden; the Museo Reina Sofia in Madrid; the Museum Moderner Kunst in Vienna, and the Mie Prefectural Art Museum in Japan. In the United States, the Richard Gray Gallery in Chicago had sponsored several shows of Plensa's art. Described as "contextually diverse, layered and dualistic," Plensa

16.7. *Bridge of Light* at Mishkenot Sha'ananim, in Jerusalem, Israel (1998).

sculptures were noted for attempting to draw viewers into participating with the work of art itself.[17]

Born in Barcelona in 1955, Plensa grew up in Spain and lived throughout Europe as an adult. His work reflected late twentieth-century shifts in Spanish culture and his Catalonian origins. By the 1980s, Plensa had emerged as an influential figure, in part because his work reflected the pluralistic culture of Barcelona and Catalonia. Inhabited at various times by Iberians, Phoenicians, Greeks, Carthaginians, Romans, Celts, Visigoths, Arabs, and Jews, Barcelona has long been cognizant of its multiplicity of sometimes-conflicting cultures, especially compared to the rest of the Iberian peninsula. The hybrid heritage of Catalonia encouraged Plensa to confront and explore the increasingly temporal and rootless life of late twentieth-century Europe. Whereas migration and transience are defining characteristics for North Americans, Plensa believed that Europe lacked such experiences and traditions. As rootlessness epitomized European life at the end of the century, so it defined much of Plensa's art. "As an artist I'm in a state of permanent nomadism," he declared. "The journey is a fundamental part of everyday life."[18]

Plensa's nomadic predisposition was manifested in his refusal to adopt a signature style. His art passed through various stages. In the 1980s, Plensa's works of cast, forged, and recycled iron, as well as bronze and copper, attracted attention for their voluptuous, anthropomorphic qualities. Although many artists considered cast iron a second-rate industrial material, Plensa was attracted to its historical associations with earth, rocks, and magma. Most significant was Plensa's use of "junkyard" materials and his penchant for transgressive art. Early on, for example, he rebelled against the emphasis on form among late twentieth-century artists. He wanted to replace the centrality of form with what he considered far more interesting: the ungraspable. For Plensa, form was an obstacle preventing viewers from seeing or "grasping" the content of a work.[19]

In Plensa's mind, too many artists and critics linked form with beauty. He acknowledged that one value of art was in creating beauty, but beauty did not "necessarily lie in the form." Plensa wanted to develop an art that addressed the beautiful but was also transformative. Good art, he argued, challenged the viewer to interact with the object, to question tradition and preconceptions, and thereby generated, in his words, "an exchange of energy."[20]

Plensa's disregard for form was echoed in his reluctance to work in one specific medium. For Plensa, issues of proportion, materials, and technical procedures never defined his work. They simply served as "equipment" for "viewing the world." Whether he employed cast iron or resin, tempered glass or mirrors, stainless steel or neon tubes, Plensa's primary interest remained the expression of ideas in a physical space, how to make abstract thought a concrete reality, discovering a connection between ideas and materials. A sculpture or any physical form of art was, for Plensa, "a great container of memory which enables us to explore our most global memory, the development of opposites, of dualities."[21]

Indeed, dualism was the dominant and ongoing theme in much of Plensa's work prior to the *Crown Fountain*. Dualism defined much of his daily existence; living and working in Paris and Barcelona, he was both a part of and apart from each, speaking in regional and international languages. In time, Plensa developed a body of sculpture seeking to invest intangible ideas with a tangible structure. Dualities such as public/private, interior/exterior, absence/presence, opaque/translucent increasingly attracted his interest.[22]

In 1993, while in residence at the Henry Moore Sculpture Trust in England, Plensa developed his first fountain. Installed in a former woolen mill at Dean Clough, Halifax, England, Plensa's fountain questioned traditional ideas of progress. In one room, visitors confronted *Twins*: two huge, steel-mesh nets containing a total of seventy-four cast iron balls with rough, rusted surfaces bearing letters and numbers in relief. In one net, the balls displayed numbers and the most popular first names of the nineteenth-century men and women who worked at Dean Clough. In the second net, visitors found a matching numbered ball with a disease that corresponded to the name. Plensa implied that the transition from an agricultural to industrial society brought untold benefits alongside material inequality and social ills.

Juxtaposed to *Twins* was the adjoining building with an interior spine of cast iron columns extending the entire length. An earthen floor made with 140 tons of local soil was partly flattened to make a path to an egg-shaped, bronze fountain standing alone. Water emerged from the top and flowed evenly down the sides to a collecting tank in the base. Water also poured from a spout near the bottom of the object. Herein was the duality of industrial society: the material world of disease and death in one room, the spiritual and supernatural symbolism of water in another. The presence of death coexisted with life.[23]

16.8, 16.9. *The Personal Miraculous Fountain* (1993) at the Camellia House at Breton Hall in the Yorkshire Sculpture Park in West Bretton, U.K.

Plensa's fascination with dualism expanded as his artistic mediums multiplied. By the 1990s, the artist's palate of melted materials included synthetic resin, melted glass, and alabaster. Plensa's sculptures were formed into containers, cabins, and hollow spaces. *The Porter* (1995), *Waiting Room* (1997), and several other works, for example, employed clear resin boxes. *The Porter*'s four resin panels were etched with texts from *Macbeth*, transforming abstract ideas into concrete reality. Reading the text visually and conceptually generated an interactive dialogue. Viewers were outside, the text was inside; in between was anticipation, projection, imagination. To comprehend the work, viewers were forced to circumambulate the object. At each facade, the sculpture and text changed, providing another viewpoint. A central light in the conceptually active void indicated potential for enlightenment through exchange between Plensa, Shakespeare, and the spectator. Thick but clear polyester resin transformed the sculpture into a glowing tower at night.[24] These elements ultimately appeared in the *Crown Fountain*.

Equally influential and predictive of Plensa's *Crown Fountain* creation were his outdoor public projects. *The Star of David* (1998) in Raoul Wallenberg Square in Stockholm, *Bridge of Light* (1998) at Mishkenot Sha'ananim in Jerusalem, a sculpture of iron and light at *Escalier monumental* and *Place Barbès* (1991), in Auch, France, and *Blake in Gateshead* in England (1996) enabled Plensa to experiment with light and a multiplicity of physical materials: cast iron, glass, stainless steel, mirrors, teak, and resin. In *Gläserne Seele & Mr. Net in Brandenburg* (1999–2000), Plensa employed LED technology, videos, and a computer in the design. "Thanks to all those projects, I got the capacity to do the project for the Crowns," Plensa acknowledged in 2003. "If that invitation arrived ten years ago,

16.10. *The Porter* (1995).

16.11. *Waiting Room* (1997).

16.12. (From left) *Winter Kept Us Warm II* (1998), *Scholars of War* (1999), *Hotel Paris* (1999), *Komm mit! Komm mit!* (1999).

16.12

16.15

I would not have the knowledge to do it.[25] Like Anish Kapoor, Plensa came to realize that public art presented distinctive problems, especially in relation to gallery art. "In an exhibition," he said in 1996, "works engender their own space, as if to protect themselves." By contrast, public art presents a more compelling challenge: how to integrate the viewer into an interactive relationship with the art, or in Plensa's words, "to succeed to be as one with it."[26]

The public settings of these projects also shaped Plensa's distinctive urbanism. The city, according to Plensa, "is an alive body, a geography in transformation, an accumulation of datum points particular and, in each case, unique." Similarly, "Each human being is a 'place,' an inhabitable space in itself that moves and develops; a 'place' in time, geography, volume and color."[27] Like Frank Gehry, Plensa views cities as chaotic beauty.

16.13, 16.14. *Escalier Monumentale* and *Place Barbès*, in Auch, France (1990–1991).

16.15. *Blake in Gateshead* at the Baltic Centre for Contemporary Art, in Gateshead, U.K. (1996).

16.16

16.17 | 16.18

16.16, 16.17. *The Star of David*, in Raoul Wallenberg Square, in Stockholm (1998).

16.18. *Gläserne Seele & Mr. Net* in Brandenburg (1999–2000).

"[I]f something characterizes cities," he declares, "it is the permanent friction between all these facets: romantic and practical, right and unjust, public and prevailed, exotic and daily, new and old, static and fleeting." In the emerging global city, architects and artists confront a rapidly evolving social fabric, full of "new attitudes" and distinctive "places of encounter."[28]

The Crowns were attracted to Plensa for many reasons. According to Plensa's gallery representative, Paul Gray, at least four qualities swayed different members of the Crown family. First, they were impressed by Plensa's artistic drive and personal enthusiasm. Second, the diversity of Plensa's art—drawings, sculpture, glass, plastic, metal,

videos, electronics, sound, light, and (most important) water—indicated an ability to work with multiple mediums and engage different philosophical approaches. Plensa eschewed a predictable style, a third trait that indicated a level of flexibility critical to such a large, complicated project. Finally, they admired the ability of Plensa's art "to connect with people on a human level," remembered Gray. Most important, according to Lester Crown, "We felt that Plensa's [design] was more unique, unusual, and more appropriate for this location."[29]

The Crowns imposed virtually no restrictions on Plensa. "They gave him a blank slate," claimed Paul Gray. No budgetary conditions were mentioned; nearly a year passed before any discussion took place regarding cost. "They said dream," remembered Gray, "dream big."[30]

Although the Crowns expressly wanted a design that was both innovative and unique, Plensa began with tradition, researching the history of fountains. He was especially influenced by fountains with anthropomorphic images, fountains that included "a sense of life," in Plensa's words.[31] When he presented his proposal to the Crowns in early 2000, he began with a visual slide show of Western fountains dating from the Middle Ages to the present. Plensa discussed the history, uses, and art associated with fountains. Most important, he emphasized the philosophical meaning attached to them over time. In Plensa's mind, to create something new or unique required a deep understanding of the history of fountains.

Plensa began with a simple question: what did he wish to achieve in a public space? First, he wanted to create a new kind of fountain. "The *Crown Fountain* is not just a fountain for Chicago," Plensa insisted, "but a fountain for the entire world," a fountain for the twenty-first century. He endeavored to create something with a certain universality about it. "That's the measure of success for an artist," believes Paul Gray. "If they're

16.19. *Fountain of the Four Rivers* (1648–1651) by Gianlorenzo Bernini in Piazza Navona, Rome.

16.20. *Salamander Fountain* by Gaudi in Park Güell (1900–1914), Barcelona.

able to communicate, the more profound their work is." So while the initial references considered the *Crown Fountain*'s relationship to *Buckingham Fountain*, as Plensa and the Crown family worked on the design, "we forgot about *Buckingham Fountain*."[32]

Second, Plensa recognized that the center of any fountain is the treatment and meaning of water. The fountain is, noted Plensa, "a reminder and reference to nature in everyday public spaces." Not only is water the key element of a fountain, but it embodies many mythic elements: life, transformation, creation, the body, and communication. By way of example, Plensa argued that 75 percent of the earth's surface is water; 60 percent of the human body is water. This took on an added importance in Chicago, for, in Plensa's words, "to think about water in Chicago is a very big responsibility."[33]

Plensa wanted to evoke Lake Michigan several hundred yards to the east. "I am always fascinated with the lake that is always changing even if it is always the same," he stated. Ice in the winter, blue waves in the summer: "It's an ideal sculpture in itself." Plensa readily acknowledged than an artist cannot improve upon the beauty of nature, but "my intention was to try to offer something eternally moving to the city, . . . an alternative memory of something that every one of us would know."[34]

Plensa also envisioned a fountain that played to his youthful fantasies of water. "Since I was a child that was an image that was always on my mind—to invite people to walk on the water," he explained. For Plensa, the fountain needed to simultaneously express commemorative meaning and innocent play.[35]

A third question for Plensa—an "obsession," in his words—was, what happens when the water is turned off? Most fountains "lose any direction," when the water stops flowing, believed Plensa. "It's completely stupid as an object." Since the Chicago climate prohibited a fountain with water flowing all year, Plensa sought a design that was "as beautiful with and without water."[36]

Plensa resolved this challenge with technology. The giant, fifty-foot LED screens operate twenty-four hours a day, all year round. "That is very important, because I am keeping the memory of water in the videos," claims Plensa. "The video of nature and water is always there, even if it is not physically falling down."[37] Like nature itself, the fountain changes with the seasons. While the water is turned off during the cold weather seasons, the LED screens transform the fountain into a high-tech sculpture.

Video technology also allowed Plensa to address another concern: what could he do to insure that the fountain remained alive, not static, over time? After visiting many fountains throughout Europe, Plensa was impressed by their passive and sometimes stagnant qualities. The sculpted figures in fountains remain unchanged after centuries. To avoid this predicament, Plensa incorporated video images of Chicago residents, enabling the fountain to evolve and become a visual archive of the city. A fountain that visually changed would enable later generations to interpret and reinterpret the art itself.[38]

At the same time, Plensa relied upon certain historic European traditions. In the Middle Ages and Renaissance, fountains incorporated the faces of gargoyles, and water spouted from their mouths. "I wished to do that with the real people," Plensa admitted.

16.21. *Crown Fountain in the winter.*

In effect, the video faces on the two towers "come alive" and are engaged in conversation. Plensa suggests that when the lips purse and spit out a huge stream of water, this evokes the importance of water, namely "the giving of life."[39]

Finally, Plensa sought a fountain reflective of his personal urbanism. Cities, for Plensa, are familiar yet anonymous spaces. The "relinquishment of intimacy and personal freedom in favor of anonymity has also left a deep mark on art in public spaces," he once stated. With the *Crown Fountain*, Plensa envisioned a place that was simultaneously anonymous and public. Again, the technology of the LED towers accomplished this. "I

16.22. Computer-generated image of *Crown Fountain*.

16.23. Computer-generated image of *Crown Fountain* plaza, looking northeast.

film the face of an old person living in Chicago who is not my father or your father," believed Plensa, "but he could represent perfectly your father or my father. He becomes a symbol of something wider than itself."[40]

But Plensa's vision of a fountain that simultaneously evoked the city and the new millennium was briefly threatened by its spiraling price tag. "I remember after two years working on the project, we got the final estimate for the piece," recounted Plensa. "It was a big meeting. Everybody was surprised about the cost of the piece." Plensa remembers Lester Crown speaking up.

"Jaume, I think it is more than I expected," Crown admitted. "Could you reduce the size of the piece just to be on the right price?"

Plensa hesitated, momentarily crestfallen, and then responded: "Look Lester, my piccc is in the right scale of the city," he charged. "If you could reduce Chicago, I could reduce my piece."[41] Plensa's resolve persuaded the Crowns; the project continued.

More than any other enhancement, the *Crown Fountain* generated the most criticism and opposition, although much of this resistance was out of the public eye. Some, such as Art Institute president James Wood, feared that the columns of glass were too tall. Others worried that the digital imaging would quickly become outmoded. Mayor Richard Daley raised two concerns: would the spectacular lighting of the fountain "Disneyfy" that part of the park, giving it a glitzy Times Square feel? On another occasion, Daley questioned whether the *Crown Fountain* presented a First Amendment issue: is the video display a public forum?[42] In both instances, appropriate authorities convinced the mayor that such worries could be resolved.

Michael Lash of the Public Art Committee was the most critical. After a full-scale model of the proposed fountain was set up in 2002, Lash wrote a letter to John Bryan objecting to the height and scale of the project. He was especially critical of Plensa, whom Lash accused of getting into "a pissing match" with the other artists in the park. Plensa, Lash believed, was trying to "one-up Kapoor."[43]

To Plensa's American representative, Paul Gray, these fears were expected. "This project opens a lot of new doors," he reminded observers. "Most people, when they think of a large video image, have really only a few references to go by. One would be a Times Square sign, or a ballpark billboard. It's understandable why people might find that objectionable in an environment like this." But Gray quickly pointed out that Plensa was attempting something completely different. "You can't design something like this by committee," insisted Gray. "Somewhere along the line you have to decide that you trust the artist."[44]

Despite the radical differences among Taft's *Fountain of Time* (1922) and *Fountain of the Great Lakes* (1914), Bennett and Loyau's *Buckingham Fountain* (1927), and Plensa's *Crown Fountain*, they share certain characteristics: they are not simply fountains, but architectural structures designed by sculptors.[45] Each celebrates water, serves as commemorative art, incorporates the latest forms of technology, provides a sense of spectacle and entertainment, and acts as an urban oasis.

But the *Crown Fountain* is distinctive from its aquatic and artistic predecessors. First, the *Crown Fountain* is a video sculpture. The water ceases flowing during cold-weather seasons, but the fountain remains an active, changing, and evolving piece of video art. Second, like the water itself, the "message" of the *Crown Fountain* is always in motion. "All is flux," wrote Heraclitus, "nothing stays still." Such is the *Crown Fountain*. Traditional, historic fountains are physically and sometimes philosophically static. But for their water, their singular themes remain the same over decades and centuries. By contrast, the faces and scenes that pass over the *Crown Fountain*'s LED towers constantly change. Plensa agreed to determine the images for only the initial two years of the fountain's existence,[46] insuring that future generations will redesign and transform the fountain to reflect their own values. As Plensa intended, the *Crown Fountain* is "an endless project."

Finally, the *Crown Fountain* promotes a unique level of interactivity. Traditional fountains discourage visitors from touching, much less splashing, in the water. *Buckingham Fountain* is surrounded by a fence. Lorado Taft's *Fountain of the Great Lakes* and *Fountain of Time* include moats that discourage citizens from touching the sculpture. By contrast, the *Crown Fountain* invites pedestrians to shower beneath the "spittle" of a video gargoyle, to remove one's shoes and cool off, to literally walk on water.

Some of this was unintentional. Plensa admitted his surprise that within hours of opening on July 16, 2004, children transformed the *Crown Fountain* into an informal water park. Kids played and splashed; adults watched and smiled. The dense pedestrian traffic destroyed the surrounding grass landscape within days. This unintended consequence of artistic creativity had given Chicago a new piazza. "What drew the kids to the

16.24, 16.25. In less than a week after opening on July 16, 2004 (16.24), the overwhelming crowds had trampled and destroyed portions of the grass lawn surrounding the *Crown Fountain* (16.25).

16.26. The Crown family, Jaume Plensa, and Richard Daley at the dedication of the *Crown Fountain*. Lester Crown is on the far left.

fountain was the dream, the dream to walk on the water," Plensa proclaimed. "Dreams, that is something that artists work with."[47]

But the fountain encourages more than childish recreational interactivity. As in other Plensa works, water and light are the main components of the *Crown Fountain*. "The light is an intense light from within, a light glowing inside the massive body and burning right through," according to Plensa. "This is the 'inner light,' the soul or the dream, the bright aura visible under the tattooed resin skin." By turning water and light on and off, the fountain embodies basic contradictions of human existence: life and death, day and night, love and hate.[48]

"Jaume took a risk," suggested Crown family representative Steve Crown. "He was working with a lot of ideas from the older school of fountains and updating them. The result is very different, very contemporary, and yet it also has traditional themes running through it."[49]

Only time will determine whether the *Crown Fountain* ranks as a pinnacle of creative achievement or "the relic of a willfully forgotten era's bad taste," as one critic predicted.[50] But only the most cynical will dispute that Jaume Plensa devised a new adventure for downtown pedestrians, enlivened Grant Park with water and diverting entertainment, offered people a sometimes tranquil respite, and challenged Chicago and the world with his distinctive vision of creativity at the millennium.

16.26

Chapter 17

THE LURIE GARDEN

Lurie Garden represents the most daring element in the Millennium Park design: an elaborate horticultural experiment with approximately 30,000 plantings which include more than two hundred varieties of plants, shrubs, and trees, all of which sit atop a parking garage and railroad line. The broad outlines of the three-acre garden were in place upon opening, but many of the 130 perennials would not mature for two years; the massive fifteen-foot Shoulder Hedge will require another five to ten years to fill out. Yet, as architecture critic Blair Kamin reported, the garden remains "a richly textured, metaphorically powerful space." The garden also visually connects the work of two great architects at the millennium—Frank Gehry and Renzo Piano—while simultaneously echoing the historic geography of Grant Park: the railroad and the lake.[1]

Lurie Garden was the only element in Millennium Park resulting from a formal competition. The winning proposal was the Shoulder Garden, designed by Gustafson Guthrie Nichol Ltd. (GGN) with plant specialist Piet Oudolf and lighting designer Robert Israel, collapsing the separate disciplines of architecture, horticulture, and theater. Described by the competition jury as "bold, intellectual, daring, cutting edge," the Shoulder Garden evokes Carl Sandburg's famous poem on Chicago and represents a unique combination of spatial structure, plantings, and lighting design. GGN shaped the overall organization and enclosure of the garden. Oudolf's passion for texture, color, and grouping plants was reflected in the garden's palettes and the seasonal change. Israel advised GGN on illumination methods and schemes, allowing the garden to include a day-to-night transformation as well as those of the four seasons. Just as theater lighting evokes changes in day, time, or mood, so would the Shoulder Garden. Moving through the garden was to be a dramatic experience.[2]

More than the competing designs, the Shoulder Garden moved with equal confidence between the largest spatial structure of the site and the smaller-scaled spaces of the plantings, thereby addressing the design challenge of accommodating on one hand thousands of concertgoers passing through the park to Monroe Street, as well as scattered visitors on a weekend morning. The jury was impressed with the design's sculpted contours, references to Chicago's history, and Oudolf's gardens. According to Ed

[T]he sweet breath of plant life so abundant in nature and so agreeable to man should give greeting to those who seek the refreshment of the parks.

DANIEL BURNHAM AND

EDWARD BENNETT

17.1

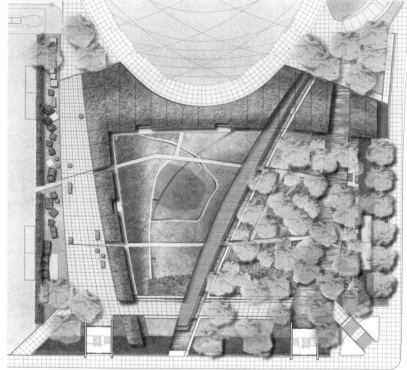

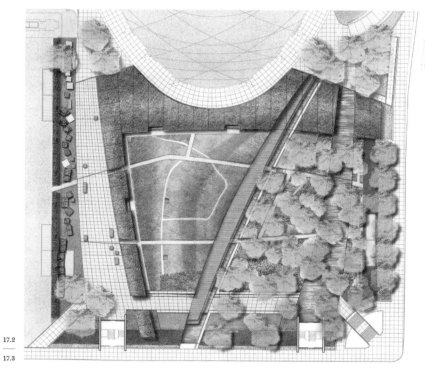

17.1. Kathryn Gustafson, Robert Israel and Piet Oudolf at the Lurie Garden dedication ceremony.

17.2. Overview of Shoulder Garden—summer/fall. The Light Plate is to the left of the diagonal seam. The Dark Plate, with its many trees and shading, is to the right of the seam.

17.3. Overview of Shoulder Garden—winter.

17.2
—
17.3

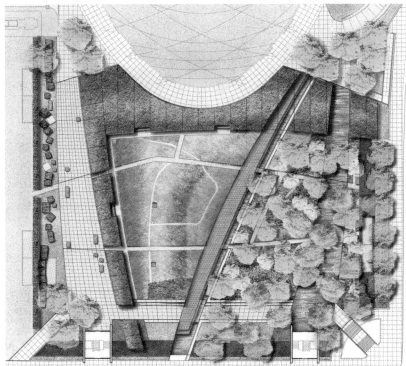

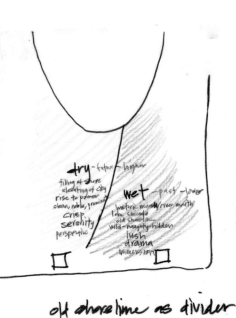

17.4. Overview of Shoulder Garden—spring.

17.5. This drawing provides a simple template for the garden: the former shoreline divides the garden into dry (later designated "light") and wet (later designated "dark") plates.

Uhlir, American nurserymen had never seen some of the plants employed by Oudolf.[3]

GGN and Israel had previously worked independently on a design for the Seattle Opera House. Kathryn Gustafson was also familiar with Oudolf's work, and was considering contacting him after the initial invitation for submissions was sent. When she read that the committee wanted "unusual plantings," she thought he was the ideal person with whom to collaborate. Literally within minutes of reading the list of invited participants, Oudolf called Gustafson on the phone. "We both had the same thought across continents," remarked Gustafson.[4]

Gustafson's earlier projects ranged in scale from one-acre gardens to reclamation works of more than two hundred acres. She first attracted international attention with her designs in France: Morbras Meeting Point Park, a thirty-five-hectare recreational park outside Paris (1986); the Shell Petroleum Headquarters in Rueil-Malmaison, France (1992); and the Esso/Exxon Corporation Headquarters in Rueil, France (1992).[5] By the turn of the millennium, her award-winning work included widely acclaimed parks, gardens, and community spaces throughout Europe, North America and the Middle East: the Gardens of Imagination in Terrasson, France (1995); the Arthur Ross Terrace at the American Museum of Natural History in New York City (2000); the Great Glasshouse at the National Botanic Garden in Wales (2000), in collaboration with Sir Norman Foster; the fifteen-hectare Westerpark, a cultural park for the city of Amsterdam (2003); and the

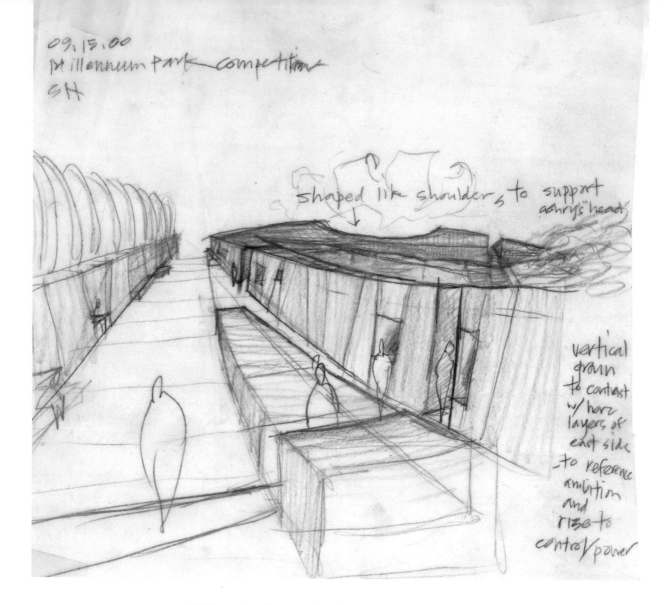

shaped like shoulders to support achry's "head"

vertical grain to contrast w/ horz layers of east side to reference ambition and rise to control/power

17.6. This schematic rendering illustrates how Kathryn Gustafson and Shannon Nichol of Gustafson Guthrie Nichol, Ltd. envisioned the hedge to serve as a support for the Gehry-designed pavilion's headdress.

Bridge at South Coast Plaza in Costa Mesa, California (2000). The *Diana, Princess of Wales, Memorial Fountain* in London's Hyde Park, designed by Gustafson and her London office (Gustafson Porter) was completed a few weeks before Millennium Park opened.[6]

Gustafson was born in 1951 and raised in Yakima, Washington. She briefly attended the University of Washington before moving to New York City to study at the Fashion Institute of Technology. Throughout the 1970s, she worked as a fashion designer, specializing in fabric drapery. In 1977, her fascination with the fluidity of forms led her to begin studies in landscape architecture under Alexandre Chemetoff at the *Ecole Nationale Supérieure du Passage* at Versailles, the leading French school of landscape design. In 1980, she opened her own office in Paris.

Some observers contend that Gustafson's landscapes reflect her earlier background in textile design, particularly with her emphasis on organic forms.[7] Gustafson, however, rejects that interpretation. "I think that's a common mistake a lot of people make be-

17.7. Esso/Exxon Corporation Headquarters in Rueil-Malmaison, France (1992).

17.8. Arthur Ross Terrace at the American Museum of Natural History in New York (2000).

17.9. Overview plan of Westerpark in Amsterdam (2003).

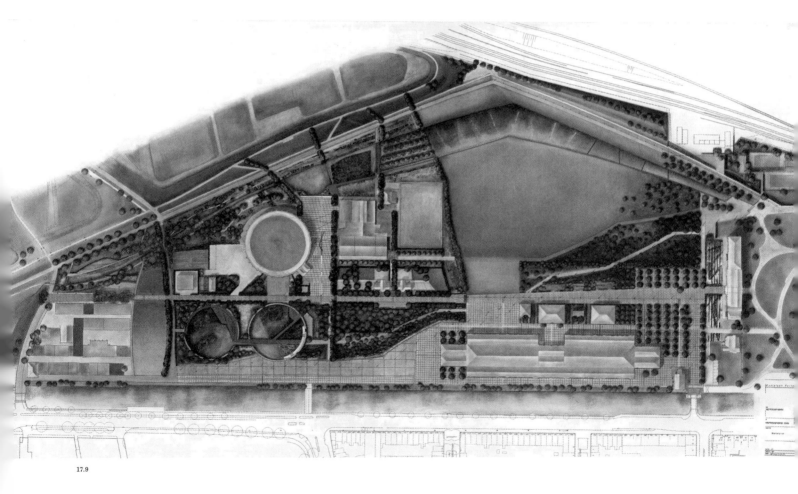

17.9

17.10. *Princess Diana Fountain* in Hyde Park, London (2004). These gardens reveal the multiple ways Gustafson incorporates moving water into her designs.

17.11. Gardens of Imagination (with Ian Ritchie Architects) in Terrasson, France (1995).

17.12. South Coast Plaza in Costa Mesa, California (2000). From rural European gardens to California shopping malls, Gustafson has created innovative landscapes.

17.10

17.11

17.12

cause I do so much land movement that they connect it immediately back to drapery and fashion." Gustafson believes that Yakima, Washington, plays a more significant role in her designs than contemporary fashion. "We have all these naked, very sculptural hills, and I think that has more to do with my childhood than it does with fashion."[8]

More specifically, Gustafson grounds her designs in emotional rather than intellectual concepts. "Most of the spaces I have designed, that we have designed, . . . are very experiential." She admits to being more philosophically interested in form, feelings, and scents than in any specific ideological agenda or political message. "I work with the ground," insists Gustafson. "From the contact with the ground I try to evoke emotions."[9]

After 1980, Gustafson committed herself to functional designs that integrated beauty and livability. She attracted attention for finding ways to transcend modernist formalism with a close reading of a particular site. Her work integrated land art motifs influenced by minimalism, ecological history, and artistic studies for reprogramming derelict and marginal sites. Like *Crown Fountain* designer Jaume Plensa, Gustafson never developed a signature style or became identified with a specific design genre. Her projects included public parks, corporate office campuses, factory grounds, urban plazas, roadways, and structural installations. Gustafson's designs were acclaimed for their sculptural and sensual qualities: rolling lawns, garden floors, changing levels of plazas and squares. According to one observer, "Gustafson's discipline is sculpting and the land is her medium."[10]

Piet Oudolf, described as a "detail-scale landscape designer" and the author or coauthor of four books, is renowned for elevating natural gardening theory to new heights. Oudolf's *Designing with Plants* (1999) revealed his philosophy of "New Wave planting," a landscape design philosophy emphasizing the architectural aspects of plants—leaf, flower, and stem structure, lateral and vertical growth characteristics, and rhythmical function. Some critics believed Oudolf's gardens represented "a middle ground" in that they contain formal traditions and order while creatively recasting classical shapes and forms. Whereas the Dutch de Stijl art movement of the 1920s emphasized primary colors and geometrical forms, noted one critic, new wave planting gave precedence to sculptural planting schemes.[11]

Prior to the opening of Millennium Park in 2004, Oudolf's work included plantings at the Botanical Garden in Utrecht; the Royal Horticultural Society gardens at Wisley; the entrance to the Pensthorpe Waterfowl Trust in Fakenham, England; a public park in Rotterdam; the Dromparken in Enkoping, Sweden; the greenscape for the headquarters of ABN AMRO Bank in Amsterdam; and the redesign of the Battery Park City gardens in New York City.[12] His award-winning "Evolution Garden" (with Arne Maynard), sponsored by *Gardens Illustrated* at the Chelsea Flower Show in 2000, impressed critics with how the design evolved and changed right up to the moment the judges entered the garden. Elements of this design, specifically the strong structure of the planting and the massive box "cloud hedge," were later incorporated into the Lurie Garden.[13]

Oudolf views landscape garden design as a distinctive art. Painters work with palettes of colored pigments, while garden designers select from a palette of plants. For

Oudolf, plant selection does not rest primarily on colors, but first on the shape of their flowers and seed heads, and second on their leaf shape and texture. Color is tertiary, "only an added extra," according to Oudolf. "Without structure, color makes no sense." Consequently, few roses are found in Oudolf-designed gardens because of their weak form and foliage. Flower color usually lasts for only a short season, whereas the shape of plants—perennials from spring until winter—endure much longer. Structure and form thus precede color in Oudolf's garden design.[14]

Oudolf's sculptural view of garden design, however, does not see the garden as a static piece of art. Gardening, emphasizes Oudolf, "is a living process." Many traditional landscape designs serve as frozen monuments, seeking a consistent image. "A garden that shows the cyclical nature of the garden process," argues Oudolf, "is one that has emotion and mood." Consequently, he addresses issues long ignored in landscape design, like lighting and plant movement. According to Oudolf, plants experience life cycles that need to be addressed and incorporated into the design of any garden. The ideal garden is one that changes through the years, if not day to day. The plants that work best are those which "live well and die well."[15]

The third contributor to the Shoulder Garden design was Robert Israel, an international theater and opera designer affiliated with the University of California at Los Angeles (UCLA). A collaborator with composer Philip Glass on four world-premier operas, Israel had designed sets and costumes for more than sixty productions in opera houses worldwide, including the Paris Opera, the National Theatre of London, the Netherlands Opera, the Vienna Statsoper, and the Metropolitan Opera in New York. Israel's stage designs attracted enough attention that his works were exhibited at numerous museums and galleries, some of which were later incorporated into permanent collections.[16]

History was an instrumental element in the Lurie Garden design. Gustafson, in particular, was well known for immersing herself in the local history of a site when preparing a garden or landscape. "One of the most important aspects of design for me is creating a project that emerges from its place," argued Gustafson. "A design cannot be something parachuted into its place from somewhere else, but it must rise out of the unique place it holds in the world."[17]

Her previous works illustrated that philosophy. In the Rights of Man Square in Evry, France (1991), Gustafson took her inspiration from article 11 in the Declaration of the Rights of Man—freedom of expression. The square was conceived as a space for private and public activities, encompassing civic gatherings, individual oratory, and cultural programs ranging from dance to theater to music.[18] In her "Gardens of Imagination" in Terrasson Lavilledieu, France, Gustafson included multiples iterations of garden history. A glass house designed by Ian Ritchie was situated in the landscape so that it "disappeared" when viewed from above and afar, disguised as a body of shimmering water (glass). At Shell Petroleum Headquarters, in Rueil-Malmaison, France, Gustafson designed undulating, rolling hills to reflect the sinuous waves of fossil fuels moving up and out of the earth.[19]

17.13 | 17.14

Lurie Garden incorporates this reliance on inspiration from history and place. The garden is "site-specific," insists Gustafson, and represents a landscaping dialogue with nineteenth-century Chicago. "For me, the Midwest has always been the strength of this country, that distributes through the rail everything that feeds this country," believes Gustafson. "We wanted something that talked about industry, talked about steel, about building, about all the energy that comes from the city."[20] Lurie Garden attempts to link and address Chicago's urban core, major cultural institutions, the role of the railroad, Grant Park, and Lake Michigan.[21]

In their preliminary research, GGN discovered that the proposed garden was almost directly above the site of a nineteenth-century breakwater wall constructed by the Illinois Central Railroad to protect the rail tracks from Lake Michigan. GGN's Shannon Nichol then devised a diagonal walkway, or "seam," alongside a parallel stream of water to represent the evolution of the successive lines between the natural and man-made landscapes of Chicago. When lit from underneath, the glowing seam and lapping water evoke the historic water edge.[22]

The placement of the seam also refers to Chicago's 1855 ordinance requiring future builders to elevate the grade level of the entire city five to ten feet. Over the ensuing two decades, city residents and businesses jacked up buildings, lifted streets and sidewalks, and installed new drains and pavings. For Gustafson and Nichol, the park and plates symbolize that "rising." Extending diagonally from Gehry's pedestrian bridge in the northeast corner to the southwest corner at Monroe Street, the path breaks the rectan-

17.13. Rights of Man Square in Evry, France (1991).

17.14. Shell Petroleum Headquarters, in Rueil-Malmaison, France (1992).

17.17

17.15. Lurie Garden's seam evokes the nineteenth-century breakwater that separated Lake Michigan from the city, as seen in this 1871 bird's-eye view of Chicago.

17.16. The wooden step along the seam encourages pedestrians to stop and cool their feet.

17.17, 17.18. The seam at night.

17.19

17.21

17.20. This 1857 lithograph of Lake Street between Clark and LaSalle illustrates how nineteenth-century builders raised Chicago's street grade.

17.21. Kathryn Gustafson explains a model of the Lurie Garden to mayor Richard M. Daley.

17.22. Planting schema for Lurie Garden by Piet Oudolf.

17.20

gular pattern of the city's grid. The placement of the seam links not only the garden's Dark and Light Plates, but also Gehry's contemporary bridge with Chicago's historic past: the seam's wooden path echoes the first wooden walkways built over Chicago's swampy terrain while tracing the historical shoreline of Lake Michigan and the railroad right-of-way below. "Chicago made that important civic decision to rise up and rebuild at a higher height out of the muck," remarks Gustafson. The seam serves as "a symbolic gesture of how it happened."[23]

The large hedges on the west and north sides of Lurie Garden also reflect this theme. The fifteen-foot metal framework shapes and organizes a variety of plants (including cedar, beech, and hornbeam trees) into a single, sculpted hedge feature, while supporting snow-filled branches in winter. The northern hedge is deliberately indented or concave, so that when viewed from the Art Institute, the hedge visually supports the headdress of Pritzker Pavilion. "I wanted something that had the strength of Chicago," recounted Gustafson. "That's where the 'big hedge' comes from, [it] comes from out of the ground."[24]

Inside Lurie Garden, the hedges simultaneously provide a rigid separation and an invitation to the curious through openings, or "doors," which create rooms, much like a Renaissance garden. The placement of the hedges enables the various openings to tantalize visitors as they move along the edge or outside the garden. In determining the planting design and plant selection , the Lurie Garden designers wanted to capture the native ecology of the upper Midwest, especially the soft movements found in various prairie grasses. Oudolf and Gustafson divided the garden's interior into two distinctive "plates," slightly tilted to face southern sunlight and enhance visibility from the future Art Institute addition across Monroe Street. The Dark Plate to the east represents Chicago "before the city rose up," in Gustafson's words. The land form evokes humankind's immersion in nature. The ambiance of the Dark Plate is conveyed through broad leaves and shade, giving that part of the garden a lush, baroque, even romantic feeling. In the spring and summer, the Dark Plate will be filled with ferns, angelicas, shrubs, and other moisture-loving perennials emphasizing primitive shapes and colors. In the fall, the complexity of the mixture will reach, according to Oudolf, "a crescendo" with the changing colors. The presence of evergreens will generate still more new contours and spaces in the winter months.[25]

By contrast, the Light Plate to the west is radiant and abstract, a representation of the Midwest plains, the construction of Chicago, the domination over nature, and the future. This was the most challenging element of the garden's design. The vegetation is more typical of the plains—open and sunny, filled with coneflowers, bluestem, and more than 130 species of perennials and grasses. The Light Plate is organized in blocks and curves to form a multicolored quilt of Midwestern vegetation. Few, if any, annuals are used. Combined with the tilted landscape, the multiple vista angles, and the many entrances, Oudolf considered Lurie Garden to be by far his most complex garden design.[26]

17.22

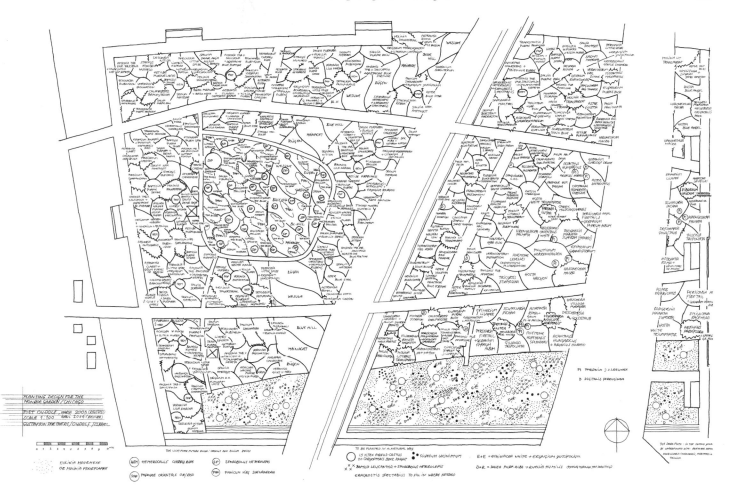

17.23 | 17.24

17.23. Inside the Light Plate. Note how the metal scaffolding for the shoulder hedge in the back serves as a "shoulder" for the pavilion's head-dress.

17.24, 17.25. Flowers and butterflies in the Light Plate.

17.26, 17.27. The Dark Plate at night.

17.25

Robert Israel added an element of drama to all of this. Lighting inside the garden creates a nighttime theatrical ambiance, thereby distinguishing the garden by night and day, season to season. Equally important to Israel, Lurie Garden treats visitors as players in a theater of their own devising. They are invited to follow the wooden walkway—"the seam"—between the Dark and Light Plates, between sun and shade, over shallow water. They can move through doorways perforating the volumetric hedges and physically engage the serene spaces and expansive garden vistas. "We wanted something that was very theatrical," admits Gustafson, "something that didn't happen to you but you happened to it."[27]

The Lurie Garden designers also addressed the garden's relationship with adjoining areas of the park. For example, the northeast corner was redesigned in order to address the BP Bridge, specifically coordinating pedestrian movement from the bridge. GGN

17.26

17.27

17.28. Eventually the shoulder hedge will fill up the steel frame outline.

17.29. Extrusion Plaza. The shoulder hedge is on the right.

was concerned with accommodating up to ten thousand people attending concerts at Pritzker Pavilion. Pedestrians are encouraged to walk to the sides of the garden. Extrusion Plaza on the west side of the garden thus serves as the main exit from the Great Lawn. The designers did not wish to force park users into a delicate garden area. Consequently, Lurie Garden is a closed, tightly knit space with its own distinct identity, a dramatic spatial contrast to the large, open expanse of the lawn immediately adjacent. Once you enter the garden, remarks Gustafson, "you are in another environment."[28]

GGN also addressed the garden's relationship to a future structure immediately south—Renzo Piano's addition to the north side of the Art Institute. Piano and Gustafson balanced the "natural" habitat of the garden and the architectural elements of limestone and glass in the Art Institute addition. Gustafson designed a "half wall" in order to provide an "urban edge" and offer a space to incorporate a future bridge, if necessary. Finally, GGN tilted the garden up at the northern end, providing a distinctive vista from the future Art Institute addition.[29]

The combination of these elements in the Lurie Garden reflects several changing themes within contemporary landscape architecture. First, Lurie Garden illustrates the increasing emphasis on garden landscapes as mediating elements in contemporary urban infrastructure. At the beginning of the twentieth century, gardens were associated with health and a sanctified view of nature. Ebenezer Howard's *Garden Cities of To-morrow* (1898) was an influential source for a movement that shaped landscape architecture, garden design, and even suburbanization for nearly a century.[30]

By contrast, the "natural" landscape of Lurie Garden is not divorced from the surrounding city, but rather aligned with the infrastructure that supports it, both fiscally and physically. Gustafson has written that recent landscape design is "radical" in emphasizing the largely unrecognized role of physical infrastructures in urban and personal environments. In Lurie Garden, cultural ideas and beliefs are allied with a public works project and public policy, forming one element in a single, massive architectural construction. Architectural historian Charles Waldheim argues that Lurie Garden is "a roof terrace above an enormous cultural and entertainment complex." In this respect, the destination garden marks a new conception of landscape design.[31]

Lurie Garden also departs from two other garden traditions: modernism, with its emphasis on quantitative analysis and ecological deference to natural cycles, and the older pastoral values epitomized by Frederick Law Olmsted and Jens Jensen. Like a seventeenth-century French garden, the Lurie Garden design displays an interest in the theatrical potential of a garden site by generating multiple levels of interactivity, by engaging the pedestrian in the design with forgotten or fresh ensembles, by encouraging contemplation and reflection.[32] Just as Andrew Jackson Downing in the mid-nineteenth century directed the prevailing taste in landscaping away from geometric and classical patterns to less formal picturesque and romantic designs, the Lurie Garden moves away from the traditional grid of Chicago and the classical, beaux arts style of Grant Park.[33]

Several horticultural neighbors illustrate this departure. Most notable is Daniel Kiley's Art Institute Garden (1962) a few hundred yards to the south. Facing Michigan Avenue and bounded by the Art Institute's original building and the newer Morton wing, Kiley's garden epitomizes the modern, twentieth-century garden with its symmetrical arrangement of trees organized around an axis from Michigan Avenue to Lorado Taft's

17.30. Art Institute South Garden.

Fountain of the Lakes sculpture on the dark facade of the Morton wing. Kiley's affection for precise geometry is revealed by the central axis cutting a path between planters containing honey locust trees. The garden's hardscape evokes its urban setting while the rigid geometry extends Chicago's grid streetscape into the garden itself. The variety of finely textured materials, interesting tree forms, constantly changing patterns of light and dappled shade, and a brilliant succession of seasonal flowers create a hospitable and serene environment in the center of the city.[34]

Kiley's Art Institute Garden is a fitting contrast to the Lurie Garden. At the end of the twentieth century, many historians considered Kiley to be the leading landscape designer. Along with James Rose and Garrett Eckbo, he virtually invented modern landscape architecture. All three challenged the flatly picturesque nature of design. They longed for involvement in the spaces, for a fully rounded appreciation of proportions, textures, light, and shade. Most of Kiley's designs attempted to address these questions, finding new ways to integrate ground covers, trees, shrubs, space, and light. Kiley's gardens were distinguished for integrating natural and structural elements. His innovations made him popular with architects. "I think architects tend to like Kiley's kind of stuff," admits Frank Gehry, "because it's organized and architectural."[35]

In what some will consider poetic irony, Kiley came in second in the Millennium Park garden competition. He proposed a reprise of his Art Institute Garden with a quiet, serene space of formally ordered and axially aligned Hawthorn trees.[36] In the process, he extended the skeletal structure of the Gehry trellis with a thin, crisp line of water and allée of trees terminating in a serene cascade of water at Monroe Street reflecting the new building of the Art Institute on the opposite side. The emphasis on quiet contemplation and simplicity, however, worked against Kiley. The jury acknowledged that the design indeed reflected the modernist elements perfected by Kiley, but thought it remained "indistinguishable from the less well-maintained trees and lawns of Grant Park." Some jury members felt that Kiley's plan simply echoed the Art Institute South Garden design of nearly forty years earlier and failed to acknowledge changes in contemporary culture. "With few exceptions," wrote one observer, "Kiley's scheme is absolutely bereft of flowing plants, and is sedate to the point of sedation."[37]

Lurie Garden has more in common with two nearby Alfred Caldwell–designed landscapes: Lily Pool in Lincoln Park (1936–1938) and Lake Point Tower Garden (1968). For Caldwell (1903–1998), the garden area concept was "a biographical footnote on the meaning of the Chicago Plain." He sought to recreate a garden reflecting the native ecology and geology, a landscape which was simultaneously a pleasure ground and a geological manifesto. Caldwell equated nature with history, envisioning himself as a kind of environmental historian long before professional academics created such a field. For that reason, he filled his gardens with trees, flowers, and shrubs native to the Chicago region, plants which, with thousands of years of adaptation to the native climate and soil, were not just beautiful, vigorous, and healthy, but "the most practical and the most poetic."[38]

The 11.5-acre Lily Pool, three miles north of Lurie Garden in Lincoln Park, epitomizes

the prairie-style landscape. Inspired by the work of Jens Jensen and Frank Lloyd Wright, Lily Pool's limestone walls appear to emerge from the very ground upon which they sit. Caldwell's design evoked the flat, seemingly endless Midwestern topography by incorporating native plants, stratified stone outcroppings, and horizontal landscaping. A pavilion, waterfall, and other features arranged around a lily pool are meant to replicate a creek running through a Midwestern landscape. Like most Caldwell designs, the quiet, naturalistic urban oasis was to serve as a sanctuary for native flora and fauna in the midst of the hustle and bustle of Chicago. Lily Pool was a refuge from the city, "a place sequestered from Megalopolis, the jungle of profound ugliness," in the words of Caldwell.[39]

By contrast, Lurie Garden devotes less attention to the native Midwestern landscape. Gustafson and Oudolf do incorporate prairie themes in different elements of the garden,

17.31. Alfred Caldwell's Lily Pool in Lincoln Park.

17.32. Alfred Caldwell's plaza-level plan in Lake Point Tower Garden. Two significant prairie-style gardens are within close proximity to Lurie Garden. Alfred Caldwell's Lily Pool is three miles north in Lincoln Park, while Caldwell's Lake Point Tower Garden is a quarter-mile northeast.

17.33–17.35. The simple stone walls in Lurie Garden depart from the stratified rock outcroppings in prairie-style landscapes (like Lily Pool in Lincoln Park, fig. 17.35). Lurie Garden encourages passers-by to stop and sit.

17.35

illustrated by the wide variety of Midwestern fauna and plantings. But the designers are less concerned with precisely replicating the prairie landscape, evidenced by the introduction of new plants not found in the Midwest and the absence of indigenous stonework. For prairie landscape designers, the stratified ledges and rock outcroppings were, according to Caldwell, "the structural essence of the landscape." In Lurie Garden, the plantings themselves—from the massive hedges to the small perennials—provide the fundamental structure of the garden.[40]

Lurie Garden seeks to evoke a different kind of inspiration. The garden does not represent a serene space devoted to quiet contemplation, a romantic, pastoral retreat, or a respite from the surrounding urban "chaos," like a prairie landscape. Rather, Lurie Garden strives to visually and emotionally stimulate pedestrians passing through. The combination of running water (the seam), shading trees (the Dark Plate), the open prairie (the Light Plate), massive and small hedges (Extrusion Plaza), and the changing foliage within a small, three-acre site aspires to generate new experiences for visitors with each new encounter. The Light Plate, a tilted palate of more than 130 perennials, is virtually a horticultural museum, an art gallery of ever-changing color and fauna.

This appeal to emotional reaction over a transcendental experience with the natural world (as in an Olmsted- or Caldwell-designed park) united the designers, despite their differing disciplinary backgrounds. "Every time you move through it," emphasizes Kathryn Gustafson, "you discover something else, and this is an essential part of the design." The distinct spaces, combined with lighting and plantings that change with the seasons, transform the garden into "an organic entity in itself," believes Robert Israel. Or as simply put by Piet Oudolf: "Every space has its own experience."[41]

17.36. The garden in the city. Looking west, one can see the Dark Plate (foreground), the Light Plate (center), the shoulder hedge, and the famed Michigan Avenue streetwall.

17.37. John Bryan addresses the crowd at the dedication of the Lurie Garden as mayor Richard M. Daley and Ann Lurie listen. Looming in the background is Daley's future residence under construction, the Heritage at Millennium Park.

Chapter 18

THE SUBTLE AMENITIES OF MILLENNIUM PARK

In an early review, architecture critic Fred Bernstein described Millennium Park as "a sculpture garden on steroids." Chicago was, blared a *New York Times* headline, a city of "Big Shoulders, Big Donors, Big Art."[1]

Such a characterization of Millennium Park assumes that the massive public art of Gehry, Plensa, and Kapoor represents the entire project. Just as few would equate Chicago architecture with solely the skyscraper, and thereby ignore Frank Lloyd Wright's Prairie-style houses, Millennium Park is more than just gigantic art and architecture. Many visitors will be drawn to the park because of the major enhancements; yet Millennium Park includes a variety of subtle amenities that may prove equally important to the success of the park. They reflect the importance of transportation, environmental planning, increasing park usage, and making the park accessible to all citizens in the design of the park.

Transportation

Millennium Park originated as a transportation project. Planners and city officials long imagined the area south of Randolph Drive as part of an intermodal transit site linking conventioneers in downtown hotels with McCormick Place.[2] Millennium Park realized that dream. Located mostly out of sight and below the park along a former railroad line route, the intermodal transportation center links automobile, bus, and rail traffic. Conventioneers departing from the McCormick Center can now jump on a bus, avoid surface-level street traffic, ride directly to a bus station on the lower level of Randolph Drive, and visit the Harris Theater or any other part of Millennium Park. Since the station is connected to multiple underground pedways, visitors can also walk to a Metra train station, Butler Field, Daley Bicentennial Plaza, the Art Institute, the Cultural Center, and the Monroe Street Garage, and never go above ground.

When the Lakefront Millennium Project plans were publicly released in 1998, Chicagoland Bicycle Federation executive director Randy Neufeld urged that bike parking be incorporated into the overall transportation plan. Neufeld and others recommended

18.1. The tunnel and roadway connecting Millennium Park's intermodal transit station with McCormick Place occupies the site of a former Illinois Central Railroad line.

that bicycle racks be dispersed throughout the site, perhaps integrating them into the fencing designs and other structures. He advocated the creation of a large bicycle area for secure, attended parking for large events, something that would discourage bikers from bringing bikes into crowded areas.[3]

The Bicycle Station represented the realization of Neufeld's dream. City officials claimed that the facility was the nation's first bicycle parking commuter station designed to simultaneously serve a major event venue and a multimodal transit center. With the opening of Millennium Park, for the first time, bicyclists can ride to Grant Park, lock their bikes in a protected facility, take a shower, buy a cup of coffee and breakfast, and head to work in the Loop. The station is connected to the Randolph Drive Pedestrian Way, a hub for Chicago Transit Authority and Metra trains, and the McCormick Place busway on Lower Randolph Drive. Together, these physical links allow the facility to cater to bike commuters, recreational cyclists, runners, and in-line skaters. "If you're coming to a concert at Grant Park and want your bike securely locked, it's a gem," admitted Randy Warren, program director for the Chicago Bicycle Federation.[4]

The Bicycle Station also embodied mayor Richard M. Daley's desire to transform Chicago into the most bicycle-friendly city in the United States. In 1991, he established the Mayor's Bicycle Advisory Council. Over the next decade, the Daley administration not only adopted policies to give bicyclists access to public buses and trains, but spent millions on bike-related infrastructures. Promotional events like Bike to Work and Bike the Drive received municipal support. By 2004, the city's 125 miles of bikeways and 9,400 public bike racks were reportedly the most of any American city (by comparison, Pittsburgh has less than five miles of bike paths). In 2002, *Bicycle Magazine* named Chicago the best big city in the United States for bicycling.[5]

The Bicycle Station is a three-hundred-bike parking facility complete with lockers, showers, bike rentals, a repair area, a café, and the Chicago Police Department's Bike Patrol Group. The $3.1 million, 16,448-square-foot facility sits on the top two levels of the Millennium Park parking garage at the northeast corner of the park at Randolph and Columbus Drives. The original scheme was completed by David Dillon of O'Donnell Wicklund Pigozzi & Peterson[6] (the designer of the peristyle and rink), while the final plan was authored by David Steele of Muller & Muller. The Bicycle Station has a simple purpose: to encourage bike commuting to downtown Chicago. It works. Less than two weeks after opening, all 200 memberships were sold.[7]

The station is supported by steel frames and composed of glass organized around an atrium that leads to the underground facilities. A steeply pitched roof contains visible solar energy panels, which advertise the structure's "green" identity and provide shade for the glass structure below. The horizontal stainless steel cables on the exterior will eventually be filled with plants, changing the station's seasonal appearance and adding to its environmentally sensitive design.[8]

The Bicycle Station was not the only Millennium Park structure that combined environmental planning and transportation. Millennium Park designers needed to provide

three entrances to the underground garage, as well as a visitor center. Rather than non-descript elevator boxes, Exelon, the parent company of Commonwealth Edison, donated four structures along Randolph Drive and Monroe Street. The $7 million Exelon Pavilions incorporate solar panels to exemplify the green architecture theme of Millennium Park. Photovoltaic technology quietly converts light energy into direct-current electricity with no moving parts, burning fuel, or pollution.[9]

Thomas Beeby designed the Randolph Drive structures to echo his simple, sleek design of the Harris Theater. Located immediately on the east and west sides of the theater,

18.2. The Millennium Park Bicycle Station.

18.3

18.4

18.3. The Bicycle Station café.

18.4. The Bicycle Station design includes grooved ramps for bikes.

18.5. Inside the Bicycle Station.

18.5

the pavilions appear to be independent wings of the theater. The east pavilion encloses the elevator to the underground garage, while the west pavilion includes offices, restrooms, and venues for special events. The dark, photovoltaic walls not only produce their own power and alternative energy sources, but are the first curtain walls in the Midwest to generate electricity. The two pavilions are among the first structures with solar panels on all four sides.[10] At night, they glow from within.

The Monroe Street pavilions were designed by the Pritzker-prize-winning architect Renzo Piano of Italy. The sleek, modernist boxes anticipate his design for the Art Institute's addition across the street in 2008. Clad in light-colored limestone slabs, they also echo the stonework in Lurie Garden. The transparent glass walls on the north and south

18.6. Thomas Beeby's Exelon Pavilion and Visitor Center on Randolph Drive.

18.7. The Exelon Pavilions on Monroe Street were designed by Renzo Piano.

facades provide views of the garden upon entering and exiting the pavilions. In contrast to their counterparts on Randolph Street, the solar panels are on their roofs.

Café Society and Park Usage

In 1978, the famed urbanist William H. Whyte acknowledged Grant Park's success as a piece of physical planning and development. At the same time, however, the park failed to fulfill its potential as a social gathering place for city residents and workers. The

18.9

18.8

18.10

18.8. Skidmore, Owings & Merrill's model with ice rink and pavilions behind the music pavilion.

18.9. A winter rendering of the ice rink after it was relocated to Michigan Avenue.

18.10. The opening of McCormick Tribune Plaza on December 20, 2001, marked the completion of the first Millennium Park enhancement. From left to right are mayor Richard M. Daley, actress Bonnie Hunt, Millennium Park chairman John Bryan, and Tribune Corporation CEO John Madigan.

18.11, 18.12. (facing, top left and right) McCormick Tribune Plaza in winter. The classical-style lampposts echo the beaux arts features of adjacent Wrigley Square.

18.13. (facing, bottom) Ice skating in Millennium Park.

"trouble with Grant Park," Whyte concluded, "is not so much what the park has got as what it hasn't got enough of—people."[11]

Richard Daley, early in the planning of Millennium Park, insisted that the park serve as a year-round venue, that planners devise ways to attract people during all seasons. McCormick Tribune Plaza, the first Millennium Park enhancement completed, was the manifestation of those plans. The original park design authored by Skidmore, Owings & Merrill placed an ice rink along Randolph Street, approximately at the site of the Harris Theater. But shortly after assuming his role as Millennium Park project director, Ed Uhlir suggested moving the facility to Michigan Avenue. This not only presented a more accessible location for the rink, but eliminated visible warming and food service pavilions by placing them beneath SBC Plaza and Anish Kapoor's *Cloud Gate* just east of the rink. The move also provided a more central location for use of the plaza as an outdoor, summertime venue for eating and music. In early 1999, the McCormick Tribune Foundation agreed to donate $5 million for construction of the rink and plaza.[12]

After opening in December 2001, the skating structure replaced the "Skate on State" venue on Block 37 as one of Chicago's most popular winter attractions. From Thanksgiving to March, the plaza is occupied by a professional hockey-size ice rink measuring 200 by 80 feet, considerably larger than Rockefeller Center's 120-by-60-foot facility in New York City. McCormick Tribune Plaza quickly rivaled Rockefeller Center as the most popular downtown ice rink in the United States. In the winter of 2003–2004, the rink rented 77,667 skates, an average of more than 550 per day.[13]

Eating facilities were a second element of Daley's vision to attract patrons to Millennium Park all year round. When Millennium Park opened on July 16, 2004, McCormick Tribune Plaza was transformed into a large, 350-seat, outdoor café. With Parisian-style steelwork, the Park Grill on the Plaza became Chicago's largest outdoor eatery. The restaurant not only included a separate outdoor kitchen, a distinct menu ("ethnic barbeque cuisine"), and waiting staff, but provided live musical entertainment throughout the summer months.[14]

18.14. (above) Midway Gardens.

18.15–18.18. (facing) As these seasonal views attest, Millennium Park planners envisioned McCormick Tribune Plaza as a year-round facility.

Ever since Frank Lloyd Wright's Midway Gardens (1914–1929) was destroyed, Chicago had lacked a large outdoor garden and entertainment venue. Located just off the southwest corner of the Midway Plaisance on the city's South Side, the five-tier concert garden was one of Chicago's most popular places to dine, dance, and relax in the early twentieth century. The facility included an outdoor terrace with a bandstand, an indoor restaurant and dance hall, and a private club. When Midway Gardens was razed, no similar facility replaced it. In 1977, University of Chicago historian Neil Harris complained, "The city does need a kind of Rockefeller Plaza with activities as well as spectators." McCormick Tribune Plaza was envisioned as Chicago's pleasure garden for the twenty-first century.[15]

The outdoor café on McCormick Tribune Plaza was an extension of the adjacent Park Grill restaurant. Millennium Park planners recognized that the amenities surrounding the plaza were critical in attracting patrons into the park. While the park was under con-

18.19

18.20 | 18.21

18.19. The Park Terrace on McCormick Tribune Plaza.

18.20. The Park Grill exterior.

18.21. The Park Grill interior.

struction, city and park district officials issued requests for qualifications and requests for proposals to anyone interested in operating a major restaurant facility in Millennium Park. A selection committee interviewed three finalists before selecting two experienced Chicago restaurateurs: Matthew O'Malley, the proprietor of three nearby restaurants along South Michigan Avenue and South Wabash Avenue, joined Jim Horan, who operated a restaurant a few blocks away on East Adams Street and a catering service. The $6 million, three-hundred-seat Park Grill opened in November 2003 beside McCormick Tribune Plaza and beneath *Cloud Gate* in SBC Plaza. With floor-to-ceiling windows, the restaurant had a scaled-back interior: tile floors, muted colors, and minimal decorations.[16]

At first, some worried that the restaurant was situated in an isolated location, set back from Michigan Avenue. Horan, in particular, worried that the ice skating rink would draw only skaters to that part of the park, and discourage potential restaurant customers. But the popularity of the ice skating drew surprising numbers of patrons.[17]

18.22 | 18.23

18.24 | 18.25

The plaza, whether used as an ice skating rink in the winter or café in the summer, succeeded in making this part of Millennium Park an ongoing urban theater. Diners watched skaters in the winter from the indoor restaurant, while patrons in the summer months observed the famed Michigan Avenue skyline on one side, or Kapoor's sculpture on the other. "The view alone is sublime," described one reporter.[18]

Less visible were two other eating venues incorporated into the Jay Pritzker Pavilion, both designed to serve smaller and more private functions and generate revenue for park programming. The first was a rooftop terrace located between the pavilion's steel headdress and the Harris Theater's above-ground entrance. A second facility was the enclosed stage of the pavilion itself. In order to accommodate private receptions and parties, the massive window curtains of the stage can be closed, transforming the stage into a large, indoor banquet facility. A smaller chorus rehearsal room on the second level and accessible to the stage can be used for similar but smaller events.

18.22, 18.23. Closing the glass stage doors of the Pritzker Pavilion allows for smaller events—ranging from formal dining to dancing—all year round.

18.24. Receptions and smaller musical events can take place in the Jay Pritzker Pavilion Choral Room.

18.25. The rooftop terrace behind the Pritzker Pavilion and the Harris Theater provides space for outdoor receptions during the summer months.

Disability Access

Millennium Park is one of the first, large-scale parks designed to be fully accessible to disabled patrons. In ways little noticed by most visitors, virtually no section of the park is inaccessible. Sidewalk-level ramps and walkways allow wheelchair visitors to enter the park along all three entry streets. Elevators in the Exelon Pavilions provide routes to the underground garage; all levels of the Harris Theater include elevators. Once inside the park, people in wheelchairs never confront the difficult gravel parkscape near Buckingham Fountain. The three-block stretch of Chase Promenade from Monroe Street to Randolph Drive is completely flat and covered with concrete. Disabled patrons can easily maneuver from the promenade to Lurie Garden or the oval surrounding the Great Lawn. Once in the garden or lawn area, easy access is provided to and across the BP Bridge. If they prefer to move west toward Michigan Avenue, ramps expressly designed to accommodate individuals unable to use the steps connect the Michigan Avenue enhancements to the upper level of the park. A barely visible ramp behind the Millennium Monument allows for complete access around the peristyle and Wrigley Square.

Some early criticisms of the park charged that Chase Promenade epitomized how park planners overemphasized the major enhancements at the expense of creating more intimate spaces. The promenade, some complained, acted more like a barrier dividing the east and west sections than a seam that united them. Compared to the artist renderings of Chase Promenade prior to construction, full of colorful plants and happy pedestrians, the three-block-long plaza appeared stark and lifeless.[19]

Within months, Millennium Park officials addressed some of these criticisms. First, seventy "Maggie benches"—320-pound plate- and cast-aluminum seats designed by Kathryn Gustafson and named in honor of mayor Richard Daley's wife—were added to the promenade and other parts of the park. Second, two 200-foot cedar-log benches with stainless-steel legs were installed on both sides of the skin pool at Crown Fountain. Third, "Bob's Hedge," a $500,000 wood-and-topiary feature named after Lurie Garden design-team member Robert Israel, was installed at the edge of the garden. Officials also pointed out that, like Lurie Garden, the trees and plantings along the promenade's border needed to mature and grow before evolving into a grand urban space.[20]

The most significant improvement appeared in 2006. Millennium Park officials redesigned the grass-and-gravel-covered terraces separating Chase Promenade from the enhancements along Michigan Avenue. With a $5 million donation from the Boeing Company, the terraces were landscaped into 80-foot-wide, granite-paved promenades lined with sycamore trees. The North Gallery's 14,400 square feet and the South Gallery's 19,200 square feet were transformed into spaces to accommodate rotating exhibitions of public art, aided in part by an endowment included in the Boeing gift. The terrace design added Maggie benches to provide a place for park patrons to relax and observe the exhibits. The South Gallery also featured a 30-foot-wide black granite stairway from

18.26

18.27

18.28

18.29

18.30

18.26. Chase Promenade extends for three city blocks.

18.27. Access ramp into SBC Plaza.

18.28. The access ramp behind the Millennium Monument.

18.29. Wheelchair-confined individuals can move about Lurie Garden.

18.30. Access ramp along South Terrace.

18.31. Ramp leading from Randolph Street to Pritzker Pavilion, Great Lawn, BP Bridge, and Lurie Garden.

18.32. Chase Promenade was designed, in part, to accommodate large gatherings and celebrations.

18.33. An artist rendering of the Millennium Park promenade in 1998.

18.34, 18.35. The Boeing Galleries transformed the north and south terraces into outdoor art venues. The south gallery (figs. 18.34 and 18.36) provided better visibility of and accessibility to the *Crown Fountain*.

18.34

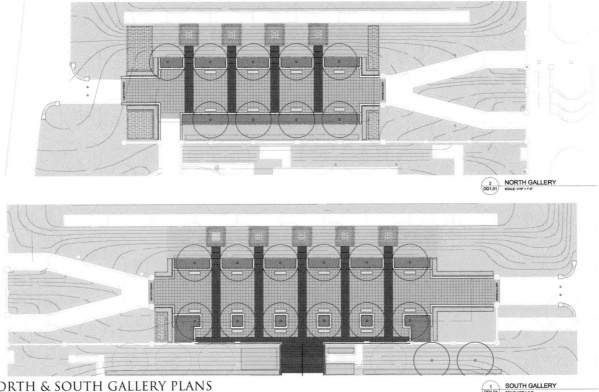

NORTH & SOUTH GALLERY PLANS

18.35

the *Crown Fountain* plaza up to the terrace gallery. Benches behind an open railing facing the *Crown Fountain* allowed people to observe activity in the fountain pool and discourage spectators from gravitating to the grassy slope and damaging the sod.[21]

18.36. The south terrace of the Boeing Gallery provides access to the Crown Fountain.

The Millennium Monument in Wrigley Square

Millennium Park's subtle amenities related to transportation, environmental design, park usage, and disability access reflect issues that drove municipal planning at the turn of the millennium. Yet planners recognized that the park was situated on a site long rooted in the history of Chicago. How could such a project with overpowering enhancements, corporate largess, and modern design innovations address that history? The peristyle design of the Millennium Monument at the corner of Randolph Street and Michigan Avenue was their answer.

Peristyles are popular in Chicago. The symbolic center of the World's Columbian Exposition of 1893 included Daniel Chester French's famed statue, *The Republic*, located in the Grand Basin and situated in front of a classical peristyle 500 feet long and 50 feet high. In 1895, Peter Wight, Daniel Burnham, and Charles Atwood proposed replicating this element of the fair along the downtown waterfront of Chicago, roughly where Queen's Landing is located in Grant Park today. And in 1917, Burnham's partner and coauthor of *Plan of Chicago* (1909), Edward Bennett, designed a more modest peristyle for the corner of Michigan Avenue and Randolph Street.[22]

The Millennium Monument is Millennium Park's bow to this history. Employing the classical design vocabulary of the beaux arts style, the monument is a peristyle: a semi-circular row of twenty-four paired Doric columns atop a base which curves around a circular fountain and pool. The structure's symmetry is reinforced with the inclusion of twenty-four flutes on each column. The peristyle's classicism mirrors that of the Chicago Cultural Center across Michigan Avenue.

The monument replicates Edward Bennett's original peristyle, which occupied the same site from 1917 to 1953. That structure also included a fountain, but in 1941 the

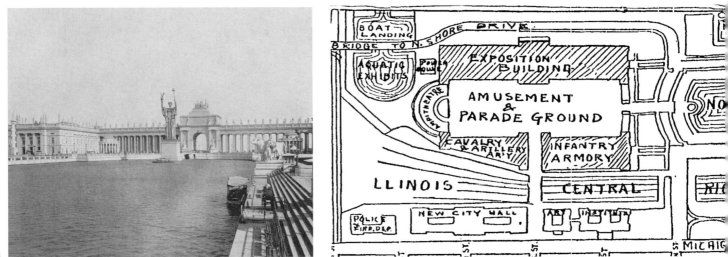

18.37. The Peristyle at the World's Columbian Exposition of 1893.

18.38. In 1895, Peter Wight and the Municipal Improvement League proposed connecting an exposition building and an armory with a peristyle.

18.39. The Millennium Monument.

18.39

fountain was replaced with Albin Polasek's sculpture *Spirit of Music* (1923). Commissioned by the Ferguson Fund to memorialize Theodore Thomas, the founder of the Chicago Symphony Orchestra, Polasek sought to convey the majesty and sweep of symphonic and classical music. "Music is divine, a positive thing," he wrote, "not a hope or a faith." In time, the statue was better known as the Theodore Thomas Memorial. After the peristyle was destroyed in 1953 for the construction of the Grant Park North garage, Polasek's sculpture was eventually removed to Congress Drive Plaza, where it sits today.[23]

18.40

18.41

18.42

18.43

18.40. The old Peristyle along Michigan Avenue in 1937.

18.41. The Peristyle and Theodore Thomas Memorial in 1944. The original peristyle pool was immediately in front of the base of the peristyle, while the front edge of the pool was only a few inches above the surface grade of the park.

18.42. Peristyle in winter, from rear, 1920s.

18.43. A rear view of the peristyle in the 1920s. The peristyle served as the gateway to Grant Park for pedestrians approaching from the north along Michigan Avenue. Note the wall of the railroad cut, later covered with the construction of Millennium Park.

18.44. The construction of the Grant Park North Garage in 1953 resulted in the destruction of the peristyle.

Architects David Dillon and Michael Patrick Sullivan of O'Donnell Wicklund Pigozzi & Peterson (OWP&P) were charged with designing the peristyle and ice rink. Relying on Chicago Park District documents authored by Edward Bennett, Dillon and Sullivan replicated as much of the original peristyle as possible. This new version is slightly smaller because the architects provided a ramp for disabled pedestrians onto the tightly confined site. The only way to accomplish this was to shrink the entire structure by approximately 20 percent. While the height is roughly the same, the original peristyle was one hundred feet in diameter. The current peristyle is approximately eighty feet.[24]

In contrast to the earlier peristyle, Dillon and Sullivan provided a level of interactivity. Separating the fountain from the peristyle itself, they enabled pedestrians to approach and read the names of the private-sector patrons who contributed to the creation of Millennium Park. A low and accommodating ledge enables pedestrians to sit along the entire perimeter of the fountain's pool.

William Wrigley, Jr., and other Wrigley officials were attracted to sponsoring the peristyle, fountain, and surrounding square by a number of features. The original peristyle (1917) and the Wrigley Building (1920–1924) were constructed in the same era. Both Wrigley Square and the Wrigley Building are located on North Michigan Avenue within sight of each other. But the historical lineage symbolized by the peristyle was perhaps most influential. "It's that sense of history, that sense of bringing back some element," claimed Wrigley's communications director Chris Perille, "the idea of a bridge between the old and the new," that made the peristyle attractive to Wrigley officials.[25]

By the time Wrigley and his company's foundation agreed to sponsor the peristyle, Dillon and Sullivan had nearly completed the design of the northwest corner of Millennium Park. Wrigley's motivation in sponsoring the peristyle, according to the president of the Wrigley Company Foundation, William Piet, "wasn't to put an image of the founders of the Wrigley Company out there, or to advertise our products." Rather, company

18.45

18.46

18.47

18.45. The Wrigley Building (1920–1924).

18.46. Pedestrians can see the Wrigley Building and the peristyle in Wrigley Square while standing along Michigan Avenue.

18.47. The Wrigley Square fountain head is modeled after a finial on the Wrigley Building.

officials primarily wanted to be associated with Millennium Park. "It's more than just a park," added Piet. "It's an attraction."[26]

Most of Dillon and Sullivan's design was acceptable to Wrigley officials, with the exception of one significant feature. Chicago Park District documents reveal that the original fountain had only a simple nozzle that the architects intended to recreate in bronze. Wrigley and Millennium Park officials elected to replicate a terra cotta finial on the Wrigley Building as the fountain's nozzle and head.[27]

Dillon and Sullivan rejected notions that the peristyle was backward-looking. The corner of Randolph and Michigan has been a meeting place for contrasting architectural styles for over half a century. Central Michigan Avenue was developed between 1890 and 1930, with most of the buildings following a classical style, best exemplified by the Chicago Cultural Center (formerly the Chicago Public Library). Randolph Street east of Michigan Avenue, however, developed after 1950 and remains a boulevard of modern skyscrapers: the Prudential Building (1954), the Aon Center (1973), Prudential Plaza Two (1990) and other structures in the Illinois Center. That tension between the classical and the modern is repeated within Millennium Park itself, between the peristyle and the Gehry-designed music pavilion. "To have the juxtaposition and the kind of dialogue between those two pieces," Sullivan concludes, "speaks to the pluralism of our time."[28]

18.48

18.49

18.48. Aon Building seen through the columns of the peristyle. According to peristyle designer Michael P. Sullivan, the view of the Aon Center with its pure, modern lines through the fluted Doric columns of the peristyle reconciles the stylistic conflict between the classical beaux arts design of Grant Park with the postmodern elements of Millennium Park.

18.49. John Bryan, William Wrigley, Jr., and Richard M. Daley at the dedication of Wrigley Square on October 30, 2002.

18.50. The Millennium Monument at night.

18.50

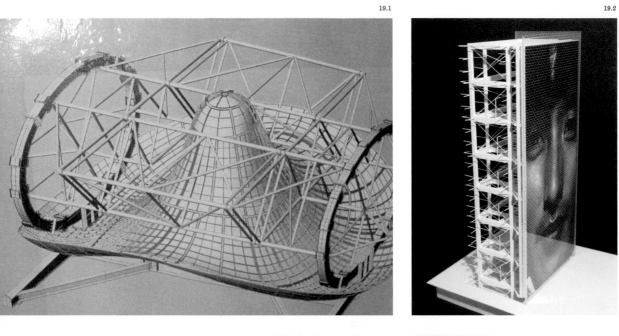

19.1

19.2

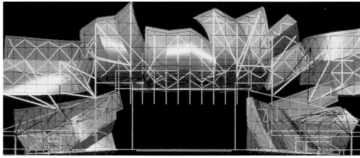

19.3

Chapter 19

CONCLUSION   THE MULTIPLE MEANINGS OF MILLENNIUM PARK

"What other city in America," asks Frank Gehry, "has a venue like this in its downtown?"[1] Compare Millennium Park with the leading outdoor music venues in the United States: the Hollywood Bowl in Los Angeles; Merriweather-Post Pavilion in Columbia, Maryland; the Chronicle (formerly Concord) Music Pavilion outside San Francisco; the Amphitheatre at Regency Park near Raleigh, North Carolina; the Meadow Brook Festival Pavilion near Detroit; the Riverbend Music Center in Cincinnati; the Blossom Music Center near Cleveland; and the Ravinia Festival north of Chicago. None combines architectural enthusiasm and superlative acoustics as well as the Jay Pritzker Pavilion. None incorporates public art with a distinctive urbanism like Millennium Park.

But what does Millennium Park reveal about culture, art, and urban space at the millennium? More precisely, what is the relationship of public art, private philanthropy, and state patronage in urban cultural development at the onset of the twenty-first century? First, Millennium Park is a cultural hybrid, a vivid illustration of the intersecting relationship of art, corporate sponsorship, urban politics, and globalization. As a cultural landscape, the park embodies no singular theme; it advertises no consistent message. Like much "global" art in the postindustrial age, Millennium Park presents multiple, even paradoxical, messages. It lacks the certitude of beaux arts works in the early twentieth century or landmark private projects like Rockefeller Center (organized around the theme "New Frontiers and the March of Civilization"). Millennium Park does not celebrate progress, stability, or nationalism. It avoids the traditional themes of commemorative art. Moreover, the art of Millennium Park eschews modernism's tendency to emphasize the artist's singular right to self-expression.

Millennium Park offers something distinctive. Through the use of scale and color, the pavilion, bridge, fountain, garden, and sculpture relate to and engage in an architectural dialogue with the surrounding skyscrapers and lake. Each component was designed to stimulate a reaction from viewers. Observers look into a sculpture, walk on water, listen to music, pass through a prairie landscape, or cross a bridge. The art still privileges the individual (like much of the modern movement), but the viewer, not the artist, interprets the art. "To a large extent, all work is incomplete," believes Anish Kapoor. "It's completed by the person who is looking at it."[2]

It is the destiny of the Lake Front to become a mighty park.

CHICAGO TRIBUNE,

30 DEC. 1894

19.1. Computer model of *Cloud Gate*.

19.2. Computer-generated image of *Crown Fountain* with steel interior support exposed.

19.3. Computer model of Pritzker Pavilion. Millennium Park reflects the ever-growing impact of the computer on art, design, and architecture.

The artistic and personal careers of Gehry, Gustafson, Kapoor, and Plensa reflect the hybrid qualities embedded in Millennium Park. For example, all experienced conflict and paradox regarding their professional and self-identities. Kapoor has discussed internal tensions regarding the Jewish, Indian, and English elements of his past; Gehry, his Jewish, Canadian, and American roots. Gustafson's training originates not in the formalism of landscape architecture but in fashion design. Plensa has said, "As an artist, I'm in a state of permanent nomadism." Indeed, each is a cultural nomad in a sense, perplexed by uncertainty and duality, intrigued by the chaos of the world. They have all spent much of their careers challenging traditional conceptions of artistic and architectural form. "We are all in exile," Kapoor contends, "in a positive sense of cultural ambiguity."[3]

This ambiguity reflects their resistance to formalism and efforts to classify their art. Plensa and Kapoor are sculptors who reject being defined solely as sculptors. "I am a painter who is a sculptor," states Kapoor. Similarly, Plensa insists, "I also believe that on occasion the form prevents us from seeing the content, . . . that beauty does not necessarily lie in the form." Gustafson dismisses claims that her organic forms are rooted in formal textile designs; rather, her landscapes originate in abstract and emotional experiences. And Gehry's resistance to traditional architectural form, for an architecture inspired by sculpture, is a defining element of his work.[4]

This antagonism to traditional categories is reflected by the artists' inclination to employ so-called ordinary materials in their earlier works. Each experimented with paraphernalia that was, at the time, conveniently at hand and considered cheap or available at low cost. Kapoor used patterned pigment and stone. Plensa designed with cast iron, considered to be a second-rate industrial material. Gehry's use of chain link, exposed pipe, and corrugated aluminum made him a controversial figure in the 1970s.

19.4. The Kapoor and Gehry families in front of *Cloud Gate*: Millennium Park artists and symbols of a hybrid Jewish diaspora at the millennium.

To Gehry, such artistic transgression was no accident. "When you start out as an architect or an artist with the kind of world we're in, we react to it," he states. The sculptures of Henry Moore and Barbara Hepworth, or the architecture of Frank Lloyd Wright, had, in Gehry's opinion, "a kind of precious character to them." But many artists in the late twentieth century rejected that vision. "The world was chaotic, and the world available to me was very cheap," remembers Gehry. "The buildings I got to look at were very inexpensive, cheap, and it was frustrating because I was trained to do fancy details and stuff." If the building process (indeed the creative process) generates hammer marks and chain link, why fight it? Why not embrace it? "If that's what the culture produces, why not flip it around and say, 'okay, turn it into a virtue.'" Influenced by artists like Jasper Johns and Robert Rauschenberg who employed "junk" in their art, Gehry moved in a different direction. "It angered people," he admits.[5]

These dissident cultural patterns are embedded in Millennium Park. The parks of Frederick Law Olmsted or Jens Jensen, the beaux arts classical projects of the City Beautiful movement, and even many post–World War II urban development programs (inspired by planners like Robert Moses and Edward Logue) reflected the vision of a single planner, architect, or artist. Quite the contrary with Millennium Park. The park was "planned" by a series of committees, informal negotiations with mayor Richard M. Daley, and the organizational talents of John Bryan and Ed Uhlir. The array of artists was unplanned, part of a decentralized, evolving process. John Bryan later acknowledged that this approach to Millennium Park's design presented aesthetic challenges. He openly worried that the inclusion of so many grand works by prominent artists in such close proximity would produce a final product where "all the artists were screaming at each other."[6]

To some critics, they are. Millennium Park is "a sculpture garden on steroids," claimed Fred Bernstein of the *New York Times*. The crowds filling the Great Lawn, complained *New City Chicago*, made it "as pleasant as any overcrowded city bar." Millennium Park "feels more like attending a splashy Pop Art exhibit than settling into a vital public place," complained Jay Walljasper of the Project for Public Spaces. "Your eyes are dazzled by all the strange and shiny objects, but your soul feels a bit underfed."[7]

Such criticisms were no surprise to architect Adrian Smith. Early on, he warned that Grant Park was being transformed into "a sort of sculpture gallery and extravaganza." While Smith sympathized with efforts by wealthy civic leaders "to contribute something very important and meaningful to the city," he nevertheless contended that the project would have been more successful if the various enhancements had been distributed throughout Grant Park. By placing a monumental sculpture, an eye-catching bandshell, and an irregular bridge in one area, maintained Smith, "all the goodies were put into one little block of the park."[8]

Such criticisms, however, ignore how the physical density of art in Millennium Park renders those elements more powerful. Grant Park already included a considerable amount of public art, much of it created by some of the greatest artists of the nineteenth and twentieth centuries. Within a short walk of Millennium Park are works by Richard

19.5. Henry Moore's *Large Interior Form* (1982) "in conversation" with Jaume Plensa's *Crown Fountain*.

19.6. Richard Serra's *Reading Cones* on Monroe Street is rarely noticed by passers-by, in part, because of its size and location.

Serra, Isamu Noguchi, Lorado Taft, Henry Moore, Augustus Saint-Gaudens, and Edward Bennett. Yet, with the exception of Bennett's *Buckingham Fountain* (perhaps because of its explosive size?), the average pedestrian is oblivious to much of this art.[9]

By contrast, the scale of the Pritzker Pavilion, the *Crown Fountain*, and *Cloud Gate* works to the advantage of each structure. Some will lament the mammoth size of these pieces, but good public art usually needs to be large in size.[10] Such is the case for Millennium Park, surrounded on two sides by some of the world's tallest skyscrapers and on another by the seemingly endless inland sea of Lake Michigan. Here massive art is a virtual necessity. Both the *Crown Fountain* and *Cloud Gate* are large designs located in spacious, open plazas. The Pritzker Pavilion is adjacent to the vast 625-yard expanse of the Great Lawn and at the foot of the 1,136-foot Aon skyscraper. All share a distinctive combination of scale and siting that enables viewers both near and far, on foot or in vehicles, to observe and react to them.

The characteristic interactivity of Gehry's, Gustafson's, Kapoor's, and Plensa's art was a motivating factor in their selection by park planners, an unconscious reflection of the hybridity of the park itself. As artists, they produce public art that not only is considered sculptural, but encourages (if not requires) a level of participation not found in traditional or gallery art. Kapoor's work, for example, openly sees participation as a primary quality, encouraging viewers to "let go," to let the piece act upon them. "This park encourages people to participate in their world," concluded Rebecca Hoffman of the Institute of Design Chicago, "from stepping into the water between video gargoyles, to picnicking at the Pritzker Pavilion while watching music and dance performances, to strolling under 'The Bean.'" *Cloud Gate*, the *Crown Fountain*, BP Bridge, and even Lurie Garden generate ongoing, multilevel, participatory dialogues between artists and viewers. In the view of their creators, art that provides multiple ways for viewers to partake of and participate in the art itself makes it "democratic."[11]

But some critics offer a different definition of democracy. Does interactive art in a public space, they ask, make it democratic? Does the privatization associated with Millennium Park undermine accessibility to genuine democratic, public spaces in cities like Chicago? Is Millennium Park only the most recent example of another American municipality ceding a public space to private control?[12]

Some critics contend that Millennium Park was a Faustian bargain. Chicago, by abdicating so much control to John Bryan and the private sector in return for more money and a more spectacular landscape, lost control of the park's development and later use. "When the private sector pays for public space," concluded Brent Ryan, codirector of the City Design Center of the University of Illinois at Chicago, "you get demands on that space you wouldn't otherwise." The park, for example, closes at night (from 11 p.m. to 6 a.m.); certain recreational activities (skateboarding and bicycle riding) are prohibited. A private security force polices the space. The lawn and pavilion are too small to accommodate the largest music festivals, such as the Chicago Jazz Festival and the Gospel Music Festival. Nor is it likely to be a space for political rallies. To critics, Chase (formerly Bank One) Promenade, the BP Bridge, the Exelon Pavilions, the Boeing Galleries, and the McCormick Tribune Plaza represent tasteless examples of corporate branding. Rather than a civic center visually divorced from private wealth, as Daniel Burnham envisioned, the Millennium Monument's roll call of millionaires advertises not only the excess bounty of a society organized around the private market, but the private usurpation of public space. Closing the park for the inaugural gala celebration on July 24, 2004, illustrated how private interests now controlled a highly visible public space. "Whose park is it, anyway?" queried Kelly Kleiman in the *Christian Science Monitor*.[13]

Others maintain that Millennium Park's privatized planning process produced a design akin to a theme park, a new kind of "Logo Land" that was "built to generate buzz." Many visitors in the park will passively move from "attraction to attraction," much like those in an amusement park. Precisely the same global forces of the "postmodern" tourist economy that created Navy Pier a few blocks to the northeast motivated city officials to build Millennium Park. The art fairs and festivals along Chase Promenade foster certain varieties of consumption, as do the information kiosk in one of the Exelon Pavilions and the gift shop facing McCormick Tribune Plaza, selling its Millennium Park and Chicago memorabilia. Millennium Park, critics contend, is not primarily a place for art and culture, but rather a space organized around spectatorship, supervision, and spectacle.[14]

But these criticisms ignore a more complex history and urban reality. Most parks and playgrounds in Chicago close during the evening hours. Skateboarding and bike riding are prohibited or segregated to specified parks or areas in many public spaces throughout Chicago. Temporarily closing a public facility one evening for a private event hardly represents an abdication of public power—Park District authorities regularly rent public spaces from Café Brauer on the North Side to the South Shore Cultural Center on the South Side for private events, and city officials routinely close public streets for private activities (such as street festivals or filmmaking). In the case of Millennium Park, the inaugural gala raised more than $2 million for the park's maintenance and endowment. In all these examples, the revenue generated ultimately benefits the public taxpayer.

Furthermore, displaying the names of wealthy donors in Chicago's public spaces is hardly a new phenomenon, nor is it a threat to public access. Grant Park alone is home to private museums named for millionaire businessmen Max Adler, Marshall Field, and John Shedd; the park has a popular and publicly accessible fountain named after Clarence Buckingham. Along the lakefront, the name of a sometimes controversial but historic Chicago family graces McCormick Place. The Ida Crown Natatorium sits in Eckhart Park, the Peggy Notebaert Nature Museum in Lincoln Park. Throughout the city are parks christened after their benefactors: Bosley, Commercial Club, Ellis, and Wicker parks, to name a few; others such as Arcade, Leland Giants, and Washington Square parks were private bequests to the city. Few Chicago residents consider these to be violations of public accessibility. Most believe they enhance civic life and encourage park usage.

The same applies for much of the city's public art. From 1913 to 1980, for example, seventeen of Chicago's most notable public monuments and sculptures were funded by a $1 million private gift from Benjamin Franklin Ferguson, including works by Lorado Taft, Isamu Noguchi, and Henry Moore.[15] Rather than representing a new threat to public access, the $173.5 million raised by John Bryan and Millennium Park, Inc., and the $63 million raised by the Music and Dance Theater are emblematic of how art and dance are subsidized in American cities. Millennium Park is only the latest and perhaps most spectacular example of a municipal culture and park system long reliant on private philanthropy.

Most striking was the largess of Millennium Park's philanthropy: more than seventy-five families or individuals contributed $1 million or more, a rare event for a single project in any city. Why? Some probably enjoyed having their family's name inscribed on the Millennium Monument. But in a city with many cultural institutions competing for philanthropic dollars (many of which list the most generous supporters on their walls), why contribute to Millennium Park? More often than not, donors invoked their gratitude and loyalty to the city of Chicago. A certain cultural idealism underlay many donors' willingness to support Millennium Park. This was especially true for those who were the descendants of immigrants who arrived in the United States with little wealth: the Crowns, the Guthmans, the Harrises, the Kaplans, the Minows, and the Pritzkers, for example. "Their children prospered and feel an obligation to repay their community in thanks for their freedom and open door," wrote one donor. "We as a family have done very well by the city and this was an opportunity to give back to the city," insisted Thomas Pritzker. "I view this not as something that we're doing for the city as much as a recognition of what the city has done for us."[16]

Consumerist critiques of Millennium Park downplay the positive impact of consumption in transforming an urban space. Jane Jacobs, in her classic manifesto *The Death and Life of Great American Cities* (1962), argued that storefronts, vendors, and other street-level establishments were responsible for much of the social vibrancy and street life in urban centers. The absence of commercial and other street-level activity rendered many city spaces dangerous, including Grant Park. In 1973, for example, two women were murdered in the park. Planners such as architect Harry Weese responded that city officials needed to develop strategies to both attract citizens and provide safety in Chicago's lakefront parks. Civic activists such as Friends of the Parks founder Lois Weisberg advocated introducing more private concessions into the city's parks. Such commercial activity, believed the famed urbanist William H. Whyte in 1978, would give the park what it lacked: people.[17]

Millennium Park's solution was to provide a variety of activities—some organized around consumption and some not—to attract a diverse population of both tourists and residents. Visitors may have to pay to eat at the park's restaurant or outdoor café, attend the Harris Theater, rent ice skates or space in the Pritzker Pavilion, or park in the underground garage. But for many, the most enjoyable elements of Millennium Park are free: a walk through the Lurie Garden or across Frank Gehry's bridge, observing one's reflection in *Cloud Gate*, ice skating beneath the sculpture, watching children splashing in the *Crown Fountain*, or listening to the Grant Park Orchestra on the Great Lawn.

In any case, not all consumption is equal. A park and a cultural complex organized around art is not a shopping mall. The pleasures derived from patronizing Water Tower Place are hardly the same as listening to orchestral, choral, or other music. Nor is Millennium Park a reprise of Navy Pier, however similar the economic and planning forces behind them. Rather than offering storefront venders and other opportunities for consumer spending, Millennium Park encourages visitors to interact with some form of art. How many Disneyland or theme park visitors contemplate their "nothingness," as Kapoor asks? Do any ponder the duality of life posed by Plensa? Who examines the chaos of music and urbanity posed by Gehry's music pavilion? "We want to make people think and react," challenges Craig Webb of Gehry Partners.[18]

By comparison, theme park planning is organized around deception and subterfuge. Projects ranging from Southern California's Disneyland to Boston's Faneuil Hall are full of references to myths and to histories that never happened. Rather than mythifying or manufacturing a past, or ignoring the beaux arts style of Grant Park, as some claim, elements of Millennium Park genuflect to and evoke history: Kathryn Gustafson's Shoulder Hedge refers to Carl Sandburg's historic poem *Chicago*. Shannon Nichol's seam in Lurie Garden mimics the nineteenth-century seawall separating the railroad from the lake that once existed on the site. The Millennium Monument recreates the peristyle from 1917. The fountain in Wrigley Square replicates a finial from the Wrigley Building. Plensa's

Crown Fountain includes LED faces that echo the gargoyles of Renaissance-era fountains. In sum, the park builds upon a variety of historic and public memories within and beyond Chicago.

Millennium Park is more rooted in the landscape ideals of Andrew Jackson Downing than recent theme park planning. For Downing and other nineteenth-century landscape architects, public parks were to serve civic, educational, and associational purposes. Such parks, Downing argued in 1851, enshrined "noble works of art, the statues, monuments and buildings commemorative at once of the great men of the nation, of the history of the age and country, and the genius of our highest artists." John Bryan echoed Downing in explaining Millennium Park. The project had "a great educational component," he insisted, and was "all about elevating people's vision of what can be done." For Bryan, a cultural project like Millennium Park "does something to the spirit of the city that almost is impossible to define."[19]

By some measures, Millennium Park *expands* the public sphere. First, what was once a private, corporate-controlled space is now public land. Real estate owned by one of the most powerful and influential corporations in U.S. history for approximately 150 years is now mostly free, open to the public, and administered primarily by municipal authorities. Private gifts exceeding $200 million built the park, but the space remains under city or park district supervision. Indeed, John Bryan was openly reluctant to create a private, nonprofit conservancy to operate and maintain Millennium Park. "We don't know how to run parks, and the city's very good at it," he admitted on behalf of the donors' group. Bryan's primary concern was to build an endowment devoted to maintaining certain enhancements: Lurie Garden, *Cloud Gate* and the *Crown Fountain*.[20] By comparison, the Art Institute across Monroe Street represents a far more extensive incursion into public space: a private institution governed largely by wealthy donors sits on public land and charges entry fees to all who enter.[21] The underlying fact of Millennium Park is that Chicago's private philanthropic and corporate elites "gave it away."

Second, the park conforms to *The Grant Park Framework Plan*, the product of an ongoing, participatory planning process and debate during the 1990s.[22] By covering the historic railroad tracks and constructing a bridge over Columbus Drive, Millennium Park physically reconnects Michigan Avenue and Randolph Street with the lakefront. The intermodal transit station and bike station offer new accessibility to and within Grant Park while reorganizing vehicular traffic in a physically congested inner city. Millennium Park also addresses earlier criticisms regarding the "lack of people" in Grant Park. The Jay Pritzker Pavilion and the Harris Theater combined sponsor twelve months of music and dance programs, some of which are free. McCormick Tribune Plaza—a popular skating rink in the winter, a vibrant outdoor café in the summer—attracts patrons year-round.

Third, the Harris Theater challenges cultural traditions of exclusion. The theater's founders deliberately sought to create a space of "racial and economic neutrality," one designed to foster civic engagement and gathering. Joan Harris openly stated that her goal was to avoid the class, gender, and race-based ideologies associated with classical and Western styles of music and dance.[23] In the theater's first two seasons of operation, performing companies included the New Black Music Repertory Ensemble, *Ballet Folklorico de la Universidad Veracruzana*, the Chicago Gay Men's Chorus, and the Arab American Action Network. Furthermore, the Music and Dance Theater of Chicago offered an institutional home and downtown presence for historically marginalized groups like the Mexican Fine Arts Center Museum, the Muntu Dance Theatre, and the Old Town School of Folk Music. Repertoires previously relegated to less centrally located neighborhoods—chamber music, opera theater, jazz, modern dance, baroque music, quartets—were incorporated into Millennium Park. Genres of music and dance long made invisible by racial, ethnic, religious, or sexual discrimination are now part of the downtown cultural landscape.

HOW DID CHICAGO PLANNERS and citizens create such a grand public space? Millennium Park's genesis and construction illustrate the dominating influence of the private sector—Chicago's global institutions—in "creating culture" in the United States. For better or worse, museums, universities, art institutes, and other educational and cultural institutions rely heavily upon private philanthropy and user fees to grow and flourish. By contrast, European municipal, state, and federal governments offer more substantial financial support for cultural development. In Spain, for example, the Basque government spent more than $170 million to build the Guggenheim Museum in Bilbao. The result after 1997 was 1.4 million annual tourists, another $200 million spent locally by visitors, and an additional $1 billion in new development.[24]

But Chicago, as Richard M. Daley reminds critics, is not Bilbao. The mayor saw no political benefit in asking taxpayers to spend even $30 million to build a small park on top of the garage that became Millennium Park. In fact, Daley understood that such a request was political suicide. Architect Laurence Booth remembered discussing the public funding for Bilbao's Guggenheim Museum with Daley on one occasion. "If you had spent $170 million on an art museum," Booth queried, "what would have happened to you?" The mayor responded that "he'd probably be ridden out of town on a rail."[25]

This was the fundamental urban political reality of the millennium. Taxpayer resistance to municipal spending, two decades of federal disinvestment from American cities, tight city budgets, and global competition presented big-city mayors like Daley with few options. His predicament was hardly unusual. Like many other U.S. cities, Chicago evolved from a transportation and commercial center and a city of industrial production to a metropolis of cultural and tourist consumption. After 1980, North American and European cities adopted aggressive cultural policies designed to redevelop and revive central core areas, stimulate tourism, and generate revenue. This strategy required redeveloping older, inner-city neighborhoods to include what some observers described as a downtown "trophy collection": a festival mall, a convention center, an atrium hotel, an aquarium, a domed stadium, a restored historic neighborhood, a redeveloped waterfront, and new office towers.[26]

19.7. The multiple languages on this Park Grill sign reflect the goal of attracting international tourists.

These circumstances persuaded Daley to privatize the construction of Millennium Park, to ask Chicago's corporate and foundation communities—its global players—to give a gift to the city. Such a project would render downtown Chicago a more attractive place to live, invigorate lakefront cultural institutions, enhance real estate values, and, he hoped, become a destination for both tourists and residents. The mayor predicted that the park would eventually generate at least $100 million of annual revenue from the two to three million expected tourists.[27]

Millennium Park represents the crown jewel in Daley's downtown development strategy. Since assuming office in 1989, the Daley administration has encouraged or directly subsidized a lakefront tourist and leisure landscape. Witness the expansion of McCormick Place, the opening of Navy Pier as a renovated waterfront and festival mall, the redesign of Soldier Field, creating an integrated Museum Campus in Grant Park with an expanded Shedd Aquarium, Adler Planetarium, and Field Museum, and the restoration of State Street to its historic mid-twentieth-century form.[28]

This symbiosis of economic and cultural development demands attracting world-renowned artists. Gehry's Guggenheim Museum in Bilbao illustrated the economic benefits of large-scale public art. The process has occurred elsewhere: Moshe Safdie's Vancouver Library Square, Rem Koolhaas's Seattle Public Library, Santiago Calatrava's Milwaukee Art Museum, and Zaha Hadid's Contemporary Arts Center in Cincinnati, Ohio, for example, represent significant, high-profile cultural structures. In contrast to public buildings constructed in earlier periods of austere budgets and simplified architecture, these structures are flamboyant and distinctive.[29]

The privatization of Millennium Park's construction process also illuminates the nature of political power in Chicago. Precisely who governs Chicago? The influence of the private sector—embodied by John Bryan and Millennium Park, Inc.—demonstrates that municipal government lacks the resources and power to govern without the support or cooperation of private groups, that growth-oriented alliances between municipal authorities and business interests remain a central feature of Chicago politics. "Millennium Park wouldn't have happened if it wasn't for the private sector really wanting to create something for the public," admits project director Ed Uhlir.[30]

But neither the private sector nor city officials associated with Millennium Park ever enjoyed a blank check. Uhlir pointed out that municipal and Millennium Park officials consistently opened the plans to public scrutiny. As in many such projects, however, "the people who are engaged in commenting on these things are not the general public." As with the debate over Lakefront Gardens in the 1970s, civic groups—Friends of Downtown, Friends of the Parks, Central Michigan Avenue Association, the Grant Park Council, North Michigan Avenue Association—represented "the public." When civic groups generated good suggestions, Millennium Park officials tried to incorporate them. When new elements were added—the Music and Dance Theater, Gehry's music pavilion, Plensa's fountain—the public or public authorities were invited to offer comment.[31]

The problem is that few individual citizens regularly participate in such forums. Interested and organized civic groups are left to scrutinize and criticize municipal planning activity. These are, as Uhlir noted, "the people who are organized to give opinions." For this reason, the planning structure for Millennium Park "wasn't ideal." The Grant Park and Lincoln Park framework plans which Uhlir helped author offered better models for citizen participation, but those were long, four-year processes. "Although I would have liked to have done it that way," concedes Uhlir, "it evolved in a much different way."[32]

Most important, mayor Richard M. Daley had the final say over all important Millennium Park decisions: the initiation of the project, selection of Ed Uhlir as manager and John Bryan as head of Millennium Park, Inc., the invitation to Frank Gehry to participate in the project, the snakelike shape of Gehry's BP Bridge, the unusual technological features of the *Crown Fountain*, the introduction of the Music and Dance Theater, the decision to hold a garden competition, and the adoption of a fundraising strategy focusing on million-dollar gifts. "This never would have happened unless Rich Daley was mayor of Chicago," summarizes architect Laurence Booth. Frank Gehry was mystified at points regarding who was in charge, but for Ed Uhlir and John Bryan there was no mystery: the mayor was "the client."[33]

Lost in the debates and controversies over Millennium Park was Richard Daley's broader vision. After assuming office in 1989, Daley's administration supported and subsidized a cultural renaissance in Chicago. With Lois Weisberg, Daley transformed the Department of Cultural Affairs into one of Chicago's most active and popular municipal agencies. The city sponsors major musical events like the Grant Park Music Festival, the Blues Festival, the Gospel Festival, the Country Music Festival, Viva Chicago, and the Chicago Jazz Festival, all with entirely free admission. Other programs, such as Gallery 37 for the Arts and special events like "Cows on Parade" are now considered models for

19.8. Richard Daley and his culture-makers. (Left-right): Daley, Anish Kapoor, Frank Gehry, Jaume Plensa, Kathryn Gustafson, and John Bryan.

other cities. Under Daley and Weisberg's stewardship, the Chicago Sister Cities International Program became the most active sister cities organization in the world.[34]

This was no accident on Daley's part. Cultural institutions and art "will really define Chicago as we look back on what the artist community has done to make this a better city," he declared. The renovations of the Harris and Selwyn theaters into the new Goodman Theatre (2000), the revival of the Ford Oriental Theater (1998) and the Cadillac Palace (1999), and the openings of the Museum of Contemporary Art (1996), the Shakespeare Theater (1999) at Navy Pier and the Lookingglass Theatre (2003) at the Water Tower Pumping Station exemplified Daley's enthusiasm for cultural development. "Politicians come and go; business leaders come and go," the mayor said, "but the artists really define a city."[35]

19.9. (facing) Side view of pavilion, looking west from Daley Bicentennial Plaza.

Art may define a city or an era, but Millennium Park will long be identified with Richard M. Daley. For over a century, Chicago planners and Park District officials envisioned a magnificent music pavilion in Chicago's lakefront park. Architects, from Daniel Burnham and Olmsted Brothers in the 1890s to Richard Bennett, Bruce Graham, and Harry Weese in the 1960s to Gene Summers and Robert Hutchins in the 1970s, offered innovative proposals to transform Grant Park into such a cultural center. After 1975, the ambitious Lakefront Gardens plan generated support from the city's civic groups, executives from Chicago's most powerful corporations, philanthropic foundations, and public officials. None of these plans was ever realized.[36] In completing Millennium Park, Richard Daley accomplished a feat that had eluded all of his predecessors.

Some predict that private philanthropy like that witnessed in the creation of Millennium Park will become ever more critical to park and cultural development in American cities.[37] But the philanthropic generosity that generated Millennium Park is unlikely to be repeated. The project was a one-time millennial event, the result of historical contingency. At numerous points in the planning and development of Millennium Park—indeed before one spade of earth was overturned to begin construction—events could have transpired altogether differently. If Lakefront Gardens had been built in the 1970s, there would have been no need for a Millennium Park. Without Randy Mehrberg's curiosity regarding the nineteenth-century contract between the City of Chicago and the Illinois Central Railroad, the city would never have repossessed the land where Millennium Park sits today. Richard M. Daley might have invited a different corporate leader without the vision of John Bryan to lead the fundraising campaign. Wrigley Company Foundation president William Piet spoke on behalf of many insiders when he said that Bryan "was probably the only one that could have carried this off."[38]

Once construction began, it was John Bryan's good fortune that Cindy Pritzker was both a friend and admirer of Frank Gehry. But Gehry might never have built the pavilion and bridge without Ed Uhlir's and James Feldstein's opportune visit to Santa Monica in December 1998. Without Gehry's participation, Bryan never would have raised so much money so quickly. If the fundraising campaign had started three years later, Bryan later admitted, he would have never attracted such financial support. And what if Ed Uhlir

had proved unconvincing to city officials and civic groups that Gehry's music pavilion was a piece of art? What if a contemporary acolyte of A. Montgomery Ward had sued the city, insisting that the pavilion was indeed a structure? Without Irving Harris's gift to initiate construction of the Music and Dance Theater, there might still be a hole in the north end of Millennium Park. If any of this had happened, Millennium Park would look completely different; it might not even exist. As Field Museum president John McCarter summarized, "All the planets were aligned."[39]

On April 13, 1897, Daniel Burnham spoke before the Merchants' Club to promote his vision of Chicago, later encapsulated in his *Plan of Chicago* (1909). Burnham issued a challenge to Chicago's economic leadership: "Why not establish here physical conditions which will make this the pleasure-town of the country, and thus enable our citizens to avail themselves of the fact?" Burnham proposed that the seven miles of lakefront from the Chicago River to Hyde Park should be "made beautiful" and developed for the general public. But the anchor of any lakefront development, he emphasized, had to be Grant Park—"the intellectual center of Chicago, . . . for art everywhere has been a source of wealth and moral influence."[40]

More than a century later, Millennium Park completes this part of Burnham's dream.

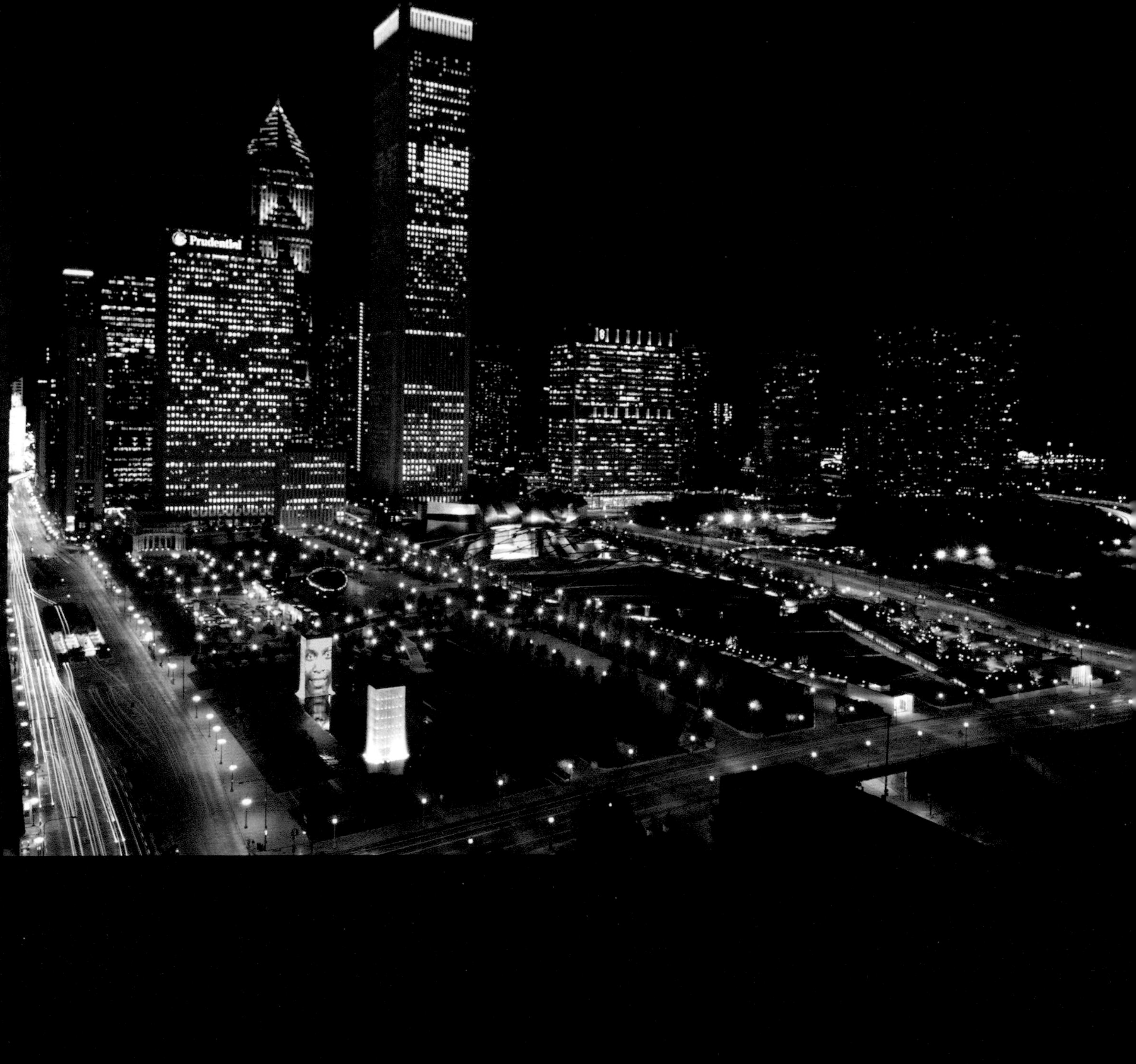
Prudential

ACKNOWLEDGMENTS Like Millennium Park itself, numerous individuals contributed their time and ideas in the conception, development, and writing of this book. I am particularly grateful to the various participants in the Millennium Park project and earlier efforts to construct a music pavilion in Grant Park who spoke with me and allowed the transcription of those interviews to be deposited in the collections of the Chicago Historical Society (now Chicago History Museum): James Alexander, Edward J. Bedore, Thomas Beeby, Laurence O. Booth, John H. Bryan, Lester Crown, Steven Crown, Susan Crown, Richard M. Daley, David Dillon, James Feldstein, Marshall Field V, Frank Gehry, Nicholas Goodban, Paul Gray, Richard Gray, Jack Guthman, Sandra Guthman, Kathryn Gustafson, Irving Harris, Joan Harris, Robert Hutchins, Robert Israel, Edgar D. Jannotta, Sr., Jonathan Laney, Donna LaPietra, Michael Lash, John McCarter, John M. McDonough, Randall Mehrberg, Joyce Moffatt, James J. O'Connor, Piet Oudolf, Judith Paulus, Christopher Perille, William Piet, Jaume Plensa, Cindy Pritzker, Thomas Pritzker, George Ranney, Jr., Alan Schachtman, Adrian Smith, Michael Patrick Sullivan, Rick Talaske, Richard L. Thomas, Edward K. Uhlir, Lella Vignelli, and Craig Webb. I am especially grateful to Ed Uhlir and John Bryan. While both were critical actors in the creation of Millennium Park, they took time away from their own work to share materials with me and willingly discussed their roles in shaping the final design of the park. When I discovered unflattering events related to the park, John Bryan never tried to suppress their revelation. "Just tell the truth," he advised. I have tried to do that.

In a project like this, a writer relies heavily on individuals who save time, provide access to sources, and offer suggestions for other relevant material. They are the hidden people who made this book a reality. Amanda Berman and Janice Llereza transcribed interviews. Paul Clausen, Roark Frankel, and Alan Schachtman took many hours out of their days to explain the complexities of building and engineering when Millennium Park was a construction site. Patricia Bakunas and the Special Collections Department at the University of Illinois at Chicago helped me through the massive collections of the Metropolitan Planning Council. Peter Skosey of the Metropolitan Planning Council allowed me to examine records related to Lakefront Gardens. Forest Claypool offered useful advice regarding the politics of construction in Chicago. Joan Tomlin of the Shedd Aquarium, Bill Wilhelm of the Adler Planetarium, and Christine Giannoni of the Field Museum helped me locate attendance statistics on those respective institutions. Keith Palmer at Murphy/Jahn allowed me to examine and reproduce documents regarding the bandshell proposal designed by Gene Summers in 1972. Heidi Hewitt at the Chicago Humanities Festival secured a relevant festival poster. Jon Daniels shared his research with me regarding the nineteenth-century baseball field located on the site of Millennium Park. Martha Briggs and JoEllen Dickie helped locate materials in the Illinois Central Railroad Collection of the Newberry Library. Doug Warrick and Loretta Hill of the Chronicle Pavilion in Concord, California, generously shared their time and expertise regarding the history of that structure. Anna Fitzloff at the Harris Theater provided access for photographing the theater. Henry Kleeman, Seth Traxler, and David York explained the mysteries of copyright law as it applied to Millennium Park. When I lost a chapter through a corrupted computer file, Adam and Devin Stewart performed a technological miracle and resurrected it. David A. Marks at Loebl Schlossman & Hackl provided materials and advice related to the Montgomery Ward Memorial bandshell proposal in 1961–1962, as well as the firm's proposals in the mid-1980s for a park over the current Millennium Park site. He also bought me lunch, for which I am most grateful. Rob Omori in John Bryan's office answered my many pestering and esoteric queries. If he is not the happiest to see this book completed, he is surely the most relieved.

Numerous people helped me obtain photographs that visually document much of this book. Jim Hedrich and Scott McDonald of Hedrich Blessing not only provided much of the visual material, but answered my requests for specific images. I am especially appreciative of Robert Wislow of U.S. Equities Realty for sharing his firm's immense archive with me. Sharon L. Burge and Rose Auriemma located relevant construction photographs. Julia Sniderman Bachrach and Bob Middaugh at the Chicago Park District and David Phillips of Chicago Architecture Photographing Company offered help in locating historic illustrations. Adam Ottavi helped me obtain images of Anish Kapoor's sculptures, Thomas Beeby for his Harris Theater, Keith Mendenhall for Frank Gehry's architecture, Erin Bakunas and Paul Gray for Jaume Plensa's art, Jeannie Ernst for Kathryn Gustafson's landscapes, and David Troszak for the Millennium Park terraces and galleries. Jack Guthman, Sandra Guthman, Robert Hutchins, Cindy Pritzker, George Ranney and Rick Talaske shared photographs from their personal collections with me.

Certain individuals took time out of their busy schedules to read the book in manuscript form. Robin Bachin, Erin Bakunas, John Bryan, Susan Crown, Lewis Erenberg, James Feldstein, Paul Gray, Kathryn Gustafson, Henry Kleeman, Shannon Nichol, Ted Karamanski, Jane Rodriguez, and Jan Toftey read portions of the manuscript, offered constructive and useful suggestions, and prevented me from committing many egregious errors. I am especially grateful to the anonymous readers at the University of Chicago Press, Rosemary Adams, Joseph Bigott, James Grossman, Russell Lewis, Newton Minow, Josephine Minow, Rob Omori, David Schuyler, and Edward Uhlir, who not only read the entire manuscript, but challenged many of my assumptions while offering insightful and positive criticisms.

This book would never have been written but for an extremely generous financial grant from the Minow Family Foundation. I am grateful to Loyola University Chicago for granting me a leave of absence from my teaching responsibilities to research and write this book. My students Laura Milsk and Tim Neary offered research assistance, directed me to sources, and provided insightful advice based on their expertise on Chicago history. My colleagues in the Department of History were especially supportive, even as they wondered what a nineteenth-century historian was doing wandering around a twenty-first-century construction site.

I owe many debts to the Chicago Historical Society. Luciana Crovato arranged for transcriptions and answered my many administrative questions. I dragged photographer Jay Crawford to various hidden parts of Millennium Park—from the loading dock and fly space of the Harris Theater to the restroom facilities—and he never complained. Jordan Walker and Gwen Ihnat arranged and organized over six hundred of these and other images prior to publication. Kathy Fredrickson, Garrett Niksch, and Matt Simpson at Studio Blue offered early ideas for layout and publication. Rosemary Adams and Russell Lewis lived with this project for four years and directed it through its many stages and problems. As always, Lonnie Bunch's enthusiasm and support made it come to fruition.

Robert Devens at the University of Chicago Press was more than just an editor. He facilitated a cooperative publishing arrangement with the Chicago Historical Society. He offered many insightful criticisms of the manuscript. He promptly answer my many production questions, both big and small. He did all of this and remained my friend. Daniel Yancz made sense of my requests regarding illustrations. Elizabeth Branch Dyson helped me negotiate the complexities of the Press at every stage of the editorial process. Jill Shimabukuro transformed a plain, colorless manuscript into an artistic masterpiece in record time. Carol Saller proved to be more than a copy editor; she offered numerous cogent and insightful suggestions on how to improve the manuscript. The Press is lucky to have her. Series editor James Grossman asked me some of the hardest questions regarding Millennium Park. I am grateful for his honest skepticism and cogent criticism, for forcing me to rethink many of my assumptions about the park and urban history.

My greatest professional debt belongs to Newton and Josephine Minow. When Millennium Park was only a hole in the ground and I had only a tangential interest in the project, they predicted and convinced me that the construction of the park was a historic event. They were right. For more than five years, they provided financial support and unbounded optimism. They opened doors and provided access to individuals who were otherwise reluctant to discuss their roles in Millennium Park. They perked up my spirits when I was discouraged. When I reached conclusions different from theirs, they listened and disagreed, but never imposed their interpretations on me. Few writers (dare I say artists) ever had better patrons. My sincere appreciation for their support, infectious enthusiasm, and love of history is exemplified by the dedication of this book.

My greatest debt is to my family. My children Danielle and Maria have grown up with Millennium Park. This book, like the park itself, is part of their lives in more ways than one. When I was busy with the book, Reyna Cerrato played with and entertained my children. She is now a part of my extended family. Most important is my wife Mary Rose Alexander. She enthusiastically joined me in many of my Millennium Park adventures, even when she had better things to do. When I needed time and money to finish the book, she gave me both. When I needed support, sympathy, and love, she gave me all three. No husband has a better wife.

APPENDIXES

1836 } Board of Canal Commissioners set aside open space along the lakefront from Randolph Street south to Park Row (11th Street) and east of Michigan Avenue with the notation on the map designated "Public Ground—A Common to Remain Forever Open, Clear and Free of Any Buildings, or Other Obstruction Whatever."

1844 } Canal Commissioners transfer control of the open, undeveloped space to the City of Chicago.

1847 } The narrow strip of land east of Michigan Avenue is designated "Lake Park" (although over the next half century, the terms "Lake Park" and "Lake Front Park" were both used).

1852 } City of Chicago grants a right-of-way to the Illinois Central Railroad in return for constructing a breakwater in the lake north of 12th Street.

1856 } Great Central Depot, a four-story, 500-foot long terminus for the Illinois Central Railroad designed by Otto Matz, opens just north of Randolph Street.

1871 } Union baseball grounds constructed at the north end of Lake Park, but destroyed later that year in the Great Chicago Fire.

1878-1884 } Union baseball grounds rebuilt at the north end of Lake Park.

OCT. 1890 } Aaron Montgomery Ward initiates the first of a series of lawsuits to keep the park free of new buildings.

1892 }	Art Institute constructed in Grant Park. U.S. Supreme Court rules that the State of Illinois does not have the right to grant appurtenant riparian rights to the Illinois Central Railroad. Such rights belong to the city "in trust for public use."
1897 }	Illinois Supreme Court approves the right of the Art Institute to build in Lake Park if permission of the abutting landowners is obtained.
1901 }	Lake Park renamed in honor of Ulysses S. Grant.
1909 }	Illinois Supreme Court reinforces Ward's opposition to development in the park when he seeks to prevent the erection of the Field Museum of Natural History. Daniel Burnham and Edward Bennett's *Plan of Chicago*, the "Burnham Plan," published.
1916 }	Municipal Pier (later renamed Navy Pier) opens.
1917-1929 }	Edward Bennett and partners William E. Parsons, Cyrus Thomas, and Harry T. Frost design elements of Grant Park.
1919 }	Illinois Central railroad tracks lowered below street level.
1921 }	Monroe Street Parking Station opens. Completed in 1938, it remained the largest single-fee parking facility in the United States into the 1950s. A pedestrian subway under Michigan Avenue near Randolph Street is completed.
1923 }	Eliel Saarinen proposes a 47,000-car underground "parking terminal" in Grant Park.
1927 }	*Buckingham Fountain* opens in Grant Park.
1931 }	In anticipation of the Century of Progress Exposition in 1933–1934, the city erects a "temporary" 43-foot-high bandshell on the south end of the park. Modeled after the Hollywood Bowl in Los Angeles, the structure costs $15,000.
1935 }	First Grant Park concert, on the Fourth of July.
1952-55 }	Prudential Building constructed on Randolph Street at north end of Grant Park.
1953 }	Peristyle at northwest corner of Grant Park destroyed for construction of underground garage.
1954 }	Grant Park North Garage opens with spaces for 2,359 vehicles.
1961 }	A. Montgomery Ward Foundation offers to donate $1.5 million for a new bandshell on Butler Field.
1964-65 }	Outer Drive East Apartments, just east of Lake Shore Drive on Randolph Street, constructed. The $27 million, 940-unit structure is the world's largest residential structure upon completion.
1965 }	Grant Park South Underground Garage opens with spaces for 1,241 vehicles.
1972 }	Gene Summers of C. F. Murphy Associates proposes an 85-foot, translucent, half-coned bandshell over a new 3,700-car underground garage on the existing site of the Monroe Street parking lot.
1976 }	Grant Park music shell named after James Petrillo.
1977 }	Lakefront Gardens proposed. The Monroe Street Underground Garage opens on the site of the old Monroe Street Parking Terminal and below Daley Bicentennial Plaza. With a capacity of 3,700 vehicles, the new facility more than doubles the total automobile capacity of Grant Park to over 7,000.

1978 }	New "temporary" Petrillo bandshell opens on Butler Field.
1984 }	Navy Pier closes.
1986 }	Lake Shore Drive at the north end of Grant Park is realigned between the Chicago River and Randolph Street, eliminating the infamous "S-curve.
1989 }	City of Chicago and the State of Illinois create the Metropolitan Pier and Exposition Authority and commit $150 million for the reconstruction of Navy Pier.
1992–1994 }	Renovation of Navy Pier by Benjamin Thompson & Associates.
1993 }	Music and Dance Theater Chicago formed with nine affiliated performing arts companies.
1994 }	Navy Pier's 1,500-seat Skyline Stage opens. Lakefront Gardens, Inc., dissolves.
1995 }	Music and Dance Theater Chicago expands to twelve affiliated performing arts companies.
1996 }	City of Chicago sues the Illinois Central Railroad to regain land south of Randolph Street.
1997 }	Estimated annual attendance at Navy Pier reaches 7 million, more than double the second leading attraction in Chicago, the Lincoln Park Zoo with 3 million annual visitors.
SEPT. 1997 }	During a reception for the mayor of Mexico City at Mid-America Club in the Amoco Building, mayor Richard M. Daley pulls John Bryan, CEO of Sara Lee, over to the window, points to the Illinois Central Railroad tracks, and says, "We should build a park there."
NOV. 1997 }	McDonough Associates Lakefront Transportation Study recommends development of a busway in the Illinois Central Railroad bed from Randolph Street to McCormick Place. John Bryan suggests that Chicago build a monument to the millennium in his acceptance speech for the Daniel H. Burnham Award from the Chicagoland Chamber of Commerce.
DEC. 1997 }	In response to the city's lawsuit, the Illinois Central Railroad donates rights, title, and interest in the land that eventually becomes Millennium Park. The IC also donates all their rights south to McCormick Place.
FEB. 1998 }	Canadian National Railway purchases the Illinois Central Railroad for $2.4 billion.
MARCH 1998 }	Mayor Richard M. Daley asks John Bryan to lead a private fundraising campaign to build a park on top of the new garage over the site of the Illinois Central Railroad tracks. Bryan sees the model for the park designed by SOM for the first time. Mayor Richard M. Daley announces the Lakefront Millennium Project with John Bryan to serve as the chief fundraiser for the donors' group.
SPRING 1998 }	Bryan forms art and garden committees to develop plans and fundraising strategies for Millennium Park.
MAY 1998 }	SBC announces merger and purchase of Ameritech for $62 billion. Chicago Plan Commission approves the Lakefront Millennium Project. Chicago City Council approves plans to float $150 million in bonds to construct Millennium Park. Millen-

nium Park is expanded from 16 to 24 acres in order to include the Grant Park North
Garage renovation.

JUNE 1998 } City of Chicago issues $150 million Lakefront Millennium Project Parking Facilities
Bonds (Limited Tax), Series 1998.

JULY 1998 } John Bryan convenes first meeting of the Art Committee to discuss what types of
public art should be included in Millennium Park.

SUMMER 1998 } Cindy Pritzker, James Feldstein, and John Bryan meet to discuss the possibility of inviting Frank O. Gehry to design a decoration for the proscenium over the music pavilion.

AUG. 1998 } Daley asks Ed Uhlir of the Chicago Park District to serve as the project director of
Millennium Park.

SEPT. 1998 } Construction begins on Millennium Park garage. Adrian Smith offers to let Gehry
do an "application" or decoration to the proscenium of the music pavilion. Gehry
says he is not interested. Edward Uhlir officially begins working as project director
of Millennium Park. John Bryan, James Feldstein, and Marshall Field V conceive of
a plan to invite Music and Dance Theater Chicago to build a theater in Millennium
Park. Thomas Beeby determines that Music and Dance Theater can fit into Millennium Park space.

OCT. 1998 } Ed Uhlir persuades SOM and Millennium Park officials to move the skating rink and
plaza from behind the music pavilion to a more prominent location along Michigan
Avenue.

NOV. 1998 TO } Ed Uhlir, Jack Guthman, Tom Beeby, and others make presentations to landlords
MARCH 1999 surrounding Millennium Park to win approval of Music and Dance Theater.

DEC. 1998 } Anish Kapoor reveals his sculpture proposal to the Millennium Park Art Committee. Drawings unveiled for inclusion of the Music and Dance Theater in Millennium
Park. Edward Uhlir and James Feldstein travel to Santa Monica to invite Gehry to
design the music pavilion. Shortly after, Gehry signs a contract.

FEB. 1999 } McCormick Tribune Foundation signs an agreement to fund an ice skating rink and
plaza, the first major gift to Millennium Park.

MARCH 1999 } William Wrigley dies; shortly after William Wrigley, Jr., agrees to fund the peristyle
and square. Anish Kapoor presents a model and prospectus for his sculpture to the
Millennium Park Art Committee. City submits revised plan for Millennium Park to
include the Music and Dance Theater to the Chicago Plan Commission, which ap-
proves the revisions.

APRIL 1999 } John and Mildred Boaz of 360 E. Randolph Drive sue the City of Chicago on behalf
of other condominium owners, charging that the Music and Dance Theater violates
the Montgomery Ward height restrictions. Daley announces that the Pritzker Foundation will donate $15 million for a Frank Gehry–designed bandshell for Millen-
nium Park.

SPRING 1999 } U.S. Equities retained by Millennium Park, Inc., to act as their representative for the
donor-funded enhancements to the park. The city issues $33 million of additional
bonds for Millennium Park.

| MAY 1999 } | Grant Park North Garage closed for a two-year reconstruction financed by garage fees and Loop TIF funds. Anish Kapoor signs agreement to design a sculpture for Millennium Park. |

MAY 1999 } Grant Park North Garage closed for a two-year reconstruction financed by garage fees and Loop TIF funds. Anish Kapoor signs agreement to design a sculpture for Millennium Park.

JULY 1999 } Illinois Central Railroad officially merges with Canadian National Railway. Frank Gehry begins designing Millennium Park music pavilion and pedestrian bridge. Harston/Schwendener hired to build 2,500-car parking garage and concrete bridge over Metra tracks for $105 million.

OCT. 1999 } Ameritech signs an agreement to fund the plaza on which will sit Anish Kapoor's sculpture. Ameritech CEO Richard Notebaert delivers the first $600,000 installment.

NOV. 1999 } Gehry publicly displays initial music pavilion design. Anish Kapoor's sculpture revealed to public.

DEC. 1999 } Ed Uhlir presents Frank Gehry's music pavilion design to the Public Art Committee and they agree that the decorative elements above the proscenium are not "structures" but "art," thereby complying with the Montgomery Ward restrictions on structures in the park. The Crown family agrees in principle to fund a "water feature" in Millennium Park. BP America signs an agreement to fund the pedestrian bridge.

JAN. 2000 } Jaume Plensa is invited by the Crown family to come to Chicago to meet the family and present a proposal. Judge Albert Green dismisses the lawsuit filed by John and Mildred Boaz, finding that the Montgomery Ward cases were not violated by the Music and Dance Theater.

APRIL 2000 } Patrick and Shirley Ryan withdraw their initial commitment to endow the Millennium Park garden.

MAY 2000 } Daley uses $35 million from Central Loop TIF for garage construction debt repayment.

JUNE 2000 } Joint venture contractor Harston/Schwendener is removed from Millennium Park garage contract after over 1,000 revisions to original plans.

JULY 2000 } Management of construction of Millennium Park shifts from Chicago Department of Transportation to the Chicago Public Buildings Commission. Invitations are issued to potential designers for the Millennium Park garden design competition. Walsh/II in One joint venture hired as replacement contractor for garage.

OCT. 2000 } Bank One agrees to fund the promenade.

NOV. 2000 } Grant Park North Garage reopens after the reconstruction is completed six months ahead of the initial schedule. Daley requests an additional $28 million from Fund 925 (Grant Funds for the Year 2000) for Millennium Park.

DEC. 2000 } Wrigley Foundation makes first payment on pledge to fund Wrigley Square.

JAN. 2001 } Bryan raises $85 million, and increases goal to $125 million. Joint venture contractor Harston/Schwendener sues the City of Chicago. *Tribune* discloses that Millennium Park garage columns cracked during construction and had to be replaced.

FEB. 2001 } Millennium Park Garage opens with 250 spaces.

MARCH 2001 }	Winning *Shoulder Garden* design of Kathryn Gustafson, Piet Oudolf, and Robert Israel is publicly displayed for first time.
APRIL 2001 }	Art Institute of Chicago announces plan to construct $200 million addition designed by Renzo Piano along Monroe Street facing the southern end of Millennium Park.
JULY 2001 }	City uses $280,000 from Central Loop TIF to pay for garage construction debt repayment.
AUG. 2001 }	*Chicago Tribune* publishes highly critical article on Millennium Park on front page of August 7 Sunday edition. Millennium Park gifts number sixty-three for a total of $103 million. Daley blames Frank Gehry for Millennium Park cost overruns.
OCT. 2001 }	Jaume Plensa and Crown family publicly announce design for *Crown Fountain*.
NOV. 2001 }	Park District officials announce plans for two restaurants—the Park Grill and the Park Cafe—in Millennium Park, adjacent to the ice rink.
DEC. 2001 }	McCormick Tribune Foundation Ice Skating Rink opens. Millennium Park garage net revenue for 2001 totals $1.69 million.
JAN. 2002 }	City uses $3.1 million from Central Loop TIF to pay for garage construction debt repayment. Express shuttle bus road running from Randolph Street to 25th Street opens, linking Millennium Park with McCormick Place. Millennium Park garage completed with 2,181 parking spaces.
FEB. 2002 }	Irving and Joan Harris announce $15 million gift and $24 million construction loan to Music and Dance Theater. Groundbreaking ceremony for the Harris Theater for Music and Dance.
JUNE 2002 }	Harris Theater reaches $45.7 million of $62.7 million goal.
JUNE-SEPT. 2002 }	*Earth from Above* photography exhibit on the McCormick-Tribune Plaza attracts 1.5 million visitors.
SEPT. 2002 }	Official gifts and pledges to Millennium Park amount to $115 million.
OCT. 2002 }	Wrigley Square dedicated and officially opened. Official gifts and pledges to Millennium Park amount to $118 million.
DEC. 2002 }	Millennium Park garage net revenue for 2002 totals $4.08 million.
MAY 2003 }	Ann Lurie verbally agrees to fund the garden for $10 million.
JUNE 2003 }	Music and Dance Theater named the Joan W. and Irving B. Harris Theater for Music and Dance.
AUG. 2003 }	City officials announce that Ann Lurie will endow the *Shoulder Garden* with $10 million and that the garden will be named the Lurie Garden.
SEPT. 2003 }	Official gifts and pledges to Millennium Park amount to $134 million.
NOV. 2003 }	Harris Theater for Music and Dance opens.
DEC. 2003 }	Park Grill Restaurant opens in Millennium Park.
FEB. 2004 }	Millennium Park officials reveal that the music pavilion will be named after Jay Pritzker.
MAY 2004 }	Mayor Richard M. Daley and architect Frank Gehry lead the dedication and first walk across the BP Bridge. Bryan announces total private contributions of $143 million from eighty-nine donors.

JUNE 2004 } City announces that Millennium Park will remain a city property operated by a private, not-for-profit organization. Anish Kapoor names his sculpture *Cloud Gate* when the final panel is installed on the elliptical sculpture.

JULY 2004 } Millennium Park officially opens. Millennium Park Inaugural Gala Celebration raises $2 million for the park's endowment. An estimated 400,000 to 500,000 people visit Millennium Park.

MARCH 2005 } Boeing donates $5 million to Millennium Park for two outdoor galleries on the Millennium Park terraces and an endowment for public programming. Bryan announces that total private contributions exceed $160 million from 104 donors.

JUNE 2005 } Fundraising by Millennium Park, Inc., ends after raising $173.5 million from 115 founders.

YEAR	MONROE ST. STATION	GRANT PARK NORTH	GRANT PARK SOUTH	TOTAL
1935	452,235			452,235
1940	859,206			859,206
1945	660,444			660,444
1955	906,680	1,346,369		2,253,049
1960	881,856	1,612,466		2,494,322
1965	934,179	1,531,370	603,860	3,069,409
1969	1,026,000	1,500,000*	1,046,000	3,572,000*
1976	No data	No data	No data	2,565,000*
1980	825,000	No data	No data	2,674,000*
1985	No data	No data	No data	3,000,000*

SOURCES: Chicago Park District, *Annual Reports* (Chicago: 1935–1988).

NOTE: For the purpose of brevity, I included only five-year intervals of data. No data was available for 1970 and 1975, as well as for many other years. First portion of new underground Monroe Street Garage opened in March 1976, while the Richard J. Daley Bicentennial Plaza opened a year later.

*Approximation.

APPENDIX 3 UNDERPARK PARKING GARAGES IN U.S. CENTRAL BUSINESS DISTRICTS

PARK	CAR CAPACITY
Union Square, San Francisco (1850, 1940)	1,700
Pershing Square, Los Angeles (1951)	2,150
Mellon Square, Pittsburgh (1953)	896
Grant Park North Underground Garage (1953)	2,359
Portsmouth Square, San Francisco (1963)	
Grant Park South Underground Garage (1965)	1,241
Market Square, Alexandria, Va. (1967)	263
O'Bryant Square, Portsmouth, Oregon (1971)	
Monroe Street Underground Garage (1977) (Daley Bicentennial Plaza above)	3,700
Chicago total by 1977	7,300
Chicago total in 1985	7,700
Memorial Plaza, Cleveland (1991)	900
Post Office Square, Boston (1992)	1,400

SOURCES: Alexander Garvin and Gayle Berens, eds., *Urban Parks and Open Space* (Washington: Urban Land Institute and Trust for Public Land, 1997), 13–14, 156. For Chicago facilities, see CPD, *[Eighteenth] Annual Report for 1952* (Chicago, 1953), 12; idem, *Annual Report 1978* (Chicago, 1979), 6; Chicago Central Area Committee Transportation Task Force, *Final Report* (Jan. 1985), 10, in Folder 1297, Box 73, Accession 94–5, MHPC papers, UIC.

TRUSTEE	AFFILIATION
Roger E. Anderson	Continental Bank
Angelo R. Arena	Marshall Field's
John W. Baird	Baird & Warner Real Estate
Edward K. Banker	President, Harris Bank
Mrs. Lee Philip Bell	
James F. Bere	Borg-Warner Corp.
Miles L. Berger	Mid-America Appraisal & Research Corp.; Chicago Plan Commission member
Charles M. Bliss	Harris Bank
Joseph L. Block	Inland Steel Co.
Franklin A. Cole	Walter Heller International Corp.
Victor J. Danilov	Museum of Science and Industry
John D'Arcy, Jr.	Quaker Oats Co.
O. C. Davis	Peoples Gas Co.
Emmett Dedmon	Hill & Knowlton, author and writer
Edward S. Donnell	Montgomery Ward & Co.
Robert M. Drevs, Chairman	People's Gas Co.
Mrs. Harold M. Florsheim	Metropolitan Housing and Planning Council
Stanley M. Freehling	Freehling & Co.
Joan Harris	Cultural Affairs Director, City of Chicago
William E. Hartmann	Skidmore Owings, & Merrill
Robert M. Hunt	Tribune Co.
John H. Johnson	Johnson Publishing Co.
Clayton Kirkpatrick	Tribune Co.
Alvin W. Long	Chicago Title and Trust Co.
Lewis Manilow	Sachnoff Schrager Jones Weaver & Rubenstein
Charles Marshall	Illinois Bell Telephone Co.
Brooks McCormick	International Harvester
John M. McDonough	Secretary-Treasurer, Sidley & Austin
James J. O'Connor	Commonwealth Edison Co.
Richard B. Ogilvie	Governor of Illinois; Isham, Lincoln & Beale
George A. Ranney, Jr.	Inland Steel
Nancy Ryerson Ranney	
Arthur W. Schultz	Foote, Cone & Belding Communications, Inc.

TRUSTEE	AFFILIATION
E. Norman Staub	Northern Trust Co.
Allen P. Stults	American National Bank & Trust Co. of Chicago
Louis Sudler	Sudler & Co.
Bonnie Swearingen	wife of John Swearingen of Standard Oil of Indiana
A. Dean Swift	Sears, Roebuck & Co.
Richard L. Thomas	First National Bank of Chicago

SOURCE: Robert Hutchins Papers; Lakefront Gardens files, MPC; "For the Use and Pleasure of All" (typescript), 4 April 1979, in Lakefront Gardens Folder, Walter Netsch (unprocessed) Collection, CHS.

SOURCES: *Sightlines* (2003)

Individuals and Families

FINANCE, INSURANCE AND REAL ESTATE		SERVICE	RETAIL	INDUSTRY	
Borwell	Heineman	Duchossois	Comer	Bere	Krehbiel
Brinson	Hull	Filipowski	Field	Bernick/Lavin	Krehbiel
Bucksbaum	Istock	Guthman	Guthman	Bryan	Loucks
Clinton	Jannotta	Kurtis/LaPietra	Kaplan	Buchbinder	Morrow
Cooper	Jordan	Levy	Kaplan (Kohl)	Buntrock	Nichols
Crown	Lurie	Minow	Keller	Crown	O'Connor
Dimon	Mabie	Otterbeck	Krasny	Dixon (Searle)	Port
Driehaus	McCormack	Pedersen		Duchossois	Prince
Duncan	Newman	Schwartz		Gantz	Pritzker
Field	Osborn	Trienens		Graham	Searle
Foreman	Prince	Winfrey		Granoff	Searle
Glasser/	Pritzker			Gray	Sick
Rosenthal	Rauner			Irving Harris	Stone
Gottlieb	Ryan			Neison Harris	Stuart
Granoff	Sick			Heineman	
Gray	Steans			Jordan	
Griffin	Thomas			Kaplan	
Ira Harris	Wislow			Kaplan (Kohl)	
Irving Harris	Zell			Keiser	
Nelson Harris	Zennie			Knight	

Businesses

FINANCE, INSURANCE AND REAL ESTATE		SERVICE	RETAIL	INDUSTRY
Allstate	Harris Bank	Andersen	Sears	Abbott
Aon	JMB Realty	Deloitte	Target	Boeing
Ariel	LaSalle Bank	McDonald's		BP Amoco
Bank One	Northern Trust	Pricewaterhouse		Exelon
CNA Insurance	UBS	Coopers		Sara Lee
Goldman Sachs		SBC		Wrigley

Foundations

FINANCE, INSURANCE AND REAL ESTATE	SERVICE	RETAIL	INDUSTRY
MacArthur (old)	McCormick Tribune	Polk Bros. (old)	Fry (old)
Morse Trusts (old)	Lederer	Kovler (old)	Morse Trusts (old)
Lurie			Regenstein
			Scholl (old)
			Searle (old)
			Siragusa (old)
53 (46%)	18 (16%)	11 (10%)	46 (40%)

NOTES: Service = communications, entertainment, accounting, law, and education. Names may appear in more than one category. Survey included one anonymous founder and one founder (Slezak) whose source of wealth could not be determined.

APPENDIX 7 METROPOLITAN CHICAGO'S FORTUNE 500 COMPANIES, 2000
(MILLENNIUM PARK FOUNDING DONORS IN RED)

CORPORATION	U.S. RANK	HEADQUARTERS
Boeing	10	Chicago
State Farm Insurance	15	Bloomington
Sears Roebuck	16	Hoffman Estates
Motorola	37	Schaumburg
Allstate	47	Northbrook
Bank One Corporation	50	Chicago
Sara Lee	79	Chicago
UAL	94	Elk Grove
Walgreen	95	Deerfield
McDonald's	132	Oak Brook
Abbott Laboratories	135	Abbott Park
Illinois Tool Works	181	Glenview
Navistar	202	Warrenville
Smurfit-Stone Container	240	Chicago
Baxter	243	Deerfield
Aon	248	Chicago
R. R. Donnelly	291	Chicago
Exelon	306	Chicago
Quaker Oats	341	Chicago
USG	347	Chicago
W. W. Grainger	355	Lake Forest
Brunswick	373	Lake Forest
Comdisco Holding	380	Rosemont
Tribune	476	Chicago
Ace Hardware	482	Oak Brook

SOURCE: http://www.fortune.com/fortune/subs/500archive/fulllist/0,19389,2000,00.html, accessed May 2004.

U. S. RANK	COMPANY	WORLD RANK	REVENUES ($MILLIONS)	HEADQUARTERS
	BP	5	178,721.0	London
17	Boeing	43	54,069.0	Chicago
22	State Farm Insurance	56	49,653.7	Bloomington
28	SBC Communications	76	43,138.0	San Antonio
	UBS	79	42,329.7	Zurich
31	Sears Roebuck	81	41,366.0	Hoffman Estates
46	Allstate	128	29,579.0	Northbrook
47	Walgreen	132	28,681.1	Deerfield
61	Motorola	156	26,679.0	Schaumburg
77	Goldman Sachs Group	186	22,854.0	New York
82	Bank One Corp.	198	22,171.0	Chicago
102	Abbott Laboratories	263	17,684.7	Abbott Park
103	Sara Lee	266	17,628.0	Chicago
128	McDonald's	321	15,405.7	Oak Brook
129	Exelon	335	14,955.0	Chicago
135	UAL	346	14,286.0	Elk Grove

SOURCE: Fortune, July 21, 2003

APPENDIX 9 MILLENNIUM PARK'S AND CHICAGO'S LEADING PRIVATE COMPANIES, 2000 (MILLENNIUM PARK FOUNDING DONORS IN RED)

U. S. RANK	COMPANY	INDUSTRY	REVENUES ($MILLIONS)	HEADQUARTERS
3	PricewaterhouseCoopers	Business services	20,000	New York
8	Deloitte Touche	Business services	12,300	New York
14	Andersen	Business services	8,400	Chicago
20	Marmon Group	Misc. Fabricated Products	6,530	Chicago
23	Alliant Exchange	Food Processing	6,500	Deerfield
41	Reyes Holding	Food Processing	3,500	Rosemont
50	Eby-Brown	Food (Grocery)	2,773	Naperville
69	Allied Worldwide	Trucking & Travel Services	2,212	Westmont
71	H Holding Group	Hotels (Hyatt)	2,200	Chicago
88	BCom3 Group	Advertising	1,933	Chicago
99	Grant Thornton Inter.	Business Services	1,800	Chicago
106	Amsted Industries	Misc. Fabricated Products	1,774	Chicago
111	BDO Inter.	Business Services	1,700	Chicago
122	Comark	Computer Services	1,550	Bloomingdale
127	Duchossois Industries	Misc. Capital Goods	1,500	Elmhurst
134	Clark Retail	Retail (Grocery)	1,450	Oak Brook
138	Follett	Retail	1,401	River Grove
149	CC Industries (Crown family)	Auto & Truck Parts	1,360	Chicago
159	Dade Behring	Medical Equip. Manuf.	1,309	Deerfield
160	Frank Consolidated Enter.	Business Services	1,300	Des Plaines
169	Hewitt Assoc.	Business Services	1,275	Lincolnshire
171	Heico Companies	Electronic Instruments	1,254	Chicago
185	Ty	Recreational Products	1,200	Oak Brook
201	Outboard Marine	Recreational Products	1,111	Waukegan
218	Walsh Group	Construction Services	1,056	Chicago
234	Coca-Cola Bottling of Chicago	Beverages	1,015	Chicago
263	Baker & McKenzie	Business Services	940	Chicago
269	Motor Coach Industries	Auto & Truck Manuf.	911	Schaumburg
270	Medline Industries	Medical Products	909	Mundelein
280	Specialty Foods	Food Processing	882	Deerfield
281	Chemcentral	Chemical Manuf.	881	Bedford Park
282	Wirtz	Beverages and Recreation	880	Chicago

U. S. RANK	COMPANY	INDUSTRY	REVENUES ($MILLIONS)	HEADQUARTERS
295	Home Life	Retail	850	Hoffman Est.
333	Jordan Industries	Conglomerates	777	Deerfield
375	Pepper Companies	Construction Services	723	Chicago
382	US Can	Containers & Packaging	714	Lombard
414	TTC Illinois	Business Services	660	Kankakee
445	Charles Levy	Printing and Publishing	615	Chicago
452	Goss Holdings	Misc. Capital Goods	602	Westmont
459	Boler	Auto & Truck Parts	600	Itasca
482	Kimball Hills Homes	Construction Services	580	Rolling Meadows

SOURCE: http://www.forbes.com/lists/results.jhtml

ILLINOIS RANK	DONOR	TOTAL ASSETS ($)	AWARDED IN METROPOLITAN CHICAGO ($)
1	John D. and Catherine T. MacArthur Foundation	4,479,153,951	27,115,610
2	Robert R. McCormick Tribune Foundation	1,855,000,000	32,442,443
3	The Chicago Community Trust and Affiliates	1,302,626,633	23,382,744
5	Pritzker Foundation	617,670,485	21,153,441
	SBC Foundation (Texas)	328,100,000	5,759,737
9	Polk Bros. Foundation, Inc.	286,883,450	11,635,505
	Goldman Sachs Foundation (New York)	230,721,571	
12	Prince Charitable Trusts	197,188,349	
13	Lloyd A. Fry Foundation	196,349,955	5,235,201
14	Arie and Ida Crown Memorial	192,915,307	5,325,833
16	Dr. Scholl Foundation	186,645,652	6,564,000[g]
22	Regenstein Foundation	124,614,962	
23	Abbott Laboratories Fund	117,763,266	3,707,893
31	Blum-Kovler Foundation	93,390,235	
32	The Irving Harris Foundation	93,165,626	
33	The Richard H. Driehaus Foundation	87,865,858	
34	BP Amoco Foundation, Inc.	86,644,858	16,109,292
41	Elizabeth Morse Genius Charitable Trust	67,784,702	
47	The Elizabeth Morse Charitable Trust	58,404,048	
50	Wm. Wrigley, Jr., Company Foundation	51,695,716	
	Field Foundation of Illinois, Inc.	47,281,702[a]	
	Ann and Robert H. Lurie Foundation of Chicago	44,052,302[b]	3,045,145
	Siragusa Foundation	39,766,499[c]	
	Brinson Foundation	39,137,039[a]	
	Baxter International Foundation	34,471,129[a]	
	Mayer and Morris Kaplan Family Foundation	32,000,000[a]	
	Zell Family Foundation	29,222,568[b]	4,279,303[h]
	Steans Family Foundation	20,440,650[a]	
	Lavin Family Foundation	19,315,760[b]	1,289,226[i]
	Sara Lee Foundation	18,072,000[d]	
	J. Ira and Nicki Harris Family Foundation	15,607,078[e]	
	Rauner Family Foundation	11,889,206[f]	590,000[j]
	The Comer Foundation	8,562,333[i]	4,461,150

ILLINOIS RANK	DONOR	TOTAL ASSETS ($)	AWARDED IN METROPOLITAN CHICAGO ($)
	Marshall and Jamee Field Family Foundation	6,869,656[b]	301,700
	Duchossois Family Foundation	6,593,556[b]	3,694,911
	Cooper Family Foundation	5,558,629[b]	297,350[i]
	Stuart Family Foundation	3,489,048[b]	
	The Francis L. Lederer Foundation	3,140,493[b]	1,100,000[i]
	Minow Family Foundation	2,048,042[b]	126,603[i]
	Howard and Carol Bernick Family Foundation	1,753,423[b]	74,812[i]
	Theodore G. and M. Christine Schwartz Family Found	449,967[b]	657,321[i]

SOURCE: The Foundation Center Statistical Services, at http://fdncenter.org/fc_stats/pdf/09_top50_aa/2000/il_00.pdf; Donors Forum of Chicago, available at: http://www.donorsforum.org/forms_pdf/MFPdemographics.pdf; http://www.guidestar.org/search/; and the Center for Consumer Freedom, at: ActivistCash.com, accessed from 2003 to 2005.

[a]http://www.donorsforum.org/forms_pdf/MFPdemographics.pdf.

[b]http://documents.guidestar.org/2000/363/486/2000-363486274-1-F.pdf.

[c]Siragusa Foundation, Annual Report 2002 (Chicago, 2002), 62, at: http://dww.siragusa.org/images/annualReport/other/TSF_AR2002.pdf.

[d]ttp://www.gcir.org/resources/funding_directory/sara_lee_foundation.htm.

[e]This report is from 1997. See http://www.guidestar.org/search/report/summary.jsp.

[f]For year 2002. See ActivistCash.com.

[g]Total grants for Illinois, 2000.

[h]Total giving, 2000, for Samuel Zell Foundation.

[i]Total giving, 2000.

[j]Total giving, 2002.

FREQUENTLY USED ABBREVIATIONS

CDN   *Chicago Daily News*
CHS   Chicago Historical Society (now Chicago History Museum)
CPD   Chicago Park District
CST   *Chicago Sun-Times*
CT   *Chicago Tribune*
HWC   Harry Weese Collection, Chicago Historical Society
MHPC   Metropolitan Housing and Planning Council
NYT   *New York Times*
UIC   University of Illinois at Chicago

Oral history interviews are identified by the surname. For the full name and date of the interview, see the bibliography.

NOTES

PREFACE

1. Daley interview.

2. Joel Henning, "And Frank and Anish and Jaume and Kate," Wall Street Journal, 20 July 2004.

3. The $235 million figure is based upon $173.5 million raised by millennium Park, Inc., and $63 million raised by Music and Dance Chicago. E-mail communication, Rob Omori (Office of John Bryan) to Tim Gilfoyle, 12 July 2005, in author's possession.

CHAPTER ONE

1. Sniderman and Tippens, "Grant Park," 13 July 1992, sec. 8, p. 23. The current boundaries are Randolph Drive on the north, McFetridge Drive on the south, Lake Michigan on the east, and Michigan Avenue on the west. See ibid., sec. 7, p. 1.

2. For example, see Robert Bruegmann, "When Worlds Collided: European and American Entries to the Chicago Tribune Competition of 1922," in Zukowsky, Chicago Architecture, 303–18; and "Three Events That Shaped Chicago: The World's Columbian Exposition, the Plan of Chicago, and the Tribune Tower Competition," ibid., 397–428.

3. CPD, Grant Park Design Guidelines, 23.

4. The historical literature on parks is voluminous. I have been most influenced by Bender, Toward an Urban Vision, 59–146; Bluestone, Constructing Chicago, 183–204; Cranz, Politics of Park Design; Blackmar and Rosenzweig, The Park and the People; Schuyler, New Urban Landscape; idem, Apostle of Taste; idem, "Andrew Jackson Downing," in Birnbaum and Karson, Pioneers of American Landscape Design, 96–100; Sloane, Last Great Necessity.

5. Joshua Hathaway, Jr., Chicago with the School Section, Wabansia and Kinzie's Addition (1834), Graff Collection, no. 1817; J. S. Wright, Chicago (1834), Graff Collection, no. 4755, both in Newberry Library; J. S. Wright, Chicago (1834), CHS G4104 C4 1834 W8.

6. Wille, Forever Open, Clear and Free, 22–23; Fink, Grant Park Tomorrow, 11–17; Mayer and Wade, Chicago, 14, 26; Bachin, Cultural Boundaries, chap. 4.

The official date given in case law for the "open, clear and free" provision, or Fort Dearborn addition, is 6 June 1837. See *John and Mildred Boaz v. City of Chicago, Chicago Park District and Plan Commission of the City of Chicago*, case 99l, no. 3804, 5 April 1999. The 1836 date is based on Wille.

7. Chicago, Special Park Commission, *Report of the Special Park Commission*, 22–24; South Park Commission, *Report . . . [for 1896]*, 6 (Lake Front Park), 16 (Lake Park); Andreas, *History of Chicago*, 3:168 (Lake Park); 3:192 (Lake Front Park). For other examples of "Lake Park," see *CT*, 5 Feb. 1871, 7 March 1871; Currier & Ives, *The City of Chicago* (1892); Theodore R. Davis, "Bird's-Eye View of Chicago as It Was Before the Great Fire" (New York, 1871), CHS; Rand, McNally & Co., *Map Showing the Boulevards and Park System and Twelve Miles of Lake Frontage of the City of Chicago* (Chicago, 1886); *Blanchard's Guide Map of Chicago and Suburbs* (Chicago, 1886), all four maps in Newberry Library. For examples of "Lake Front Park" and "Lake Front Grounds," see *CT*, 12 Feb. 1871, 24 March 1878, 7 April 1878; *Railroad Gazette* 24 (22 April 1892): 301; *Harper's Weekly*, 12 Nov. 1892, 1091; *Inland Architect and News Record* 27 (Feb. 1896): 8. For maps designating Lake Park as extending only between Park Row and Peck Court, see Sheahan and Upton, *Great Conflagration*, map after p. 62; Charles Shober, "Map of Chicago" (1864–1865); "Chicago" (1872), Fitzgerald Map2F, both in Newberry Library. For maps failing to designate any part of the lakefront as a park, see Sheahan and Upton, *Great Conflagration* , map after p. 16; "The City of Chicago" (1855), Fitzgerald Map2F; Rees & Kerfoot, *Map of the City of Chicago* (Chicago, 1854), all in Newberry Library. Washington Park (1842) was established at Dearborn Street and Walton Place. According to the "Fort Dearborn Addition to Chicago" the "public ground" along the west side of Michigan Avenue between Washington and Randolph Streets was designated "for ever to remain vacant of Buildings." In 1839, this became Dearborn Park, the city's first formal park. The site later was used for the construction of the Chicago Public Library (now the Chicago Cultural Center). A map can be found in Asa F. Bradley, County and City Surveyor, "Fort Dearborn Addition to Chicago," 6 June 1837, in *Maps, Correspondence, and Papers*, Illinois Central Railroad Collection, IC 2 .71, vol. 1, p. 52, Newberry Library.

8. Illustration caption, Michigan Avenue (from Park Row), in Sheahan, *Chicago Illustrated*, part 2; Cook, *Bygone Days*, 339–40 ("breathing-space"; I am indebted to Ted Karamanski for directing me to this source); Bluestone, *Constructing Chicago*, 13–20.

9. Cook, *Bygone Days*, 339–40; and Colton, "Chicago's Waste Lands"; Mottier, "History of Illinois Central Passenger Stations," 69–70.

10. Illustration caption, Michigan Avenue (from Park Row), in Sheahan, *Chicago Illustrated*, part 2 (finest in West; gone elsewhere); Bluestone, *Constructing Chicago*, 13–20; *The Illinois Central Railway: A Historical Sketch*, 17–18 (500 feet); Sheahan and Upton, *Great Conflagration*, 80 (finest in U.S.); Waldheim, *Constructed Ground*, 7; Stover, *History of the Illinois Central*, 44–45, 76–78; Wille, *Forever Open, Clear and Free*, 26–30; Skidmore, Owings & Merrill and C. F. Murphy Associates, *Lakefront Development Plan*, 24. On the historical importance of the Illinois Central Railroad in the growth of Chicago, also see Cronon, *Nature's Metropolis*, 69–71. In December 1851, the city council approved a right-of-way to the Illinois Central in return for constructing a breakwater in the lake north of Twelfth Street. Mayor Gurnee vetoed the measure, changes were made, and final passage was approved on 14 June 1852. Shortly after acquiring the property north of Randolph, the IC sold two large plots (250 feet by 657 feet and 165 feet by 2,118 feet) immediately west of its holdings to the Michigan Central Railroad. See *Illinois Central Railway*, 18.

11. Sniderman and Tippens, "Grant Park," sec. 7, p. 8. When the Illinois Central constructed a new terminal at 12th Street (later Roosevelt Road) in 1892, another switchyard north of the terminal reduced the track width from 600 feet at 12th Street to 200 feet at 9th Street, before widening again at Adams Street.

12. John N. Jewett, *Illinois Central Railroad Company Opinion on the Rights on the Lake Front, Chicago* (Chicago, 10 Dec. 1884), 6 (three blocks), in Reports and Legal Papers, Chicago Lake Front, 1852–1900, box 2.7, Illinois Central Railroad Collection, Newberry Library; Stover, *History of the Illinois Central*, 179–81; Cremin, "Building Chicago's Front Yard," 75–80; Mottier, "History of Illinois Central Passenger Stations," 71. On the legal implications of Illinois Central efforts to control lakefront property, see Kearney and Merrill, "The Origins of the American Public Trust Doctrine," 799–931. Other legislation reconfirmed the land east of Michigan Avenue as open space. One piece of legislation allowed property owners and other interested persons to enjoin the IC, the city, and others from violating this provision. Another law conveyed the title of the submerged lands east of the IC right-of-way to the city "in trust for the public and the abutting property owners on Michigan Avenue." See Fink, *Grant Park Tomorrow*, 20.

13. "Report of B. F. Ayer, General Solicitor of the Illinois Central Railroad Co., to the U.S. Secretary of War," 25 July 1881; Report of G. J. Lydecker, Major of Engineers, U.S. Army, 24 Aug. 1881, in *Annual Report upon the Improvement of the Harbors of Chicago and Calumet, Lake Michigan, and of the Illinois River* (Washington, D.C., 1882), appendix FF, 2211, 2213; *Daily Inter Ocean*, 6–10, 12–14 July 1887 (for court arguments); and many other briefs and reports in Reports and Legal Papers, Chicago Lake Front, 1852–1900, box 2.7, Illinois Central Railroad Collection, Newberry Library.

14. Sheahan and Upton, *Great Conflagration*, 80, 394a; Colton, "Chicago's Waste Lands," 126–28.

15. *Inter-State Exposition Souvenir*, 38 (165 feet); Sheahan, *Chicago Illustrated*, 20; Lowe, *Lost Chicago*, 135.

16. Baltimore and Ohio Railroad Co., *Forty-ninth Annual Report*, 21 (description); Andreas, *History of Chicago*, 3:191, 222; Mottier, "History of Illinois Central Passenger Stations," 73. The B&O apparently used the IC terminal north of Randolph Street for passenger traffic and the new facility for freight. In 1891, just prior to the IC's building a new terminal at 12th Street in 1892, the B&O moved to the new Grand Central Station at Harrison Street and Fifth Avenue. See Hungerford, *Story of the Baltimore and Ohio Railroad*, 108, 197; Stover, *History of the Baltimore and Ohio Railroad*, 152, 172. The facility was located to the east of the Exposition Building in *Blanchard's Guide Map of Chicago and Suburbs*; and in Rand, McNally & Co., *Map Showing the Boulevards and Park System*. The Currier and Ives map of 1892, however, places it between the Exposition Building and baseball grounds. Also see Cremin, "Building Chicago's Front Yard," 101. On the "inadequate terminal facilities" for the B&O before 1891, see "Remarks of Charles Mayer," in Baltimore and Ohio Railroad Co., *Sixty-fifth Annual Report*, after p. 6 (quote); idem, *Sixty-sixth Annual Report*, 10. (I am indebted to Laura Milsk for bringing these sources to my attention.) City directories from 1876 to 1891 gave the address of the B&O depot as "Michigan Avenue, foot of Monroe Street." See Cremin.

17. Cremin, "Building Chicago's Front Yard," 90–128; Blanchard's Guide Map of Chicago and Suburbs; Rand, McNally & Co., Map Showing the Boulevards and Park System.

18. Lowry, Green Cathedrals, 42 (Randolph).

19. Benson, Ballparks of North America, 80–83 (180, 196); Gershman, Diamonds, 19–20, 30–31; Lowry, Green Cathedrals, 42–43. The debate over leasing the park, constructing the grounds, and improving the facility after 1880 are covered in CT, 30 Oct. 1877; 13, 25, 27 Nov. 1877; 23 Dec. 1877; 20 Jan. 1878; 24, 31 March 1878; 20 June 1880; 22 April 1883. I am indebted to Jon Daniels for providing these citations. Correspondence of Jon Daniels to Cheri Heramb (30 April 1998) and Edward Uhlir (20 Sept. 1998), in author's possession.

20. Benson, Ballparks, 83; CT, 22 April 1883; Harper's Weekly, 12 May 1883, 299. A good overview of the baseball grounds appears in Cremin, "Building Chicago's Front Yard," 115–20. The seating capacity of the stands was eight thousand with room for two thousand more standing. "The Map of Chicago Harbor, 30 June 1883," in W. H. H. Benyaurd (Major of Engineers), Annual Report upon the Improvement of the Harbors of Chicago and Calumet, Lake Michigan, and the Illinois River . . . Being Appendix GG of the Annual Report of the Chief of Engineers for 1883 (Washington, D.C.: GPO, 1883), after p. 1744, shows "Base Ball Grounds" between Randolph and Washington streets. A similar map in Appendix JJ of Benyaurd's Annual Report . . . for 1885 (Washington, D.C.: GPO, 1885), after p. 2050, shows no baseball grounds. Nor does Illinois Central Map "On Lake Front Question" (1885), based on Mr. Ayer's Report, 13 Dec. 1884, Illinois Central Railroad Collection, Newberry Library (call no. 2F 0G4104 .C6P3 1885 I5). Both Benyaurd reports are in Reports and Legal Papers, Chicago Lake Front, 1852–1900, box 2.7, Illinois Central Railroad Collection, Newberry Library.

21. Illinois Central Railroad v. State of Illinois and City of Chicago, nos. 419, 508, 609, 5 Dec. 1892; "The Ordinance: Final Draft as Agreed Sept. 3, 1895," 13 (quote); and printed correspondence between Stuyvesant Fish, president of Illinois Central Railroad, and mayor George B. Swift of Chicago, 1895, in "Lake Front Park" (1895), in Reports and Legal Papers, Chicago Lake Front, 1852–1900, box 2.7, Illinois Central Railroad

Collection, Newberry Library. Related documents and briefs on this subject are in this box. Also see Kearney and Merrill, "The Origins of the American Public Trust Doctrine."

22. Railroad Gazette, 21 July 1891, 537 (ruin); 9 Sept. 1892, 657 (eyesore); 14 April 1893, 275–76 (I am indebted to Laura Milsk for these citations); Stover, History of the Illinois Central, 218–21.

23. Sniderman and Tippens, "Grant Park," sec. 8, p. 27.

24. Wille, Forever Open, Clear and Free, 71–81; Sniderman and Tippens, "Grant Park," sec. 8, p. 27; Bachin, Cultural Boundaries, chap. 4. The "Montgomery Ward cases" are City of Chicago v. A. Montgomery Ward, 169 Ill. 392 (1897), referred to as Ward I; E. R. Bliss v. A. Montgomery Ward, 198 Ill. 104; A. Montgomery Ward v. Field Museum of Natural History, 241 Ill. 496 (1909); and South Park Commissioners v. Ward & Co., 248 Ill. 299.

25. South Park Commissioners, "Map of Grant Park Showing Areas of Land Made Each Year from 1897 to 1907," Grant Park folder, CPD Archives; South Park Commissioners, Report . . . from March 1, 1909, to February 28, 1910, inclusive, 13. The landfill east of the IC tracks between Monroe and Randolph Streets was created in 1902. South Park Commission reports are confusing in that reports prior to 1901 consistently claimed Lake Park was 186 acres. See South Park Commissioners, Report for 1896, 16; Report for 1897, 18; Report for 1898, 16; Report for 1899, 16; Report for 1900, 18; Report for 1901, 18.

CHAPTER TWO

1. CT, 16 Dec. 1894 (greatest park; Madden), 30 Dec. 1894, 12 May 1895 (Madden plan); Brent, Martin B. Madden, 182 (200 acres).

2. Daily Inter Ocean, 10 Aug. 1895; CT, 10 Aug. 1895; CPD, Grant Park Design Guidelines, 11. The most thorough coverage of these debates is in Bluestone, Constructing Chicago, 183–89. On Wight's earlier career in New York City, see Stern et al., New York 1880, 168–73, 390–91, 450, 525, 532–33, 575–76, 677, 854–55, 864–65, 954–57. The Municipal Improvement League was founded expressly for "securing the Lake Front to the city, and then for the proper improvement of the site," and the plan was commissioned by the city council. Normand S. Patton, the father of the movement to develop the lake front, was president of the league and worked in conjunction

with the Illinois chapter of the American Institute of Architects.

3. Daily Inter Ocean, 10 Aug. 1895.

4. Ibid.; CT, 10 Aug. 1895 (another kind of park). The Chicago Architectural Club Plan in 1896 was prepared in conjunction with the Municipal Improvement League. See Chicago Architectural Club Plan (1896), in Chicago Architectural Club, Catalogue of Ninth Annual Exhibition, 1896, [10, 27].

5. Chicago, Special Park Commission, Report of the Special Park Commission, 75 (Perkins); CT, 11 Feb. 1897 (outrival Paris), quoted in Draper, "Paris by the Lake," in Zukowsky, Chicago Architecture, 107; CPD, Grant Park Design Guidelines, 12; CT, 4 June 1895; Bluestone, Constructing Chicago, 188–89. Bluestone presents convincing evidence that Burnham's plans of 1895 and 1896 were derivative of Normand Patton's and the Improvement League's. Central elements of Burnham's lakefront plans were prompted by input from others. Burnham did not really originate many of the lakefront plans, but later took credit for them. Burnham also insisted on keeping the Field Museum in the center of the park, despite criticism from Wight and others who wanted the center left open.

6. South Park Commissioners, Report . . . from December 1, 1906, to February 29, 1908, inclusive, 8, 32, 82–90. On the influence of Versailles, see South Park Commissioners, Report . . . from March 1, 1908, to February 28, 1909, inclusive, 26–29; Sniderman and Tippens, "Grant Park," 13 July 1992, sec. 8, pp. 30–31. On the McMillan Plan, see Reps, Making of Urban America, 502–14.

7. South Park Commission, Chicago, Ill., Olmsted Brothers, "Revised Preliminary Plan for Grant Park," no. 31, 22 Sept. 1903, CPD Special Collections; and Map no. 2818, Chicago Parks—Grant, 1903, CHS. Map no. 31 was published in South Park Commission, Annual Report for 1904, 38a.

8. South Park Commission, Chicago, Ill., Olmsted Brothers, "Revised Preliminary Plan for Grant Park," no. 20, 22 Sept. 1903, CPD Special Collections. This plan also placed the Crerar Library in the park along Michigan Avenue at the terminus of Madison Street. At the same time, the South Park Commissioners developed a new system of neighborhood parks with swimming pools, outdoor gymnasia, ball fields and "field houses" (a new building type). Fourteen of these parks

were laid out by Olmsted Brothers, but D. H. Burnham and Company later received the architectural commission for the new neighborhood parks. The two firms collaborated and designed twelve new neighborhood parks from 1904 to 1910. The development of these neighborhood parks also convinced the South Park Commissioners that Grant Park should be a more formalized space, with fewer playfields and athletic facilities than initially proposed by Olmsted Brothers. See Sniderman and Tippens, "Grant Park," sec. 8, p. 32.

9. Bluestone, *Constructing Chicago*, 183, 188, 190–91. Also see Burnham and Bennett, *Plan of Chicago*. Historical analysis of the *Plan of Chicago* is considerable. I have been influenced by Hines, *Burnham of Chicago*; Boyer, *Urban Masses*, 261–76; Foglesong, *Planning the Capitalist City*; Boyer, *Dreaming the Rational City*; Wilson, *The City Beautiful Movement*; Draper, "Paris by the Lake," in Zukowsky, *Chicago Architecture*, 107–15; Bach, "A Reconsideration of the 1909 'Plan of Chicago,'" 132–41; Mumford, *City in History*, 401; Reps, *Making of Urban America*, 517–19; Wille, *Forever Open, Clear and Free*; Art Institute, *Plan of Chicago*; Bachin, *Cultural Boundaries*, chap. 4.

10. The Ward cases set the stage for a variety of lakefront protection measures. The Lake Front Ordinance of 1919 prepared the way for larger lakefront development by creating procedures for the City of Chicago, the South Park Commission, and the Illinois Central Railroad to develop the shoreline south of the city center. Eight miles of beaches and park were later built between Grant and Jackson parks. See Mayer and Wade, *Chicago*, 294. In 1948, the Chicago Plan Commission passed the Lakefront Resolution, declaring "that the entire lakefront should be used for recreations and cultural purposes, except for the sections between Grand Avenue and Randolph Street, and south of 79th Street." This policy was reconfirmed in 1964 in *Basic Policies for the Comprehensive Plan of Chicago*. See Development of Policies for the Chicago Lakefront, 18 Jan. 1966, in folder 4, box 24, accession 80-49, MHPC papers, UIC. In 1973, the Chicago City Council passed the Lake Michigan and Chicago Lakefront Protection Ordinance, which required Chicago Plan Commission approval "for any physical change, whether temporary or permanent, public or private," inside a mapped zone that in most places extends two blocks inland. But in April 1981, the Illinois Appellate Court ruled that the Chicago Park District was not bound by the city's lakefront protection ordinance. See *CT*, 29 April 1981.

11. Harry Weese, "The Chicago Plan Commission," *Inland Architect* 24 (April 1980): 18; Sniderman and Tippens, "Grant Park," sec. 8, pp. 23 (Bennett), 36 (Bennett); Mayer and Wade, *Chicago*, 292. Between the two world wars, over a billion dollars went into new landfill on the Lake Michigan shoreline in Chicago. See the following renderings by Edward H. Bennett: Terrace walls, balustrade, and fountain at north end of Grant Park, 2 drawings, 25 Feb. 1915; Colonnade at north end of Grant Park, 2 drawings, May 1915; Balustrade and steps, at north side of approach to the Monroe Street viaduct, Sketches and details, 2 drawings, 21 Aug. 1915. Also see South Park Commissioners, General Plan for the Improvement of Grant Park, 1920 ; idem, "Map of Grant Park." Plat showing subsurface areas sought for station facilities at Randolph Street by the ICRR, 18 June 1920, all in Chicago Park District Special Collections.

12. Sniderman and Tippens, "Grant Park," sec. 7, pp. 8–9. A drawing dated 1922 appears to be the firm's first full intent for the park, envisioning Grant Park as a formal landscape inspired by the French Renaissance. See ibid., sec. 8, p. 36. Bennett's firm was Bennett, Parsons, Frost and Thomas.

13. Sniderman and Tippens, "Grant Park," sec. 7, p. 1; CPD, *Grant Park Design Guidelines*, 27 (trees), 29.

14. Sniderman and Tippens, "Grant Park," sec. 7, p. 16.

15. pp. 10, 15 (new bandshell); sec. 8, p. 40 (art deco); CPD, *Grant Park Design Guidelines*, 16. In 1934, the South Park Commission was consolidated into the Chicago Park District, which completed improvements using federal relief funds. The park district is a municipal corporation, chartered and empowered to levy property taxes by the State of Illinois, and governed by a board of commissioners appointed to staggered five-year terms by the mayor of Chicago. The day-to-day operations are the responsibility of the general superintendent and his staff. See CPD, *Grant Park Design Guidelines*, 3.

16. CPD, *Grant Park Design Guidelines*, 11.

17. South Park Commissioners, *Report . . . from March 1, 1909, to February 28, 1910, inclusive*, 17 (Foster); Idem, *Report . . . from March 1, 1913, to February 28, 1914, inclusive*, foldout, "Map of South Park District Showing Parks and Boulevards."

18. Saarinen, "Project for Lake Front Development," 488, 491, 493, 500, 505; Sniderman and Tippens, "Grant Park," sec. 8, p. 37.

19. Saarinen, "Project for Lake Front Development," 489–90, 504–7. A discussion of this project appears in Christ-Janer, *Eliel Saarinen*, 59–65.

20. Chicago Association of Commerce and Industry, *Parking Plan*, 10–11, copy in folder 33, box 2, accession 80-59, MHPC papers, UIC. On the origins of the Monroe Street Garage, see Wille, *Forever Open, Clear and Free*, 92. In the 1920s, plans for the realignment of Lake Shore Drive were developed, which culminated in curves around the Field Museum (1936) and completion of the Outer Drive Bridge (1937), making Lake Shore Drive a key north-south axis. Previously, Michigan Avenue served as the boulevard linking the South Parks and Lincoln Park. On the development and construction of Lake Shore Drive, see Chicago Plan Commission, *The Outer Drive*. The Bronx River Parkway (constructed between 1906 and 1925) in Westchester County, just north of New York City, is regarded as the nation's first limited-access, scenic automobile parkway. See New York State Office of Parks, Recreation and Historic Preservation, *New York State Historic Preservation Plan, 2002–2006* (Albany, N.Y., 2002), 8.

21. Noonan, *Railway Passenger Terminal Problem*, 27–34; "Lakefront Passenger Terminal for Chicago Railroads," *Engineering News-Record*, 25 Jan. 1934 (I am indebted to Laura Milsk for this citation). For earlier reports on a terminal south of the Loop, see Arnold, *Report*.

22. "Large Suburban Terminal Built for Illinois Central Railroad," *Engineering News-Record*, 3 Sept. 1931. The expansion of the Randolph Street viaduct was constructed from 1926 to 1931. During the construction, the IC opened a temporary terminal south of Randolph, roughly at the future site of the Music and Dance Theater.

23. Chicago Association of Commerce and Industry, *Parking Plan*, 10–11, copy in folder 33, box 2, accession 80-59, MHPC papers, UIC; CPD, *Fourth Annual Report*, 47; CPD, *General Information* (Chicago, 1947), 12; idem, (Chicago, 1950), 12; idem, (Chicago, 1956), 12; idem (Chicago, 1961), 14–15. The fee for the Monroe Street lot was 35 cents in 1947, 50 cents in 1950, 60 cents in 1956.

Capacity statistics on the Monroe Street Parking Area were inconsistent. The *General Information* reports for 1947, 1950, and 1956 gave a capacity of 3,500 cars. The report in 1961 listed capacity at 2,700 cars. Chicago Association of Commerce and Industry, *Parking Plan*, 49 (largest in U.S.), copy in folder 33, box 2, accession 80-59, MHPC papers, UIC, gave the Monroe Street Garage a capacity of 3,000.

24. CPD, *[Eighteenth] Annual Report for* 1952, 5, 12 ($8.3 million bonds); Memos, Park District treasurer Thomas Purcell to Board of Commissioners, 14 March 1961, folder 6, box 5; 13 March 1962, folder 6, box 6, both in Jacob Arvey Papers, CHS; Uhlir interview (Burke); Sniderman and Tippens, "Grant Park," sec. 8, p. 41. The number of automobiles entering the Loop increased from 90,000 in 1926 to 160,000 in 1950. See Hillman and Casey, *Tomorrow's Chicago*, 101. Efforts to invoke the Ward cases to prevent construction of underground parking garages failed. See *Michigan Boulevard Building Co. v. Chicago Park District*, 412 Ill. 350 (1952).

25. Garvin and Berens, *Urban Parks and Open Space*, 13–14. Mellon Park was the first to provide an income stream to cover debt service on the capital borrowed to pay the cost of developing and maintaining a new 1.37-acre park. The Mellon family paid $3.65 million for land acquisition and demolition, and $650,000 for construction of the surface park. The Pittsburgh Parking Authority financed the $3.5 million garage construction from parking fees and commercial rents.

26. Presentation of Grant Park Improvement Program by Harold Moore, 25 May 1960, before Michigan Boulevard Association, p. 7; Schroeder, *The Issue of the Lakefront*, 26; Ruth Moore, typescript titled "Moore Park II," 1961, all in Central Area Chicago folder, box 2, Ruth Moore Papers, CHS.

27. Chicago Central Area Committee and Chicago Department of Planning, *Downtown Parking*, 4. The CPD paid off the debt on both Grant Park garages in 1973. See unmarked clipping, 28 Nov. 1972, folder 2, box 14, accession 80-59, MHPC papers, UIC. Ultimately, all three Grant Park garages were revenue bond operations whose bond redemption requirements were satisfied according to schedule. See CPD, *Annual Report* 1981, 16; Skidmore, Owings & Merrill and C. F. Murphy Associates, *Lakefront Development Plan*, 28. In

1978, the three Grant Park garages generated $6.3 million in revenue, and a total of 2,589,000 autos parked in the three garages, a 12.7 percent increase over 1977. Combined, the three garages held 7,300 cars. See CPD, *Annual Report 1978*, 15. On the growing importance of the automobile in the Chicago region in the postwar era, see Mayer and Wade, *Chicago*, 438–48.

28. Department of City Planning, *Development Plan*, 34, 40; Idem, *Annual Report, 1958*, 11–12; Chicago Central Area Committee, *Grant Park and Burnham Park Study*; Presentation of Grant Park Improvement Program by Harold Moore, 25 May 1960, before Michigan Boulevard Association, 7–14; Michigan Boulevard Association Press release, 25 May 1960, all in Central Area Chicago folder, box 2, Ruth Moore Papers, CHS. For a proposal to build more expressway features on Lake Shore Drive, see Burke, *Preliminary Report on Lake Shore Drive Improvements*. On the park district considering inclusion of Lake Shore Drive in the interstate highway system, see CPD, *Annual Report for 1957*, 18. On how parts of the 1958 and 1960 plans were implemented, see CPD, *Grant Park Design Guidelines*, 18.

29. Philip J. Maggio of Transportation Research, Confidential Report on the Illinois Central Railroad, 12 Sept. 1961, p. 10, in folder 2, box 7; *Southtown Economist*, 26, 29 July 1959, in folder 12, box 60, both in accession 80-49, MHPC papers, UIC. On predictions regarding the escalating value of air rights in the 1930s, see *Engineering News-Record*, 3 Sept. 1931. (I am indebted to Laura Milsk for this citation.)

30. "The Prudential Building," pamphlet (350 spaces), 1956, Map no. 2685, Chicago—Historical and Pictorial, CHS; Department of City Planning, *Development Plan*, 32; CT, 25 July 1972 (eighty-three acres); *Southtown Economist*, 29 July 1959 (Johnson), in folder 12, box 60, accession 80-49, MHPC papers, UIC. A confidential report by Transportation Research estimated that the value of the IC's air rights north of Randolph exceeded $135 million in 1961. See Philip J. Maggio of Transportation Research, Confidential Report on the Illinois Central Railroad, 12 Sept. 1961, pp. 1, 10, in folder 2, box 7, accession 80-49, MHPC papers, UIC. Although the full potential of the air rights were not realized for over a decade, Maggio recognized that "the extraordinary underlying value" of the air rights would remain a potent and "vitalizing influence" in marketing Illinois Central securities. A good introduction to the complicated history of Illinois Central air rights and the development of the Illinois Center

can be found in the newspaper clippings and documents in box 2, Ruth Moore Papers, CHS.

31. News release, 31 Jan. 1969, MHPC, folder 3, box 29, accession 80-49, MHPC papers, UIC. For discussions of the development of the IC yards, see CDN clippings for 9 July 1969, 23, 30 Sept. 1966 (illustrations), 30 July 1969, 4 Sept. 1969; CST, 29, 30 Sept. 1966, 21 Feb. 1967; CT, 5, 24 Sept. 1966, all in folder 3, box 31, accession 80-49, MHPC papers, UIC. In 1966, the Illinois Supreme Court ruled that the IC owned the air rights over its lakefront right-of-way, rejecting claims that the land was public property. The above claim that the Illinois Central began selling the land under the rail yards and warehouses in 1968.

32. CT, 23 July 1972 (greatest deal); CT, 24 July 1972; Wille, *Forever Open, Clear and Free*, 138–40; Chicago Plan Commission and Department of City Planning, *Annual Report*, 1963, 42 (world's largest apt.); Skidmore, Owings & Merrill and C. F. Murphy Associates, *Lakefront Development Plan*, 28.

33. CPD, *Annual Report 1974*, 17–18. For a brief description of these and surrounding developments, see Sinkevitch, *AIA Guide to Chicago*, 34–36. The Illinois Central Railroad also agreed to vacate a portion of its track yard in Grant Park to permit construction of a new underground garage on East Monroe Street. In 1974, the Illinois Central Railroad Station south of Grant was demolished, allowing for expansion of the park to 12th Street.

34. "Report of the Mayor's Committee on the Lakefront Gardens," final draft, 7 Nov. 1977, p. 1, appendix I(1), in files of MPC.

35. Harry Weese to George Ranney, 11 Nov. 1977, Grant Park Bandstand folder, box 16, HWC.

CHAPTER THREE

1. CT, 30 Dec. 1894, quoted in Bluestone, *Constructing Chicago*, 187. The historical literature on the City Beautiful movement is vast. See Wilson, *The City Beautiful Movement*; Peterson, *The Birth of City Planning in the United States*; Hines, *Burnham of Chicago: Architect and Planner*; Boyer, *Urban Masses and Moral Order in America*, 261–76; Foglesong, *Planning the Capitalist City*; Boyer, *Dreaming the Rational City*; Cronon, *Nature's Metropolis*, 341–69; Mary Corbin Sies and Christopher Silver, "The

History of Planning History"; and idem, "Planning History and the New American Metropolis," both in Sies and Silver, *Planning the Twentieth-Century American City*, 1–34, 449–73; Bachin, *Cultural Boundaries*.

2. Wille, *Forever Open, Clear and Free*. On Burnham's views regarding parks and other forms of city planning as vehicles to mitigate class conflict, see Bluestone, *Constructing Chicago*, 190; Hines, *Burnham of Chicago*, 331–34.

3. *CT*, 10 Aug. 1895; *Daily Inter Ocean*, 10 Aug. 1895. Chicago Architectural Club Plan for Proposed Lakefront Park and Civic Center (1896), in Chicago Architectural Club, *Catalogue of Ninth Annual Exhibition*, 1896, [27], in CHS. Bluestone, *Constructing Chicago*, 226n21, points out that this plan was the product of a Chicago Architectural Club competition to design a lakefront music pavilion. See *Inland Architect and News Record* 27 (Feb. 1896): 8.

4. *CT*, 4 June 1895. Alderman Martin B. Madden's 1894 proposal included no music facility.

5. Burnham and Bennett, *Plan of Chicago*, 100 (single composition), 110–12; Bluestone, *Constructing Chicago*, 194–98.

6. CPD, *Annual Report 1978*, 5; *CT*, 11 June 1978; Rob Cuscaden, "Grant Park's Bandshell Bombshell," *Chicago Guide*, Aug. 1972 (50,000); Skidmore, Owings & Merrill and C. F. Murphy Associates, *Lakefront Development Plan*, 27. The Century of Progress Exposition lasted from April 1933 to October 1934. In the ensuing decades, park commissioner James Petrillo, who was also president of the Chicago Federation of Musicians, actively promoted the concerts. In 1976, the city named the shell for him.

7. "Summer in Grant Park," *Central Manufacturing District Magazine*, June 1957, 40, copy in CHS; CPD, *General Information* (Chicago, 1947), 10; "The History of the Chicago Park District's Grant Park Music Festival" (101 concerts). The eight-week season extended from late June to late August.

8. CPD, Sketch of Proposed Open Air Music Garden and Amphi-Theatre, 14 Sept. 1936, in Grant Park folder, CPD Special Collections. CPD annual reports never discussed designs completed by CPD architects. This and the other undated proposals were most likely examples of "a long list of worthy projects" prepared by the CPD at the invitation of the Works Progress Administration in 1935. See CPD, *First Annual Report*, 22, 63. Minchin was a draftsman and architect with his own practice (Sidney Minchin, Inc., at 139 North Clark Street) by 1928. *Lakeside Directory of Chicago* (Chicago, 1917), 2:1243 (draftsman); idem (1923), 2:2038 (Minchin-Spitz, Co. at 19 West Jackson); idem (1938), 2:2157. The directories published in 1917 and 1928 spelled his name "Minchen."

9. Photo of Model of Proposed Outdoor Amphitheater in Grant Park, undated [1936?], Traffic Engineering Section, Neg. X-1–38–207-A; Study of Stage Setting, Outdoor Amphitheater, Grant Park, 24 Feb. 1936; Plan for Outdoor Amphitheater in Grant Park, undated [1936?], all in CPD Special Collections.

10. Chicago Park District, Study of Stage Setting, Outdoor Amphitheater, Grant Park, 24 Feb. 1936; other undated and unattributed drawings in Grant Park folder, CPD Special Collections. The park district halted all improvement plans when the United States entered World War II. See CPD, *Seventh Annual Report* (1941), 16.

11. Model of Proposed Music Court and Amphitheater, Grant Park, 17 Dec. 1945, Neg. 6796–64, 6796–63, 6796–46 (dated 17 Dec. 1946), 6796–68, CPD Special Collections.

12. *CT*, 29 Aug. 1961; CPD, *Annual Report for 1961*, 4, 10; idem, *Annual Report for 1962*, 2, 14, 38; CPD, Proposed Music Amphitheater in Grant Park, E. V. Buchsbaum, architect, 15 Oct. 1961, in CPD Special Collections; Memorandum of Agreement, between CPD and Loebl, Schlossman & Bennett, 14 Nov. 1961; Study for Proposed Music Center for CPD, Dec. 1961, by E. V. Buchsbaum (architect), Robert Black (chief engineer), Lyman Riggle (assistant chief engineer), and Loebl, Schlossman & Bennett (architects); Same study, sec. B-B, 7 Nov. 1961, all in private records of Loebl, Schlossman & Hackl. Also see various architectural drawings of CPD Amphitheater, dated 22 Dec. 1961; 10 Jan. 1962; 1 March 1962; 17 April 1962; 18 July 1962, private records of Loebl, Schlossman & Hackl. The CPD has no records regarding the multiple proposals Bennett submitted to the CPD. The firm of Loebl, Schlossman & Hackl (the successor to Loebl, Schlossman & Bennett) has extensive records on the proposals, all of which indicate that Bennett was the lead architect in this proposal. I am indebted to David Marks for generously sharing these records with me and his extensive knowledge of Richard Bennett and the firm. The band-

shell stage was rebuilt in 1959. See Memo from Robert Black, CPD Chief Engineer, 31 Dec. 1959, folder 6, box 4, Jacob Arvey Papers, CHS. Coverage of the Ward Pavilion plan appears in Wille, *Forever Open, Clear and Free*, 131–32.

13. Although many of the published accounts of these proposals attributed them to Jerrold Loebl, David Marks assures me that Richard Bennett was the lead architect on the proposal. Also see CPD, *A. Montgomery Ward Memorial*; Memo on Proposed Music Amphitheater, General Superintendent Daniel Flaherty to Jacob Arvey, 2 May 1962, folder 8; Jerrold Loebl of Loebl, Schlossman & Bennett to Robert Black, 6 April 1962, folder 7, both in box 6, Jacob Arvey Papers, CHS; Memorandum of Agreement (between CPD and Loebl, Schlossman & Bennett), 14 Nov. 1961; Lyle F. Yerges of Bolt Beranek & Newman to Richard M. Bennett of Loebl, Schlossman & Bennett, 29 Dec. 1961, in private records of Loebl Schlossman & Hackl (I am indebted to David Marks for sharing these documents with me); *CDN*, 25 Oct. 1962; *CST*, 25 Oct. 1962; *Chicago American*, 15 Nov. 1961, 14 July 1963; clippings in folder 6, box 61, accession 80-49, MHPC papers, UIC.

14. *CST*, 23 Nov. 1962 (Reich), 28 March 1963 (Lincoln Center), 23 Aug. 1963 (cultural wasteland), 23 Sept. 1963 (Berlin); *Daily News*, 30 Oct. 1962; *NYT*, 7 July 2001; Donal J. Henahan, "Grants and Dance: Another Ford Passes Us By," *CDN* clipping, 1963; Peter Jacobi, "On Theaters and Cultural Centers: Maybe This Time," undated [1964?], all in box 3, Ruth Moore Papers, CHS; *Chicago's American*, 16 Nov. 1961, in Scrapbook, box 1, MHPC papers. On Chicago's desire to replicate Lincoln Center, see Ruth Moore's articles in *CST*, 17 Nov. 1959, 17 & 19 Feb. 1961, 17 Sept. 1961, 10 & 11 Dec. 1961, 31 Dec. 1961, 7 Jan. 1962, 9 March 1962, 29 April 1962 (Center for Performing Arts on Block 37); *Midwest Magazine*, 17 Sept. 1961; Robert Ahrens, Executive Director of Adult Education Council of Greater Chicago, to Board of Directors, 16 Feb. 1961; John Phillips, "The Arts Center in Tomorrow's Chicago," 28 July 1961 (typed manuscript), all in box 3, Ruth Moore Papers.

15. *CDN*, 25 Oct. 1962, 29 May 1963, 9 Oct. 1963, 27 Nov. 1963, 11 Dec. 1963; *CST*, 25 Oct. 1962, 21 May 1963, 1 July 1963, 21 Aug. 1963, 11, 12, 24 Sept. 1963; *National Observer*, 17 June 1963; Calvin P. Sawyier (MHPC vice president), Statement regarding proposed Grant Park Music Bowl, 12 Sept. 1963, in folder 22, box 15; correspondence and internal memoranda in folders 4 and 7, box

28; clippings in folder 2, box 60, all in accession 80-49, MHPC papers, UIC. Property owners in opposition included the Orchestral Association (owner of Orchestra Hall), the Chicago Community Trust (owner of the University Club) and the landlord of the Fine Arts Building. The ten-group coalition also included the Chicago Federation of Musicians, the Garden Club of Illinois, the Planning Committee of the Chicago chapter of the American Institute of Architects, the American Institute of Planners, the Chicago Heritage Committee, the Midwest Open Land Association, the Prairie Club, and the Chicago Community Music Foundation.

16. *CST*, 21 May 1963 (green grass); *Chicago's American*, 28 Nov. 1963; "Recent Music Bowl Proposals," undated [1972], folder 3, box 28; clippings on Lakefront Issues, 1958–1963, folder 6, box 61, both in accession 80-59, MHPC papers, UIC; Schroeder, *The Issue of the Lakefront*, 26–28 (10,700 seats); Murray B. Woolley, Vice President of the City Club of Chicago, to James H. Gately, President of the CPD, 1 Feb. 1963, 26 Nov. 1963, both in box 38; Minutes of Board of Governors of the City Club of Chicago, 7, 9, 14 Nov. 1962, 23, 30 Jan. 1963, 6 Feb. 1963, box 8, all in City Club of Chicago Collection, CHS. By the end of the year, the civic groups identified in the previous note called upon the Chicago Plan Commission to begin feasibility studies on "the engineering and financing aspects of covering the Monroe Street parking lot." See final draft (letter) as approved by cooperating groups to Chicago Plan Commission, 25 Sept. 1963, folder 22, box 15, accession 80-59, MHPC papers, UIC. The park district reportedly rejected an offer by air rights developers north of Randolph Street to carry part of the burden of financing the music bowl if it were located over the Monroe Street parking lot because the park district did not want another interest involved. See Minutes of the Joint Committee on the Music Bowl, 18 Sept. 1963, folder 7, box 28, accession 80-59, MHPC papers, UIC.

17. *Chicago's American*, 2 Oct. 1963, in folder 9, box 61, accession 80-59, MHPC papers, UIC. Tigerman was chairman of the planning committee of the Chicago chapter of the American Institute of Architects at the time. See *CST*, 21 May 1963; final draft (letter) as approved by cooperating groups to Chicago Plan Commission, 25 Sept. 1963, folder 22, box 15, accession 80-59, MHPC papers, UIC. Even though the site for Lake Point Tower was east of Lake Shore Drive, property between Grand and Randolph

streets fell within one of the two exceptions for limiting private development east of the Drive in the Lakefront Resolution of 1948. See Chicago Department of Development and Planning, "Development Policies for the Chicago Lakefront," 1 Dec. 1965, p. 7, folder 11, box 27, accession 80-59, MHPC papers, UIC. Directly related to this concern was the development of Illinois Central air rights at *both* ends of the park. Not only was the railroad encouraging new high-rise construction north of Randolph Street after 1950, but numerous development proposals appeared concerning the IC's air rights between Roosevelt Road and 23rd Street south of Grant Park, including McCormick Center. For debates regarding whether Grant Park should be treated as a "preservation project," or part of "an innovative master planning" approach (in the words of Harry Weese), see Minutes of the combined meeting of the Lakefront and Parks Committee and the Transportation Committee, 10 Jan. 1973, folder 10, box 27, accession 80-59, MHPC papers, UIC; Discussion of Traffic and Transportation, Joint Meetings of the Transportation and Lakefront-Parks Committee, 10 Jan. 1973, p. 4, box 33, HWC.

18. *CST*, 29 Nov. 1963; Harry Weese memorandum, "Grant Park Traffic," 8 Aug. 1968; Weese, "Grant Park, 1963–1968: A Proposition for Settling the Issues of Grant Park," 5 Aug. 1968, p. 4 (Forest Preserves), 6, copies of both in folder 6, box 28, accession 80-59, MHPC papers, UIC; and Grant Park Bandstand folder, box 16, HWC; *CST*, 29 Nov. 1963. Weese and others were concerned that up to this point (and later) that city maps designated Lake Shore Drive as an expressway. See Harry Weese, memorandum to file, 1 Dec. 1972; Mark Dirolhi, Nagle, Hartray & Associates, to Harry Weese, 11 Dec. 1981, both in Lake Shore Drive folder, box 170, HWC. For examples of city plans emphasizing traffic control in Grant Park, particularly redesigning Grant Park and Lake Shore Drive to improve pedestrian access and more use, see Basic Policies for the Comprehensive Plan of Chicago, Aug. 1964, in folder 11, box 27, accession 80-59, MHPC papers, UIC.

19. *CST*, 28 March 1963, 21 May 1963, 29 Nov. 1963; *CDN*, 11 Dec. 1963. The plan also included an underground garage, gardens, ice skating rinks, and other recreational facilities. In 1963, the Chicago Department of City Planning proposed covering the Monroe Street Parking Station and the Illinois Central tracks with a series of disk-shaped gardens and terraces dropping down from a new arts center north of Randolph Street. See *CST*, 29 Nov. 1963.

20. Skidmore, Owings & Merrill and C. F. Murphy Associates, *Lakefront Development Plan*, 39–40, 49; Confidential Comment, "Proposed Music Bowl in Grant Park," 12 May 1972, folder 8, box 14; "Recent Music Bowl Proposals," undated [1972]; "A Park for All Seasons," 1972 typescript, p. 9, both in folder 3, box 28; Minutes of the Meeting of the Grant Park Committee, 19 Jan. 1966 (Bruce Graham, IC interest), folder 1, box 30, all in accession 80-59, MHPC papers, UIC; *CST* editorial, 1966 (new Burnham plan), folder 9, box 61, accession 80-59, MHPC papers, UIC. Elements of the SOM-Murphy proposal first appeared in 1963. See *CST*, 29 Nov. 1963. The Chicago Central Area Committee and SOM later authored both the *Chicago 21 Plan* (1975) and the *Central Area Plan* (1982) with some participation by the Department of Planning. See Ira J. Bach, director of city development, "A Short History of Planning in Chicago" (typescript), 6 June 1984, in Chicago City Planning folder, box 2, Ira J. Bach Papers, CHS. On support for decking over the Monroe Street Parking Station, see Openlands Project, "Lake Front Policy for the City of Chicago," Adopted by the Board of Directors, Welfare Council of Metropolitan Chicago, 20 Oct. 1965, Parks folder, box 6, Ruth Moore Papers; folder 1, box 17, Openlands Project Collection, both in CHS; all in accession 80-59, MHPC papers, UIC. The decking over of the Monroe Street parking lot and IC tracks remained a topic of discussion within the MHPC during the 1960s and 1970s. See Agenda, Meeting of the Lake Front Committee, 17 March 1966, folder 11; Key Lakefront Issues and Proposals, 20 June 1972, p. 4; Goals for Chicago's Lakefront, undated [1971], both folder 7, all in box 27, accession 80-59, MHPC papers, UIC. In 1972, the City went on record supporting covering the entire depressed railroad right-of-way in Grant Park. See City of Chicago, *Lakefront Plan of Chicago*, 34b.

21. *CDN*, 2–3 Dec. 1972, 10, 11 Feb. 1977; *CT*, 17 Oct. 1977, 17 Nov. 1977 (musicians complaints); *New Art Examiner*, 19 Feb. 1978 (hated music, noise); Kiriazis, "Musical Chairs." For support of the new bandshell, see WGN Editorial, no. 77–119, 17 May 1977.

22. C. F. Murphy Associates, *Grant Park Music Facility*, in Records and Files, Murphy/Jahn, Chicago, Ill. I am indebted to Keith Palmer for allowing me to examine and reproduce these materials. Also see Rob Cuscaden, "Grant Park's Bandshell Bombshell," *Chicago Guide*, Aug. 1972; *CDN*, 19, 22 June 1972, 21 Oct. 1972; *Chicago*

Today, 20 June 1972; and other clippings in folder 2, box 14, accession 80-59, MHPC papers, UIC.

23. CDN, 21 Oct. 1972; "A Park for All Seasons," 1972 typescript, p. 3; "Recent Music Bowl Proposals," undated [1972]; Confidential Comment, Proposed Music Bowl in Grant Park, 12 May 1972, all in folder 3; Minutes of the Lakefront and Parks Committee, MHPC, 24 March 1972, p. 2, folder 6, all in box 28, accession 80-59; CST, 21 June 1972, 30 Nov. 1972 (opposition due to height); Press release, Chicago chapter American Institute of Architects, "Proposed Music Bowl in Grant Park," 3 Aug. 1972 (opposed until adoption of a master plan); other clippings, all in folder 2, box 14, accession 80-59, all in MHPC papers, UIC; Rob Cuscaden, "Grant Park's Bandshell Bombshell," *Chicago Guide*, Aug. 1972.

24. CST editorial, 27 June 1972 (Art Institute 82 feet); CDN editorial, 28 June 1972, 29 June 1972, each in folder 2, box 14, accession 80-59; Michigan Boulevard Association, "Bandshell," undated, folder 8, Grant Park Bandshell, box 14; "Recent Music Bowl Proposals," undated [1972], folder 3; Daniel J. Shannon, Park District President, to Mrs. Frederick H. Rubel, MHPC Director, 23 June 1972, folder 6, both in box 28, each in accession 80-59, all in MHPC papers, UIC; Rob Cuscaden, "Grant Park's Bandshell Bombshell," *Chicago Guide*, Aug. 1972 (Art Institute 85 feet). The Michigan Boulevard Association included representatives of Michigan Avenue property owners. The group argued that the bandshell, with a zero elevation at the southern extremity and 59-foot elevation on the north, averaged only 29 feet in height. The bandshell remained below tree level and did not impede sight lines from Michigan Avenue toward Lake Michigan. Some later pointed out that sight lines from Michigan Avenue to Lake Michigan have been blocked ever since the Illinois Central sunk its tracks and created a ridge to allow roads to pass over the tracks.

25. MHPC, "Grant Park: A Park For All Seasons" (1972), 2–5, 8; John Bailey, President, MHPC, to Daniel Shannon, President, CPD, 25 Oct. 1972 (living park); Bailey to Mayor Richard J. Daley, 27 Oct. 1972; John Womer, Chairman, MHPC, to Michigan Avenue Property Owners, 1 Nov. 1972, all in Lakefront Gardens files, MPC; Confidential Comment, "Proposed Music Bowl in Grant Park," 12 May 1972; WGN Editorial no. 72-083, "A Bigger Band-Shell?" 8–11 July 1972, all in folder 8, Grant Park Bandshell, box 14; "A

Park for All Seasons," 1972 typescript, folder 3, box 28, all in accession 80-59; 24 July 1972 (downtown Ravinia), in Scrapbook, box 1, accession 74-011, all in MHPC papers, UIC. Michigan Avenue property owners opposed to the proposal included the Borg-Warner Corp., the Community Arts Foundation, and the John M. Smyth Co. See unmarked clipping, 28 Nov. 1972, folder 2, box 14, accession 80-59, MHPC papers, UIC. Summers's proposal was not completely in vain, as his design for the underground garage beneath the bandshell was later adopted when the East Monroe Drive Underground Garage beneath Daley Bicentennial Plaza was constructed on the site from 1975 to 1977. See C. F. Murphy Associates, *People Places* (Chicago, 1973 or 1974). I am indebted to Keith Palmer for allowing me to examine these and other related documents from C. F. Murphy.

26. Lois Weisberg Oral History Interview, 22 May 2000, deposited in the collections of the Chicago Historical Society; CST, 24 Dec. 1972; CT, 29 Nov. 1972 (plan scrapped), in Scrapbook, box 1, accession 74-011, MHPC papers, UIC.

27. CDN, 10, 11 Feb. 1977; CT, 17 Oct. 1977; *New Art Examiner*, 19 Feb. 1978. The demountable bandshell was conceived by park district chief engineer Maurice Thominet, designed by architectural designer Alan Melsky, and directed by park district chief architect Ed Uhlir, with the support of Grant Park concert series manager Robert Wilkins. Unrecorded conversation with Ed Uhlir, 7 March 2005.

28. CST, 3 April 1977; CT, 21 Aug. 1977. An approximate total of 350,000 attended 37 concerts in 1972. An estimated 25,000 attended on 1, 7, and 8 August. See Attendance Figures for 1972 Grant Park Concerts, folder 6, box 28, accession 80-59, MHPC papers, UIC; CPD, [*Eighteenth*] *Annual Report for* 1952, 25. An estimated 634,600 had attended the 31 concerts in 1952.

29. CST, CT, 20 July 1978; David Farber, *Chicago '68* (Chicago, 1988), 184, 189, 191. Coverage of the disturbance associated with Sly and the Family Stone appears in *New York Times*, 29 July 1970; CT, CST, 28, 29 July 1970 (I am indebted to Ted Karamanski for directing me to this event). For a survey showing that a bandshell located "closer to Randolph Street" would be more heavily used, see Patricia P. Rosenzweig, Perkins & Will, to Jack Cornelius, Chicago Central Area Committee, 30 Nov. 1977, in Lakefront Gardens files, MPC. For earlier criticisms on the lack of pedestrian traffic in Grant Park, see Harry Weese,

"Grant Park, 1963–1968: A Proposition for Settling the Issues of Grant Park," 5 Aug. 1968, p. 3, copies in folder 6, box 28, accession 80-59, MHPC papers, UIC; and Grant Park Bandstand folder, box 16, HWC. On concerns regarding park safety, see *Chicago American*, 17 May 1964; CST, 24 June 1960. On racial fears in Grant Park, see Hutchins interview.

30. *New Art Examiner*, 19 Feb. 1978; McDonough interview (civics); Hutchins interview (civics); Ranney interview; George Ranney to Julian Levi, 15 Feb. 1977; Memo by George Ranney to Laurence Booth et al., 15 Feb. 1977, both in folder 15, box 7, accession 81-81, MHPC papers, UIC. For other criticisms of the park district proposal, see Walter Netsch, SOM, to Larry Christmas, MHPC, 18 Feb. 1977, folder 15, box 7, accession 81-81, MHPC papers, UIC; CDN, 10 Feb. 1977 (Weese); CST, 14 Feb. 1977. On growing opposition by the Metropolitan Planning Council, see CST, 1 June 1977, 5 Aug. 1977. The *New Art Examiner* article describes Ranney as "enraged" and confrontational in conversations with Levi, an unlikely occurrence given that Ranney was a student of Levi's, that they collaborated later on other projects, and that Ranney's sister married a nephew (a son of Edward Levi) of Julian Levi's. See Ranney interview.

31. Ranney interview; *Who's Who in America* (1999).

32. Ranney interview; *New Art Examiner*, 19 Feb. 1978.

33. MHPC, press release on Lakefront Gardens for the Performing Arts, 6 Oct. 1977; George Ranney to Miles Berger, 11 Oct. 1977; Evaluation of Chicago Park District Proposal for a New Grant Park Music Shell by American Institute of Architects (Chicago chapter), Friends of the Parks, MHPC, and Openlands Project for the Chicago Plan Commission, March 1977, all in folder 15, box 7, accession 81-81, MHPC papers, UIC. Ranney believed that $7 million would be provided by the federal government, $1 million by the park district, and $2 million by the private sector. Hutchins also estimated that the performance facilities and gardens would cost $4 million, decking and tunneling over the IC tracks another $4 million, and the proposed extension over Columbus Drive $2 million. Potential sources of federal funding included the Bureau of Outdoor Recreation, the Urban Park and Recreation Recovery Program and the Consent Degree Capital Improvement Fund, the

federal highway program, and the Department of Housing and Urban Development. See *New Art Examiner*, 19 Feb. 1978; *CT, CST*, 7 Oct. 1977; *CDN*, 7, 8 Oct. 1977; *CPD, Annual Report 1984* (Chicago, 1985), 13–20. On the Feb. 1977 request for bandshell designs from the Plan Commission to the MHPC, see *CDN*, 15 Oct. 1977. As late as 1976, the MHPC remained opposed to "permanent structures in the park, particularly a permanent bandshell." See Minutes of the Environmental Committee Meeting, 28 July 1976, folder 8, box 27, accession 80-59, MHPC papers, UIC. Later Lakefront Garden designs cut the acreage from 20 to 14 acres, and the seating capacity from 10,000 to 2,000 in an inner circle, 8,500 on an adjoining grass terrace, and 30,000 in a listening garden. See Lakefront Gardens, Inc., Project Description for Lakefront Gardens (typescript), 13 Dec. 1978, p. 4; Lakefront Gardens, "For the Use and Pleasure of All" (typescript), 4 April 1979, both in Lakefront Gardens folder, Walter Netsch (unprocessed) Collection, CHS.

34. Neil Harris to George Ranney, 29 June 1977, folder 16, box 7, accession 81-81, MHPC papers, UIC. On Midway Gardens later serving as a model for Lakefront Gardens, see Plan for Festival Performance Center Lakefront Gardens, Jan. 1981, in Lakefront Gardens file, MPC.

35. *New Art Examiner*, 19 Feb. 1978; Ranney interview; McDonough interview; Hutchins interview; Harold Jensen, IC Industries vice president, to Ranney, 20 May 1977, Lakefront Gardens files, MPC.

36. Harold Jensen, IC Industries vice president, to Ranney, 20 May 1977, Lakefront Gardens files, MPC. Press release on Lakefront Gardens for the Performing Arts, 6 Oct. 1977, folder 15, box 7, accession 81-81, MHPC papers, UIC (Freehling); *CDN*, 7, 9 Oct. 1977. Harry Weese and Laurence Booth's criticism of Lakefront Gardens as too "grandiose" and ambitious appears in Kiriazis, "Musical Chairs" (Booth); Harry Weese to George Ranney, 18 Oct. 1977, Grant Park Bandstand folder, box 16, HWC; Booth interview.

37. Ranney interview; McDonough interview; Harry Weese to Bill Lacy, National Endowment for the Arts, 1 Sept. 1976, Grant Park Bandstand folder, box 16, HWC; *CDN*, 13 Oct. 1977; *Chicago Today, CST*, 14 Oct. 1977, 17 Nov. 1978 (incompetent dictatorship); *CT*, 17 Oct. 1977. For other editorials supporting Lakefront Gardens, see *CST*, 8, 17 Oct. 1977; *CDN*, 8–9 Oct., 15 Oct. 1977;

CT, 10 Oct. 1977; *NBC5 News*, broadcast 18 Oct. 1977.

38. *New Art Examiner*, 19 Feb. 1978 (ornament); *CT, CDN*, 20 Oct. 1977; *CST*, 18, 20 Oct. 1977. Several days later Harry Weese, past president of the Chicago chapter of the AIA and chair of its Task Force on the Burnham Plan, offered to raise the money to rehabilitate the existing Grant Park bandshell to allow its operation for several more summers. See *CDN*, 20 Oct. 1977.

39. "Report of the Mayor's Committee on the Lakefront Gardens," final draft, 7 Nov. 1977, p. 1, appendix I(1), in files of MPC.

40. *CT*, 11 June 1978 (permanent part), 3 Nov. 1978; *New Art Examiner*, 19 Feb. 1978. In December, a Skidmore, Owings & Merrill design for the new, lightweight, translucent, demountable bandshell was released, which included accommodations for 30,000 spectators, including 4,000 seats. See *CDN*, 14 Nov. 1977 (temporary), 16 Dec. 1977; *CST*, 13 Nov. 1977, 17 Dec. 1977; *CT, CDN* ($20 million), 11 Nov. 1977; *CPD, Annual Report 1977*, 2; Metropolitan Housing and Planning Council, *Issues and Positions* 4, no. 4 (Nov. 1977). Within weeks after opening the new Petrillo Music Shell on 24 June 1978, the largest crowd ever to attend a Chicago concert took place there on 3 July, when 200,000 heard the Chicago Symphony and the Grant Park Orchestra. Exactly a year later, 300,000 came out to hear the Grant Park Orchestra. *CPD, Annual Report 1978*, 6, 20; idem, *Annual Report 1979*, 8; *CST*, 6 July 1978. The $389,000 cost was determined by competitive bidding for the dismantling, storage, and reerection in a one-year cycle. Unrecorded conversation with Ed Uhlir, 7 March 2005.

41. *New Art Examiner*, 19 Feb. 1978; Ranney to Julian Levi and Lewis Hill, 14 Sept. 1977, folder 7, box 15, accession 81-81, MHPC papers, UIC; A Timetable for 1979, in Lakefront Gardens, "For the Use and Pleasure of All" (typescript), 4 April 1979, in Lakefront Gardens folder, Walter Netsch (unprocessed) Collection, CHS; Kiriazis, "Musical Chairs" (federal funding); unrecorded conversation with James Feldstein, 19 Jan. 2001 (formation of Lakefront Gardens, Inc.). Levi also worked with Edward Banker, John McDonough, and James F. Feldstein in the fundraising campaign. See Ranney interview.

42. Feldstein interview (Klutznick, MacArthur Gardens); Joan Harris interview (MacArthur Gardens); "Scenario," Lakefront Gardens, 28 Aug. 1980, Lakefront Gardens file, MPH; Presentation

to the Commercial Club of Chicago of the Lakefront Gardens for the Performing Arts (typescript), 25 Jan. 1978, Chicago Club, Lakefront Gardens folder, Walter Netsch (unprocessed) Collection, CHS. The Lakefront Gardens proposal also stimulated competing designs. William Brubaker and Laurence Booth each separately proposed locating a new public library on the site. In 1989, Donald Hackl designed a threestory garage over the rail yard, on top of which would be a simple park filled with water pools and a promenade. On the Brubaker proposal, see William Brubaker, "A New Home for the Chicago Public Library," 3 March 1980, in Lakefront Garden files, MPC. On the Booth proposal, see McDonough interview; Booth interview. In 1986, Friends of the Parks successfully opposed construction of the central library on 10 acres of land in Grant Park. See Friends of the Parks, *Annual Review* (Chicago, 1986). On the Hackl proposal, see Untitled drawing; side view looking east for "A Proposal for the Extension of the Extension of Grant Park" (caption "N-S Section") by Loebl, Schlossman & Hackl (undated; Aug. 1989) by Donald Hackl; "A Proposal for the Extension of Grant Park" by Loebl, Schlossman & Hackl (undated; Aug. 1989) by Donald Hackl, both in records of Loebl, Schlossman & Hackl.

43. The potential federal funding sources were in the Urban Parks Program and the Land and Water Conservation Fund, both in the U.S. Department of the Interior. See *CST*, 17 Dec. 1977 ($30 million); Feldstein interview (no formal campaign); Minutes of the Meeting of the Board of Trustees of Lakefront Gardens, Inc., 20 March 1980, Lakefront Gardens files, MPC. Drevs was involved with the formation of Lakefront Gardens, Inc. See Robert Hutchins to Robert Drevs, 18 April 1978, Lakefront Gardens folder, Walter Netsch (unprocessed) Collection, CHS. Byrne later endorsed the project, describing the plan as "a unique opportunity for Chicago" and "a magnificent example of government and private citizens working together in partnership on behalf of Chicago." See Mayor Jane Byrne to the People of Chicago, 5 Dec. 1980, in plan for Festival Performance Center Lakefront Gardens, Jan. 1981, in Lakefront Gardens file, MPC; Feldstein interview.

44. Lakefront Gardens: Functional and Construction Elements, SOM, 30 April 1983, in author's possession (I am indebted to Robert Hutchins for sharing this and other Lakefront Gardens material with me); Memo from Tom Cokins and Bill Martin, CCAC, to Adrian Smith,

16 Jan. 1998, in Public Process Documentation for the Lakefront Millennium Project Binder, Office of the Millennium Park Project, Suite 1600, 200 South Michigan Avenue, Chicago, Ill (hereafter Binder). The $15 million cost is mentioned in Lakefront Gardens memo, Skidmore, Owings & Merrill, 19 Oct. 1983, in Lakefront Gardens files, MPC.

45. "Grant Park: A Vision for the NorthWest Corner," draft memo, 20 March 1992; Robert Hutchins to Deborah Stone, Metropolitan Planning Council, 2 March 1992, both in Lakefront Gardens files, MPC.

46. Robert Hutchins to Deborah Stone, Metropolitan Planning Council, 2 March 1992, Lakefront Gardens files, MPC; Chicago Central Area Committee Transportation Task Force, *Final Report* (Jan. 1985), 10, in folder 1297, box 73, accession 94-5, MHPC papers, UIC. On the Lakefront Gardens board rarely meeting after 1985, see Feldstein interview; Thomas interview; O'Connor interview.

47. See appendix 4 for a list of Lakefront Gardens trustees. John McDonough remembers that by the early 1990s, less than $1,000 was left in the bank account of Lakefront Gardens, Inc. See McDonough interview. On Byrne's support, see McDonough interview; Feldstein interview. After 1975, SOM, in the personages of Robert Hutchins and William Hartmann, donated a decade of service valued at over $100,000. On SOM's importance to the various Lakefront Gardens proposals, see Hutchins interview; Ranney interview. By the beginning of 1978, some claimed that SOM had donated $75,000 worth of time to Lakefront Gardens. See *New Art Examiner,* 19 Feb. 1978.

48. McDonough interview; Ranney interview; Hutchins interview. The park district came under attack from other sources during the 1980s. After a series of news accounts revealed a systematic pattern of racial discrimination in park district policies, a threatened federal lawsuit produced a consent decree between the park district and Justice Department in 1983. The result generated long-awaited reforms: the creation of local advisory councils, better relations with private citizen groups, the opening of concessions bidding. U.S. District Court for the Northern District of Illinois (Eastern Division), Civil Action 28 C 7308 "Consent Decree," 7 Dec. 1983; and "Implementation Committee Report to the

Court," 24 Jan. 1985. Discussion of consent decree monitoring is in Friends of the Park, *Annual Reports* (Chicago, 1985–1991). After 25 years of a no-bid process, the park district agreed to an open bidding process in 1980. See idem, *Annual Report for 1989–1990.* A copy of "Consent Decree Task Force Preliminary Report" appears in CPD, *President's Report,* 131–37.

49. *New Art Examiner,* 19 Feb. 1978 (Butler); O'Connor interview; Mehrberg interview; CT, CST, 20, 21, 22 June 1986; CPD, *President's Report.* Chicago mayoral administrations covered the following years: Richard J. Daley, 1955–1976; Michael Bilandic, 1976–1979; Jane Byrne, 1979–1983; Harold Washington, 1983–1987; Eugene Sawyer, 1987–1989; Richard M. Daley, 1989-present. In 1980, after a dispute regarding patronage hiring in the park district with recently elected mayor Jane Byrne, O'Malley resigned as park district board president. He was immediately replaced by fellow board member Raymond F. Simon, a former assistant to mayor Richard J. Daley and in 1965 the youngest corporation counsel in the United States. Later, Simon was briefly a principle in the law firm of Simon and Daley, formed with the then-mayor's son Richard M. Daley in 1969. Known for his ability to handle tough political assignments, Simon's ascension to the park district presidency marked the beginning of reform in park district politics. See *Tribune,* 5, 10 May 1979. Details of Simon's career before 1980 are in *Tribune,* 18 July 1980. Simon was replaced by Byrne in 1982. See *Tribune,* 8, 12, 21 May 1982, 13, 17 June 1982. On the racial and ethnic discriminatory patterns in park district programs, see the reports in *Chicago Reporter,* May 1978, April 1980; CST, 17–22 June 1979. Also see CPD, *Master Plan,* vol. 1.

50. Kiriazis, "Musical Chairs" (Butler); *New Art Examiner,* 19 Feb. 1978 (Levi); McDonough interview ($5 million); Ranney interview ($10 million); Feldstein interview; CST, 17 Jan. 1988 (Harris); Julian Levi, "Civic Power in Times of Crises: The Past and Future Role of the Private Sector in Planning," Address before MHPC, 11 Oct. 1984, pp. 14–15 ($50,000 from CCT), in folder 20, box 2; accession 89-30; Lakefront Gardens Financial Statement, 20 Feb. 1981 ($50,000), folder 236, box 22, accession 89-30, all in MHPC papers, UIC; Lakefront Gardens Milestones, no date, in author's possession. Most (over $36,000) of the $50,000 CCT grant went to Charles Feldstein & Co. from 1 Feb. 1978 to Dec. 1980. See Lake Front [sic] Gardens (financial report), 20 Feb. 1981, folder 236, box 22, accession 89-30, MHPC papers, UIC.

51. Feldstein interview. This was hardly an unprecedented problem.

52. John M. McDonough to Mary Sue Barrett, president, Metropolitan Planning Council, 5 Sept. 1996, in Lakefront Garden files, MPC; Confidential Letter, George A. Ranney, Jr., President of the Metropolitan Housing and Planning Council, to Mayor Michael Bilandic, 10 August 1977, in author's possession.

CHAPTER FOUR

1. The dentist story appears in Bedore interview; Mehrberg interview (every six months); Smith interview; Daley interview; McDonough interview; Uhlir interview no. 3; Waldheim, *Constructed Ground,* 3 (1997). On the lack of historical memory regarding Lakefront Gardens in the development of Millennium Park, see Feldstein interview; Thomas interview; O'Connor interview; Bedore interview.

2. Mehrberg interview. Mehrberg was park district counsel from 1993 to 1997. He joined Exelon in 2000. For more on Mehrberg, see Krysten Crawford, "Punch the Clock," *New York Lawyer,* 19 Nov. 2002. The subsidiary was the Chicago Missouri & Western Railroad.

3. Mehrberg interview.

4. Ibid.

5. Ibid.

6. Ibid. CPD superintendent Forrest Claypool kept Mayor Daley informed of the status of the negotiations. Telephone conversation with Mehrberg, 17 Sept. 2003 (IC relinquished all control); Waldheim, *Constructed Ground,* ix. An article describing the closing of the seven-dollar-a-day parking lot appears in CT, 3 Sept. 1998.

7. Mehrberg interview.

8. Bedore interview; Thomas interview.

9. Mehrberg interview; telephone conversation with Mehrberg, 17 Sept. 2003 (Uhlir on envelope).

10. Ranney interview.

11. LaPietra interview; Ulrich, "Green Roofs and Blue Trees," 44–53 (median plantings); *CT*, 11 July 1999 (55 school parks); *CT*, 28 Aug. 2002; http://www.edcmag.com/CDA/ArticleInformation/news/news_item/0,4124,116627,00.html, accessed May 2004. Also see Chamberlain, "Mayor Daley's Green Crusade." In 1999, Daley received the J. Sterling Morton Award from the National Arbor Day Foundation, as well as the Garden Club of America Award. In 2003, the American Horticultural Society recognized Daley for his significant contributions to urban horticulture with the Urban Beautification Award. See Ulrich, "Green Roofs and Blue Trees," 53. Daley also received an environmental award from the U.S. Conference of Mayors in 2005.

12. Paulus interview; Daley interview.

13. Garvin, *The American City*, 30–71; Garvin and Berens, *Urban Parks and Open Space*, ix–x, 2.

14. Spirou and Bennett, *It's Hardly Sportin'*, 159–60.

15. SOM Press release, 12 Aug. 1999.

16. *SOM: Adrian Smith, FAIA of Skidmore, Owings & Merrill LLP* (Korea, no date), 262–77.

17. Bryan interview no. 2.

18. Smith interview; Uhlir interviews no. 1, no. 3.

19. Bedore interview.

20. Smith interview.

21. Ibid.; Forrest Claypool to Adrian Smith, 16 April 1997, CPD records, in author's possession. Burnham's harbor plan was never feasible because of the large size. The current harbor is only one-fourth the size of Burnham's proposal and suffers from large wave buildup at times. Unrecorded conversation with Ed Uhlir, 7 March 2005.

22. Smith interview; SOM press release, 12 Aug. 1999.

23. Lash interview; Smith interview; unrecorded conversation with Ed Uhlir, 7 March 2005 (Friedman).

24. Plan for Festival Performance Center Lakefront Gardens, Jan. 1981, in Lakefront Gardens file, MPC. Compare this with Richard M. Daley, *Lakefront Millennium Project* (Chicago, 1998), unpaginated color brochure; News release, Mayor Richard J. Daley Press Office, 30 March 1998, in Binder; *Daily Southtown*, 31 March 1998; *Chicago Daily Defender*, 1 April 1998; *Inside Gold Coast*, 22 April 1998. For Millennium Park planners who believe Lakefront Gardens had little influence on Millennium Park, see Field interview; O'Connor interview; Thomas interview.

25. Smith interview; Richard Gray interview. Breslau was the most involved from SOM; Adrian Smith was less involved. Uhlir interview no. 3.

26. Lash interview; Dillon and Sullivan interviews.

27. Uhlir interview no. 1. Later studies revealed that sounds moving from the south would indeed hit the Randolph Street structures and reverberate. See Bedore interview; Smith interview.

28. *North Loop News*, 14 May 1998, 16 July 1998; News release, Mayor Richard J. Daley Press Office, 30 March 1998, in Binder; *Showtimes: News from the Metropolitan Pier and Exposition Authority* 9 (Fall 1998): 1. Early projections estimated $120 million in cost would come from parking fees. Landscaping and enhancements were estimated to cost $30 million, which were to be paid for from private donations. The bus lane was planned and constructed by the Chicago Department of Transportation for the MPEA. Also see *Daily Southtown*, 31 March 1998; *Chicago Daily Defender*, 1 April 1998; *Inside Gold Coast*, 22 April 1998. Organizations which joined Daley in support of the project at the press conference included the Art Institute of Chicago, Building Trades Council, Chicago Convention and Tourism Bureau, Chicago Federation of Labor AFL-CIO, Chicagoland Chamber of Commerce, Chinatown Chamber of Commerce, Chinese Consolidated Benevolent Association of Chicago, Friends of Downtown, Friends of the Parks, Illinois Central Railroad Company, Metra, Metropolitan Pier & Exposition Authority, Metropolitan Planning Council, National Center for Latinos with Disabilities, Inc., Near South Planning Board, and Openlands Project. See also chapter 4, note 64, below.

29. *CT*, 15 April 1962. On complaints about the poor transportation facilities in the Grant Park area, see Metropolitan Planning Council, *Urban Development: Fact Sheet no. 1*, May 1997; Metropolitan Planning Council, *Lakefront Alliance Issue Brief no. 2*, April 1998; McDonough Associates, *Lakefront Transportation Study Prepared for the City of Chicago Department of Transportation* (draft), May 1997; idem, *Central Lakefront Transportation Study Prepared for the City of Chicago Department of Transportation* (draft), Nov. 1997.

30. The initial proposal required raising the bonding cap for the MPEA, which failed to pass the Illinois Senate in the fall of 1997. See *Skyline*, 29 Jan. 1998. In 2000 and 2001, Taste of Chicago attendance exceeded 3.5 million. See *CT*, 9 July 2001. The busway reportedly would cut convention-related busing costs by one-third, making the Chicago cheaper than other convention cities. See *CT*, 14 Jan. 2002.

31. News release, Mayor Richard J. Daley Press Office, 30 March 1998, in Binder; *Daily Southtown*, 31 March 1998; *Chicago Daily Defender*, 1 April 1998; *Inside Gold Coast*, 22 April 1998; e-mail communication from Rob Omori (Office of John Bryan) to Timothy Gilfoyle, 11 July 2003, in author's possession.

32. Discussion of Traffic and Transportation, Joint Meetings of the Transportation and Lakefront-Parks Committee, 10 Jan. 1973, p. 3, both in box 33, HWC.

33. Chicago Department of Planning, *Tourist Industry*, 27 (stepchild); Chicago Department of Planning and Chicago Plan Commission, *Chicago 1992*, 29–32 (one million square feet); Regional Agenda Project, *The State of the Region*, VI-6, copy in MHPC publications folder, box 33, HWC. Also see Chicago Department of Planning and Chicago Plan Commission. *Comprehensive Plan: Goals and Policies* (Chicago, 1981), 47–50; Chicago Department of Planning and Chicago Plan Commission, *Chicago 1992*, 59–63, on the need for greater public and corporate investment in the arts and cultural institutions. None of these reports specifically addressed Lakefront Gardens. In 1985, one report concluded that Chicago had not done as well as the rest of the nation in attracting visitors, "pleasure visitors in particular." Compared to neighboring states, Chicago appeared to be falling behind. The Chicago Tourism Council, representing a cross section of the city's civic and business communities, was established in 1985 to improve relations among the Chicago Convention and Tourism Bureau and Illinois Office of Tourism. See Chicago Department of Planning, *Tourist Industry*, i, 8, 28.

34. Susan S. Aaron, Executive Director, to Grant Park Cultural and Educational Community

Board of Directors, 26 Oct. 1988; Mary Decker, MHPC, to Susan Aaron, 23 June 1988 (quote), both in folder 1358; Lynn Minich, WFMT, to Gretchen Miller Reimel, Sara Lee Foundation, 18 Aug. 1988; and other correspondence and promotional literature in folder 1359, all in box 78, accession 94-5, MHPC papers, UIC. Member organizations in 1985: Adler Planetarium, Art Institute, Field Museum of Natural History, Shedd Aquarium, Chicago Symphony Orchestra, Grant Park Concerts, Columbia College, DePaul University, Roosevelt University, Spertus College of Judaica, Chicago Public Library, Chicago Office of Fine Arts. See Grant Park Cultural and Educational Community pamphlet, 1985, folder 1359, box 78, accession 94-5, MHPC papers, UIC.

35. CDN, 7–8 May 1977.

36. Chicago Mayor's Task Force on Navy Pier, *Window on the Future,* 5–6; Judd, "Promoting Tourism in U.S. Cities," 175–76; Bruce Ehrlich and Peter Dreier, "The New Boston Discovers the Old: Tourism and the Struggle for a Livable City" (12 million in Boston), in Judd and Fainstein, *The Tourist City,* 155–78.

37. Chicago Mayor's Task Force on Navy Pier, *Window on the Future,* 5–6.

38. Ibid., 12.

39. Plans for conventional private development (exemplified by a casino, condominiums, or shopping markets) were rejected in the proposal. See ibid., 19, 54.

40. *Showtimes: News from the Metropolitan Pier and Exposition Authority* 8 (Fall 1997): 4. On "fun zones," see CT, 10 Nov. 2002, real estate section.

41. Chicago Office of Tourism, 1998.

42. *Showtimes: News from the Metropolitan Pier and Exposition Authority* 9 (Winter 1998): 1.

43. *Millennium Park News,* Winter 2001–2002. In my interview with Richard M. Daley, he stated that Navy Pier had little impact on the planning of Millennium Park. See Daley interview. Yet in his introduction letter in his *Lakefront Millennium Project,* an unpaginated color brochure released on 30 March 1998, he linked the project to Navy Pier and McCormick Place for generating "tens of thousands of jobs for working Chicago families, millions of dollars in tax revenues, and billions more in economic activity. With the Lake-

front Millennium Project, Chicago will become an even better place in which to live, work, raise our families, and visit."

44. Metropolitan Planning Council, *Urban Development: Fact Sheet no. 1,* May 1997.

45. CT, 14 July 2003.

46. Ibid.

47. Caraley, "Washington Abandons the Cities," 8 (46 percent); Felbinger, "Conditions of Confusion and Conflict," and Mier, "Economic Development and Infrastructure," both in *Building the Public City,* ed. Perry, esp. 71–96 and 109–17. Terry Nichols Clark, introduction to Clark, *Urban Innovation,* 1, claims that U.S. government grants to cities dropped by more than half from 1977 to the early 1990s.

48. Clark, "Innovations That Work: A Menu of Strategies," in Clark, *Urban Innovation,* 216–17, 219. On "taxpayer revolts" in Chicago, see CT, 23 Oct. 2003, 1 Nov. 1995.

49. Mayor Richard M. Daley's Remarks, Civic Federation 1991 Annual Luncheon, June 5, 1991, available at http://www.lib.niu.edu/ipo/im910719.html, accessed June 2003.

50. Spirou and Bennett, *It's Hardly Sportin',* 51; James Atlas, "The Daleys of Chicago," *New York Times Magazine,* 25 August, 1996 (our goal). On the emergence of a "new political culture" in American cities, see Clark and Hoffmann-Martinot, *New Political Culture;* Clark, "Race and Class versus the New Political Culture," in Clark, *Urban Innovation,* 21–78. On the global spread of this culture, see Clark and Rempel, *Citizen Politics in Post-Industrial Societies.*

51. William D. Eggers, ed., "Revitalizing Our Cities: Perspectives from America's New Breed of Mayors," February 7, 1996, Washington Institute for Policy Studies, available at http://www.ncpa.org/pd/private/privb3.html, last accessed 22 March 2005.

52. CT, 25 June 2004 (public schools); Paul Glastris, "Chicago's Hands-On Mayor," *City Journal* 3 (Autumn 1993), available at http://www.city-journal.org/article01.php?aid=1456, last accessed 23 May 2005; Spirou and Bennett, *It's Hardly Sportin',* 51; *Catalyst Chicago,* Feb. 2001 (Claypool), available at http://www.catalyst-chicago.org/02-01/0201claypool.htm, last accessed 22 March 2005. Daley entertained privatizing parts of the public

schools as early as 1994. See CT, 6 Oct. 1994. For discussion of privatized services, see CT, 5 March 2003 (building permit reviews); 1 Aug. 2003 (utility services); 26 Oct. 2000 (Midway; O'Hare); 14 Sept. 1999 (data processing); 27 March 1997 (school capital program); 30 Nov. 1994; 20 Nov. 1993 (abandoned cars); 29 May 1991 (stump removal; tree trimming); 25 Oct. 1990 (sewers); Rowan A. Miranda, "Contracting Out: A Solution with Limits," in Clark, *Urban Innovation,* 197–212. For Alderman Edward M. Burke's support of Daley's privatization programs, see CT, 23 Oct. 1991. On the successful results of privatization in California parks, see Callahan, "The Basics of Privatization," 56–59.

53. James Atlas, "The Daleys of Chicago," *New York Times Magazine,* 25 August 1996 (Holleb). On the importance of patronage in Richard J. Daley's regime, see Cohen and Taylor, *American Pharaoh,* 155–63. Daley blamed layoffs in 2002 on certain unions' refusal to accept unpaid furloughs. At least 87 percent of city jobs were covered by union contracts. See CT, 1 Aug. 2003; 23 May 2003 (threat). On Teamster Union complaints of Daley privatizing municipal towing operations, see CT, 10 Oct. 1996. On perceptions of Daley's hostility to organized labor, see CT, 28 Nov. 2004. The literature on urban political machines and patronage is vast. I have been most influenced by McDonald, *Parameters of Urban Fiscal Policy;* Teaford, *Unheralded Triumph;* Riordan, *Plunkitt of Tammany Hall,* introduction. A summary of recent historical debates on machines and patronage appears in Gilfoyle, "White Cities."

54. Judd, "Promoting Tourism in U.S. Cities," 175–76 (like railroads); Judd and Fainstein, *The Tourist City.* For more on urban development strategies promoting tourism and leisure activity, see Spirou and Bennett, *It's Hardly Sportin',* esp. 39–58; Zukin, *Culture of Cities;* Beauregard, "Tourism and Economic Development Policy in U.S. Urban Areas," 220–34; Clark et al., "Amenities Drive Urban Growth," 493–513; Lloyd and Clark, "City as an Entertainment Machine," 357–78; Florida, *Rise of the Creative Class,* 224–29. On nineteenth-century urban boosters, see Abbott, *Boosters and Businessmen.*

55. Private-sector support for the New Jersey Performing Arts Center topped $60 million, while federal, state, and city contributions amounted to some $125 million. See http://www.njpac.org/sitegenerator.cfm?dir=about&page=history, last accessed 23 March 2005; Strom, "Let's Put on a Show," 423–35. For similar and related

discussions in other cities, see NYT, 30 Oct. 2001 (on Pulitzer Foundation for the Arts in St. Louis); *Miami Herald*, 3 Nov. 2003 (Miami-Dade Performing Arts Center); *Puget Sound Business Journal*, 13 Nov. 1998 (Benaroya Hall).

56. http://www.glasgow.gov.uk/en/About-Glasgow/History/Cultural+Renaissance.htm, last accessed 23 March 2005.

57. http://www.asiaweek.com/asiaweek/maga-zine/nations/0,8782,103424,00.html, last accessed 23 March 2005.

58. Daley interview. On Millennium Park and the "Bilbao effect," see CT, 4 Nov. 1999. Also see Judd and Fainstein, *The Tourist City*.

59. Daley interview. For more on Gehry, see Ragheb, *Frank Gehry*, 349. Studies show that 80 percent of the visitors to Bilbao come to see the museum, making a single building responsible for a 500 percent increase in tourism. See *Columbia University Record*, 9 May 2003.

60. *Millennium Park News*, Winter 2001–2002 (Andersen report); "One-on-One with Frank Gehry," *Chicago Tonight*, no. 17121, WTTW-TV (PBS), Channel 11, Chicago, 3 Feb. 2000; Elmer W. Johnson, *Chicago Metropolis 2020* (Chicago, 2001), 168, note 5 (Arts Council report); *North Loop News*, 16 April 1998 (Natarus). Chicago commissioner of cultural affairs Lois Weisberg repeated the 2–3 million estimate in tourists when Millennium Park opened. See CT, 12 July 2004. Also see *Midwest Construction*, May 2004 (2–3 million tourists), available at http://midwest.construction.com/features/archive/0405_cover.asp, accessed July 2004.

61. John McCarron used the term "Pax Daleyorum" in CT, 4 June 2004.

62. In 1958, CCAC supported development of a new amphitheater and bandshell in Grant Park. A similar proposal was included in CCAC's Chicago 21 Plan in 1973 and in the Chicago Central Area Plan of 1983, both done in concert with the City's Department of Planning. In 1978, they supported the MHPC Lakefront Gardens proposal. See Tom Cokins, Executive Director, CCAC, to Mayor Richard M. Daley, 27 April 1998, in Binder. Adrian Smith was president of the CCAC at this time. CCAC literature claims that "CCAC joined forces with the Metropolitan Planning Council to develop 'Lakefront Gardens'" in the 1970s. See Minutes of the Joint Meeting, CCAC

and Chicago Central Area Research and Study Committee, 13 April 1998, page 2, in Binder.

63. Letters to Editor, CST, 22 April 1998 (Alba quote); Erma Tratner, Executive Director, and Eleanor Roemer, General Counsel, Friends of the Parks, to Transportation Commissioner Thomas Walker, 28 April 1998, in Binder; *Daily Southtown Southwest*, 15 May 1998 (Beck quote); CST, 1 April 1998 (What's not to like). For other endorsements, see Carolyn Williams Meza, General Superintendent, Chicago Park District, to Peter Bynoe, Chair, Chicago Plan Commission, 1 April 1998; Gerald Adelmann, Executive Director, Openlands Project, to Commissioner Christopher Hill, Chicago Plan Commission, 12 May 1998; TRW Remarks, Zoning Committee, 4 June 1998, all in Binder. The *Chicago Tribune's* architecture critic Blair Kamin defended the early Millennium Park proposal, especially because the Petrillo bandshell suffered from poor acoustics and loud, nearby traffic, while turning into a mud flat whenever it rained. The new project promised to be a sharp improvement. See CT, 5 April 1998. Among the most widely cited criticisms on "theme park planning" is Sorkin, *Variations on a Theme Park*. On "theme park" planning in Asia, see Ian Buruma, "Asia World," *New York Review of Books*, 12 June 2003.

64. CT, 2 April 1998. CT, 2 April 1998 (visual knockout);

65. Daley interview; News release, Mayor Richard J. Daley Press Office, 30 March 1998, in Binder. Some, like Ed Bedore, insist that the park was always a critical component of the design. See Bedore interview.

66. Lakefront Millennium Project, Resolution of Approval, 14 May 1998, Chicago Plan Commission; *Daily Southtown Southwest*, 15 May 1998; Uhlir interview no. 3. The three principal construction contracts went to McDonough (contract), Kenny, and SOM (subcontract).

CHAPTER FIVE

1. In Bryan interview no. 2, Bryan said that he believed this incident took place during the 1996 Democratic National Party Convention in Chicago. However, no record of Bryan attending the Mid-America Club during the convention appears in his calendar. He did introduce South African deputy president Thabo Mbeki at a dinner at the Mid-America Club on 25 July 1996, but Bryan's records do not indicate whether Daley

was in attendance. E-mail communications, Rob Omori (Office of John Bryan) to Timothy Gilfoyle, 14 July 2003, in author's possession.

2. Bryan interview no. 1 (quote); Feldstein interview.

3. Field interview (moon); Paulus interview.

4. Bryan interview no. 2. The official name of the campaign was the Lyric Opera of Chicago/Chicago Symphony Orchestra Facilities Fund; it enabled the Lyric to purchase their office and performance space in 1993. See Paulus interview; CT, 5 March 1993; http://www.lyricopera.org/about/history.asp, last accessed 23 March 2005.

5. Bryan interview no. 2; *Lyric Opera News*, Spring 1993.

6. CT, 26 Oct. 1997; 3 May 1992 (Cummings); *Who's Who in America, 1999* (New Providence, N.J., 1998), 1:571. Details on John Bryan's life here and hereafter are found in John Bryan, Making History Oral History Interview, 5 May 1999, in Collections of the Chicago Historical Society (hereafter Bryan, Making History Interview); and Timothy J. Gilfoyle, "Corporate Consciences: Interviews with John H. Bryan and Newton Minow," *Chicago History* 29 (Summer 2000): 54–65.

7. CT, 26 Oct. 1997.

8. Bryan, Making History Interview; *Economist*, 14 Nov. 1992; *Financial World*, 4 Jan. 1994; CT, 3 May 1992; *Fortune*, 6 Feb. 1995; Sara Lee Narrative History, http://www.saralee.com/history/content_intro.html, accessed May 2003; Gilfoyle, "Corporate Consciences." By 1996, Sara Lee had operations all over the world and employed 150,000 workers. See *Economist*, 25 May 1996. Bryan stepped down as CEO in 2000 and retired as chairman of the board in 2001.

9. *Wall Street Journal*, 13 Oct. 1997; Bryan, Making History interview.

10. *Jet*, 21 Feb. 1994 (Young quote); *Economist*, 25 May 1996; *USA Today*, 27 April 1998.

11. *Business Wire*, 16 Nov. 1998; O'Connor interview.

12. Bryan interview no. 1; LaPietra interview. Bryan was not the first to suggest completion of the breakwater envisioned in Burnham and Bennett's *Plan of Chicago*. Skidmore, Owings &

Merrill and C. F. Murphy Associates had made a similar proposal in 1966. See Skidmore, Owings & Merrill and C. F. Murphy Associates, *Lakefront Development Plan*, 46–49. Adrian Smith had a similar idea. See Smith interview.

13. John H. Bryan's Remarks, Sara Lee Corporation, to Chicagoland Chamber of Commerce, Daniel H. Burnham Award Dinner, Chicago Hilton and Towers, 18 Nov. 1997. Bryan also mentioned earlier plans for a performing arts center on Chicago's lakefront, as well as the Chicago Millennium Project (led by John McCarter and Richard Gray) to erect a sculptural icon for the city and John Borling's (United Way) proposal for a grand millennium structure. Bryan's speech reportedly encouraged Richard M. Daley to think about Lakefront Gardens. Adrian Smith may have also planted the seed in Daley's head when they traveled to Paris together. See Smith interview; unrecorded telephone conversation with Tom Cokins, CCAS, 18 July 2001. On Burnham and Bennett's treatment of Chicago as a work of art, see Burnham and Bennett, *Plan of Chicago*, esp. 78, 100, 118.

14. McCarter interview.

15. Ibid.; Richard Gray interview; Reidy, *Chicago Sculpture*, 260.

16. Bryan interview nos. 1 and 2.

17. Bedore interview.

18. Garvin and Berens, *Urban Parks*, 205–7.

19. Ibid, 149–56.

20. Uhlir interview no. 1. Also see news release, Mayor Richard J. Daley Press Office, 30 March 1998, in Binder. Early projections estimated that $120 million in cost would come from parking fees. Landscaping and enhancements were estimated to be $30 million, which was to be paid from private donations.

21. Feldstein interview; Memo on Mayor Richard M. Daley's Lakefront Millennium Project, Presentations and Discussion Meeting, 16 June 1998 (in author's possession).

22. Feldstein interview; Thomas interview.

23. Bryan interview no. 1; LaPietra interview; Feldstein interview (Lakefront Millennium Gardens).

24. Bryan interview no. 1; Field interview.

25. LaPietra interview; Bryan interview nos. 1 and 2; Field interview; Feldstein interview.

26. Bryan interview no. 1.

27. Ibid.

28. Richard Gray interview; Daley interview; O'Connor interview.

29. Paulus interview.

CHAPTER SIX

1. For a longer discussion of the growing role of art in public planning, see Florida, *Rise of the Creative Class*; Fleming, *Place Makers*.

2. Craig Nakano, "Chicago's Art and Soul," *Los Angeles Times*, 15 June 2001.

3. See the description of Chicago's Public Art Program at http://www.cityofchicago.org/CulturalAffairs/PublicArt/, accessed July 2003. On the 1978 ordinance, see Gray, *Guide to Chicago's Murals*, xxvii; Chicago Department of Cultural Affairs, *Chicago Public Art Locations*, pamphlet. On the early history of public sculpture, see Bogart, *Public Sculpture and the Civic Ideal*.

4. Bryan interview no. 1; Osgood File (CBS Radio Network), "Urban Herds and Murals," 20 Feb. 2002, in *ACFNewssource*.

5. Paulus interview; Bryan interview no. 1.

6. *CT*, 4 June 1895; Bluestone, *Constructing Chicago*, 193–94; Reidy, *Chicago Sculpture*, 9–40, 44–46, 50–51; Bogart, *Public Sculpture and the Civic Ideal*, 298 (Ferguson Fund). *Buckingham Fountain* was designed by architect Edward H. Bennett, the sculpture was completed by Marcel Loyau, and the fountain was renovated in 1994 by Harry Weese Associates.

7. Paulus interview.

8. Lash interview.

9. Richard Gray interview; Bryan interview no. 2; E-mail communication from Rob Omori (Office

of John Bryan) to Timothy Gilfoyle, 11 July 2003, in author's possession (date).

10. Richard Gray interview.

11. Bryan interview nos. 2 and 3; unrecorded conversation with Ed Uhlir, 7 March 2005 (Strick)

12. Bryan interviews no. 1, no. 2 and no. 3.

13. *Crain's Chicago Business*, 2 June 1997; *Innovative Solutions Worldwide: Aon Annual Report for 1997* (1998), 6–17. Ryan received the Horatio Alger Association of Distinguished Americans Award in 1987. See *CT*, 15 May 1987. For more on Ryan, see Gilfoyle, "Wisconsin's Finest," 54–72; *NYT*, 31 Oct. 2004.

14. *NYT*, 2 Oct. 2003; http://www.wavehill.org/horticulture.html, accessed October 2003.

15. *NYT*, 2 Oct. 2003; *CT*, 15 May 1987; *Crain's Chicago Business*, 2 June 1997.

16. Bryan interview no. 2; Lash interview (symmetrical dropping).

17. Paulus interview (initial discussions); Bryan interviews no. 1 (Smith suggested Gehry) and no. 2; Uhlir interview no. 3; Richard Hunt, Making History interview; Paulus interview. Attendees of the first meeting of the Millennium Park Art Committee, 10 July 1998, 8 a.m., included John Bryan (Sara Lee Corp.), Amina Dickerson (Kraft Foods, Inc.), Richard Driehaus (Driehaus Capital Management), Bernard Ford (McDonough Associates), Richard Gray (The Richard Gray Gallery), Sandra Guthman (Polk Bros. Foundation), Michael Lash (for Commissioner Lois Weisberg, Chicago Department of Cultural Affairs), William Parke (for Arthur Martinez, Sears, Roebuck & Co.), Judith Paulus (Sara Lee Corp.), Adrian Smith (Skidmore, Owings & Merrill), Jeremy Strick (Art Institute of Chicago), Marge Susman (former Sotheby's Chicago representative), John Vinci (Vinci/Hamp Architects), and James Wood (Art Institute of Chicago). See E-mail communication, Rob Omori (Office of John Bryan) to Timothy Gilfoyle, 14 July 2003, in author's possession.

18. Bryan interview no. 1; Paulus interview. The fish first appeared in Gehry's work in 1981 in the colonnade of the Smith Residence project. Gehry claimed this initial fish was a "kind of comment

on postmodernism." For an interpretation and examples of "Gehry's fishes," see Dal Co and Forster, *Gehry: Complete Works*, 11–13, 22–24, 54–55, 272, 278–79, 302, 325–32 (quote), 430–33.

19. Friedman, *Gehry Talks*, 8; Ragheb *Frank Gehry*, 13 (quotes on Guggenheim); Greenberg and Jordan, *Frank O. Gehry*, 6 (Think Different).

20. Cindy Pritzker interview.

21. Ibid.

22. Ibid.; Tom Pritzker interview (wife no. 2); *CT*, 24 May 2004 (wife).

23. For biographical details on Pritzker, see Gilfoyle, "Philanthropists as Civic Activists," 60–72.

24. Cindy Pritzker interview; *CS*, 8 Jan. 1998; *CT*, 8 Jan. 1998, 20 Sept. 1989; biographical statement from Cindy Pritzker (in author's possession).

25. *CT*, 12 April 1990; Coburn, "The Prize Pritzker."

26. *CST*, 8 Jan. 1998; *CT*, 8 Jan. 1998, 19 April 1994; Chicago Historical Society Making History Award Citation, 17 May 2001.

27. Feldstein interview.

28. Cindy Pritzker interview; Tom Pritzker interview.

29. Gehry interview (quotes); Smith interview; Frank Gehry interview with Katherine Bliss, on *News 2 at Ten*, WBBM-TV (CBS), Channel 2, Chicago, 24 July 2001; Uhlir interview no. 1.

30. Feldstein interview.

31. Ibid.

32. Uhlir interview no. 2; *Corlands Connection*, Summer 2001. Upon retiring, Uhlir was by law unable to work directly for the city. Instead, he worked for Knight Infrastructures, which in turn billed the city for his services. See *CT*, 15 July 2004.

33. Edward Keith Uhlir resume, in author's possession. Uhlir was technically a consultant and not listed on the city payroll. See Uhlir interview no. 3. The "Lincoln Park Framework Plan" (1993) won awards from the American Society of Landscape Architects and the American Planning Association. "Shoreline Reconstruction Plans for Chicago" (1993), and the "Grant Park Design Guidelines" (1992) contributed to the selection of Uhlir's office for the Burnham Award in Excellence in Planning from the Metropolitan Planning Council of Chicago (1993). His office received the same award in 1998 for "City Spaces—Turning Abandoned Land into Green Assets." Uhlir also received the Distinguished Service Award from the Chicago chapter of the American Institute of Architects in 1999, and the Mary Ward Wolkonsky Award from Friends of Downtown in 2000.

34. Uhlir interview no. 1; Feldstein interview.

35. Gehry claims he was never approached by Cindy Pritzker prior to meeting with Uhlir and Feldstein. See Gehry interview. He reiterated this publicly at "The Architecture of Millennium Park," Millennium Park Symposium, 23 July 2004, Rubloff Auditorium, Art Institute of Chicago. Feldstein and Bryan, however, both believe Gehry was aware of Pritzker's offer. Bryan believes he discussed the proposal with Gehry in the fall of 1998 when they were guests at the White House and recipients of the National Medal of Arts. Pritzker "was the one who really bugged him so much to get him engaged. We worked behind her pushing." See Bryan interview no. 2; Feldstein interview. Craig Webb also thought that Cindy Pritzker made the initial offer to Gehry. See Webb interview.

36. Feldstein interview; Uhlir interview no. 1.

37. Feldstein interview; *CST*, 7 Oct. 2003 (Daley quote).

CHAPTER SEVEN

1. Uhlir interview no. 1.

2. Field interview.

3. Lash interview; Richard Gray interview.

4. Bryan interview no. 2; Field interview.

5. Lash interview.

6. Ibid.; Richard Gray interview.

7. *CT*, 25 Feb. 2000; E-mail communication from Rob Omori (Office of John Bryan) to Timothy Gilfoyle, 14 July 2003, in author's possession

(date of Kapoor visit); Lash interview (drop of mercury).

8. *CT*, 25 Feb. 2000; E-mail communication from Rob Omori (Office of John Bryan) to Timothy Gilfoyle, 14 July 2003, in author's possession.

9. Paulus interview.

10. Bryan interview no. 1 (too confusing) and no. 2; Paulus interview; Uhlir interview no. 3.

11. Lash interview.

12. Bryan interview no. 2; E-mail communication from Rob Omori (Office of John Bryan) to Timothy Gilfoyle, 14 Sept. 2004, in author's possession (April 2000).

13. Lash interview.

14. Millennium Park, Inc., *Invitation to Participate in a Garden Design Competition*, 5–6; Bryan interview no. 2; Waldheim, *Constructed Ground*, ix, 12–13. The garden competition jury consisted of Gerard T. Donnelly, executive director of the Morton Arboretum; Posy Krehbiel, a garden enthusiast; Donna LaPietra, Kurtis Productions; Michael Lash, director of public art for the Chicago Department of Cultural Affairs; Deborah Needleman, editor at large, *House and Garden Magazine*; Janet Meakin Poor, director, Chicago Botanic Gardens; Adrian Smith, SOM; Maria Smithburg, president, Artemisia Landscape Architecture; James Wood, Art Institute; Xavier Vendrell, professor of architecture, UIC; John Vinci, Vinci/Hamp Architects; John Bryan (chair); Edward Uhlir (ex officio). See Millennium Park, Inc., Garden Committee Design Competition, The Jury (no date).

15. Smith interview; Feldstein interview. Also see Cindy Pritzker interview; Uhlir interview no. 1.

16. Gehry interview.

17. Bryan interview no. 1.

18. Smith interview.

19. Gehry quoted in Jean-Louis Cohen, "Frankly Urban: Gehry from Billboards to Bilbao," in Ragheb, *Frank Gehry*, 326; Frank Gehry interview with Katherine Bliss, on *News 2 at Ten* (best architectural city).

20. Van Bruggen, "Leaps into the Unknown," 125–27.

21. Gehry interview.

22. Johnson, Johnson & Roy, *Progress Report on the Future of Chicago's Lakefront*, 15. According to Judith Paulus, the Millennium Park committee spent a great deal of time discussing the Burnham Plan in its early meetings. See Paulus interview.

23. Thomas Pritzker interview.

24. Thomas interview.

25. Gehry interview; Cindy Pritzker interview; Uhlir interview no. 2.

26. Daley interview. On Daley's belief that the sound system was critical, see Talaske interview; Laney interview.

27. Gehry interview. Also see Cindy Pritzker interview.

28. Smith interview. When Smith was interviewed, the estimated costs of the sculpture and pavilion were $5 million and $50 million, respectively. Those enhancements eventually cost in excess of $20 million and $60 million, respectively. On Burnham and Bennett's views of Grant Park, see Bluestone, *Constructing Chicago*, 183, 188, 190–91; Burnham and Bennett, *Plan of Chicago*. For historical analysis of the *Plan of Chicago*, see chapter 2, note 10, above.

29. Smith interview; Lash interview; Field interview.

30. Uhlir interview no. 1.

31. Webb interview.

32. Lash interview.

33. Lash interview. Also see Richard Gray interview. Marshall Field V remembered only limited discussion and influence of the Burnham Plan on Millennium Park. See Field interview.

34. Richard Gray interview; *CT*, 4 Nov. 1999 (Daley). Also see Cindy Pritzker interview.

35. *Daily Inter Ocean*, 10 Aug. 1895; *CT*, 10 Aug. 1895 (another kind of park).

36. *Who's Who in America, 1999* (New Providence, N.J., 1998), 1:571; John H. Bryan Biography, Sara Lee Corp. (in author's possession); Sara Lee website, December 2000.

37. Others in attendance in room 5E at the Chicago Cultural Center included Karen Hansen (for Robert Allgyer and Arthur Andersen), Jill Carter (for Vernon R. Loucks of Baxter International), Chryssa Sanford (for Dennis H. Chookaszian of CNA Financial), Susan Levy (for William L. Davis of R. R. Donnelly & Sons), Richard Driehaus (Driehaus Capital Management), Sue Gin (Flying Food Fare), John Johnson (Johnson Publishing), Adele S. Simmons (MacArthur Foundation), Juanita Jordan (The M&J Endowment Fund), Langdon Neal (for Earl Neal of Earl Neal & Associates), Ron Culp (for Arthur Martinez of Sears), Patricia Asp (for Carlos H. Cantu of ServiceMaster Co.), James J. O'Connor (Unicom), Bob Webb (for Robert Pritzker and the Marmon Group), Gerald M. Greenwald (UAL Corp.), William Piet (for William Wrigley), Maria Bechily, Judy Block, Rosemarie Buntrock, Sandra Guthman (Polk Bros. Foundation), Posy Krehbiel, Donna LaPietra (Kurtis Productions), Susan Manilow, Ella Strubel, and Paula Trienens. Invited but absent were Laurence Fuller (Amoco), Patrick Ryan (Aon), Marshall Field V (Field Corporation), Lester Crown (Material Service Corporation), Ramsey Lewis, Jerry Pearlman, Susan Stone, and Oprah Winfrey. See Memo on Attendance for Presentations and Discussion Meeting, 16 June 1998.

38. Ibid. On Chicago's nineteenth-century cultural philanthropy, see Horowitz, *Culture and the City*; McCarthy, *Noblesse Oblige*. More recent overviews are the essays in Adam, *Philanthropy, Patronage, and Civil Society*; and McCarthy, *American Creed*.

39. E-mail communication, Rob Omori (Office of John Bryan) to Timothy Gilfoyle, 14 July 2003, in author's possession.

40. On McCormick, see Smith, *The Colonel*. While Tribune Company stock remains the key asset of the foundation to this day, the institution is a separate nonprofit organization, independent from Tribune Company. Information on the McCormick Tribune Foundation can be found at http://www.rrmtf.org/mtf/programs.htm, last accessed 23 March 2005.

41. By the twenty-first century, the company's global reach extended to fourteen factories worldwide—three in North America, four in Europe, one in Africa, and five in Asia and the Pacific region. See http://www.wrigley.com/wrigley/about/about_story.asp, accessed January, 2002. *CT*, 9 March 1999.

42. http://www.wrigley.com/wrigley/about/about_story.asp.

43. Piet interview; Bryan interview nos. 1 and 2; *GMA News*, 11 June 2001, available at http://www.gmabrands.com/news/docs/NewsRelease.cfm?docid=774, accessed July 2003. Business reporters sometimes complained that the only time William Wrigley would talk with them was when they cornered him at annual shareholder's meetings. See *CT*, 9 March 1999.

44. Paulus interview; Bryan interview no. 1. Because of the civic nature of the project, Wrigley originally appointed William Piet, president of the Wrigley Company Foundation, to represent the firm at various meetings. Shortly thereafter, Piet was named to the garden committee. See Piet interview.

45. Perille interview; Piet interview; Bryan interview nos. 1 and 2; *CT*, 9 March 1999 (Wrigley obituary). The Wrigley Company Foundation, the company's charitable foundation, traditionally supports not-for-profit causes in education and youth programs. But it also has a component for civic projects, particularly in locales where the Wrigley Company has facilities. See Perille interview.

46. Stephane Fitch, "Pritzker vs. Pritzker," *Forbes*, 24 Nov. 2003; *Sun On-Line*, 24 Jan. 1999, http://www.morningsun.net; Tritsch, "Family Circus," available at http://www.bostonmagazine.com Archives.

47. *CST*, 28 Sept. 1998, based on the Forbes 400; "Forbes Billionaires List (1998)" in Forbes.com; *NYT*, 24 Jan. 1999; *CT*, 24 Jan. 1999; http://www.marmon.com/Profile.html, last accessed 23 March 2005; Coburn, "The Prize Pritzker."

48. *NYT*, 24 Jan. 1999 (napkin); *CST*, 28 Sept. 1998, based on the Forbes 400; "Forbes Billionaires List (1998)" in Forbes.com; *NYT*, 24 Jan. 1999; *CT*, 24 Jan. 1999; http://www.marmon.com/Profile.html; Coburn, "The Prize Pritzker." Another source identified Jay Pritzker as the twentieth-richest American with a fortune of $5 billion. See *Sun On-Line*, 24 Jan. 1999, http://www.morningsun.net, accessed May 2003.

49. Petrakis and Weber, *Henry Crown*, 1:ix, 1–7,; 2:18–30, 48–58, 88–109, 133; *Business Week*, 31 March 1986, 50–54; *Financial World*, 10 Jan. 1989, 34–35; *Forbes*, 13 Oct. 1997, 194.

50. E-mail communication, Rob Omori (Office of John Bryan) to Timothy Gilfoyle, 14 July 2003 (water feature), in author's possession. The annual donations of these and other nonprofit foundations are available in tax form 990-PF for the years 1998 to 2002, available at http://www.guidestar.org/controller/search.gs, last accessed 23 March 2005. Precise figures on the total philanthropic donations by the Crowns and Pritzkers are difficult to find. By 1986, the Crown family had donated more than $75 million to charities, according to one source. See *Business Week*, 31 March 1986, p. 54. From 1991–1998, the Pritzkers pledged $140 million to charities, museums and cultural institutions. See *CT*, 24 Jan. 1999; Coburn, "The Prize Pritzker."

51. E-mail communication, Rob Omori (Office of John Bryan) to Timothy Gilfoyle, 14 July 2003, in author's possession.

52. Field interview; Bryan interview no. 2. On Speyer and Broad as culture power brokers, see *NYT*, 2 June 2004; *Los Angeles Magazine*, June 2003. On Charles Hutchinson, see Horowitz, *Culture and the City*, 50–58.

53. The new (January 2001) goal of $125 million included an endowment of $25 million to manage, maintain, and preserve various enhancements in the park. See Bryan interview no. 1; LaPietra interview.

CHAPTER EIGHT

1. The original SOM plan included an underground 300-seat "performance space" behind the stage of the music pavilion, and another 300-seat outdoor amphitheater at the south end of the Great Lawn. See Chicago Plan Commission, "Report on Lakefront Millennium Project," 14 May 1998, 3.

2. Feldstein interview. The date is based on an e-mail communication from James Feldstein to Timothy Gilfoyle, 29 June 2004, in author's possession, and confirmed by James Alexander's minutes of MDTC directors meeting, 9 Nov. 1998.

3. Joan Harris interview; Sandra Guthman interview; *NYT*, 3 Dec. 2003 (1,000–2,200). By the 1990s, midsized companies were also defined as those with annual budgets ranging from $500,000 to $3 million. See Sandra Guthman interview.

4. Joan Harris interview.

5. Ibid.; Sandra Guthman interview.

6. *CT*, 2 Nov. 2003.

7. Music and Dance Theater Press release, 3 June 2003, at http://www.madtchi.com/03jun03.shtml, accessed July 2003; *CT*, 2 Nov. 2003.

8. Regional Agenda Project, *State of the Region*, VI-2, copy in MHPC publications folder, box 33, HWC.

9. Sandra Guthman interview.

10. Joan Harris interview; Moffatt interview; Music and Dance Theater Press release, 3 June 2003 (1991 date).

11. Joan Harris interview; Moffatt interview; Music and Dance Theater Press release, 3 June 2003 (1991 date).

12. Joan Harris interview; Sandra Guthman interview.

13. On Chicago Opera Theater as the primary impetus behind the creation of MDTC, see *CT*, 23 Dec. 2001.

14. *Hemispheres Magazine*, March 2001; *CT*, 25 Oct. 1999; *Nation's Restaurant News*, 5 March 2001, at http://articles.findarticles.com/p/articles/mi_m3190/is_10_35/ai_71564009, accessed September 2003. The Cadillac Palace Theater (originally 1926) is located at 151 West Randolph Street. The Ford Center for the Performing Arts, Oriental Theater (originally 1926) is at 24 West Randolph Street. The Chicago Theater is at 175 North State Street. Storefront Theater is at 66 East Randolph Street.

15. *Chicago Philanthropy*, Sept. 1996.

16. Sandra Guthman interview.

17. Moffatt interview; Joan Harris interview.

18. Uhlir interview no. 1; Joan Harris interview.

19. *Chicago Philanthropy*, Sept. 1996.

20. Bryan interview no. 1; Feldstein interview. The date is based on an e-mail communication from James Feldstein to Timothy Gilfoyle, 29 June 2004, in author's possession, and confirmed by James Alexander's minutes of MDTC directors meeting, 9 Nov. 1998.

21. Uhlir interview no. 1; Moffatt interview; Sandra Guthman interview; Uhlir interview no. 3.

22. Ironically, Beeby had been an apprentice architect at C. F. Murphy Associates in 1972 and worked in the same room as Gene Summers while the latter designed an outdoor music pavilion on the site of the Monroe Street Garage. The project was eventually shelved because civic groups and landlords surrounding Grant Park considered the 59-foot-high translucent pavilion to be too tall. See Beeby interview; chapter 3, notes 22–25, above.

23. Sandra Guthman interview; Uhlir interview no. 3.

24. Beeby interview.

25. Beeby interview; Sandra Guthman interview (25 percent).

26. Mayer and Wade, *Chicago*, 294.

27. Sandra Guthman interview.

28. Uhlir interview nos. 1, 3. On Joan Harris asking Guthman to represent the MDTC, see Jack Guthman interview.

29. *Chicago* Magazine, March 2002, p. 66.

30. Ibid.

31. Jack Guthman interview.

32. Ibid.

33. Ibid.; Moffatt interview; *City of Chicago v. Ward*, 169 Ill. 392 at 420; 48 N.E. 927 at 936 (1897), generally referred to as *Ward I*; *John and Mildred Boaz v. City of Chicago, Chicago Park District and Plan commission of the City of Chicago*, Case 99L, Number 3804, 5 April 1999 (hereafter *Boaz v. Chicago*).

34. Uhlir interview no. 1.

35. Jack Guthman interview.

36. Ibid.

37. Uhlir interview no. 1; Institutional/Transportation Planned Development no. 677, as Amended, Longitudinal Section at Stage center Line Looking East, in Chicago Plan Commission, "Lakefront Millennium Project, revised," 11 March 1999.

38. Moffatt interview; Uhlir interview no. 3.

39. Jack Guthman interview.

40. Ibid.

41. See Advocates of Change on Symphony Orchestra Institute, http://www.soi.org; Program for Annual Conference for Conductors, 3–6 Jan. 2002, Chicago, Ill.

42. CST, 6 April 1999.

43. Jack Guthman interview.

44. Ibid.; *Boaz v. Chicago*.

45. Feldstein interview; Moffatt interview.

46. Field interview.

47. CT, 23 Dec. 2001 (complaints, Kalver), 12 Jan. 2003 (Lipman), 5 Dec. 2004 (Lipman).

48. CT, 23 Dec. 2001 (Chicago Opera Theater), 12 Jan. 2003 (Hubbard), 5 Dec. 2004.

49. NYT, 23 July 2001.

50. Field interview; Moffatt interview; Alexander interview. The 16 donations shared between Millennium Park and the Music and Dance Theater were: Dick and Lana Cooper, Judy and Jamie Dimon, the Glasser and Rosenthal family, Sandra and Jack Guthman, the Kaplan family, the Kovler family, John and Alexandra Nichols, Helen and Sam Zell, the Lloyd A. Fry Foundation, JMB Realty Corp., the Francis L. Lederer Foundation, LaSalle Bank, the Morse trusts, Polk Bros. Foundation, the Prince Charitable Trust, and the Siragusa Foundation. See Moffatt interview.

51. Alexander interview.

52. CT, 2 Nov. 2003; *Sightlines* (undated).

53. Music and Dance Theater Press release, 3 June 2003, at http://www.madtchi.com/03jun03.shtml, accessed July 2003; Biographical sketch of Irving B. Harris (in author's possession); *University of Chicago News*, 23 Nov. 1998; NYT, 16 Nov. 1986; CT, 22 Sept. 1996. Of all philanthropists in the United States, Harris was ranked 57th in 1999, 67th in 2000. See *Worth*, April 1999, April 2000. For more on Irving Harris, see Irving Harris interview; Gilfoyle, "Philanthropists as Civic Activists," 60–72.

54. CT, 23 Dec. 2001; Moffatt interview; *Sightlines* (undated).

55. *Sightlines*, Jan. 2003.

56. Moffatt interview; Alexander interview.

57. CT, 4 June 2003. Moffatt interview; Alexander interview. By June 2004, the MDTC had raised over $62 million. In December 2004, Harris Theater trustees announced that the institution had raised enough money to pay off the construction loan made by Irving Harris. See CT, 5 Dec. 2004. A list of trustees appears in appendix 5.

CHAPTER NINE

1. LaPietra interview. Blair Kamin used a similar term in his review of Millennium Park. See CT, 18 July 2004. The beneficence and patronage of the Medici family, particularly Lorenzo de Medici, is a subject of historical debate. Nevertheless, the Augustine Church of San Lorenzo, designed by Brunelleschi with a pulpit by Donatello and the sacristy with tombs by Michaelangelo, was a product of Medici patronage, as were the literary works deposited in Michelangelo's Laurentian Library. Lorenzo was also a financial supporter of various musicians. See Kent, *Medici and the Art of Magnificence*. A brief summary of Medici patronage appears at http://www.vanderbilt.edu/htdocs/Blair/Courses/MUSL242/f98/robing.htm, accessed 23 March 2005.

2. On the "new economy," see Alcaly, *New Economy*; Florida, *Rise of the Creative Class*.

3. Fifteen donations from Forbes 400 members listed from 1998 to 2003 included Robert Pritzker, Thomas Pritzker, William Wrigley, Lester Crown, Samuel Zell, Oprah Winfrey, Neil Gary Bluhm, Michael Krasney, John Krehbiel, Fred Krehbiel, Patrick Ryan, Gary Comer, Ken Griffin, Theodore Schwartz, and the Searle family. Forbes 400 members who did not contribute to

Millennium Park included H. Ty Warner (Ty and Beanie Babies), Michael Birck (Tellabs), Robert Galvin (Motorola), Marvin Herb (Coca-Cola Bottling of Chicago), Michael Heisley, Sr. (Heico Acquisitions), and the Donnelly family.

4. On Chicago as a leading commercial center, see Cronon, *Nature's Metropolis*.

5. The total number of donors or founders was 115, of whom 80 possessed wealth derived exclusively or in part from a service-sector activity. Because of the overlapping sources of wealth of certain donors, some were included in more than one category. Consequently, the added total percentages in appendix 6 and this discussion sometimes exceed 100. Individual and family donors with a mixture of wealth from FIRE and industry include Crown, Granoff, Gray, Neison Harris, Irving Harris, Heineman, Jordan, Prince, Pritzker, Sick, and the Morse trusts. Duchossois family wealth originates in service and industrial activity, the Kaplan and Kohl families in retail and industry, the Fields in FIRE and retail, and the Guthmans in retail and service. I was unable to determine the source of wealth of the Slezak family or the anonymous donor.

6. For data on metropolitan Chicago employment, see Illinois Department of Employment Security, 2003, at http://www.ci.chi.il.us/PlanAndDevelop/ChgoFacts/Business.html.

7. Ibid. These workers were spread out over a wide array of industries, making the Chicago metropolitan area the most diverse in the United States. Sectors such as food processing (9.4% of manufacturing employment), paper and allied products (4.2%), printing and publishing (11.6%), chemicals and allied products (7.6%), rubber and other plastic products (7.2%) primary metals (3.8%), fabricated metals (12.1%), industrial machinery (12.8%), electronics (14.2%), transportation equipment (2.9%), and instrumentation (3.8%) evidenced the varieties of Chicago manufacturing. See http://www.worldbusinesschicago.com/whychi/landscape/manufacturing.asp#top, last accessed 23 March 2005.

8. On the Lloyd A. Fry Foundation, see http://www.fryfoundation.org. On the Siragusa Foundation and Admiral, see http://www.siragusa.org/aboutUs.html. On the Kaplan Family Foundation, see http://www.kapfam.com/. On the Prince Charitable Trust, see http://fdncenter.org/grantmaker/prince/. Dolores Kohl Kaplan

is a descendant of the founder of Kohl's department store. See Bryan interview no. 3.

9. http://www.marmon.com/Profile.html, last accessed 23 March 2005

10. http://www.molex.com, accessed July 2004

11. http://www.baxter.com/about_baxter/company_profile/sub/globalpresence.html, accessed July 2004.

12. Illinois Tool Works, "Company Overview," March 2001, at http://www.itw.com/about.html, accessed April 2001.

13. http://www.wrigley.com, accessed Oct. 2003.

14. Fourteen individual donors were associated with Fortune 500 companies: John Bryan (Sara Lee), Dean Buntrock (Waste Management), Jamie Dimon (Bank One), Bill Graham (Baxter), Verne Istock (Bank One), Vernon Loucks (Baxter), Richard Morrow (Amoco), John Nichols (Illinois Tool Works), James O'Connor (Exelon), Patrick Ryan (Aon), William Searle (G. D. Searle), Daniel Searle (G. D. Searle), Robert D. Stuart, Jr. (Quaker Oats), and Richard Thomas (First Bank of Chicago).

15. Bryan pointed out that although UBS was headquartered in Zurich, the firm had a large presence in Chicago. See Bryan interview no. 3. By 2004, UBS was one of the largest investment banking operations in Chicago, ranking in the top eight firms based on the number of Chicago-based investment banking professionals. See *Crain's Chicago Business*, 20 Sept. 2004.

16. This would include the Marmon Group and H Holding Group (both controlled by Pritzker concerns), Duchossois Industries, CC Industries (controlled by the Crown family), and Jordan Industries.

17. *Los Angeles Times*, 30 Aug. 2003, at http://www.calendarlive.com/cl-et-reynolds30aug30,0,3168348.story.

18. *Los Angeles Times*, 30 Aug. 2003, at http://www.calendarlive.com/cl-et-reynolds30aug30,0,3168348.story.

19. Kimmel Center Press release, 20 March 2001, available at http://www.kimmelcenter.org/news/item.php?item=2001-03-20, accessed June 2003.

Similarly, although the $98.6 million Music Center at Strathmore in North Bethesda, Maryland, advertised itself as a public-private partnership, the state of Maryland and Montgomery County paid for most of the construction, while the private sector contributed a $10 million endowment. See *Washington Post*, 3 Feb. 2005; *Washington Times*, 5 Feb. 2005.

20. John Bryan biography, Sara Lee Corporation.

21. By one account, the most prestigious Chicago boards for nonprofit institutions are Chicago Symphony Orchestra, Lyric Opera of Chicago, University of Chicago, Rush Presbyterian–St. Luke's Medical Center, Art Institute of Chicago, and YMCA of the USA. See *Worth Magazine*, March 2003, available at http://www.harvestto-day.org/topboards.htm, accessed June, 2004.

22. The specific amounts were: CSO, $200 million; Lyric Opera, $200 million; Museum of Science and Industry, $160 million; Field Museum, $134 million; Art Institute, $120 million. National giving declined 2.8 percent from 1996 to 1997. *CT*, 29 Jan. 1999. On the influence of Bryan's success in the CSO/Lyric campaign, see Goodban interview.

23. Trustees of CSO included James L. Alexander (Morse Trust), Naomi Borwell, Matthew Bucksbaum, Dean Buntrock (Waste Management), Richard Cooper, James S. Crown, Deborah De-Haas, H. Laurance Fuller, William B. Graham (Baxter), Kenneth Griffin, Ben W. Heineman, Judy Istock, Frederick Krehbiel, Arthur Martinez (Sears), Steve McMillan (Sara Lee), Newton Minow (Sidley & Austin), John D. Nichols (Illinois Tool Works and Marmon Group), James O'Connor (Exelon), William Osborn, Robert A. Pritzker (Marmon Group), John W. Rogers (Ariel), William L. Searle, Richard Thomas, Paula Trienens, and Eleanor Wood Prince. Directors of Lyric Opera include: James L. Alexander (Morse Trust), Lester Crown, William B. Graham (Baxter), William Osborn, and Sidney Port.

24. Bryan was named a trustee of the Art Institute in 1983. See Art Institute of Chicago, *Annual Report, 1983–1984*, 72. Donors serving on Art Institute committees included Gilda Buchbinder, Rosemarie Buntrock, Sue Dixon, Richard Driehaus, Catherine Graham, Kay Krehbiel, Muriel Kallis Newman, Eleanor Wood Prince, Nicholas Pritzker and Stephanie Sick. See Art Institute of Chicago, *Annual Report, 2001–2002*, 47–49; idem, *1999–2000*, 41–43; idem, *1995–1996*, 40–43.

25. Trustees at the University of Chicago included John Bryan, James Crown, Jamie Dimon, Craig Duchossois, James Glasser, William Graham, Irving Harris, King Harris, Ben Heineman, Edgar Jannotta, Dennis J. Keller, John Mabie, Richard Morrow, Thomas Jay Pritzker, John Rogers (Ariel), Byron Trott (Goldman Sachs). Trustees of Northwestern University included Lester Crown, Steven Crown, Deborah DeHaas, Ira Harris, Nancy Trienens Kaehler, Morris Kaplan, Lester B. Knight, Ann and Robert Lurie, Martha Grimes Mabie, Arthur Martinez (Sears), Newton Minow, James O'Connor (Exelon), William Osborn, John Rowe (Exelon), Patrick Ryan, D. C. Searle, D. Gideon Searle, Richard Thomas, Howard Trienens, and William Wrigley, Jr.

26. Museum of Contemporary Art trustees: Richard Cooper, Kenneth Griffin, Jack Guthman, Nicki Harris, King Harris, Joan Harris, Anne Kaplan, Sally Meyers Kovler, Muriel Kallis Newman, Penny Pritzker, and Helen Zell. See Museum of Contemporary Art, *2003 Annual Report* (Chicago, 2003), 5, available at http://www.mcachicago.org/MCA/About/pdf/AnnualReport03.pdf, accessed August 2004.

27. The Lloyd Fry, Francis Lederer, Morse/Genius, and Siragusa foundations had no representatives in the Commercial Club. Members of the Commercial Club of Chicago who contributed to Millennium Park included Carol Bernick, Howard Bernick, John Bryan, Gary Comer, James Crown, Lester Crown, Susan Crown, Wesley M. Dixon, Jr., Craig Duchossois, Jonathan Fanton (MacArthur Foundation), Marshall Field V, William B. Graham, Sandra P. Guthman (Polk Bros. Foundation), J. Ira Harris, Ben W. Heineman, Sr., Lawrence Howe (Chicago Community Trust), Verne Istock, Edgar Jannotta, Dennis Keller, Fred Krehbiel, Lester Knight, Alan J. Lacy (Sears), Leonard Lavin, John Mabie, John Madigan (Tribune Corp.), Arthur Martinez (Sears), Robert McCormack, Newton Minow, Richard M. Morrow, John Nichols, James O'Connor (Exelon), William A. Osborn, Penny Pritzker, Robert A. Pritzker, Thomas J. Pritzker, Bruce Rauner, John W. Rogers, Jr. (Ariel Capital Management), John W. Rowe (Exelon), Patrick Ryan, D. C. Searle, Harrison Steans, Donald M. Stewart (Chicago Community Trust), John Swearingen (Amoco), Richard L. Thomas, Howard J. Trienens, Byron D. Trott (Goldman Sachs), Robert A. Wislow, and William Wrigley, Jr. See Commercial Club of Chicago Membership at http://www.commercialclubchicago.org/memebers/, last accessed 23 March 2005.

28. Donors to CHF included Naomi Borwell, Henry and Gilda Buchbinder, Richard and Lana Cooper, Sandra and Jack Guthman, MacArthur Foundation, Polk Bros. Foundation, Bank One, Chicago Community Trust, Exelon Corporation, James Glasser, Judy and Verne Istock, Mayer and Morris Kaplan Family Foundation, Newton and Josephine Minow, John and Alexandra Nichols, LaSalle Bank Corporation, Lois and Harrison Steans, Lloyd A. Fry Foundation, the Harris Foundation, Janet and Richard Morrow, Abbott Laboratories, Edgar Jannotta, Muriel Kallis Newman, Sara Lee Foundation, Dennis and Connie Keller , Frederick and Kay Krehbiel, Patrick and Shirley Ryan, Richard and Helen Thomas, Eleanor Prince. See List of Donors, Chicago Humanities Festival, 2002–2003, at http://www.chfestival.org/sponsorship.cfm?Action=Donors, accessed July 2004.

29. Millennium Park donors who were members of the American Academy of Arts & Sciences included John Bryan, Lester Crown, Jonathan Fanton (MacArthur Foundation), Irving B. Harris, Ben Heineman, Sr., and Newton Minow. See http://www.amacad.org/members/searchname.htm, accessed May 2004.

30. Bryan interview no. 2.

31. Ibid.

32. Bryan personally knew at least 47 of the 75 individual and family donors through business, civic, or other relationships, 13 of the 25 corporations, and 9 of the 15 foundations. Individuals and institutions with whom Bryan enjoyed a personal friendship or civic relationship included Barbara and James Bere, Gilda and Henry Buchbinder, Kay and Matthew Bucksbaum, Rosemarie and Dean Buntrock, Francie and Gary Comer, the Crown family, Judy and Jamie Dimon, Sue and Wes Dixon, Janet and Craig Duchossois, Linda and Bill Gantz, Louise and Jim Glasser, William Graham, Perry and Marty Granoff, Sandra and Jack Guthman, Bette and Neison Harris, Natalie and Ben W. Heineman, Sr., Blair Hull, Judy and Verne Istock, Debby and Ned Jannotta, Connie and Dennis Keller, Posy and John Krehbiel, Kay and Fred Krehbiel, Bill Kurtis and Donna La Pietra, Sue and Vernon Loucks, Martha and John Mabie, Mary and Robert McCormack, Josephine and Newton Minow, Janet and Richard M. Morrow, Muriel Kallis Newman, John D. and Alexandra Nichols, James and Ellen O'Connor, Suzie and Jim Otterbeck, Sidney Port, Eleanor

and William Wood Prince, the Pritzker family, Shirley and Patrick Ryan, Sally and Bill Searle, Dan Searle, Bill and Stephanie Sick, Lois and Harrison Steans, Robert Stuart, Jerome Stone, Helen and Richard Thomas, Howard J. and Paula M. Trienens, Oprah Winfrey, Robert A. Wislow, Lisa W. and James J. Zenni, Jr., the Aon Corporation (Patrick Ryan), Arthur Andersen (Deborah DeHaas) Ariel Mutual Funds (John Rogers), Bank One (Jamie Dimon), Baxter (William Graham), BP America, Inc. (John Browne), Deloitte (Deborah DeHaas), Exelon (James O'Connor), Goldman Sachs (Byron Trott), JMB Realty (Neil and Barbara Bluhm), Sara Lee Corporation, SBC (Richard Notebaert), William Wrigley, Jr., Company Foundation (William Wrigley, Jr.), Cooper Family Foundation (Lana and Dick Cooper), Marshall and Jamee Field Family Fund (Marshall Field V), J. Ira and Nicki Harris Foundation (J. Ira Harris), MacArthur Foundation (Jonathan Fanton), Robert R. McCormick Tribune Foundation (Neil Creighton), Elizabeth Morse & Elizabeth Morse Genius Charitable Trusts (James Alexander), Polk Bros. Foundation (Sandra Guthman), The Searle Funds of the Chicago Community Trust (Donald Stewart and the Searle family), the Siragusa Foundation (John Siragusa). This is not to say Bryan was alone in attracting gifts. According to Bryan, Marshall Field was responsible for generating gifts from Wes Dixon, Bill Searle, and Dan Searle, while Richard Thomas was responsible for attracting gifts from Naomi and Robert Borwell, Gary Brinson, CNA Insurance, and others in the banking community. Sandra Guthman was instrumental in recruiting donations from Richard Cooper, Lindy and Michael Keiser, the Kovler Foundation, the Polk Bros. Foundation, and the 16 gifts shared between Millennium Park, Inc., and the Harris Theater. See Bryan interview nos. 2 and 3.

33. O'Connor interview; Thomas interview.

34. LaPietra interview.

35. Field interview.

36. Piet interview.

37. *Economist*, 14 Nov. 1992; *Wall Street Journal*, 29 Sept. 1992.

38. Based on political contributions made by individual donors to state and national party organizations, or to various candidates for elective office. Thirty-nine (53%) were primarily Republican and 27 (37%) were primarily Democrats. Seven others (10%) gave to both parties. See

publications of the Illinois Campaign for Political Reform at:

Http://www.ilcampaign.org/sunshine/patrons/profiles/; http://www.tray.com/cgi-win/x_allindiv.exe; and http://www.opensecrets.org, all last accessed March 2005. Some gave contributions to candidates from both parties. In those cases, I counted an affiliation only if they donated to a national or state party organization.

39. *Economic Focus* (published by World Business Chicago), Feb. 2001, available at http://www.worldbusinesschicago.com/about/upload/102-01-01.pdf, last accessed 23 March 2005.

40. Sassen, *Global City*, 3–7. The literature on globalization is vast. See especially Kresl and Gappert, *North American Cities and the Global Economy*; LaFaber, *Michael Jordan*.

41. NYT, 15 Jan. 2004; Thomas, Making History interview.

42. Bryan interview no. 3. Phillip Morris acquired Kraft in a 1988 hostile takeover. The $13.1 billion purchase was the largest nonoil merger in United States history at the time.

43. McCarter interview.

44. The gross regional products were: Russia, $347 billion; Taiwan, $282 billion; and Switzerland, $267 billion. See World Business Chicago, *The Global Chicago: Business Center of the Hemisphere* (Chicago, no date), available at http://www.ftaa-alca.org/tnc/submissions/tni148a1_e.pdf, accessed July 2004; *Crain's Chicago Business*, 7 April 2003.

45. *Crain's Chicago Business*, 21 April 1997. Family foundations are defined as grant-making, independent foundations with measurable donor or donor-family involvement. See *Key Facts on Family Foundations*, Feb. 2004, at http://fdncenter.org/research/trends_analysis/pdf/key_facts_ff.pdf, last accessed March 2005.

46. Bryan admitted that some donors identified as individual or family contributors to Millennium Park gave their gifts through a family foundation, but were listed on the peristyle as individuals and families, not as foundations. See Bryan interview no. 2.

47. Bryan interview no. 2; http://www.bea.gov/bea/newsrel/gsp_glance.htm (lowest quintile),

accessed July 2004; *CT*, 20 May 2003(budget deficits). Richard Thomas expressed a similar view of the Lyric/Symphony campaign as well: "When I look back at it, the timing was right. We couldn't get that done today. There aren't enough corporations left in the Loop to pull that off." See Richard Thomas, Making History interview.

CHAPTER TEN

1. *CT*, 5 Aug. 2001.

2. *CT*, 30 March 1986, 7 April 1987 (State of Illinois Center), 11 Nov. 1988, 28 Sept. 1991 (McCormick Place); Mier, "Economic Development," 93.

3. *CT*, 13 Jan. 2002. Daley administration officials countered that Millennium Park construction involved no *neighborhood* property taxes. The Central Loop Tax Increment [Financing] District was created in 1984 and obtained funds from tax increments gained from rising downtown property values that are above the base level set in 1983 when the district was created. Most of those revenues came from commercial properties and were employed for economic development and public works. Ideally, such projects increase property values in the immediate and surrounding neighborhood. See Public Building Commission, press release, 10 Jan. 2001; Neighborhood Capital Budget Group, "TIF Profile: Central Loop," undated, available at http://www.ncbg.org/tifs/tifprofile.aspx?id=15, last accessed 23 March 2005. Chicago originally designated four TIF areas; by 2003, eleven such areas existed in the city. See *CT*, 4 June 2003.

4. *CST*, 29 Aug. 2001 (Roeder); Steve Rhodes, "The Case against Daley," *Chicago Magazine*, Dec. 2002, p. 115; Metropolitan Tenants Organization flyer, 21 Aug. 2002. The Metropolitan Tenants Organization (MTO) complained that more than $38 million in TIF funds could have been used to create 2,870 units of affordable housing. In contrast to the MTO's assertion, TIF funds were frequently used in "nonblighted" areas. One North Side TIF fund, for example, financed $50,000 improvements for small businesses like the Wooden Spoon, a gourmet kitchenware store on North Clark in Andersonville. Other companies that used TIF funds include the Goose Island Brewing Co. (to repair a loading dock), and

Bernacki & Associates (to finance renovations on an art framing and restoration store). See *CT*, 4 June 2003.

5. *CT*, 17 June 2004; *NYT*, 13 July 2004. Also see Dick Simpson, "Contract, Connections and Corruption at Chicago City Hall," WBEZ Radio, 23 June 2004, available at http://www.wbez.org/audio_library/848_rajune04.asp, last accessed 23 March 2005; *CT*, 21 Dec. 2001.

6. *CT*, *CST*, 8 Aug. 2001. Less than two months after the *Tribune* editorial charged the Daley administration with corruption, reporters asked Daley if he doubted that the *Tribune*-owned Chicago Cubs had performed the million dollar repairs on Wrigley Field as they claimed, Daley responded: "I don't know. Don't ask me. 'I doubt?' Then 'The mayor doubts the Tribune.' That's the headline you want, and I will get another editorial. They will get mad and will write an editorial." See *CT*, 11 Aug. 2004; *NYT*, 26 Aug. 2004. For an interpretation of the origins of the *Tribune*-Daley feud, see *Crain's Chicago Business*, 30 Aug. 2004.

7. Feldstein interview; *CT*, 15 Aug. 2001 (conventional illiteracy).

8. Gehry interview.

9. Gehry interview. Tom Pritzker believes the media and others exaggerated the tension between Daley and Gehry. In conversations with Pritzker, Gehry reportedly said something like "I've got 142 other things going on right now. This is number 37 on my list of priorities. . . . It's not that big a deal." See Thomas Pritzker interview.

10. *CT*, 5 Aug. 2001.

11. Lakefront Millennium Project, Resolution of Approval, 14 May 1998, Chicago Plan Commission, in Binder.

12. *Daily Southtown Southeast*, 21 May 1998.

13. *CT*, 5 Aug. 2001; Bedore interview (12 subcontractors); confidential source. The three principal construction contracts went to McDonough (contract), Kenny and SOM (subcontract).

14. *CT*, 5 Aug. 2001.

15. Ibid.

16. Uhlir interview no. 2. Daley briefly considered Public Building Commissioner Ben Reyes's

suggestion to simply fill in the garage, and rely solely on the Millennium Park garage. Michigan Avenue businesses and educational institutions quickly objected, pointing out that they relied on the garage. Rather than postpone the problem, the city elected to rebuild the garage. See Uhlir interview no. 1. Construction began in May 1999. See *CT*, 2 May 1999; 7 July 1999; 10 March 2001. Reconstruction of the North Garage was done by the Public Building Commission, headed by Ben Reyes and Teng Associates (who did the Lake Shore Drive relocation). This came out of another budget funded by TIF funds and a $70 million bond issue. Expenses related to the reconstruction of the Grant Park North Garage were never included in the cost of Millennium Park. Uhlir interview no. 3. The final breakdown of car spaces in the three garages bounded by Lake Shore Drive, Randolph Street, Michigan Avenue and Monroe Street are:

Reconstructed North Garage	1,900 *car spaces*
Millennium Park Garage	2,181
Monroe Street Garage	3,800
TOTAL	7,960

17. Bryan interview no. 1.

18. Chicago Plan Commission, "Lakefront Millennium Project, revised," 11 March 1999, 2–3. A tenth change included constructing 150 additional subsurface parking spaces under the Monroe Street parking garage east of Columbus Drive and adjacent to Millennium Park, but was never completed.

19. Confidential source, July 2003. On tensions between Millennium Park officials and SOM over budgetary matters relating to the peristyle and ice skating rink, see Uhlir interview no. 1.

20. The original private contribution was estimated to be $22.5 million for projects, $7.5 million for endowment. The actual total was $150 million—$120 million for construction and $30 million for enhancements. See Uhlir interview nos. 1, 3.

21. Bedore interview; *CT*, 5 Aug. 2001.

22. The pavilion cost $60.3 million: the city contributed $25.4 million for the pavilion superstructure, while private donors paid $31.9 million for the trellis, $2.5 million for the sound enhancement system, and $500,000 for the fixed seating.

23. Bedore interview.

24. Public Building Commission, *Annual Report for 2000* (Chicago, 2001), 21; Field interview; Bedore interview; unrecorded conversation with Ed Uhlir, 7 March 2005 ($17 million for sculpture). The original 60-ton weight of Kapoor's sculpture was an estimate. No one knew the precise thickness of the steel until the design was completed. See Uhlir interview no. 2.

25. Webb interview; Bedore interview ($45 million); Gehry interview. Webb also claimed that between 1999 and 2002, the construction industry witnessed an unexpected escalation in prices. On the rising price of steel during 2000 and 2001, see *Pittsburgh Business Times*, 16 Aug. 2001, available at http://www.bizjournals.com/pittsburgh/stories/2001/08/13/daily28.html?jst=s3_rs_hl, accessed June 2003.

26. *CT*, 5 Aug. 2001. The *Tribune* also charged that city officials may have violated state purchasing law by negotiating a new price, especially since the price increased.

27. *CT*, 18 July 2004.

28. Ibid.

29. *CT*, 5 Aug. 2001; "Millennium Park Overruns," *Chicago Tonight*, no. 19023, WTTW-TV (PBS), Channel 11, Chicago, 9 August 2001. Harston, described as an influential African American contractor who served as president of Black Contractors United, was a member of Republican governor Jim Edgar's transition team in 1990. See *CT*, 6 June 2000.

30. *CT*, 14 Nov. 2001.

31. *CT*, 5 Aug. 2001.

32. Confidential sources.

33. In the rush to complete the fast-track project, city officials overlooked some of their own regulations. For example, the city reportedly failed to follow the permit process. The permit for the foundation was obtained in 1998, but the permit for the garage was not submitted until September 1999, when construction had been underway for two months. See *CT*, 5 Aug. 2001.

34. *CT*, 13 Jan. 2002.

35. Millennium Park garage revenue for 2002 totaled $4.08 million. See Public Building Com-

mission, press release, 8 Jan. 2003. In 2003, the garage generated over $4.9 million in net revenue. See http://midwest.construction.com/features/archive/0405_cover.asp, last accessed 24 March 2005. In 2004, garage revenue was $7.5 million. See *Crain's Chicago Business*, 2 May 2005. The city never again resorted to dipping into the Central Loop TIF to meet the debt service requirements on the garage. Motorist usage also dropped from 635,000 in 2003 to 602,000 in 2004. On the failure to cover bond payments in early 2005, see *CT*, 20 Jan. 2005, 16 Feb. 2005.

36. Field interview; Thomas interview; Jack Guthman interview.

37. Uhlir interview no. 2.

38. Smith interview. *Tribune* reporters Andrew Martin and Laurie Cohen conceded that the fast-track process contributed to many of the park's problems. See *CT*, 5 Aug. 2001.

39. Gehry interview.

40. Feldstein interview.

41. *CT*, 1 Aug. 2003.

42. Neighborhood Capital Budget Group, "Following the Money for Millennium Park," July 2004, available at http://www.ncbg.org/public_works/millennium_park.htm, last accessed 22 March 2005; idem., *TIF Almanac* (Chicago, 2003), 96–101, available at http://www.ncbg.org/documents/TIF%20ALMANAC%207%2003.doc, last accessed 22 March 2005.

43. Uhlir interview no. 1; unrecorded conversation with Uhlir, 7 March 2005.

44. *CT*, 5 Aug. 2001; John Bryan and Members of the Millennium Park Executive Committee to Founders of Millennium Park, 10 Aug. 2001, in possession of author.

45. *CT*, 5 Aug. 2001; John Bryan and Members of the Millennium Park Executive Committee to Founders of Millennium Park, 10 Aug. 2001, in possession of author; E-mail communication, Rob Omori (Office of John Bryan) to Timothy Gilfoyle, 14 July 2003, in author's possession; Paul Gray interview (Plensa).

46. *CT*, 5 April 1998 (Kamin review); Richard J. Daley, "Lakefront Millennium Project: The Completed Vision" (Chicago, 1998); *Notes: The Newsletter of the Lakefront Millennium Project* 1, July 1998;

Daily Southtown South, 31 March 1998.

47. *CT*, 25 July 1999 (Duff); *Chicago Magazine*, July 2004.

48. Baldassare, *When Government Fails* (Orange Co.); *NYT*, 7 Sept. 2004 (thoroughly corrupt), 2 Jan. 2005 (open sewer); *CT*, 20 Aug. 2004; Cooley, *When Corruption Was King*.

49. *The Art Newspaper*, at http://www.theartnewspaper.com/news/article.asp?idart=11604, last accessed 21 March 2005.

50. Uhlir interview no. 1; Bryan interview no. 1 ($400–$500 million). City of Chicago, "Lakefront Millennium Project Parking Facilities Bonds (for $33,868,391.20) Statement," 1 July 1999, 2. The breakdown was:

Parking facilities	$ 92,250,000
Park and performance facilities, lakefront bus route, on-site improvements	$101,400,000
Enhancements	$ 40,200,000
TOTAL CONSTRUCTION BUDGET	$233,850,000

Also see: Neighborhood Capital Budget Group, "Funding Millennium Park," undated, available at http://www.ncbg.org/public_works/park_update.htm, last accessed 24 March 2005; Neighborhood Capital Budget Group, "Following the Money for Millennium Park," July 2004, available at http://www.ncbg.org/public_works/millennium_park.htm, accessed September 2004 ($33 million bond); "Millennium Park Overruns," *Chicago Tonight* ($35 million). In August 2001, Daley wanted to take another $30–$50 million from TIF. See ibid. A later *Tribune* story claimed that the City used $280,000 in July 2001, to cover the debt and $3.1 million on 1 Jan. 2002. See *CT*, 13 Jan. 2002. At one point, Uhlir even contemplated inviting the Metropolitan Pier and Exposition Authority to take control of the park as a cost-saving measure. "Then they would have all these resources to add to the management of the park," he believed. See Uhlir interview no. 2.

51. Mehrberg interview; Booth interview.

52. Telephone interview with Richard Hanson, Mesa Development and the Heritage at Millennium Park, 17 Aug. 2004; Uhlir interview no. 2. On increased sales and real estate values surrounding Grant Park after the opening of Millennium Park, see *Crain's Chicago Business*, 6 Sept. 2004; *CT*,

17 Oct. 2004. Also see the *Crain's Chicago Business*, 3 May 2004, special advertising supplement. For early examinations of the Heritage at Millennium Park, see CT, 12 Aug. 2001, 14 June 2001; *Illinois Real Estate Journal*, 11 Feb. 2002. On Richard Daley's belief that Millennium Park would increase downtown real estate values, see *Midwest Construction*, May 2004. The 82-story Aon Center increased in value from $174 per square foot in 1998 to $186 per square foot in 2003. Next door, Shorenstein Co. LP (of San Francisco) paid $387 million ($187 per square foot) for Prudential Plaza in 2000. See CT, 25 Oct. 2002.

53. Neighborhood Capital Budget Group, *TIF Almanac* (Chicago, 2003), 96–101, available at http://www.ncbg.org/documents/TIF%20ALMANAC%207%2003.doc.

54. Bedore interview; Uhlir interview no. 1.

55. Bryan interview no. 1.

56. John Bryan and Members of the Millennium Park Executive Committee to Founders of Millennium Park, 10 Aug. 2001, in possession of author.

57. "The Sydney Opera House," at http://www.anzac.com/aust/nsw/soh.html, accessed August 2003; *Los Angeles Downtown News*, 1997 at http://www.losangelesdowtown.com/archive/archive97/Gehry.html.

58. E-mail communication, Rob Omori (Office of John Bryan) to Timothy Gilfoyle, 12 July 2005, in author's possession ($173.5 million); CT, 5 Aug. 2001; Mark Horowitz, "Taking the Fall," *Buzz*, Sept. 1995; David D'Arcy, "Why L.A. Hates Frank Gehry," *Los Angeles Magazine*, Aug. 1996; *New Times Los Angeles*, 18 Dec. 1997; *Los Angeles Times*, 19 Aug. 2001, Calendar section.

59. Deborah Wilk, "Winged Victory," *Chicago Magazine*, Sept. 2003; "A New Museum," *Milwaukee Journal Sentinel*, 7 Oct. 2001 ($120 million cost). I am indebted to Sheila DeLuca for directing me to this source.

60. Meyerson Symphony Center in Dallas, Texas, was originally projected to cost $47.7 million in 1982. By 1989 when the center opened, officials claimed the cost was $81.5 million, although some critics insisted that with the cost of land

acquisition, infrastructure, and debt service, the real price tag was $157 million. See Shulman, *Meyerson Symphony Center*, 142, 150, 269–70, 345.

61. CT, 30 Oct. 2002.

62. Thomas Pritzker interview; Frank Gehry speech at Millennium Park Founders Dinner, Jay Pritzker Pavilion, 22 May 2004.

CHAPTER ELEVEN

1. CT, 5 Aug. 2001; E-mail communication, Rob Omori (Office of John Bryan) to Timothy Gilfoyle, 14 July 2003, in author's possession (Crowns).

2. Millennium Park, Inc., *Invitation to Participate in a Garden Design Competition* (Chicago, 17 July 2000), 5–6; Bryan interview nos. 2 and 3; Ed Uhlir comments at "Landscape of Millennium Park," Millennium Park Symposium, 23 July 2004, Rubloff Auditorium, Art Institute of Chicago ($10,000 honorarium). The best overview of the competition and 11 submissions appears in Waldheim, *Constructed Ground*. The jury membership is found above in chapter 7, note 14, above.

3. Oudolf interview (season); Waldheim, *Constructed Ground*, 15; Paulus interview. Gustafson later moved her European office to London.

4. Bryan interview nos. 2 and 3.

5. Ibid.

6. Bryan interview no. 3 (quotes); E-mail communication, Rob Omori (Office of John Bryan) to Timothy Gilfoyle, 14 July 2003, in author's possession (May 2003 verbal commitment); CST, 26 Aug. 2003.

7. Coverage of Lurie's philanthropy appears at http://philanthropy.com/free/articles/v15/i09/09002401.htm; *Friends of the Parks Newsletter*, Spring 2004, at http://www.fotp.org/special_events/parks_ball.shtml, both accessed February 2005. Also see CST, 26 Aug. 2003; *Chronicle of Philanthropy*, 20 Feb. 2003; *Business Week*, 1 Dec. 2003 (top 50); CST, 26 Aug. 2003. In 1999, Lurie was ranked as the 72nd most generous philanthropist in the United States, In 2000, 78th. See *Worth*, April 1999, April 2000.

8. CST, 26 Aug. 2003.

9. Uhlir interview no. 2.

10. Beeby interview; Uhlir interview no. 2.

11. General Superintendent Daniel Flaherty to Jacob Arvey, attached to Dorothy Christerson (Arvey secretary) to Colonel Henry Crown, 30 July 1962, folder 9, box 6, Jacob Arvey Papers, CHS.

12. See chapter 3 for a longer discussion of this.

13. CPD, *Grant Park Design Guidelines*, 35.

14. Uhlir interview no. 1; unrecorded conversation with Uhlir, 7 March 2005.

15. Talaske interview. Also see CST, 11 July 2004.

16. Uhlir interview no. 2.

17. Ibid.

18. Ibid.

19. Ibid.

20. Telephone conversation with Virginia Manriquez, Chicago Public Art Program, 13 July 2004. Uhlir discussed the Millennium Park art donations at an earlier meeting on 12 Oct. 1999.

21. Uhlir interview no. 1. Uhlir also brought the sculpture designs of Anish Kapoor and Jaume Plensa before the Public Art Committee for scrutiny and criticism. In all cases, the committee unanimously approved the designs. See Uhlir interview no. 2.

22. Gehry interview.

CHAPTER TWELVE

1. Bryan interview no. 2.

2. Anish Kapoor lecture, "Landscape, Art and Architecture," Millennium Park Symposium, Rubloff Auditorium, Art Institute of Chicago, 23 July 2004.

1. *CT*, 4 Nov. 1999; Webb interview (bouquet); Frank Gehry interview with Katherine Bliss, on *News 2 at Ten* (bouquet); *Entertainment Design*, 1 Nov. 2003 (festive).

2. *Millennium Park Schedule and Map for Opening Day* (Chicago, 15–17 July 2004); PR Newswire, 4 Nov. 1999; *CT*, 3 Nov. 1999, 4 Nov. 1999, 9 June 2000; Midwest Construction, *Walking through Chicago's Millennium Park*, 7; Sharoff, *Better Than Perfect*, 28. By comparison, the Ravinia Festival seating capacity is 3,200. See http://www.ravinia.org/Media/presskitdetailpub.aspx?ID=33&parentID=12, accessed 23 March 2005.

3. Frank Gehry speech at Millennium Park Founders Dinner, Jay Pritzker Pavilion, 22 May 2004.

4. *CT*, 17 July 2004; Jean-Louis Cohen, "Frankly Urban: Gehry from Billboards to Bilbao," in Ragheb, *Frank Gehry*, 326; Frank Gehry interview with Katherine Bliss, on *News 2 at Ten* (best architectural city).

5. Gehry interview (let it unfold); Webb interview; "One-on One with Frank Gehry," *Chicago Tonight*.

6. Webb interview.

7. Gehry interview.

8. Gehry interview; Webb interview; "One-on One with Frank Gehry," *Chicago Tonight*; Blair Kamin, "How Stellar are 'Starchitects'?" *CT*, 27 Jan. 2002 (quotes). On Cindy Pritzker's preference for a more flamboyant Gehry design, see *CST*, 11 July 2004. On John Bryan's preference for an identifiable Gehry design, see Bryan interview no. 3.

9. Gehry interview; Webb interview; *CT*, 15 July 2004.

10. Webb interview. Webb remembers that this idea was originally raised and applied while they were working on a cancer center in Scotland named after Gehry's friend Maggie Cheswick Jenks. The Millennium Park pavilion, however, allowed for a much larger-scale design. On Gehry's interest in seventeenth-century Dutch painting, see Friedman, *Gehry Talks*, 44.

11. Webb interview; *Entertainment Design*, 1 Nov.

2003. All *Entertainment Design* issues cited below are available at http://entertainmentdesignmag.com, and were last accessed 23 March 2005. The Lyric Opera House capacity is 3,563, the second-largest in the United States.

12. Webb interview.

13. Gehry quote at "The Architecture of Millennium Park," Millennium Park Symposium, 23 July 2004, Rubloff Auditorium, Art Institute of Chicago.

14. "One-on One with Frank Gehry," *Chicago Tonight*.

15. *Entertainment Design*, 1 Nov. 2003.

16. Gehry interview; Frank Gehry interview with Katherine Bliss, on *News 2 at Ten* (wow).

17. Rosemarie Haag Bletter, "Frank Gehry's Spatial Reconstructions," in Cobb, *Architecture of Frank O. Gehry*, 44 (explode); Germano Celant, "Reflections on Frank Gehry," in Gehry, *Buildings and Projects*, 5; Greenberg and Jordan, *Frank O. Gehry*, 13; Dal Co and Forster, *Gehry: Complete Works*, 51, 53, 55.

18. "One-on One with Frank Gehry," *Chicago Tonight*.

19. Ross Miller, "The Master of Mud Pies," *Interview*, Jan. 1990. For a contrasting and critical view of Gehry's sense of chaos and disorder, see Davis, *City of Quartz*, 238–40.

20. Ragheb, *Frank Gehry*, 130; Friedman, *Gehry Talks*, 167.

21. Borda et al., *Symphony*, 50–54; *The Richard B. Fisher Center for the Performing Arts at Bard College* (pamphlet, 2003), in author's possession.

22. *CT*, 15 July 2004.

23. Gehry interview.

24. Friedman, *Gehry Talks*, 44.

25. *CT*, 15 July 2004; Gehry quote (shmattee) at "The Architecture of Millennium Park," Millennium Park Symposium, 23 July 2004, Rubloff Auditorium, Art Institute of Chicago; unrecorded conversation with Ed Uhlir, 7 March 2005 ($17 million cost). Mayor Richard M. Daley expressed interest in covering the Great Lawn, in part because 20 to 25 percent of outdoor events

in the spring and summer were canceled because of rain. See Bryan interview no. 1.

26. Dal Co and Forster, *Gehry: Complete Works*. Other Gehry music and concert pavilion projects include Arts Park in Van Nuys, Calif. (1976; never built); Paramount Theatre Shell project, Oakland, Calif. (1981; never built); World Expo Amphitheater, New Orleans, La. (1982–1984); and Fountain Valley School Theater, Colorado Springs, Colo. (1985).

27. *NYT*, 23 July 1967 (70 days); Gehry, *Buildings and Projects*, 34–35; Dal Co and Forster, *Gehry: Complete Works*, 84–87, 588; James Bailey, "Only in Columbia, the Next America," *Architectural Forum*, Nov. 1967 (most successful). Shortly after completion, the pavilion received a Merit Award from the Baltimore chapter of the American Institute of Architects.

28. *Los Angeles Times*, 21 Aug. 1975, 15 May 1977; *CT*, 15 March 1987 (Mies); unrecorded interview with Doug Warrick, 4 Jan. 2002. The pavilion was renovated in 1996 by Gehry Associates. Seating capacity was expanded to 7,900 seats and 4,600 on the lawn, for a full capacity of 12,500. The new seating also include 67 box seats. Demand for large-venue concerts forced pavilion administrators to replace the theater-in-the-round with a more traditional stage. The seating area now fans out beyond both sides of the roof. The facility was renamed the Chronicle Pavilion in 1998. Unrecorded interviews with Doug Warrick and Loretta Hill, 4 Jan. 2002.

29. Gehry, *Buildings and Projects*, 34–35; Dal Co and Forster, *Gehry: Complete Works*, 84–87, 588; James Bailey, "Only in Columbia, the Next America," *Architectural Forum*, Nov. 1967 (most successful). Many of the initial reviews of the Concord Pavilion never even mentioned Gehry, focusing instead on Jaffe and the high quality of the sound. For examples, see *San Francisco Chronicle*, 13 May 1975; *Berkeley Independent Gazette*, 19 May 1975; *Contra Costa Times*, 19 March 1975, 1 May 1975; 21 March 1976. Some, however, were critical of the sound at Concord. *San Francisco Examiner* critic Alexander Fried concluded that the pavilion acoustics "still need adjustment." *San Francisco Chronicle* critic Heuwell Tircuit wrote, "The pavilion was so designed that it can be 'tuned.' It needs it." See *Los Angeles Times*, 21 Aug. 1975. Christopher Jaffe worked on the acoustics for the Meadow Brook Music Pavilion, the Ravinia Festival north of Chicago, Lincoln Center's

Philharmonic Hall, the New York State Theater, and Delacorte Theater. See *Berkeley Independent Gazette*, 19 May 1975.

30. Frank Gehry presentation of Millennium Park Donors, 9 Sept. 2003 (cheap car radio); *CT*, 3 Nov. 1999 (Hollywood Bowl structure); Webb interview; Lyle F. Yerges of Bolt Beranek & Newman to Richard M. Bennett of Loebl, Schlossman & Bennett, 29 Dec. 1961, in Records of Loebl Schlossman & Hackel. I am indebted to David Marks of LSH for providing me with this source. Craig Webb believes that the Hollywood Bowl renovation was probably the most influential of all earlier Gehry designs on the final Millennium Park product. See Webb interview.

31. *Los Angeles Times*, 19 July 1970 (Krips); Gehry, *Buildings and Projects*, 52–57; Dal Co and Forster, *Gehry: Complete Works*, 107–14; Mildred Friedman, "Fast Food," in Cobb, *Architecture of Frank O. Gehry*, 105–6.

32. Webb interview; unrecorded conversation with Ed Uhlir, 7 March 2005 (Daley objections); "One-on One with Frank Gehry," *Chicago Tonight*; *Entertainment Design*, 1 Nov. 2003.

33. Blackwood, "Architecture of Joy." On the influence of the DG Bank in this regard, see Webb interview; *CST*, 11 July 2004.

34. Gehry interview.

35. Jean-Louis Cohen, "Frankly Urban: Gehry from Billboards to Bilbao," in Ragheb, *Frank Gehry*, 333–34.

36. Webb interview.

37. Ibid.; *Entertainment Design*, 1 April 2004; Talaske interview; Laney interview.

38. Webb interview; Laney interview; Talaske interview; Frank Gehry presentation of Millennium Park Donors, 9 Sept. 2003; Talaske Group, "Pritzker Music Pavilion: Key Questions and Answers" (Roan Group, 3 May 2004); *Entertainment Design*, 1 Nov. 2003; *CT*, 6 Jan. 2000.

39. Laney interview (enjoyable); Talaske Group, "Pritzker Music Pavilion," *Entertainment Design*, 1 Nov. 2003; Talaske interview.

40. Talaske Group, "Pritzker Music Pavilion."

41. Webb interview; Laney interview; Frank Gehry presentation of Millennium Park Donors, 9 Sept. 2003; *CT*, 6 Jan. 2000; *Entertainment Design*, 1 April 2004. On Gehry devising the bridge to serve as a sound berm, see Talaske interview.

42. *CT*, 15 July 2004; *Entertainment Design*, 1 April 2004.

43. Dal Co and Forster, *Gehry: Complete Works*, 534–35, 574–75; Mildred Friedman, "Architecture in Motion," in Ragheb, *Frank Gehry*, 293.

44. Webb interview; unrecorded conversation with Ed Uhlir, 7 March 2005 (Uhlir and MacManus recommendations); *NYT*, 18 July 2004; *Midwest Construction*, *Walking through Chicago's Millennium Park*, 19.

45. Van Bruggen, *Frank O. Gehry*, 57.

46. Webb interview; *Midwest Construction*, *Walking through Chicago's Millennium Park*, 20 (pau lope).

47. Webb interview. On Gehry's urbanism, see Ross Miller, "The Master of Mud Pies," *Interview*, Jan. 1990; Friedman, *Gehry Talks*, 38; J. Fiona Ragheb, "Sites of Passage," in Ragheb, *Frank Gehry*, 339, 344 (Gehry quote)Van Bruggen, *Frank O. Gehry*, 73. On Gehry's urbanism embodied in Loyola Law School (1981–1984), the Hollywood Library (1983–1986) and the Yale Psychiatric Institute (1985–1986), see Martin Filler, "Gehry's Urbanism," *Skyline*, Oct. 1982; Pilar Viladas, "Illuminated Manuscripts," Special Issue on Frank O. Gehry, *Progressive Architecture*, Oct. 1986.

48. Gehry interview.

49. Gehry interview (lungs); Webb interview.

50. Webb interview.

CHAPTER FOURTEEN

1. *Sightlines*, Jan. 2003; http://www.chi-athenaeum.org/award2000(2).htm#page1, last accessed 23 March 2005. The other award-winning Chicago entry was Max Palevsky Residential Commons at the University of Chicago.

2. Sandra Guthman interview; Beeby interview. Guthman attributes this metaphor to Beeby, but he attributes it to Jack Duffin .

3. Beeby interview.

4. *Sightlines*, Jan. 2003.

5. Beeby interview.

6. Ibid.

7. Ibid.; Moffatt interview.

8. Beeby interview; Moffatt interview.

9. "The Architecture of Millennium Park," Millennium Park Symposium, 23 July 2004, Rubloff Auditorium, Art Institute of Chicago (Beeby quote, from Larry Booth); *Sightlines*, Jan. 2003 (Beeby quote). For criticisms that the theater is "unfriendly and foreboding to audiences," see *CT*, 5 Dec. 2004. By comparison, the Auditorium Theater has approximately 3,700 seats.

10. Beeby interview. For a favorable review of the seating structure, see *CT*, 10 Nov. 2003.

11. Beeby quote at "The Architecture of Millennium Park," Millennium Park Symposium, 23 July 2004, Rubloff Auditorium, Art Institute of Chicago; Moffatt interview.

12. Beeby interview.

13. *CT*, 10 Nov. 2003.

14. Beeby interview.

15. Chicago Plan Commission, "Lakefront Millennium Project, revised," 11 March 1999, 5; Moffatt interview.

16. Beeby interview.

17. Joan Harris interview.

18. Ibid. In the Harris Theater's first two years of operation, performing companies included the New Black Music Repertory Ensemble, *Ballet Folklorico de la Universidad Veracruza* (sponsored by the Mexican Fine Arts Center Museum), and the Arab American Action Network.

19. Beeby interview.

20. Ibid.

21. Ibid.

22. *NYT*, 3 Dec. 2003. A proposal by Linda Shelton, director of the Joyce Theater in Chelsea,

called for such a theater at Ground Zero. The plan called for a stage 150 feet wide and 50 feet deep, and approximately 1,000 seats.

CHAPTER FIFTEEN

1. *CST*, 14 July 2004; *CT*, 25 Feb. 2000; 9 June 2000; 18 July 2004; unrecorded conversation with Ed Uhlir, 7 March 2005 (27 feet); Shankarkumar, "A Silver Bean for Chicago."

2. *CT*, 25 Feb. 2000, 18 July 2004; Shankarkumar, "A Silver Bean for Chicago."

3. Richard Gray interview.

4. *CT*, 29 June 2004.

5. Lash interview.

6. For these and more biographical details, see Celant, *Anish Kapoor*, xiv–xv; Maxwell, "Anish Kapoor Interviewed," 6–12; Bhabha, "Anish Kapoor," in *Anish Kapoor*, 115; *The Independent* (London), 27 Jan. 1998.

7. Quoted in Cooke, "Between Image and Object," 34–53 (quote p. 36); Cohen, "Anish Kapoor," 30.

8. Lewallen, "Interview," 2–4.

9. Maxwell, "Anish Kapoor Interviewed," 7–11 (self-discovery); Gache, 22 (neurosis); Newman, *Objects and Sculpture*, 20 (sculpture of belief), quoted in Cooke, "Between Image and Object," 36; and Celant, *Anish Kapoor*, xx; On Kapoor's view of himself as a painter working as a sculptor, see Meer, "Anish Kapoor," 40–41.

10. *CT*, 25 April 2004.

11. Ibid. (completely different); Institute of Contemporary Arts (London) and Arnolfini Gallery (Bristol), *Objects & Sculpture* (London and Bristol, 1981), 20, quoted in Cooke, "Between Image and Object," 36, 45 (quotes); Celant, *Anish Kapoor*, xxi; Meer, "Anish Kapoor"; Paul Hughes Fine Arts, *LOVE Exhibition in Shanghai* (Exhibition catalogue, 2003), available at http://www.paulhughes.co.uk/shanghai/shanghai_proposal.pdf, last accessed 23 March 2005.

12. Lewallen, "Interview," 26; Cohen, "Anish Kapoor," 31.

13. Bhabha, "Anish Kapoor," 18; Lewallen, "Interview," 16, 21; Celant, *Anish Kapoor*, xxxii–xxxiii.

14. Celant, *Anish Kapoor*, xxxviii–xxxix.

15. Bhabha, "Anish Kapoor," 14.

16. Celant, *Anish Kapoor*, xxxix–xl.

17. Anish Kapoor lecture (hole in space), "Landscape, Art, and Architecture," Millennium Park Symposium, Rubloff Auditorium, Art Institute of Chicago, 23 July 2004; *News-Telegraph*, 8 Jan. 2001, at http://www.telegraph.co.uk/news/main.jhtml?xml=/news/2001/01/08/nsky08.xml, last accessed 23 March 2005; Lara Grieve, "Anish Kapoor" at http://www.bbc.co.uk/arts/news_comment/artistsinprofile/kapoor2.shtml, accessed November 2003.

18. Bhabha, "Anish Kapoor," 12; Celant, *Anish Kapoor*, xvii.

19. Lewallen, "Interview," 16; Celant, *Anish Kapoor*, xxx; *The Independent* (London), 27 Jan. 1998. Also Bhabha, "Anish Kapoor," 12.

20. Celant, *Anish Kapoor*, xxxviii; Donald Kuspit, "Anish Kapoor: Icon and Illusion," *Artnet* at http://www.artnet.com/magazine_pre2000/features/kuspit/kuspit4-29-98.asp, last accessed 23 March 2005 (passion).

21. http://www.chippingnorton.net/Features/kapoor.htm, last accessed 23 March 2005.

22. Anish Kapoor lecture, "Landscape, Art and Architecture," Millennium Park Symposium, Rubloff Auditorium, Art Institute of Chicago, 23 July 2004.

23. Lewallen, "Interview," 16; Celant, *Anish Kapoor*, xxviii–xxix.

24. Celant, *Anish Kapoor*, xxiii. Kapoor explicitly argues: "I feel my creative self to be feminine. I feel that creativity itself is feminine. I think this is also very Eastern." The Western tradition in modern art, by contrast, is associated with masculinity. "Western sculpture is a phallic art," he asserts. See Meer, "Anish Kapoor," 42; idem, "Art in Venice," 93.

25. On Kapoor's conception of truth and on themes of sexuality and death, see Meer, "Anish Kapoor," 40–43. On Kapoor's essentialism and on the influence of Jungian ideas on his work, see Celante, *Anish Kapoor*, xxxvi–xxviii. Writer

James Hall charged that *Blood Stone* (1988) and *Void Fields* (1989) were "an insult to women and rocks." See Cohen, "Anish Kapoor," 34.

26. Prior to the creation of *Cloud Gate*, Germano Celant believed these themes reach their "culmination" with *At the Edge of the World* (1998). See Celant, *Anish Kapoor*, xl.

27. Anish Kapoor lecture, "Landscape, Art and Architecture," Millennium Park Symposium, Rubloff Auditorium, Art Institute of Chicago, 23 July 2004.

28. Ibid.

29. Meer, "Art in Venice," 93; For more on the importance of "viewing" in Kapoor's work, see Bhabha, "Anish Kapoor," 16. On the influence of Marcel Duchamp's *The Large Glass (The Bride Stripped Bare by Her Bachelors, Even)* and *Etant Donnés*, which encourage interplay between the art and viewer, on Kapoor, see Lewallen, "Interview," 12; Bhabha et al., *Anish Kapoor*, xviii.

CHAPTER SIXTEEN

1. Paul Gray interview; unrecorded conversation with Ed Uhlir, 7 March 2005 (quarter-inch depth) *CT*, 5 Oct. 2001.

2. *CT*, 15 July 2004; 27 Jan. 2005; unrecorded conversation with Ed Uhlir, 7 March 2005 (five-minute faces); *CST*, 20 May 2004; *The Art Newspaper*, at http://www.theartnewspaper.com/news/article.asp?idart=11604, accessed March, 2002. Also see Susan Crown's description in Ahrens, *Plensa*, 282.

3. Symmes, *Fountains*, portions available at http://ndm.si.edu/EXHIBITIONS/fountains/start.htm, last accessed 23 March 2005.

4. Tatum, *Penn's Great Town*, 167–68 (c.1809), figure 41; http://www.phila.gov/fairpark/squares/penn.html, last accessed 21 March 2005. I am indebted to David Schuyler for directing me to these sources.

5. Reidy, *Chicago Sculpture*, 41; Bach and Gray, *Guide to Chicago's Public Sculpture*, 21; Symmes, *Fountains*.

6. E-mail communication, Rob Omori (Office of John Bryan) to Timothy Gilfoyle, 14 July 2003, in author's possession. SOM provided a number of

fountain designs, but none captured the support of the Crown family. Unrecorded conversation with Ed Uhlir, 7 March 2005.

7. Bryan interview nos. 2 and 3.

8. Bryan interview no. 2.

9. Feldstein interview.

10. Bryan interview.

11. Telephone conversation with Steven Crown, 1 Sept. 2004; Jack Guthman interview; Richard Gray interview; Paul Gray interview; Lester and Steven Crown interview; Susan Crown interview. Susan Crown also solicited advice from architect and Yale University's Robert A. M. Stern. Richard Gray is the American gallery representative of Jaume Plensa. Crown family members and Richard Gray alike insisted that Gray had no influence or role in the selection of Plensa for the *Crown Fountain* commission. On Wislow and U.S. Equities, see Sharoff, *Better Than Perfect*, esp. 9–11.

12. Paul Gray interview. Paul Gray is Richard Gray's son.

13. Paul Gray interview; unrecorded conversation with Ed Uhlir, 7 March 2005 (met with city and Millennium Park officials).

14. Susan Crown interview; Lester Crown interview; Uhlir interview no. 1; Bob Wislow to Tim Gilfoyle, e-mail communication, 23 Sept. 2004, in author's possession.

15. Jack Guthman interview; telephone conversation with Steven Crown, 1 Sept. 2004; Bob Wislow to Tim Gilfoyle, e-mail communication, 23 Sept. 2004, in author's possession.

16. Susan Crown interview.

17. Gray Gallery, *Jaume Plensa*; Jeu de Paume, *Jaume Plensa*; Richard Gray Gallery, "Jaume Plensa," at http://www.richardgraygallery.com. The most recent comprehensive list of Plensa exhibitions, projects, and museum works is in Ahrens, *Jaume Plensa*, 289–303.

18. Jaume Plensa, quoted in De los Santos Aunon, "Interview" (nomadism, integration); Robert J. Loescher, "Between and Within," in Gray Gallery, *Jaume Plensa*, 3. Also see Ahrens, *Plensa*,

7–40, for more on the artist's philosophy and approach to art.

19. Kim Bradley, "Jaume Plensa at the Joan Miró Foundation, Barcelona," Artnet.com (anthropomorphic); *Jaume Plensa: Public Projects*, 9 (second-rate); De los Santos Aunon, "Interview" (grasping).

20. Bradley, "Jaume Plensa at the Joan Miró Foundation, Barcelona," Artnet.com.

21. Commentary by Carsten Ahrens, "Islands of the Imagination," *Chaos-Siliva* (Museo Nacional Centro de Arte Reina Sofia, 2000), quoted in *Jaume Plensa: Public Projects*, 2 (equipment); Jaume Plensa, quoted in De los Santos Aunon, "Interview."

22. Loescher, "Between and Within," in Gray Gallery, *Jaume Plensa*, 3; "Millennium Park Announces Major Donor for Fountain and Unveils Design by Spanish Sculptor," Chicago Department of Cultural Affairs, news release, 4 Oct. 2001.

23. Hopper et al., *Personal Miraculous Fountain*, 8–10; reprinted in Ahrens, *Jaume Plensa*, 90–93.

24. Gray Gallery, *Jaume Plensa*, 5; Kim Bradley, "Jaume Plensa at the Joan Miró Foundation, Barcelona," available at: http://www.Artnet.com. On Plensa's evolution after 1990, see Ahrens, *Plensa*, 44. For more discussion on Plensa's work in resin and alabaster bricks, see Ahrens, *Plensa*, 132–37, 188–99, 208–12, 268–74.

25. Plensa interview. Also see Ahrens, *Plensa*, 54–57, 146–49, 252–61.

26. *El Pais*, 4 Aug. 2001 (quotes); "Millennium Park Announces Major Donor for Fountain and Unveils Design by Spanish Sculptor," Chicago Department of Cultural Affairs, news release, 4 Oct. 2001; *Jaume Plensa: Public Projects*; Richard Gray Gallery, "Jaume Plensa," at http://www.richardgraygallery.com.

27. *El Pais*, 4 Aug. 2001.

28. Ibid.

29. Paul Gray interview; Lester Crown interview; Richard Gray interview.

30. Paul Gray interview; Plensa interview.

31. Jaume Plensa presentation on the *Crown*

Fountain, press conference at Chicago Cultural Center, 4 Oct. 2001.

32. Ibid.; Paul Gray interview.

33. Jaume Plensa presentation, 4 Oct. 2001.

34. Plensa interview.

35. Ibid.

36. Ibid.

37. Ibid.

38. Ibid.

39. Ibid.; NYT, 18 July 2004 (giving of life).

40. Plensa interview.

41. Ibid.

42. Uhlir interview no. 1 (Wood, Disneyfy); Bryan interview no. 3 (Wood); Bryan interview no. 2 (outmoded; Times Square); untaped conversation with Ed Uhlir, 23 May 2003.

43. Confidential source. Lash's objections failed to persuade Bryan, the Crowns, and other Millennium Park officials.

44. Paul Gray interview.

45. On *Buckingham Fountain* as an architectural structure, see Reidy, *Chicago Sculpture*, 50–51.

46. Uhlir interview no. 2.

47. *CST*, 12 July 2004.

48. Commentary by Sune Nordgran, "ON OFF," *Chaos-Siliva* (Museo Nacional Centro de Arte Reina Sofia, 2000), quoted in *Jaume Plensa: Public Projects*, 3.

49. *CST*, 12 July 2004.

50. *New City Chicago*, July 7, 2004 at http://www.newcitychicago.com/chicago/3561.html, accessed 20 July 2005.

1. Piet Oudolf comments at "Landscape of Millennium Park," Millennium Park Symposium, 23 July 2004, Rubloff Auditorium, Art Institute of Chicago (140 perennials; 30,000 total plants). Waldheim, *Constructed Ground*, 15; CT, 18 July 2004.

2. Oudolf interview (season); Waldheim, *Constructed Ground*, 15; Paulus interview; Millennium Park, Inc., *Invitation to Participate in a Garden Design Competition* (Chicago, 17 July 2000); Bryan interview nos. 2 and 3. The best overview of the competition and 11 submissions appears in Waldheim, *Constructed Ground*.

3. Waldheim, *Constructed Ground*, 15; NYT, 15 July 2004.

4. Gustafson interview.

5. Levy, *Kathryn Gustafson*, 6–11; Waldheim, *Constructed Ground*, 17; Keeney, *On the Nature of Things*, 168–80.

6. *Friends of the Parks Newsletter*, Spring 2004, at http://www.fotp.org/special_events/parks_ball.shtml, June 2004; "Ian Ritchie Architects: The Greenhouse Fragment, *Terrasson Lavilledieu*, Dordogne, France," *Architectural Design* 68 (March-April, 1998): 44–47. On the Esso Headquarters, see Amidon, *Radical Landscapes*, 76–77; Spens, *Modern Landscape*, 134–37; On the Great Glasshouse of the National Botanic Garden of Wales, see Deitz, "Botanic Garden in Wales," 57. On Westerpark, see Environmental Protection Agency, "Westergasfabriek." Also see "Westergasfabriek" at http://www.westergasfabriekd.nl/w_english/fr_english.htm, accessed October 2001. Some have criticized Gustafson's projects, notably that for Westerpark in Amsterdam, for effectively redistributing public space to high-income and socially elite groups while camouflaging the project as a public park. See Paul Treanor, "Brownfield Gentrification" at http://web.inter.nl.net/users/Paul.Treanor/gasfab.html, accessed November 2001.

7. Biographical information on Gustafson appears in Levy, *Kathryn Gustafson*, 9–10; Spens, *Modern Landscape*, 134; Diedrich, "Kathryn Gustafson."

8. Gustafson interview.

9. Ibid.; Levy, *Kathryn Gustafson*, 43; Amidon, *Radical Landscapes*, 76 (evoke emotions).

10. Levy, *Kathryn Gustafson*, 6–11; Waldheim, *Constructed Ground*, 17; Keeney, *On the Nature of Things*, 168–80. The quickest introduction to Gustafson's work can be found at her firms' websites. See http://www.ggnltd.com and http://www.gpltd.com.

11. Oudolf with Kingsbury, *Designing with Plants*, 9 (middle ground), 52–55; Leopold, "Designer to Plant Hunter" (De Stijl). Oudolf's publications are listed in the bibliography.

12. Waldheim, *Constructed Ground*, 19; Gerritsen and Oudolf, *Dream Plants*; Ed Uhlir comments at "Landscape of Millennium Park," Millennium Park Symposium, 23 July 2004, Rubloff Auditorium, Art Institute of Chicago (Battery Park City). Images of Enkoping appear in Oudolf, *Designing with Plants*, 110–13.

13. "Judging at Chelsea," BBC Online, 9 Sept. 2001.

14. Oudolf interview; Piet Oudolf with Kingsbury, *Designing with Plants*, 16 (palette), 8, 30–31, 42 (added extra), 52–55; Gerritsen and Oudolf, *Dream Plants for the Natural Garden*, 5 (roses).

15. Oudolf, *Designing with Plants*, 94–95 (living process), 96–107.

16. http://www.amrep.org/people/israel.html; Waldheim, *Constructed Ground*, 21; http://www.courttheatre.org/home/plays/0304/voice/designers.shtml. Israel's costume drawings for Glass's *Satyagraha* are now part of the permanent collection of the Museum of Modern Art in New York. Israel's costumes and set designs for Speight Jenkins's *Die Walküre* of Wagner's *Ring* at the Seattle Opera in 1985 generated controversy. See http://www.seattleopera.org/wagner/jenkins/walkure_85.aspx.

17. Levy, *Kathryn Gustafson*, 8. "Interview with Kathryn Gustafson," *InSight*, May 2000.

18. Levy, *Kathryn Gustafson*, 55.

19. Keeney, *On the Nature of Things*, 168; "Ian Ritchie Architects: The Greenhouse Fragment, *Terrasson Lavilledieu*, Dordogne, France," *Architectural Design* 68 (March-April, 1998): 44–47; Levy, *Kathryn Gustafson*, 43. Gustafson argues that her designs like the Ross Terrace, the Rights of Man Plaza, or Westerpark share little in common with

Lurie Garden. See Gustafson interview. Yet each place considerable emphasis on history or civic memory.

20. Kathryn Gustafson, Videotape of Millennium Park Garden Competition Finalist, conducted by Edward Uhlir, 2001 (hereafter Gustafson interview with Uhlir).

21. Waldheim, *Constructed Ground*, 20.

22. Gustafson interview with Uhlir; Gustafson comments at "Landscape of Millennium Park," Millennium Park Symposium, 23 July 2004, Rubloff Auditorium, Art Institute of Chicago.

23. Gustafson interview; Gustafson Partners, *Monroe Garden*, 5; Waldheim, *Constructed Ground*, 15. I am indebted to Shannon Nichol for clarifying these ideas. On Chicago raising the street grade, see Mayer and Wade, *Chicago*, 94–96.

24. Gustafson interview; Gustafson interview with Uhlir; Piet Oudolf, Videotape of Millennium Park Garden Competition Finalist, conducted by Edward Uhlir, 2001 (hereafter Oudolf interview with Uhlir); Gustafson Partners, *Monroe Garden*, 6; Waldheim, *Constructed Ground*, 18; NYT, 15 July 2004.

25. Gustafson interview; Oudolf interview; Oudolf interview with Uhlir; Gustafson Partners, *Monroe Garden*, 12–13. On Oudolf's philosophy regarding flower color, see Oudolf, *Designing with Plants*, 34–39, 49–51.

26. Oudolf interview; Gustafson interview; Oudolf interview with Uhlir; Gustafson comments at "Landscape of Millennium Park," Millennium Park Symposium, 23 July 2004, Rubloff Auditorium, Art Institute of Chicago (representation of the Midwest plains, the construction of Chicago, and the future).

27. Gustafson interview.

28. Ibid.

29. Ibid.; Gustafson Partners, *Monroe Garden*, 6, 10.

30. The original title was *Tomorrow: A Peaceful Path to Real Reform*. On Howard and the garden city movement, see Howard, *Garden Cities of To-Morrow*; Schuyler and Parsons, *From Garden City*

to *Green City*. On Howard's influence on suburbanization in the United States, see Jackson, *Crabgrass Frontier*.

31. Gustafson, Foreword to Amidon, *Radical Landscapes*, 4; Waldheim, *Constructed Ground*, 11.

32. For an example of this trend, see Keeney, *On the Nature of Things*, 6.

33. The best study of Downing's influence is Schuyler, *Apostle of Taste*.

34. Kiley, "Landscape Design: Works of Dan Kiley," 52; Kiley, "Dan Kiley: Landscape Design II," 82.

35. Gehry interview (organized); Gutheim, "Natural Responses to Architectural Statements," 62 (new form of landscape art); Brown, *The Modern Garden*, 98; Kiley, "Dan Kiley: Landscape Design II," 4 (quote by Michiko Yamada). From 1963 to 1968, Kiley had worked with architect Harry Weese on a plan for redesigning Grant Park. In 1967, Kiley authored *Chicago Inland Regional Parks*, a report completed on behalf of the Chicago Park District which included a variety of recommendations later incorporated in Millennium Park, including centralized activity to bring people into the heart of park; an internal transit system; indoor park activities for year-round use; auto traffic and parking removed from park; facilities designed for more than one use; and extending the city's geometry into the park. See Kiley, *Chicago Inland Regional Parks*, 19–20; Kiley and Amidon, *Dan Kiley*, 204–19; Kiley, "Dan Kiley: Landscape Design II," 150–57.

36. Videotaped interview with Dan Kiley and Peter Meyer by Edward Uhlir, 2001.

37. Waldheim, *Constructed Ground*, 25–27; Videotaped interview with Dan Kiley and Peter Meyer by Edward Uhlir, 2001.

38. Blaser, *Architecture and Nature*, 36–38. For more on Caldwell, see Domer, *Alfred Caldwell*; Wilson and Robinson, *Modern Architecture*, 185–212.

39. On Lily Pool, esp. see Caldwell, "The Lily Pool, Lincoln Park" (published in 1942), in Domer, *Alfred Caldwell*, 158–59; http://www.archidose.org/Deco3/122203a.html; and http://www.ci.chi.il.us/Landmarks/C/CaldwellLilyPool.html.

40. Domer, *Alfred Caldwell*, 158 (quote).

41. Oudolf interview; Israel interview; and Gustafson interview, all with Uhlir.

CHAPTER EIGHTEEN

1. NYT, 18 July 2004.

2. Mehrberg interview.

3. Randy Neufeld to Cheri Heramb, 10 July 1998, in Binder.

4. CT, 21 March 2004, 16 May 2004 (Warren).

5. Randy Neufeld to Cheri Heramb, 10 July 1998, in Binder; http://www.biketraffic.org/content.php?id=178_0_16_0_C (125 miles, 9,400 bike racks), last accessed 23 March 2005; *EcoCityCleveland* (award), available at http://www.ecocitycleveland.org/transportation/bicycles/chicago_bikes.html, accessed November 2004; *Pittsburgh Post-Gazette*, 3 Feb. 2005, available at http://www.post-gazette.com/lifestyle/20030518bikesidelifestyle6p6.asp. On Daley's pro-bicycle attitudes, see *Transportation Alternatives* (Summer 2003), available at http://www.transalt.org/press/magazine/033Summer/14chicago.html, last accessed 23 March 2005.

6. Dillon interview.

7. CT, 18 May 2004; Midwest Construction, *Walking through Chicago's Millennium Park*, 21.

8. CT, 18 May 2004.

9. Midwest Construction, *Walking through Chicago's Millennium Park*, 29.

10. Untaped conversation with Ed Uhlir, 23 May 2003; Midwest Construction, *Walking through Chicago's Millennium Park*, 29.

11. CST, CT, 20 July 1978 (Whyte). For earlier criticisms on the lack of pedestrian traffic in Grant Park, see chapter 3; Harry Weese, "Grant Park, 1963–1968: A Proposition for Settling the Issues of Grant Park," 5 Aug. 1968, p. 3, copies in folder 6, box 28, accession 80-59, MHPC papers, UIC; and Grant Park Bandstand folder, box 16, HWC; *Chicago American*, 17 May 1964; CST, 24 June 1960. On racial fears in Grant Park, see Hutchins interview.

12. CT, 21 Dec. 2001.

13. Ibid. A National Hockey League-size rink is 85 by 200 feet. An Olympic-size rink is 100 by 200 feet.

14. CT, 15 July 2004. Also see the Park Grill's Web site at http://www.parkgrillchicago.com/about/index.asp, last accessed 23 March 2005.

15. Neil Harris to George Ranney, 29 June 1977, folder 16, box 7, accession 81-81, MHPC papers, UIC. On Midway Gardens, see photographs in Midway Gardens Co., *Midway Gardens* (Chicago, 1914?), unpaginated, in CHS; Lowe, *Lost Chicago*, 183–85, 203; Kruty, *Frank Lloyd Wright and Midway Gardens*.

16. CT, 29 Oct. 2003, 9 Feb. 2004; e-mail communication, Jane Rodriguez to Tim Gilfoyle, 5 Nov. 2004, in author's possession. O'Malley was the proprietor of the Chicago Firehouse at 1401 South Michigan Avenue, Grace O'Malley's at 1416 South Michigan Avenue, and the Wabash Tap at 1233 South Wabash. Jim Horan owned Rhapsody Restaurant at 65 East Adams Street and Blue Plate Catering. The Park Grill's lease became an issue of controversy in early 2005. See CST, 11, 12, 16, 17 Feb. 2005; CT, 17 Feb. 2005; Ben Joravsky, "A Percentage of Nothing," *Chicago Reader*, 18 Feb. 2005; Greg Hinz, "Park Perks," *Crain's Chicago Business*, 28 Feb. 2005.

17. CT, 30 Jan. 2004. For other reviews of the Park Grill, see CT, 3, 12 Dec. 2003.

18. Sherry Thomas, "This Ice Is Nice," *Milwaukee Journal Sentinel*, 10 Feb. 2002 (sublime); CT, 18 July 2004.

19. CT, 18 May 2004.

20. CT, 10 Jan. 2005, 16 March 2006.

21. CT, 16 March 2006.

22. The Peter Wight and Burnham-Atwood proposals are discussed in chapter 2. Also see CT, 4 June 1895; Bluestone, *Constructing Chicago*, 188–89.

23. Sherwood, *Carving His Own Destiny*, 357–58; Reidy, *Chicago Sculpture*, 240–41.

24. Sullivan interview; CT, 18 July 2004.

25. Perille interview; Piet interview.

26. Piet interview.

27. Dillon and Sullivan interview; Perille interview.

28. Dillon and Sullivan interview.

CHAPTER NINETEEN

1. Gehry quote at "The Architecture of Millennium Park," Millennium Park Symposium, 23 July 2004, Rubloff Auditorium, Art Institute of Chicago.

2. Meer, "Anish Kapoor," 40–41. On globalization, culture, and hybridization, see Kapur, "Globalization and Culture." On the ideological messages of public art in the early twentieth century, see Bogart, Public Sculpture and the Civic Ideal, esp. 309–19. On nationalism, civic unity, and stability as identifying qualities of the City Beautiful movement, see works cited in chapter 2, note 9, above.

3. Bonami, "Anish Kapoor," 82; Lewallen, "Interview," 26; Cohen, "Anish Kapoor," 31; Celant, Anish Kapoor, xvi–xvii; Jaume Plensa, quoted in De los Santos Aunon, "Interview" (nomadism). Also see Ahrens, Plensa, 7–40.

4. Meer, "Anish Kapoor," 40–41; Plensa quoted in de los Santos Aunon, "Interview." Gustafson interview; Levy, Gustafson, 43; Amidon, Radical Landscapes, 76 (emotions).

5. Gehry interview. On Plensa's admiration of the unconventional, see De los Santos Aunon, "Interview."

6. Unrecorded conversation with John Bryan, 28 March 2001; Bryan interview no. 3. On the influence of Moses, Logue, and other postwar planners, see Caro, Power Broker; Gans, People, Plans and Policies; Teaford, The Rough Road to Renaissance, esp. 1–15; Gillette, "The Evolution of Neighborhood Planning"; Bennett, Fragments of Cities; Schwartz, New York Approach; Wallock, "The Myth of the Master Builder," 339–62; Kennedy, Planning the City upon a Hill; Mollenkopf, Contested City; Frieden and Sagalyn, Downtown, Inc.; O'Connor, Building a New Boston; Fox, Metropolitan America.

7. NYT, 15 July 2004; New City Chicago, 17 July 2004; Jay Walljasper, "Town Square," Making Places (Sept. 2004), available at http://www.pps.org/info/newsletter/september2004/september2004_town_square, last accessed 24 March 2005.

8. Smith interview.

9. Richard Serra's Reading Cones (1988) along Monroe Street; Isamu Noguchi's Celebration of the 200th Anniversary of the Founding of the Republic (1976) behind the Art Institute on Columbus Drive; Lorado Taft's Fountain of the Great Lakes (1913) in the Art Institute's South Garden; Henry Moore's Sundial—Man Enters the Cosmos (1980) along Solidarity Drive; Augustus Saint-Gaudens's (Seated) Abraham Lincoln (cast 1908, erected 1926) in Court of Presidents; Augustus Saint-Gaudens's Gen. John Logan (1897) at Michigan Avenue and 9th Street axis; and Edward Bennett's Buckingham Fountain (1927) in the center of Grant Park.

10. For more on this point, see Alan G. Artner, "Lessons Lost When Placing Public Art," CT, 22 July 2001. On controversies surrounding public art, see Bogart, Public Sculpture and the Civic Ideal; Finkelpearl, Dialogues in Public Art.

11. Rebecca Hoffman quoted in "Commentary," CT, 24 July 2004.

12. Recent works that raise these and other questions include Kohn, Brave New Neighborhoods; and Mitchell, The Right to the City.

13. Christian Science Monitor, 29 Sept. 2004. For a longer critique of Millennium Park, see comments by Don Mitchell and Robin Bachin, "The Use of Public Parks," Odyssey, WBEZ-Radio, 6 Oct. 2004; "Commentary" and "Letters to the Editor," CT, 24 July 200425. The most recent and insightful critiques of privatization include Kohn, Brave New Neighborhoods; and Mitchell, The Right to the City; Turner, "The Politics of Design." The privatization of parks is a national trend. After 1980, with the formation of the Central Park Conservancy in New York, cities throughout the United States increasingly relied upon private organizations to raise money for park maintenance and programs. Forest Park in St. Louis and Piedmont Park in Atlanta are recent examples. As taxpayers refused to pay for such costs, public officials increasingly sought out wealthy individuals and philanthropic corporations to provide necessary funds to keep parks open and operating. The best historical summary of this

development is Blackmar and Rosenzweig, The Park and the People, 505–30.

14. Comments by Don Mitchell and Robin Bachin, "The Use of Public Parks"; Walljasper, "Town Square," (buzz); Christian Science Monitor, 29 Sept. 2004 (Logo Land). Political demonstrations took place in Millennium Park within months after its opening. See photograph in CT, 29 Nov. 2004. The charge that Millennium Park was a theme park was first broached by Richard Solomon of the Graham Foundation, and then by Chicago Tribune architecture critic Blair Kamin. See Financial Times, 20 July 2004 (Solomon quote); Blair Kamin comments, "The Architecture of Millennium Park," Millennium Park Symposium, 23 July 2004, Rubloff Auditorium, Art Institute of Chicago; Witold Rybczynski, "Chicago's Magic Kingdom: Is Millennium Park a Theme Park for Adults?" Slate, 11 May 2005. Kamin later criticized interpretations of Millennium Park as an example of theme park planning. See CT, 29 Aug. 2004. On theme park planning, see Eco, Travels in Hyperreality, available at http://www.transparencynow.com/eco.htm, last accessed 24 March 2005; Sorkin, Variations on a Theme Park, xiii. Also see Findlay, Magic Lands; Abbott, Metropolitan Frontier; Zukin, Cultures of Cities, 50, 64, 77; idem, Landscapes of Power, 217–50; Davis, City of Quartz; Hannigan, Fantasy City; Gilfoyle, "White Cities."

15. Reidy, Chicago Sculpture, 9; South Park Commissioners, Report for the Period of Fifteen Months from 1 Dec. 1906 to Feb. 29, 1908, inclusive (Chicago, 1980), frontispiece; idem, "Spirit of Music: Theodore Thomas Memorial," program (1924), in CHS. The works include Taft's Fountain of the Great Lakes (1913), Noguchi's Celebration of the 200th Anniversary of the Founding of the Republic (1976), and Moore's Sundial—Man Enters the Cosmos (1980). Bosley Playground (1899) was named after William Bosley donated $9,000 in 1916. Ellis Park (1855) was donated by Samuel Ellis. The Commercial Club Playground (1906) was funded by that private civic group. Leland Giants Playlot (1972) was build on land donated by the Crown family's Material Service Corporation. Wicker Park (1870) was a donation of Charles and Joel Wicker. Arcade Park (1880) was donated by George Pullman, and Washington Square Park (1842) was donated by the American Land Company. For details on these and other parks, see http://www.chicagoparkdistrict.com, last accessed 21 March 2005.

16. Newton and Josephine Minow to Timothy Gilfoyle, email, 13 Dec. 2004 (obligation), in author's possession; Thomas Pritzker interview. Similar sentiments can be found in Lester and Steve Crown interview; Susan Crown interview; Cindy Pritzker, Making History interview; Jannotta interview; O'Connor interview; Uhlir interview no. 1. Kapoor believed that Chicago's "civic pride" was "unique for an American city." See *Financial Times*, 20 July 2004. On cultural idealism in Chicago during an earlier period, see Horowitz, *Culture and the City*, 1–4.

17. CST, CT, 20 July 1978 (Whyte); Lois Weisberg Oral History Interview, 22 May 2000, Collections of the Chicago Historical Society; Jacobs, *Death and Life of Great American Cities*. For earlier criticisms on the lack of pedestrian traffic in Grant Park, see Harry Weese, "Grant Park, 1963–1968: A Proposition for Settling the Issues of Grant Park," 5 Aug. 1968, p. 3, copies in folder 6, box 28, accession 80-59, MHPC papers, UIC; and Grant Park Bandstand folder, box 16, HWC. On concern regarding park safety, see *Chicago American*, 17 May 1964; CST, 24 June 1960. On the debate over park concessions (especially the sale of liquor) in the 1960s, see Café Brauer Correspondence, Lincoln Park Neighborhood Collection, DePaul University, available at http://mimsy.itd. depaul.edu/lpncsearch/results.asp?type=cat&id= committee, accessed May 2004.

18. Webb interview. The theme park critique of recent urban development also ignores how most design is based on some form of simulation: enhancing the visual style or appearance of an object by making it conform to some more refined ideal.

19. Bryan interview no. 3 (educational); Bryan interview no. 1 (elevating). Downing, *Rural Essays*, 150; Schuyler, *New Urban Landscape*, 83–85. I am indebted to David Schuyler for raising and discussing this issue with me.

20. Bryan interview.

21. The Art Institute offers free admission on Tuesdays. On other days, admission is suggested; visitors pay what they wish, but must pay something.

22. *The Grant Park Framework Plan* enumerated three goals in restoring and redeveloping Chicago's most important park: (1) reconnect the central city, the park, and the lake, (2) reconnect the separate blocks which comprise Grant Park, and (3) develop new programs that benefit the immediate and Chicago area. See Chicago Park District, *Grant Park Framework Plan*.

23. Joan Harris interview.

24. NYT, 24 June 1997; *Crain's Chicago Business*, 2 Aug. 2004. The Basque government covered $100 million in construction costs, created a $50 million acquisitions fund, paid a one-time $20 million fee to the Guggenheim, and subsidized the museum's annual $12 million budget. More recently, European cultural institutions have started relying more on private sources of financial support. See NYT, 13 Nov. 2004.

25. Booth interview; Daley interview (Chicago not Bilbao). On the reluctance to spend public money on cultural projects for fear of taxpayer revolt, see Mehrberg interview; Beeby interview.

26. Frieden and Sagalyn, *Downtown, Inc.*, 43 (trophy collection); Zukin, *Cultures of Cities*; Clark et al., "Amenities Drive Urban Growth," 493–513; Turner, "Politics of Design." On Chicago's nineteenth-century economy and growth, see Cronon, *Nature' Metropolis*; Mayer and Wade, *Chicago*, 35–202; Miller, *City of the Century*.

27. CT, 21 Dec. 2001, 12 May 2005 (3 million tourists); *Midwest Construction*, May 2004 (2–3 million tourists), available at http://midwest. construction.com/features/archive/0405_cover. asp, last accessed 24 March 2005; Goodman Williams Group, *Millennium Park: Economic Impact Study*, 5.

28. Hotels built after 1990 included (rooms in parentheses): Sheraton (1,200), Hotel Burnham (122), Allerton Crowne Plaza Hotel (445), Sofitel (415), Embassy Suites (358), Hyatt Regency McCormick Place (800), InterContinental (844; renovated), Park Hyatt (202), Omni Ambassador (285; renovated), Swissotel (632), and the Whitehall (renovated). Room numbers are from various hotel Web sites.

29. *Seattle Times*, 31 Oct. 1999.

30. Uhlir interview no. 2. Useful works and summaries of urban regime theory are Stone, *Regime Politics*; Lauria, *Reconstructing Urban Regime Theory*; Mossberger and Stoker, "The Evolution of Urban Regime Theory."

31. Uhlir interview no. 2.

32. Ibid.

33. Booth interview. This paragraph is based on a wide range of interviews with individuals involved in various aspects of Millennium Park's design. See Bryan interviews nos. 1, 2, and 3; Uhlir interview nos. 1 and 2; Susan Crown interview; Talaske interview; Field interview.

34. On Chicago's uniqueness in supporting a jazz festival, see Ehrensaft, "Festivals and the Sustainability of Jazz," available at http://www. scena.org/lsm/sm7-9/FestivalJazz.html, last accessed 24 March 2005. On Chicago as a leader in the Sister Cities Program, see the Department of Cultural Affairs, "History of the Sister Cities International Program," available at http://egov. cityofchicago.org/city.

35. Daley interview.

36. For more on this, see chapter 3.

37. Trust for Public Land, "Local Parks, Local Financing—Gifts and Donations" (2004), available at http://www.tpl.org/tier3_cdl. cfm?content_item_id=1121&folder_id=826, last accessed 24 March 2005.

38. Piet interview. For other admiring views of Bryan's vision, see Gustafson interview; O'Connor interview; Feldstein interview; Thomas Pritzker interview.

39. McCarter interview.

40. Burnham and Bennett, *Plan of Chicago*, 101, 103, 112.

BIBLIOGRAPHY

ORAL HISTORY INTERVIEWS
(DEPOSITED AT CHICAGO HISTORICAL SOCIETY)

James Alexander, 29 June 2004
Edward J. Bedore, 11 Feb. 2002
Thomas Beeby, 12 June 2003
Laurence O. Booth, 14 Aug. 2001
John H. Bryan, 31 Jan. 2001, 3 Sept. 2002, 10 Aug. 2004
Lester Crown, 21 Nov. 2001
Steven Crown, 21 Nov. 2001
Susan Crown, 9 Aug. 2004
Richard M. Daley, 28 Aug. 2003
David Dillon, 24 June 2003.
James Feldstein, 30 Aug. 2001
Marshall Field, 7 March 2001
Frank Gehry, 31 March 2003
Nicholas Goodban, 18 Feb. 2002
Paul Gray, 4 Oct. 2001
Richard Gray, 25 Sept. 2001
Kathryn Gustafson, 18 Dec. 2001

Jack Guthman, 14 Feb. 2002

Sandra Guthman, 26 Feb. 2001

Irving Harris, 4 May 2001

Joan Harris, 20 Feb. 2001

Robert Hutchins, 5 March 2001

Robert Israel, 18 March 2002

Edgar D. Jannotta, Sr., 26 July 2004

Jonathan Laney, 29 July 2004

Donna LaPietra, 12 March 2001

Michael Lash, 21 Feb. 2001

John McCarter, Nov. 2001

John M. McDonough, 12 Feb. 2001

Randall Mehrberg, 29 Aug. 2001

Joyce Moffatt, 10 June 2004

James J. O'Connor, 13 July 2001

Piet Oudolf 10 June 2004

Judith Paulus, 26 March 2001

Christopher Perille, 31 July 2002

William Piet, 31 July 2002

Jaume Plensa, 10 Oct. 2003

Cindy Pritzker, 9 May 2001

Thomas Pritzker, 23 July 2004

George Ranney, Jr., 7 March 2001

Alan Schachtman, 10 June 2004

Adrian Smith, 20 Sept. 2001

Michael Patrick Sullivan, 24 June 2003

Rick Talaske, 29 July 2004

Richard L. Thomas, 18 July 2001

Edward K. Uhlir, 3 Aug. 2004, 13 Sept. 2001, 5 Feb. 2001 (untaped)

Lella Vignelli, 20 June 2002

Craig Webb, 28 Feb. 2002

Lois Weisberg, 22 May 2000.

VIDEOTAPED SOURCES

Blackwood, Michael, producer and director. "Frank Gehry: An Architecture of Joy." Videotape:
    Michael Blackwood Productions, 2000.
Blackwood, Michael, producer and director. "Frank Gehry." Videotape: Michael Blackwood
    Productions, 1997.
Finalists of Millennium Park Garden Competition, interviews conducted by Edward Uhlir, 2001.

Frank Gehry interview with Katherine Bliss, on *News 2 at Ten*. WBBM-TV (CBS), Channel 2,
    Chicago, 24 July 2001.
"Millennium Park Overruns." *Chicago Tonight*, no. 19023, WTTW-TV (PBS), Channel 11, Chicago,
    9 Aug. 2001.
"One-on One with Frank Gehry." *Chicago Tonight*, no. 17121, WTTW-TV (PBS), Channel 11,
    Chicago, 3 Feb. 2000.

UNPUBLISHED SOURCES

Chicago Historical Society
Aerial Albums Collection
Jacob M. Arvey Papers
Ira J. Bach Papers
City Club of Chicago Collection
Construction of the Outer Drive East Apartments Collection (photo)
Construction of the Prudential Building Collection (photo)
Charles T. Ganzer Collection (photo)
Hedrich-Blessing Collection (photo)
Illinois Central Railroad Company Land Collection (photo)
Ruth Moore Papers
Walter Netsch Collection (unprocessed)
Open Lands Project Collection, 1963–1976
Harry Weese Collection

Chicago Park District Special Collections
Grant Park plans and designs
Photographs of Grant Park

University of Illinois, Chicago
Metropolitan Housing and Planning Council papers.

Robert A. Hutchins Papers (private collection)

Metropolitan Planning Council
"Report of the Mayor's Committee on the Lakefront Gardens." Final draft, 7 Nov. 1977.

Newberry Library
Blanchard's Guide Map of Chicago and Suburbs. Chicago, 1886.
The City of Chicago. 1855, Fitzgerald Map2F.
Currier & Ives. *The City of Chicago*. New York, 1892.

Davis, Theodore R. *Bird's-Eye View of Chicago as It Was Before the Great Fire*. New York, 1871.

Hathaway, Jr., Joshua. *Chicago with the School Section, Wabansia and Kinzie's Addition*. Chicago, 1834.

Illinois Central Railroad Collection.

McComber, J. B. *Birds-Eye View of the Elevated Railroads, Parks, and Boulevards of Chicago*. Chicago, 1910.

Rand, McNally & Co. *Map Showing the Boulevards and Park System and Twelve Miles of Lake Frontage of the City of Chicago*. Chicago, 1886.

Rees & Kerfoot. *Map of the City of Chicago*. Chicago, 1854.

Wright, J. S. *Chicago*. Chicago, 1834.

PUBLISHED PRIMARY SOURCES

Amidon, Jane. *Radical Landscapes*. Forward by Kathryn Gustafson. London: Thames & Hudson, 2001.

Andreas, A. T. *History of Chicago*. 3 vols. Chicago, 1886.

Arnold, Bion J. *Report on the Re-Arrangement and Development of the Steam Railroad Terminals of the City of Chicago*. Chicago, 1913.

Art Institute of Chicago. *Annual Reports*. Chicago, 1934–2002. (Burnham Library of the Art Institute of Chicago)

Baltimore and Ohio Railroad Company. *Forty-ninth Annual Report*. Baltimore, 1875.

———. *Sixty-fifth Annual Report*. Baltimore, 1891.

———. *Sixty-sixth Annual Report*. Baltimore, 1892.

Brent, Edgar Weston. *Martin B. Madden: Public Servant*. Chicago, 1901.

Burke, Ralph H., Inc. *Preliminary Report on Lake Shore Drive Improvements*. Chicago, 1956.

Burnham, Daniel, and Edward Bennett. *Plan of Chicago*. Chicago: Chicago Commercial Club, 1909; reprinted Princeton: Princeton Architectural Press, 1993.

Chicago. Department of City Planning. *Annual Reports*, 1957 (1st). Chicago, 1958.

———. *Basic Policies for the Comprehensive Plan of Chicago*. Chicago: Department of City Planning, 1964.

———. *Development Plan for the Central Area of Chicago*. Chicago, 1958.

Chicago. Department of Cultural Affairs. *Chicago Public Art Locations*. Chicago, 2004, pamphlet.

Chicago. Department of Planning. *The Tourist Industry: A Major Economic Opportunity for Chicago*. Chicago, 1985.

——— and Chicago Plan Commission. *Comprehensive Plan: Goals and Policies*. Chicago, 1981.

———. *Chicago 1992 Comprehensive Plan: Goals and Policies and Ten-Year Capital Development Strategies, Draft for Discussion*. Chicago, 1982.

Chicago Architectural Club. *Catalogue of Ninth Annual Exhibition, 1896*. Chicago: Chicago Architectural Club, 1896.

Chicago Association of Commerce and Industry. *Parking Plan for the Central Area of Chicago*. Chicago, Dec. 1949.

Chicago Central Area Committee. *Grant Park and Burnham Park Study*. Chicago, 1960.

Chicago Central Area Committee and Chicago Department of Planning. *Downtown Parking: An Update.* Chicago, 1981.

Chicago Illustrated: Two Years after the Fire. Chicago, 1873.

Chicago Mayor's Navy Pier Task Force. *Window on the Future: Final Report.* Chicago, 1985.

Chicago Park District. *A. Montgomery Ward Memorial.* Chicago, 1962.

————. *Annual Reports.* Chicago, 1935–1988.

————. *General Information.* Chicago, 1947, 1950, 1956, 1961.

————. *The Grant Park Framework Plan: A Plan for Restoration and Development.* Chicago: Chicago Park District, 2002.

————. *Grant Park Garage.* Chicago, 1954.

————. *Master Plan: Goals, Objectives, and Policies.* Chicago, 1982.

————. *President's Report: Park District Reorganization, Phase I.* Chicago, Nov. 1986.

————. *Ten-Year Plan for New Parks and Improvements of Existing Parks.* Chicago, 1945.

————. *Traffic Accident Review.* Chicago, 1952, 1953.

Chicago Plan Commission. *Annual Reports.* Chicago, 1917, 1924 (14th), 1925 (16th), 1926 (17th), 1928 (19th), 1929 (20th), 1930 (21st), 1933 (24th), 1938, 1939, 1944 (5th), 1945 (6th), 1946 (7th), 1952, 1958, 1960–1965, 1969 (1960–1965, 1969 jointly with Department of City Planning).

————. *Downtown Parking Policies.* Chicago, 1989.

————. *The Outer Drive along the Lake Front, Chicago.* Chicago, 1929.

————. *Report of Activities.* Chicago, Jan. 1953–Aug. 1954, 1955

Chicago. South Park Commission. *Annual Reports.* Chicago, 1896–1910.

————. *Report of the South Park Commissioners of the Board of County Commissioners of Cook County for a Period of Fifteen Months from December 1, 1906, to February 29, 1908, inclusive.* Chicago: South Park Commission, 1908.

————. *Report of the South Park Commissioners of the Board of County Commissioners of Cook County for a Period of Twelve Months from March 1, 1908, to February 28, 1909, inclusive.* Chicago: South Park Commission, 1909.

————. *Report of the South Park Commissioners of the Board of County Commissioners of Cook County for a Period of Twelve Months from March 1, 1909, to February 28, 1910, inclusive.* Chicago: South Park Commission, 1910.

————. *Report of the South Park Commissioners of the Board of County Commissioners of Cook County for a Period of Twelve Months from March 1, 1913, to February 28, 1914, inclusive.* Chicago: South Park Commission, 1914.

Chicago. Special Park Commission (Dwight Heald Perkins). *Report of the Special Park Commission to the City Council of Chicago on the Subject of a Metropolitan Park System.* Chicago, 1904.

City of Chicago. *The Lakefront Plan of Chicago.* Chicago, 1972.

Coburn, Marcia Froelke. "The Prize Pritzker." *Chicago,* Sept. 1991.

Cook, Frederick Francis. *Bygone Days in Chicago.* Chicago, 1910.

De los Santos Aunon, M. Jose. "Interview with Jaume Plensa." Jan. 2001, available at: http://www.tonitapies.com.

Downing, Andrew Jackson. *Rural Essays*. Ed. George William Curtis. New York: DeCapo Press, 1974.

Field Columbian Museum. *Annual Report of the Director*. Chicago, 1895–1905.

Field Museum of Natural History. *Annual Report of the Director*. Chicago, 1906–1960.

Friends of the Parks. *Annual Report*. Chicago, 1986–1987 to 1990–1991.

———. *Annual Review*. Chicago, 1985, 1986.

———. *Chicago Park Council Network Newsletter*. 1987–1988.

Gerritsen, Henk, and Piet Oudolf. *Planting the Natural Garden*. Portland, Ore.: Timber Press, 2003.

Gray Gallery, Richard. *Jaume Plensa*. Chicago: Richard Gray Gallery, 1996.

Gustafson Partners, Ltd., with Piet Oudolf and Robert Israel. *Monroe Garden: Schematic Design Narrative*. March 2001.

Howard, Ebenezer. *Garden Cities of Tomorrow*. Cambridge, Mass.: MIT Press, 1965. (Orig. 1898.)

The Illinois Central Railway: A Historical Sketch of the Undertaking. London, 1855.

The Inter-State Exposition Souvenir; Containing a Historical Sketch of Chicago; Also a Record of the Great Inter-State Exposition of 1873. Chicago, 1873.

Jaume Plensa: Public Projects. Chicago, 2001.

Jeu de Paume, Galerie Nationale du. *Jaume Plensa*. Paris: Galerie Nationale du Jeu de Paume, 1997.

Johnson, Johnson & Roy. *A Progress Report on the Future of Chicago's Lakefront*. Ann Arbor, Mich., 1968.

Kiley, Dan. *Chicago Inland Regional Parks: Design Study Report*. Chicago, 1967.

———. "Dan Kiley: Landscape Design II—In Step with Nature." *Process: Architecture* 108 (Feb. 1993): 1–160.

———. "Landscape Design: Works of Dan Kiley." *Process: Architecture* 33 (Oct. 1982), 1–147.

Kiley, Dan, and Jane Amidon. *Dan Kiley: The Complete Works of America's Master Landscape Architect*. Boston: Little, Brown, 1999.

Leopold, Rob. "Designer to Plant Hunter." *Landscape Design* 250 (May 1996): 48–49.

Lohan Associates. *Museum Campus Plan*. Chicago, 1988.

Millennium Park, Inc., *Invitation to Participate in a Garden Design Competition*. Chicago, 17 July 2000.

Noonan, Edward J. *The Railway Passenger Terminal Problem at Chicago*. Chicago, 1933.

Oudolf, Piet, and Henk Gerritsen. *Dream Plants for the Natural Garden*. Portland, Ore.: Timber Press, 2000.

———. *Planting the Natural Garden*. Portland, Ore.: Timber Press, 2003.

Oudolf, Piet, and Michael King. *Gardening with Grasses*. Portland, Ore.: Timber Press, 1998.

Oudolf, Piet, with Noel Kingsbury. *Designing with Plants*. Portland, Ore.: Timber Press, 1999.

Perkins, Dwight. "How to Beautify Chicago." *Architectural Annual* 2 (1901): 88–90.

Perkins, Lucy Fitch. "The City Beautiful: A Study of the Artistic Possibilities." *Inland Architect and News Record* 34 (19??): 10–14.

Regional Agenda Project, *The State of the Region: Policy Issues and Options for the Chicago Metropolitan Area; Final Report of the Regional Agenda Project*. Wilmette, Ill., 1987.

Saarinen, Eliel. "Project for Lake Front Development of the City of Chicago." *American Architect: The Architectural Review* 124 (5 Dec. 1923): 487–508.

Sheahan, James W. *Chicago Illustrated*. Chicago, 1866.7

Sheahan, James W., and George P. Upton. *The Great Conflagration: Chicago; Its Past, Present, and Future.* Chicago, 1871.

Skidmore, Owings & Merrill and C. F. Murphy Associates. *Lakefront Development Plan: Central Area, Chicago, Illinois.* Chicago, 3 March 1966.

Waldheim, Charles. *Constructed Ground: The Millennium Garden Design Competition.* Urbana: University of Illinois Press, 2001.

U.S. Army Corps of Engineers [W. H. H. Benyaurd]. *Annual Report upon the Improvement of the Harbors of Chicago and Calumet, Lake Michigan, and of the Illinois River.* Washington, D.C., 1882–1884.

Periodicals and Newspapers

Architectural Record

Business Week

Chicago American

Chicago Daily News

Chicago Sun-Times

Chicago Tribune

Chronicle of Philanthropy

Crain's Chicago Business

Daily Inter Ocean, 1895.

Forbes

Fortune

Friends of the Parks Newsletter

Harper's

Inland Architect

Landscape Architecture

New Art Examiner

New York Times

El País

Progressive Architecture

ShowTimes: News from the Metropolitan Pier and Exposition Authority

Sightlines: Newsletter of the Music and Dance Theater of Chicago

Worth Magazine

SECONDARY SOURCES

Abbott, Carl. *Boosters and Businessmen: Popular Economic Thought and Urban Growth in the Antebellum Middle West.* Westport, Conn.: Greenwood Press, 1981.

————. *The Metropolitan Frontier: Cities in the Modern American West*. Tucson: University of Arizona Press, 1993.

Adam, Thomas, ed. *Philanthropy, Patronage, and Civil Society: Experiences from Germany, Great Britain, and North America*. Bloomington: Indiana University Press, 2004.

Ahrens, Carsten, ed. *Jaume Plensa*. Barcelona, Spain: Ediciones Poligrafa, 2003.

Alcaly, Roger. *The New Economy: What It Is, How It Happened, and Why It Is Likely to Last*. New York: Farrar, Straus, and Giroux, 2003.

Arcidi, Philip. "American Exotica." *Progressive Architecture* 71 (Oct. 1990): 59–61.

Art Institute of Chicago. *The Plan of Chicago: 1909–1979*. Chicago: Art Institute of Chicago, 1979.

Bach, Ira. "A Reconsideration of the 1909 'Plan of Chicago.'" *Chicago History* 2 (1973): 132–41.

Bach, Ira J., and Mary Lackritz Gray. *A Guide to Chicago's Public Sculpture*. Chicago: University of Chicago Press, 1983.

Bachin, Robin F. *Cultural Boundaries: Urban Space and Civic Culture in Chicago, 1890–1919*. Chicago: University of Chicago Press, 2003.

Bailey, James. "Only in Columbia, the Next America." *Architectural Forum* (Nov. 1967): 42–47.

Baldassare, Mark. *When Government Fails: The Orange County Bankruptcy*. Berkeley: University of California Press, 1998.

Beauregard, Robert. "Tourism and Economic Development Policy in U.S. Urban Areas." In *The Economic Geography of the Tourist Industry*, ed. Dimitri Ioannides and Keith Debbage, 220–34. London: Routledge, 1998.

Bender, Thomas. *Toward an Urban Vision: Ideas and Institutions in Nineteenth-Century America*. Baltimore: Johns Hopkins University Press, 1986.

Bennett, Larry. *Fragments of Cities: The New American Downtowns and Neighborhoods*. Columbus: Ohio State University Press, 1990.

Benson, Michael. *Ballparks of North America: A Comprehensive Historical Reference to Baseball Grounds, Yards, and Stadiums, 1845 to Present*. Jefferson, N.C.: McFarland, 1989.

Bhabha, Homi K. "Anish Kapoor: Making Emptiness." In *Anish Kapoor*, ed. Homi K. Bhabha, Anish Kapoor, and Pier Luigi Tazzi. Berkeley: University of California Press, 1998.

Birnbaum, Charles, and Robin Karson, eds. *Pioneers of American Landscape Design*. New York: McGraw Hill, 2000.

Blackmar, Elizabeth, and Roy Rosenzweig. *The Park and the People: A History of Central Park*. Ithaca: Cornell University Press, 1992.

Blaser, Warner. *Architecture and Nature: The Work of Alfred Caldwell*. Basel, Switzerland: Birkhauser Verlag, 1984.

Bluestone, Daniel. *Constructing Chicago*. New Haven: Yale University Press, 1991.

Bogart, Michele H. *Public Sculpture and the Civic Ideal in New York City, 1890–1930*. Chicago: University of Chicago Press, 1989.

Bonami, Francesco. "Anish Kapoor: Jumping into the Void." *Flash Art* 179 (Nov.-Dec. 1994): 81–82.

Borda, Deborah, et al. *Symphony: Frank Gehry's Walt Disney Concert Hall*. New York: Harry N. Abrams, 2003.

Boyer, M. Christine. *Dreaming the Rational City: The Myth of American City Planning*. Cambridge, Mass., 1983.

Boyer, Paul. *Urban Masses and Moral Order in America, 1820–1920*. Cambridge, Mass.: Harvard University Press, 1978.

Brown, Jane. *The Modern Garden*. New York: Princeton Architectural Press, 2000.

Bruegmann, Robert. "When Worlds Collided: European and American Entries to the Chicago Tribune Competition of 1922." In *Chicago Architecture, 1872–1922: Birth of a Metropolis* ed. John Zukowsky, 303–17. Munich: Prestel-Verlag, 1987.

Callahan, Larry. "The Basics of Privatization." *Parks and Recreation*, Oct. 1989, 56–59.

Caraley, Demetrios. "Washington Abandons the Cities." *Political Science Quarterly* 107 (1992): 1–30.

Caro, Robert A. *The Power Broker: Robert Moses and the Fall of New York*. New York: Knopf, 1974.

Celant, Germano. *Anish Kapoor*. Milan, Italy: Charta, 1998.

Chamberlain, Lisa. "Mayor Daley's Green Crusade." *Metropolis*, July 2004. Available at http://www.metropolismag.com/html/content_0704/chi/index.html, last accessed 14 July 2005.

Cheney, Sheldon. *The Open-Air Theater*. New York: Mitchell Kennerley, 1918.

Chicago Park District. *Grant Park Design Guidelines*. Chicago: Chicago Park District, Office of Research and Planning, 1 July 1992.

Christ-Janer, Albert. *Eliel Saarinen: Finnish-American Architect and Educator*. Chicago: University of Chicago Press, 1979.

Clark, Terry N., ed. *Coping with Urban Austerity*. Greenwich, Conn.: JAI Press, 1985.

———. *Urban Innovation: Creative Strategies for Turbulent Times*. Thousand Oaks, Calif.: Sage, 1994.

Clark, Terry N., and Vincent Hoffmann-Martinot, eds. *The New Political Culture*. Boulder, Colo.: Westview, 1998.

Clark, Terry N., Richard Lloyd, Kenneth K. Wong, and Pushpam Jain. "Amenities Drive Urban Growth." *Journal of Urban Affairs* 24 (2002): 493–516.

Clark, Terry N., and Michael Rempel, eds. *Citizen Politics in Post-Industrial Societies*. Thousand Oaks, Calif.: Sage, 1997.

Cobb, Henry N., et al. *The Architecture of Frank O. Gehry*. New York: Rizzoli, 1986.

Coburn, Marcia Froelke. "The Prize Pritzker." *Chicago*, Sept. 1991, 80–85, 119.

Cohen, Adam, and Elizabeth Taylor. *American Pharaoh: Mayor Richard J. Daley; His Battle for Chicago and the Nation*. Boston: Little, Brown, 2000.

Cohen, David, "Anish Kapoor." *Sculpture* 12 (Jan.–Feb. 1993): 30–37.

Colton, Craig E. "Chicago's Waste Lands: Refuse Disposal and Urban Growth, 1840–1900." *Journal of Historical Geography* 20 (1994): 124–42.

Cooke, Lynne. "Between Image and Object: The 'New British Sculpture.'" In *A Quiet Revolution: British Sculpture Since 1965*, ed. Terry A. Neff. New York: Thames & Hudson, 1987.

Cooley, Robert J. *When Corruption Was King: How I Helped the Mob Rule Chicago, and Then Brought the Outfit Down*. New York: Carroll and Graf, 2004.

Cranz, Galen. *The Politics of Park Design: A History of Urban Parks in America*. Cambridge: The MIT Press, 1982.

Cremin, Dennis H. "Building Chicago's Front Yard: Grant Park, 1836–1936." Ph.D. dissertation, Loyola University Chicago, 1999.

———. "Chicago's Front Yard." *Chicago History* 27 (Spring 1998): 22–43.

Cronon, William. *Nature's Metropolis: Chicago and the Great West.* New York: Norton, 1991.

Cuscaden, Rob. "Grant Park's Bandshell Bombshell." *Chicago Guide,* Aug. 1972, 37–41.

Dal Co, Francesco, and Kurt W. Forster. *Frank O. Gehry: The Complete Works.* New York: Monacelli Press, 1998.

D'Arcy, David. "Why L.A. Hates Frank Gehry." *Los Angeles Magazine,* Aug. 1996, 67–174.

Davis, Mike. *City of Quartz: Excavating the Future in Los Angeles.* London: Verso, 1990.

Deitz, Paula. "Botanic Garden in Wales Boasts One of the World's Largest Glass Spans." *Architectural Record* 187 (July 1999): 57.

Diedrich, Lisa. "Kathryn Gustafson: Imagination and Form." *Topos* 21 (1997), 16–25.

Domer, Dennis, ed. *Alfred Caldwell: The Life and Work of a Prairie School Landscape Architect.* Baltimore: Johns Hopkins University Press, 1997.

Douglas, George H. *Rail City: Chicago USA.* San Diego: Howell-North Books, 1981.

Draper, Joan E. *Edward H. Bennett, Architect and City Planner, 1874–1954.* Chicago: Art Institute of Chicago, 1982.

———. "Paris by the Lake: Sources of Burnham's *Plan of Chicago.*" In *Chicago Architecture, 1872–1922: Birth of a Metropolis* ed. John Zukowsky, 107–15. Munich: Prestel-Verlag, 1987.

Eco, Umberto. *Travels in Hyperreality.* Trans. William Weaver. New York: Harcourt Brace Jovanovich, 1986. (Orig. 1975.)

Ehrensaft, Philip. "Festivals and the Sustainability of Jazz." *La Scena Musical,* June 2002, available at: http://www.scena.org/lsm/sm7-9/FestivalJazz.html.

Environmental Protection Agency. "Westergasfabriek: Collaboration of Local Government and Community." (1998), at http://www.epa.gov/swerosps/bf/html-doc/westrgas.htm.

Felbinger, Claire L. "Conditions of Confusion and Conflict: Rethinking the Infrastructure-Economic Development Linkage." In *Building the Public City: The Politics, Governance, and Finance of Public Infrastructure,* ed. David C. Perry, 103–37. Thousand Oaks, Calif.: Sage, 1995.

Filler, Martin. "Gehry's Urbanism: Critique of Loyola Law School and Spiller House." *Skyline* (Oct. 1982): 22–23.

Findlay, John. *Magic Lands: Western Cityscapes and American Culture after 1940.* Berkeley: University of California Press, 1992.

Fink, J. Theodore. *Grant Park Tomorrow: Future of Chicago's Front Yard.* Chicago: Open Lands Project, 1979.

Finkelpearl, Tom. *Dialogues in Public Art.* Cambridge: MIT Press, 2000.

Fitch, Stephane. "Pritzker vs. Pritzker." *Forbes,* 24 Nov. 2003. Available at http://www.forbes.com/forbes/2003/1124/142a_print.html, accessed Jan. 2004.

Fleming, Ronald Lee. *Place Makers: Public Art That Tells You Where You Are.* Fern Park, Fla.: Hastings House, 1981.

Florida, Richard. *The Rise of the Creative Class.* New York: Basic Books, 2002.

Foglesong, Richard E. *Planning the Capitalist City: The Colonial Era to the 1920s.* Princeton: Princeton University Press, 1986.

Fox, Kenneth. *Metropolitan America: Urban Life and Urban Policy in the United States, 1940–1980.* New Brunswick, N.J.: Rutgers University Press, 1985.

Freeman, Allen. "Fair Game on Lake Michigan." *Landscape Architecture* 94 (Nov. 2004). Available at http://www.asla.org/lamag/lam04/november/feature3.html, last accessed 14 July 2005.

Frieden, Bernard J., and Lynn B. Sagalyn. *Downtown, Inc.: How America Rebuilds Cities.* Cambridge: MIT Press, 1989.

Friedman, Mildred, ed. *Gehry Talks: Architecture + Process.* New York: Rizzoli, 1999.

Gache, Sherry. "Interview: Anish Kapoor." *Sculpture* 15 (Feb. 1996): 22–23.

Gans, Herbert J. *People, Plans, and Policies: Essays on Poverty, Racism, and Other National Urban Problems.* New York: Columbia University Press and the Russell Sage Foundation, 1991.

Garvin, Alexander. *The American City: What Works, What Doesn't.* New York: McGraw-Hill, 1996.

Garvin, Alexander, and Gayle Berens, eds. *Urban Parks and Open Space.* Washington: Urban Land Institute and Trust for Public Land, 1997.

Gehry, Frank. *Frank Gehry: Buildings and Projects.* Compiled and edited by Peter Arnell and Ted Bickford. New York: Rizzoli, 1985.

Georgis, William Ted. "Interview: Frank Gehry." *Archetype,* Summer 1979.

Gershman, Michael. *Diamonds: The Evolution of the Ballpark from Elysian Fields to Camden Yards.* Boston: Houghton Mifflin, 1993.

Gilfoyle, Timothy J. "Chicago Fortunes: Interviews with Lester Crown and John H. Johnson." *Chicago History* 29 (Fall 2000): 58–72.

———. "Civic Entrepreneurs of Chicago: Interviews with Richard L. Thomas and Arturo Velasquez Sr." *Chicago History* 31 (Fall 2002): 54–72.

———. "Corporate Consciences: Interviews with John H. Bryan and Newton Minow." *Chicago History* 29 (Summer 2000): 54–65.

———. "Philanthropists as Civic Activists: Interviews with Irving Harris and Cindy Pritzker." *Chicago History* 30 (Fall 2001): 60–72.

———. "White Cities, Linguistic Turns, and Disneylands: Recent Paradigms in Urban History." *Reviews in American History* 26 (1998): 175–204; and in Louis P. Masur, ed. *The Challenge of American History,* 175–204. Baltimore: Johns Hopkins University Press, 1999; and available at: http://www.luc.edu/depts/history/gilfoyle/WHITECIT.HTM.

———. "Wisconsin's Finest: Interviews with William Cronon, Abner Mikva, and Patrick Ryan." *Chicago History* 28 (Summer 1999): 54–72.

Gillette, Jr., Howard. "The Evolution of Neighborhood Planning: From the Progressive Era to the 1949 Housing Act." *Journal of Urban History* 9 (1983): 421–44.

Goodman Williams Group, URS Corporation. *Millennium Park: Economic Impact Study.* Chicago: Department of Planning and Development, 21 April 2005.

Gray, Mary Lackritz. *A Guide to Chicago's Murals.* Chicago: University of Chicago Press, 2001.

Greenberg, Jan and Sandra Jordan. *Frank O. Gehry: Outside In.* New York: Dorling Kindersley, 2000.

Grese, Robert. *Jens Jensen: Maker of Natural Parks and Gardens*. Baltimore: Johns Hopkins University Press, 1992.

Gutheim, Frederick. "Natural Responses to Architectural Statements" in "Landscape Design: Works of Dan Kiley," *Process: Architecture* 33 (1982): 1–147.

Hannigan, John. *Fantasy City: Pleasure and Profit in the Postmodern Metropolis*. London: Routledge, 1998.

Harriss, Joseph. *The Tallest Tower: Eiffel and the Belle Epoque*. Boston: Houghton Mifflin, 1975.

Hillman, Arthur, and Robert J. Casey. *Tomorrow's Chicago*. Chicago: University of Chicago Press, 1953.

Hines, Thomas S. *Burnham of Chicago: Architect and Planner*. Chicago: University of Chicago Press, 1974.

Hopper, Robert, Jose Jimenez, Bruno Cora, and Gloria Moure. *The Personal Miraculous Fountain: Jaume Plensa*. Halifax, Eng.: Henry Moore Sculpture Trust, 1994.

Horowitz, Mark. "Taking the Fall." *Buzz* (Sept. 1995): 43–44.

Horowitz, Helen Lefkowitz. *Culture and the City: Cultural Philanthropy in Chicago from the 1880s to 1917*. Lexington: University Press of Kentucky, 1976.

Hungerford, Edward. *The Story of the Baltimore and Ohio Railroad, 1827–1927*. New York: Putnam, 1928.

"Ian Ritchie Architects: The Greenhouse Fragment, *Terrasson Lavilledieu*, Dordogne, France." *Architectural Design* 68 (March–April, 1998): 44–47.

"Interview with Kathryn Gustafson." *InSight*, May 2000. Available at http://www.cityofseattle.net/civiccenter/ccinsight52000.htm, accessed Nov. 2001.

Jackson, Kenneth T. *Crabgrass Frontier: The Suburbanization of the United States*. New York: Oxford University Press, 1985.

Jacobs, Jane. *The Death and Life of Great American Cities*. New York: Random House, 1962.

Judd, Dennis R. "Promoting Tourism in U.S. Cities." *Tourism Management* 16 (1995): 175–87.

Judd, Dennis R., and Susan S. Fainstein, eds. *The Tourist City*. New Haven: Yale University Press, 1999.

Kapur, Geeta. "Globalization and Culture: Navigating the Void." In *The Cultures of Globalization*, ed. Fredric Jameson and Masao Miyoshi, 191–217. Durham, N.C.: Duke University Press, 1998.

Kearney, Joseph D., and Thomas W. Merrill. "The Origins of the American Public Trust Doctrine: What Really Happened in *Illinois Central*." *University of Chicago Law Review* 71 (Summer 2004): 799–931.

Kennedy, Lawrence W. *Planning the City upon a Hill: Boston since 1630*. Amherst: University of Massachusetts Press, 1996.

Keeney, Gavin. *On the Nature of Things: Contemporary American Landscape Architecture*. Basel: Birkhauser, 2000.

Kent, F. W. *Lorenzo de' Medici and the Art of Magnificence*. Baltimore: Johns Hopkins University Press.

Kiriazis, Judith. "Musical Chairs: The Grant Park Bandshell Game." *Inland Architect* (Feb. 1978): 6–11.

Kohn, Margaret. *Brave New Neighborhoods: The Privatization of Public Space*. New York: Routledge, 2004.

Kresl, Peter Karl, and Gary Gappert, eds. *North American Cities and the Global Economy*. Thousand Oaks, Calif.: Sage, 1995.

Kruty, Paul. *Frank Lloyd Wright and Midway Gardens*. Urbana: University of Illinois Press, 1998.

LaFeber, Walter. *Michael Jordan and the New Global Economy*. New York: W. W. Norton, 1999.

Landau, Sarah Bradford. *P.B. Wight: Architect, Contractor, and Critic, 1838–1925*. Chicago: Art Institute of Chicago, 1981.

Lauria, Mickey. *Reconstructing Urban Regime Theory: Regulating Urban Politics in a Global Economy*. Thousand Oaks, Calif.: Sage, 1997.

Lewallen, Constance. "Interview with Anish Kapoor." *View* 7 (Fall 1991): 2–32.

Levy, Leah. *Kathryn Gustafson: Sculpting the Land*. Washington, D.C.: Spacemaker Press, 1998.

Lloyd, Richard, and Terry Nichols Clark. "The City as an Entertainment Machine." In *Research in Urban Sociology*, vol. 6, *Critical Perspectives on Urban Redevelopment*, ed. Kevin Fox Gotham, 357–78. Oxford: JAI Press/Elsevier, 2001.

Lowe, David. *Lost Chicago*. New York: Watson-Guptill, 2000.

Lowry, Philip J. *Green Cathedrals: The Ultimate Celebration of All 271 Major League and Negro League Ballparks Past and Present*. Reading, Mass.: Addison-Wesley, 1992.

Madigan, Charles, ed. *Global Chicago*. Urbana: University of Illinois Press, 2004.

Maxwell, Douglas. "Anish Kapoor Interviewed." *Art Monthly* 137 (May 1990): 6–12.

Mayer, Harold, and Richard Wade. *Chicago: Growth of a Metropolis*. Chicago: University of Chicago Press, 1969.

McCarthy, Kathleen D. *American Creed: Philanthropy and the Rise of Civil Society, 1700–1865*. Chicago: University of Chicago Press, 2003.

———. *Noblesse Oblige: Charity and Cultural Philanthropy in Chicago, 1849–1929*. Chicago : University of Chicago Press, 1982.

McDonald, Terrence. *The Parameters of Urban Fiscal Policy: Socioeconomic Change and Political Culture in San Francisco, 1860–1906*. Berkeley: University of California Press, 1986.

Meer, Ameena. "Anish Kapoor." *Bomb* 30 (Winter 1988): 38–43.

———. "Art in Venice: Anish Kapoor." *Interview* (June 1990): 93.

Midwest Construction. *Walking through Chicago's Millennium Park*. Special Editorial Supplement, July 2004.

Mier, Robert. "Economic Development and Infrastructure: Planning in the Context of Progressive Politics." In *Building the Public City: The Politics, Governance, and Finance of Public Infrastructure*, ed. David C. Perry, 71–102. Thousand Oaks, Calif.: Sage, 1995.

Miller, Donald. *City of the Century: The Epic of Chicago and the Making of America*. New York: Simon and Schuster, 1996.

Miller, Ross. "Euro Disneyland and the Image of America." *Progressive Architecture* 71 (Oct. 1990): 92–95.

———. *Here's the Deal: The Buying and Selling of a Great American City*. New York: Knopf, 1996.

———. "The Master of Mud Pies." *Interview* (Jan. 1990): 46–50, 101–2.

Mitchell, Don. *The Right to the City: Social Justice and the Fight for Public Space*. New York: Guilford Press, 2003.

Mollenkopf, John. *The Contested City*. Princeton: Princeton University Press, 1983.

Morgenstern, Joseph. "The Gehry Style." *New York Times Sunday Magazine*, 16 May 1982.

Mossberger, Karen, and Gerry Stoker. "The Evolution of Urban Regime Theory: The Challenge of Conceptualization." *Urban Affairs Review* 36 (2001): 810–35.

Mottier, Charles H. "History of Illinois Central Passenger Stations on the Chicago Lake Front." *Bulletin of the Railway and Locomotive Historical Society* 43 (April 1937): 69–76.

Mumford, Lewis. *The City in History*. New York: Harcourt Brace Jovanovich, 1961.

Newman, Michael. *Objects and Sculpture: New Sculpture in Britain*. Exhibition catalogue. Edinburgh, 1982.

O'Connor, Thomas. *Building a New Boston: Politics and Urban Renewal, 1950 to 1970*. Boston: Northeastern University Press, 1993.

Peterson, Jon A. *The Birth of City Planning in the United States, 1840–1917*. Baltimore: Johns Hopkins University Press, 2003.

Petrakis, Harry Mark, and David B. Weber. *Henry Crown: The Life and Times of the Colonel*. Chicago: Henry Crown & Co., 1998.

Ragheb, J. Fiona, ed. *Frank Gehry, Architect*. New York: Solomon R. Guggenheim Foundation, 2001.

Reidy, James L. *Chicago Sculpture*. Urbana: University of Illinois Press, 1981.

Reps, John. *The Making of Urban America*. Princeton: Princeton University Press, 1965.

Riordan, William L. *Plunkitt of Tammany Hall*. Edited by Terrence J. McDonald. Boston: Bedford Books of St. Martin's Press, 1994, originally 1905.

Sassen, Saskia. *The Global City: New York, London, Tokyo*. Princeton: Princeton University Press, 1991.

Schroeder, Douglas. *The Issue of the Lakefront: An Historical Critical Survey*. Chicago, 1964.

Schulz, Franz. "Sunday Afternoon in the Cyber-Age Park." *Art in America* (Nov. 2004).

Schuyler, David. *Apostle of Taste: Andrew Jackson Downing, 1815–1852*. Baltimore: Johns Hopkins University Press, 1996.

———. *The New Urban Landscape: The Redefinition of City Form in Nineteenth-Century America*. Baltimore: Johns Hopkins University Press, 1986.

Schuyler, David, and Kermit C. Parsons, eds. *From Garden City to Green City: The Legacy of Ebenezer Howard*. Baltimore: Johns Hopkins University Press, 2002.

Schwartz, Joel. *The New York Approach: Robert Moses, Urban Liberals, and the Redevelopment of the Inner City*. Columbus: Ohio State University Press, 1993.

Shankarkumar, Shanthi. "A Silver Bean for Chicago." *Rediff on the Net*, 26 Nov. 1999.

Sharoff, Robert. *Better Than Perfect: The Making of Chicago's Millennium Park*. Chicago: Walsh Construction Co., W. E. O'Neil Construction Co., U.S. Equities Realty, 2004.

Sherwood, Ruth. *Carving His Own Destiny: The Story of Albin Polasek*. Chicago, 1954.

Sies, Mary Corbin, and Christopher Silver. "The History of Planning History." In *Planning the Twentieth-Century American City*, ed. Sies and Silver, 1–34. Baltimore: Johns Hopkins University Press, 1996.

Sinkevitch, Alice, ed. *AIA Guide to Chicago*. San Diego: Harcourt Brace, 1993.

Siry, Joseph M. *The Chicago Auditorium Building: Adler and Sullivan's Architecture and the City*. Chicago: University of Chicago Press, 2002.

Sloane, David C. *The Last Great Necessity: Cemeteries in American History*. Baltimore: Johns Hopkins University Press, 1991.

Smith, Richard Norton, *The Colonel: The Life and Legend of Robert R. McCormick, 1880–1955*. Boston: Houghton Mifflin Co., 1997.

Sniderman, Julia, and William W. Tippens. "Grant Park." National Register of Historic Places Registration Form, United States Department of the Interior, National Park Service, 13 July 1992.

Sorkin, Michael, ed. *Variations on a Theme Park: The New American City and the End of Public Space*. New York: Noonday Press, 1992.

Spens, Michael. *Modern Landscape*. New York: Phaidon, 2003.

Spirou, Costas, and Larry Bennett. *It's Hardly Sportin': Stadiums, Neighborhoods, and the New Chicago*. DeKalb: Northern Illinois University Press, 2003.

Stern, Robert A. M., Thomas Mellins, David Fishman. *New York 1880: Architecture and Urbanism in the Gilded Age*. New York: Rizzoli, 1999.

Stone, Clarence N. *Regime Politics: Governing Atlanta, 1946–1988*. Lawrence: University Press of Kansas, 1989.

Stover, John F. *History of the Baltimore and Ohio Railroad*. West Lafayette, Ind.: Purdue University Press, 1987.

———. *History of the Illinois Central Railroad*. New York: Macmillan, 1975.

Strom, Elizabeth. "Let's Put On a Show! Performing Arts and Urban Revitalization in Newark, New Jersey." *Journal of Urban Affairs* 21 (1999): 423–53.

Sunderland, Edwin S. S. *Abraham Lincoln and the Illinois Central Railroad*. New York: Privately Printed, 1955.

Symmes, Marilyn, ed. *Fountains: Splash and Spectacle; Water and Design from the Renaissance to the Present*. Washington, D.C., 1998.

Tatum, George B. *Penn's Great Town*. Philadelphia: University of Pennsylvania Press, 1961.

Teaford, Jon C. *The Rough Road to Renaissance: Urban Revitalization in America, 1940–1985*. Baltimore: Johns Hopkins University Press, 1990.

———. *The Unheralded Triumph: City Government in America, 1870–1900*. Baltimore: Johns Hopkins University Press, 1984.

Tritsch, Shane. "Family Circus." *Boston Magazine*, Feb. 2003, available at www.bostonmagazine.com Archives.

Turner, Robyne S. "The Politics of Design and Development in the Postmodern Downtown." *Journal of Urban Affairs* 24 (2002): 533–48.

Ulrich, Carolyn. "Green Roofs and Blue Trees: Chicago Style." *Chicagoland Gardening*, July–Aug. 2003, 44–53.

Van Bruggen, Coosje. *Frank O. Gehry: Guggenheim Museum Bilbao*. New York: Guggenheim Museum Publications, 1997.

———. "Leaps into the Unknown." In *The Architecture of Frank O. Gehry*, 123–58. New York: Rizzoli, 1986.

Vignelli, Massimo. *Grids: Their Meaning and Use for Federal Designers*. Washington, D.C.: National Endowment for the Arts, 1976.

Viladas, Pilar. "Introduction" and "Illuminated Manuscripts." Special Issue on Frank O. Gehry. *Progressive Architecture* 67 (Oct. 1986): 69–84.

Wallock, Leonard. "The Myth of the Master Builder: Robert Moses, New York, and the Dynamics of Metropolitan Development since World War II." *Journal of Urban History* 17 (1991): 339–62.

Waugh, Frank A. *Outdoor Theaters: The Design, Construction, and Use of Open-Air Auditoriums*. Boston: Richard Badger, 1917.

Wille, Lois. *Forever Open, Clear and Free: The Struggle for Chicago's Lakefront*. Chicago: University of Chicago Press, 1979. Second edition, 1991.

Wilson, Richard Guy, and Sidney K. Robinson, eds. *Modern Architecture in America*. Ames: Iowa State University Press, 1991.

Wilson, William H. *The City Beautiful Movement*. Baltimore: Johns Hopkins University Press, 1989.

Winzenried, Rebecca. "Surround Sound." *Symphony* (May–June 2004): 24–29.

Zolberg, Vera Lechner. "The Art Institute of Chicago: The Sociology of a Cultural Organization." Ph.D. thesis, University of Chicago, 1974.

Zukin, Sharon. *The Cultures of Cities*. Cambridge, Mass.: Blackwell, 1995.

———. *Loft Living: Culture and Capital in Urban Change*. New Brunswick, N.J.: Rutgers University Press, 1982.

———. *Landscapes of Power: From Detroit to Disneyland*. Berkeley: University of California Press, 1991.

Zukowsky, John, ed. *Chicago Architecture, 1872–1922: Birth of a Metropolis*. Munich: Prestel-Verlag, 1987.

CREDITS

Mikael Bäckström, **11.6**. *Batcolumn*, 1997 by Claes Oldenburg and Coosje van Bruggen; Commissioned by the U.S. General Services Administration, Art in Architecture Program, Harold Washington Social Security Center, 600 West Madison Street, Chicago, **5.5**. Robert F. Carl, **6.15**, **16.26**. Renderings by Frank Cavanaugh, **18.15–18.18**. Chicago Architectural Photographing Company, Inc., **1.11**, **3.39**, **18.43**. Chicago Historical Society, **1.3**, **1.6**, **1.7**, **1.9**, **1.10**, **1.12**, **1.14–1.16**, **1.18**, **1.20–1.22**, **1.27–1.34**, **2.1–2.5**, **2.7**, **2.9**, **2.10**, **2.14**, **2.15**, **2.17–2.23**, **2.26**, **2.27**, **2.29–2.37**, **3.1–3.3**, **3.5**, **3.6**, **3.25**, **3.27**, **3.41**, **5.1–5.4**, **8.11**, **16.3**, **16.4**, **17.15**, **17.20**, **17.31**, **18.20**, **18.37**, **18.38**, **18.42**, **18.45**. Chicago Park District Special Collections, **2.6**, **2.16**, **2.24**, **2.25**, **2.28**, **2.38**, **3.4**, **3.7**, **3.8**, **3.10–3.19**, **3.22**, **3.23**, **3.24**, **3.48**, **18.40**, **18.41**, **18.44**. City of Chicago, **4.2**, **7.5**, **10.4**, **17.21**, **18.10**. Brooke Collins/Chicago Park District, **13.33**. Frank Costantino, Hammond Beeby Rupert Ainge, Inc., **8.3**. Jay Crawford, Chicago Historical Society, **6.1–6.6**, **13.43**, **13.44**, **14.3**, **14.4**, **18.1**, **18.3–18.6**, **18.26–18.28**, **18.30**, **18.31**. Lester Crown, **16.6**. Claire De Virieu, **17.7**. Craig Dugan/© Hedrich Blessing Photographers, **19.11**. © Steve Dunwell, **4.4**. © Denis Finnin, American Museum of Natural History, **17.8**. Attributed to Clarence Fuermann, Chicago Architectural Photographing Company, Inc., **18.14**. Furla Photography, Hammond Beeby Rupert Ainge, Inc., **8.2**. Frank O. Gehry & Associates, Inc., **6.12**, **13.4–13.7**, **13.9–13.12**, **13.17–13.19**, **13.34–13.38**, **19.3**. Timothy J. Gilfoyle, **11.7**, **13.16**, **13.39**, **13.45**, **16.2**, **17.34**, **17.35**, **18.7**, **18.11**, **18.12**, **18.46**, **18.47**, **19.5–19.7**. Richard Gray Gallery, Chicago/New York, **16.7–16.18**, **16.20**, **16.23**.

© Tim Griffith/Esto, **13.14**. Kathryn Gustafson, **17.11–17.14**. Gustafson Guthrie Nichol Ltd., **11.1**, **11.2**, **12.107–12.113**, **17.2–17.6**, **17.16–17.18**, **17.23–17.29**, **17.33**, **17.36**, **18.29**. Gustafson Porter, **17.9**, **17.10**. Jack Guthman, **8.4**. Sandra Guthman, **8.12**. Joan Hackett, **6.9**, **18.32**, **19.4**. © Roland Halbe/artur, **13.24**, **13.25**. Steve Hall/© Hedrich Blessing Photographers, **P.3**, **16.21**, **16.27**. Hammond Beeby Rupert Ainge, Inc., **8.5–8.8**, **11.4**, **11.5**, **14.7**, **14.11**. HarleyEllis and Spectrum Strategies, **18.34–18.36**. Bob Harr/© Hedrich Blessing Photographs, **18.39**, **18.50**. Hedrich Blessing Photographers/Chicago Historical Society, **16.5**, **17.32**. Robert A. Hutchins, **3.35–3.38**, **3.42–3.47**. Cheri Isenberg, **5.6**. Anish Kapoor, **15.3–15.12**. Anish Kapoor/David Morgan, **7.1**. Robert Laemle, **18.22**. Loebl Schlossman & Hackl, **3.20**, **3.21**. Anel Marchan-Montes, **18.25**. Michael McCann, **6.7**, **6.8**, **6.10**, **6.11**, **7.2**, **18.9**, **18.33**. Scott McDonald/© Hedrich Blessing Photographers, **P.1**, **P.2**, **P.4–P.7**, **13.1**, **13.2**, **13.13**, **13.31**, **13.32**, **13.40**, **13.46**, **13.47**, **15.1**, **15.2**, **15.13**, **15.14**, **15.16**, **16.1**, **17.38**, **18.2**, **18.13**, **18.51**, **19.9**, **19.10**. Scott McDonald/© Hedrich Blessing Photographers, Gustafson Guthrie Nichol Ltd, **17.19**. Brian McNally, **16.19**. Randall E. Mehrberg, **4.1**. Merriweather Post Pavilion, **13.20**. The Metropolitan Museum of Art, Marquand Collection, Gift of Henry G. Marquand, 1889 (89.15.21). Photograph ©1993 The Metropolitan Museum of Art, **13.8**. Jon Miller/© Hedrich Blessing Photographers, **14.1**, **14.2**, **14.8**. Murphy/Jahn, **3.28–3.33**. Newberry Library, **1.1**, **1.2**, **1.4**, **1.5**, **1.8**, **1.13**, **1.19**, **1.25**, **2.8**. Larry Okrent, **15.15**. Piet Oudolf, **17.22**. OWP/P, **7.3**, **7.4**, **11.8**, **18.48**. Rick Pannkoke/© Hedrich Blessing Photographers, **13.30**. Cindy Pritzker, **6.14**, **13.3**. George Ranney, Jr., **3.34**. Dan Rest, **11.3**, **13.42**, **17.1**, **18.23**, **19.8**. © Ralph Richter/Esto, **6.13**. Dennis Scanlon/Chicago Historical Society, **4.12**. Peter J. Schulz, **12.114**. Skidmore, Owings & Merrill LLP and Stuart-Rodgers Photography, **4.3**. Skidmore, Owings & Merrill LLP/Chicago Department of Transportation, **4.10**. Skidmore, Owings & Merrill LLP/City of Chicago, **4.5–4.9**, **10.3**, **18.8**. Kingen Smith, **18.19**, **18.21**. © Lara Swimmer/Esto, **13.15**. TALASKE | Sound Thinking, **13.26–13.29**. Byron Terrell, Hammond Beeby Rupert Ainge, Inc., **8.13**. U.S. Equities Realty, Walsh Construction, The men and women who built Millennium Park, **12.1–12.106**, **16.22**, **16.24**, **16.25**, **18.49**, **19.1**, **19.2**. Vignelli Associates/mapPoster.com, **5.7**. Chip Williams © 2005, **17.37**. www.rickaguilar.com, **18.24**. John Zukowsky/Chicago Historical Society, **17.30**

Historical Studies of Urban America

Edited by Timothy J. Gilfoyle, James R. Grossman, and Becky M. Nicolaides

INDEX